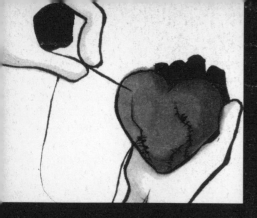

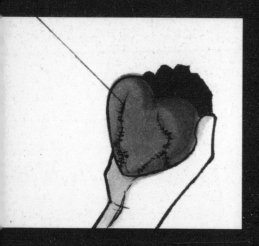

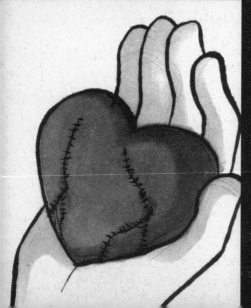

Published by SLG Publishing

President and Publisher
Dan Vado

Editor-in-Chief
Jennifer de Guzman

SLG Publishing
577 South Market St.
San Jose, CA 95159

www.slgcomic.com
www.sixkillerbunnies.com

First Printing: May 2007
ISBN 978-1-59362-064-6

Foreword

A couple of years ago Fehed told me about a story idea he was working on and handed me an early draft of *The Clarence Principle*. Although it was exciting to read the story and to imagine how it would work out, it was impossible to guage exactly how a final product will turn out. Even seeing some initial character illustrations from Shari would only come part way towards representing how the finished comic might be to read. It was obvious that a story like *The Clarence Principle* would be an analoguous process, with plenty of small changes and improvements introduced along the course of the project.

All the pieces of the story have fallen into place, and now, a couple of years later, the book is complete. The results are magnificent and in my opinion the best work to date from both writer Fehed Said and artist Shari Chankhamma.

The fact that Clarence appears to be almost entirely comfortable in his new surroundings only goes to create a mood that's even more unsettling and distinctively abstract. The world is presented as fantastic, yet credible, and even oddly familiar. We're presented with an environment that offers no guarantees and extends no apologies for its design, as we press forwards with far more trepedation than Clarence himself would ever express. Some of the themes explored within *The Clarence Principle* have been touched on in works from Fehed before, but this story establishes and retains a firm grasp of the concept throughout.

Shari's artwork captures plenty of her trademark penmanship, with elements of *Cookie* and other titles still prominent. Despite this, *The Clarence Principle* manages to maintain a unique style of its own, setting it apart from her other work. The design of characters within the story demonstrate a wonderful degree of imagination, deftly avoiding stereotypes yet producing immediately believable characters. Any small irregularities in the artwork only go to enhance the artwork and compliment the versatility of the visual style, giving the characters and the world around it an almost elastic quality, allowing the presentation of the characters to suit the scene precisely.

I hope you enjoy *The Clarence Principle* as much as I did. I had fun flicking back through the comic to my favourite scenes, to steal a few more moments with the wonderful characters found within the pages of the book. It feels as though Fehed and Shari's creative energy has been harnessed beautifully within these pages, combining imaginative storytelling and ideas with skillful illustrations, page layouts and dialogue. Most importantly, *The Clarence Principle* presents a unique set of answers to the reader, leaving the reader to ask their own questions.

- Hayden Scott-Baron,
artist/writer
www.deadpanda.com
www.sweatdrop.com

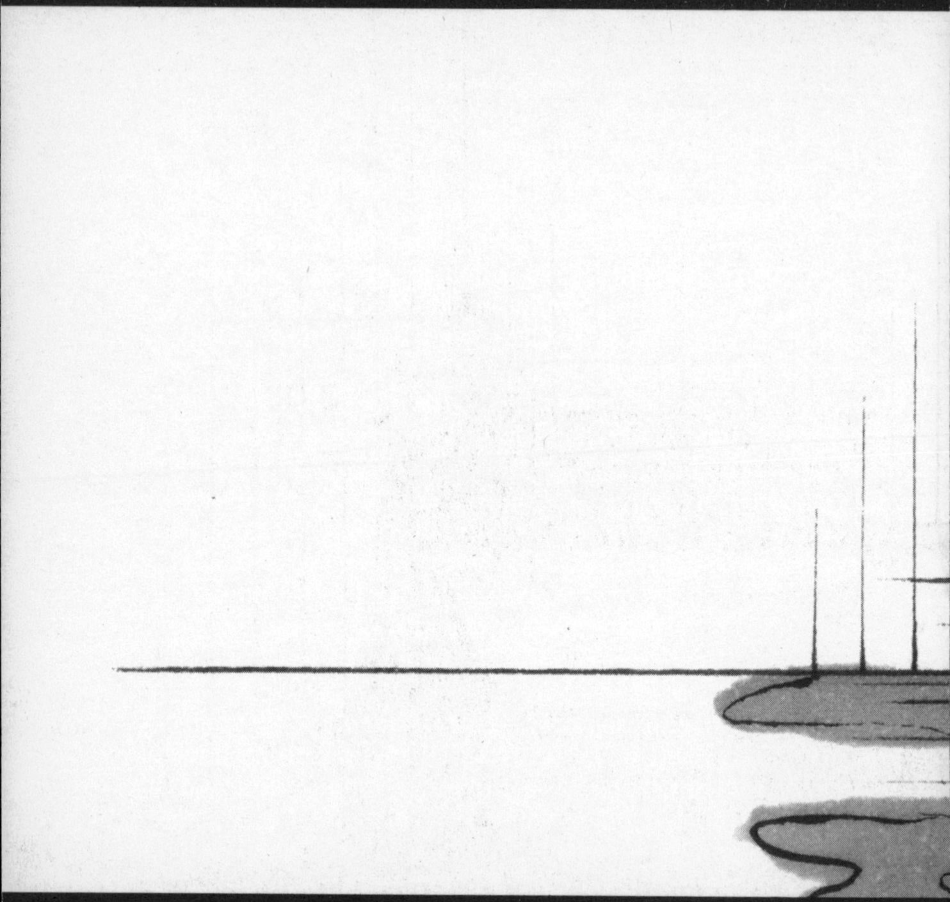

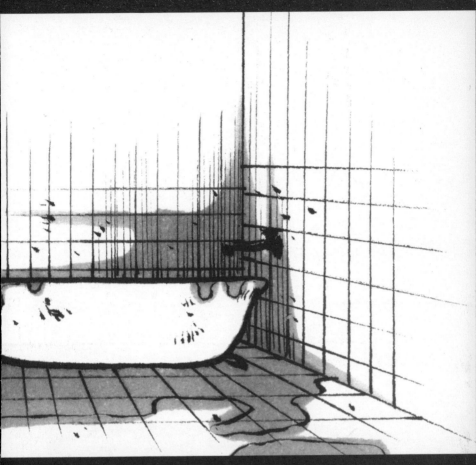

THE CLARENCE PRINCIPLE

STORY
Fehed Said

ART
Shari Chankhamma

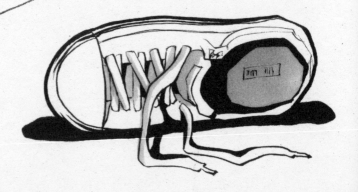

I WAS LEFT BEHIND IN A DREAM I ONCE HAD.

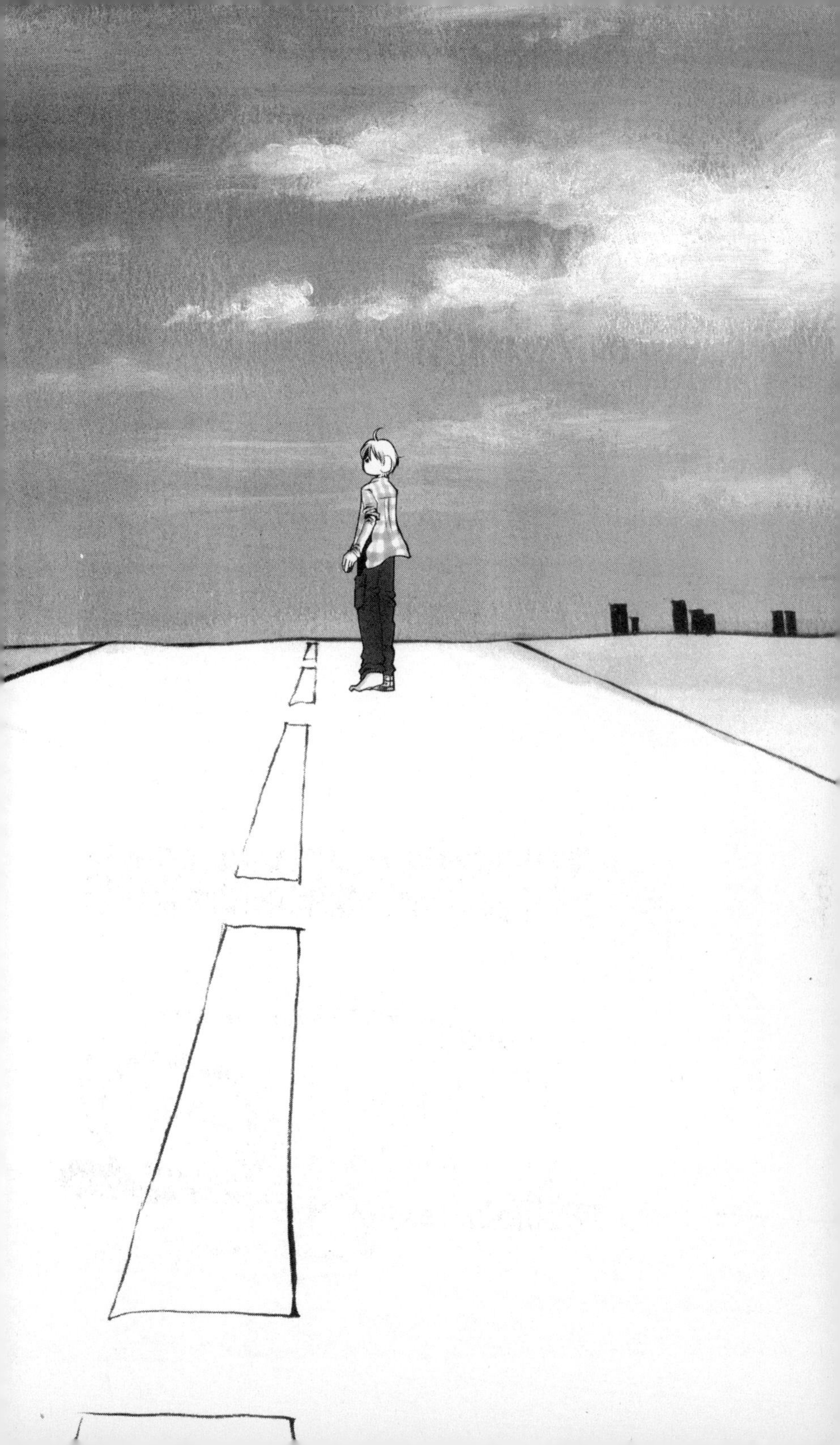

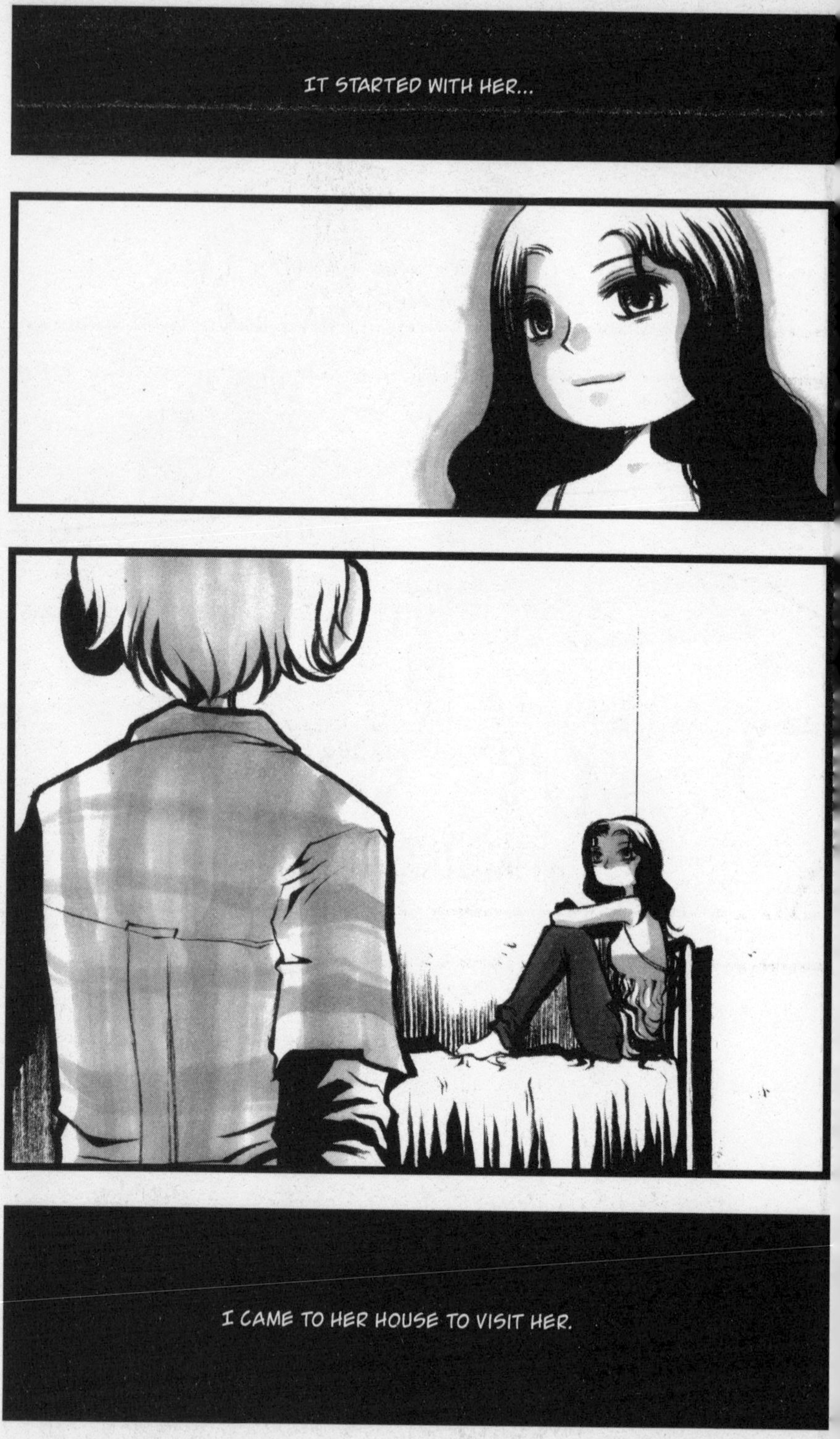
IT STARTED WITH HER...
I CAME TO HER HOUSE TO VISIT HER.

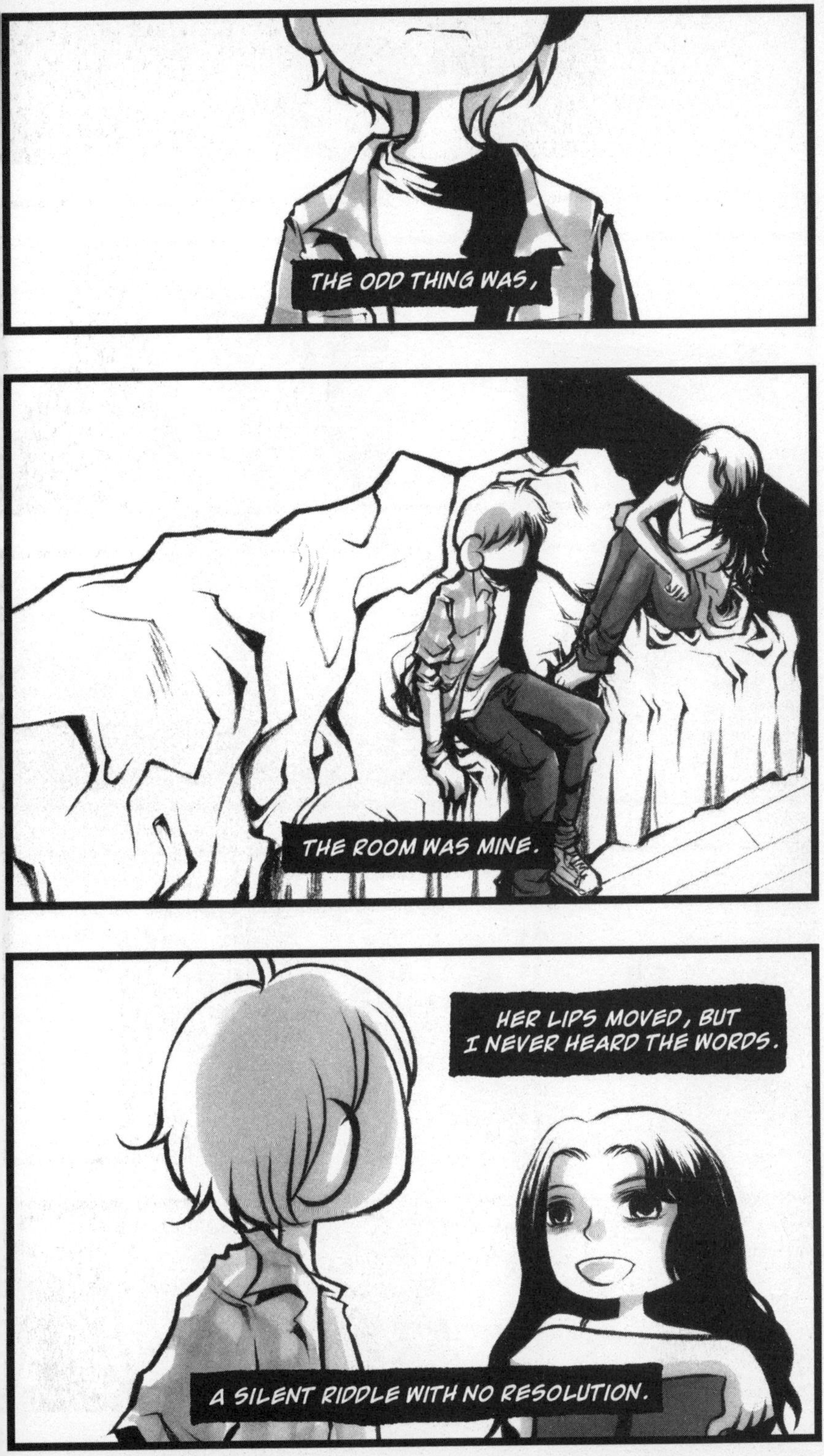
THE ODD THING WAS,
THE ROOM WAS MINE.
HER LIPS MOVED, BUT I NEVER HEARD THE WORDS.
A SILENT RIDDLE WITH NO RESOLUTION.

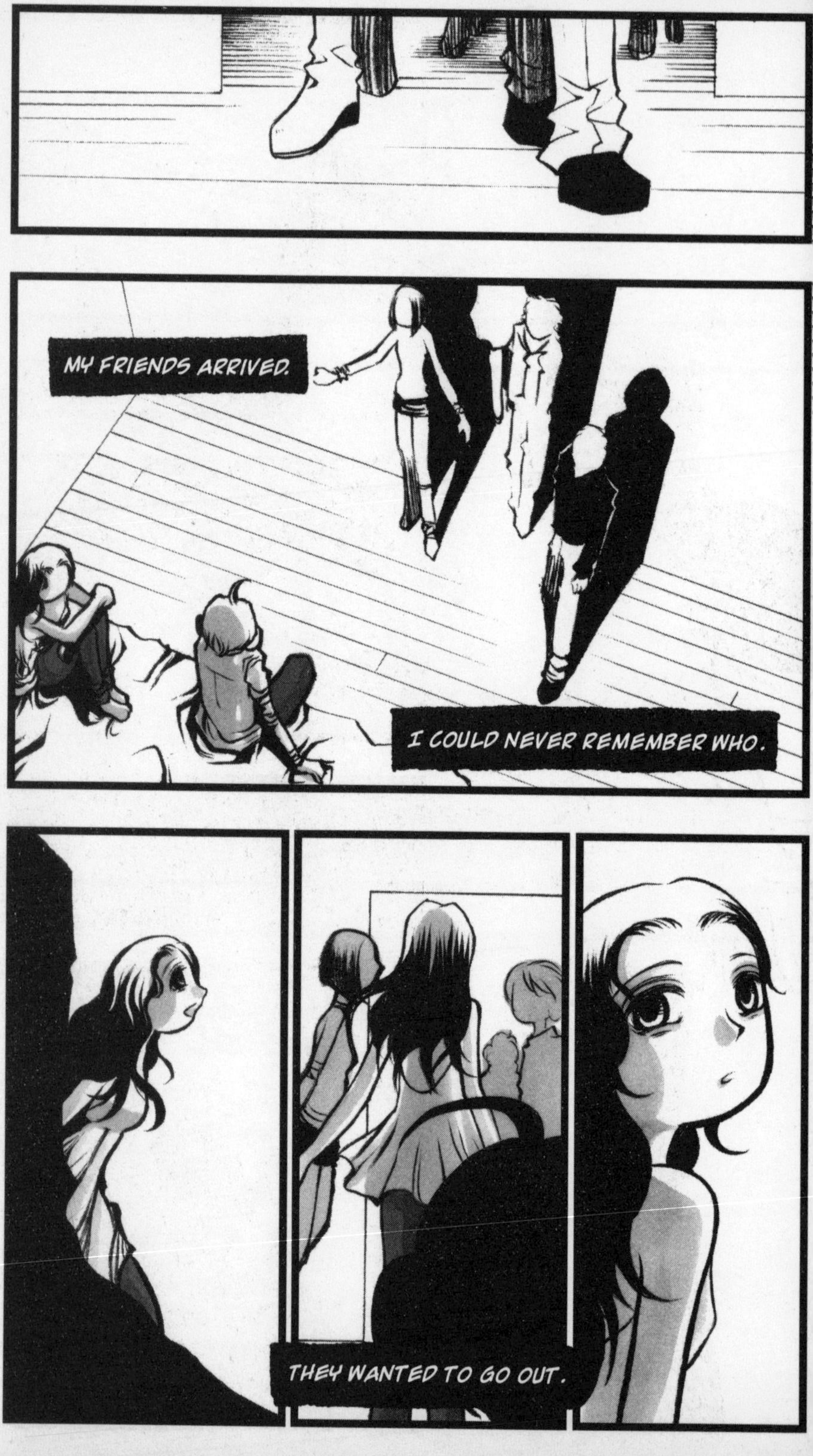
MY FRIENDS ARRIVED.
I COULD NEVER REMEMBER WHO.
THEY WANTED TO GO OUT.

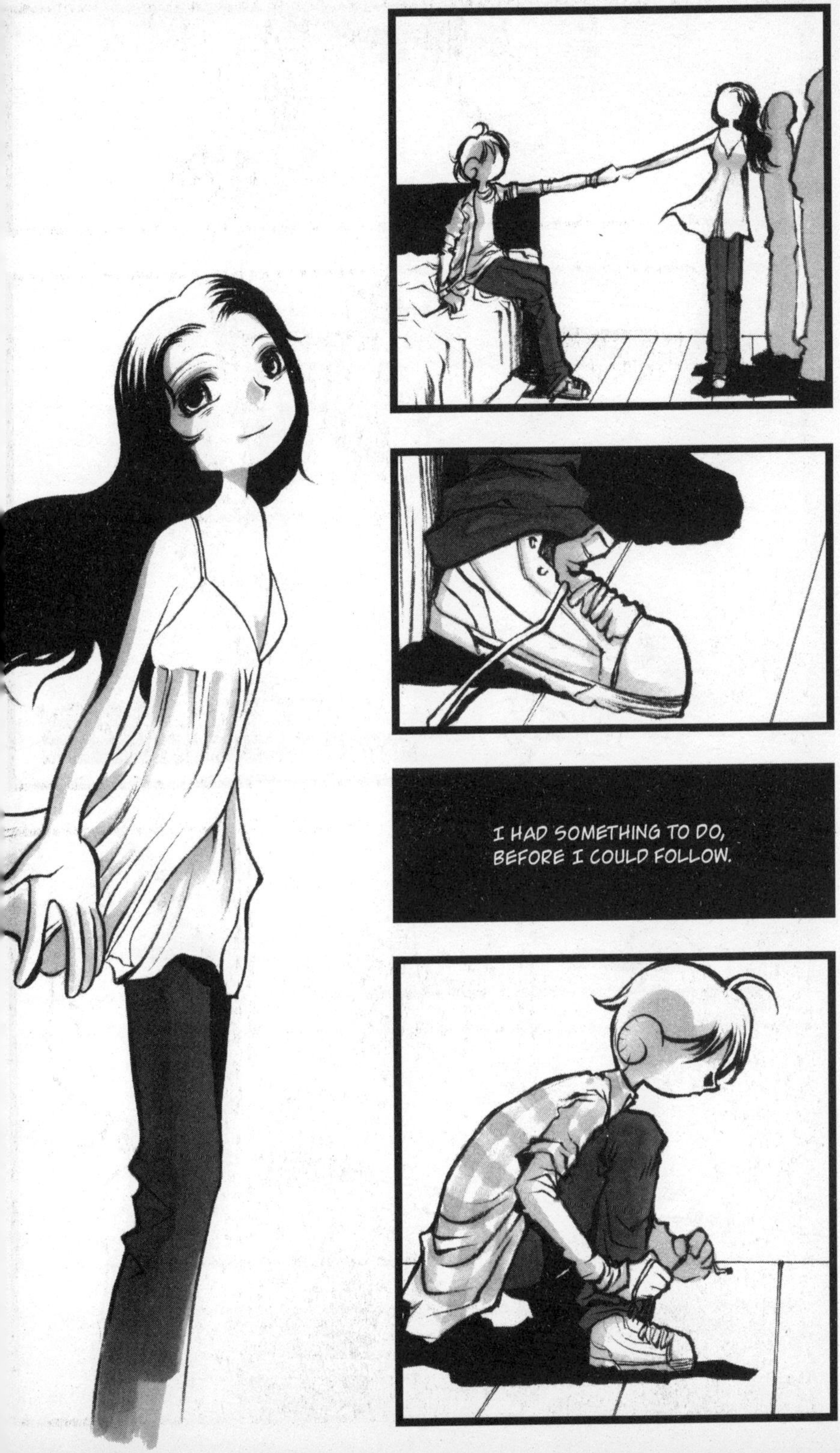
I HAD SOMETHING TO DO,
BEFORE I COULD FOLLOW.

I COULDN'T DO IT. I TRIED AND I TRIED...

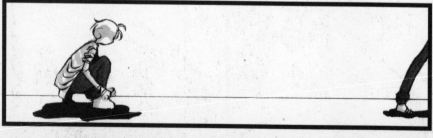

BUT I JUST COULDN'T DO IT.

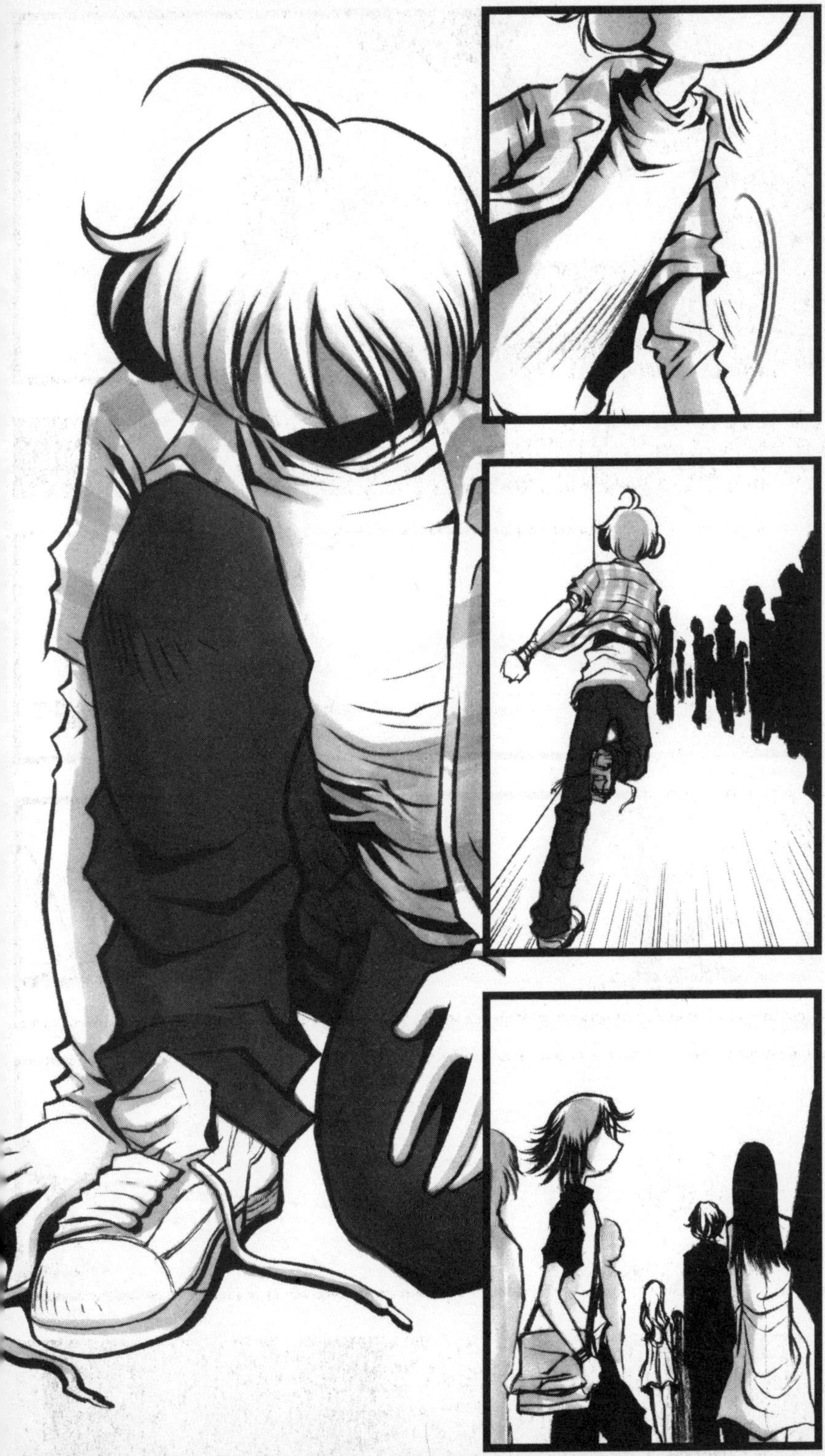

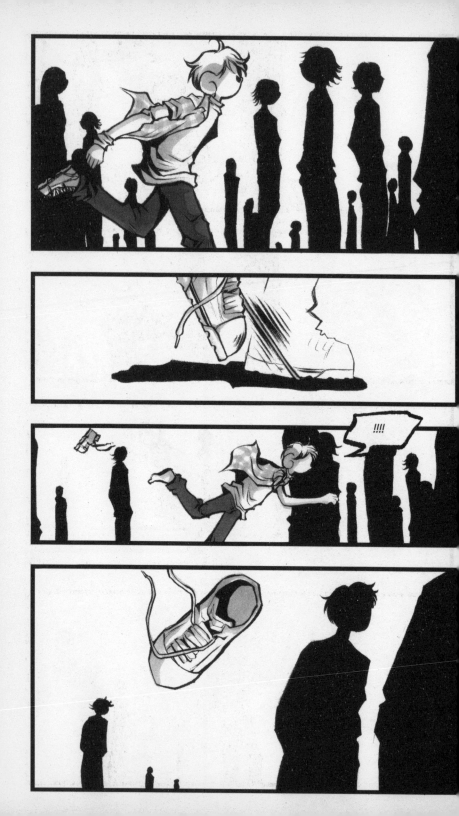

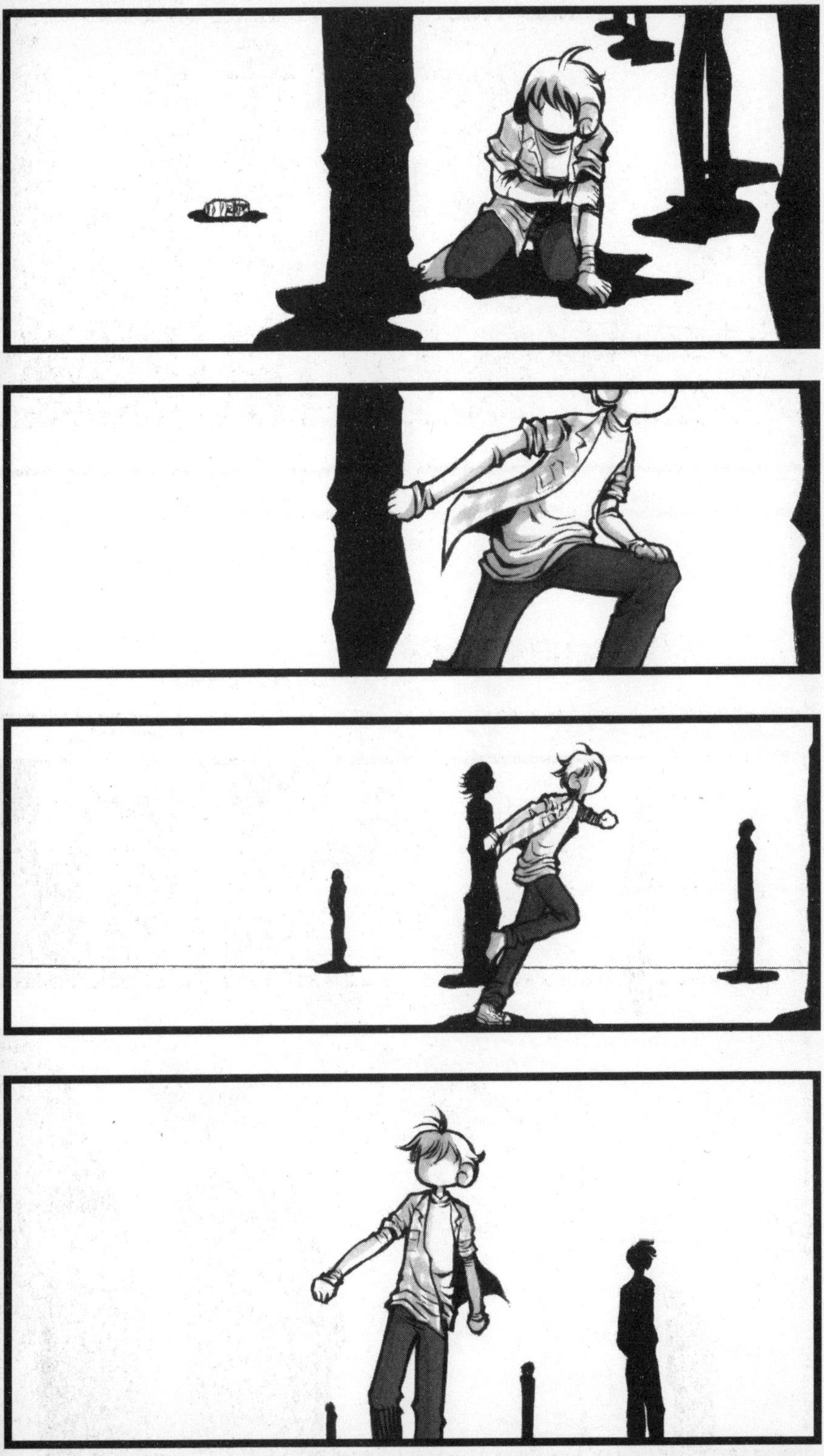

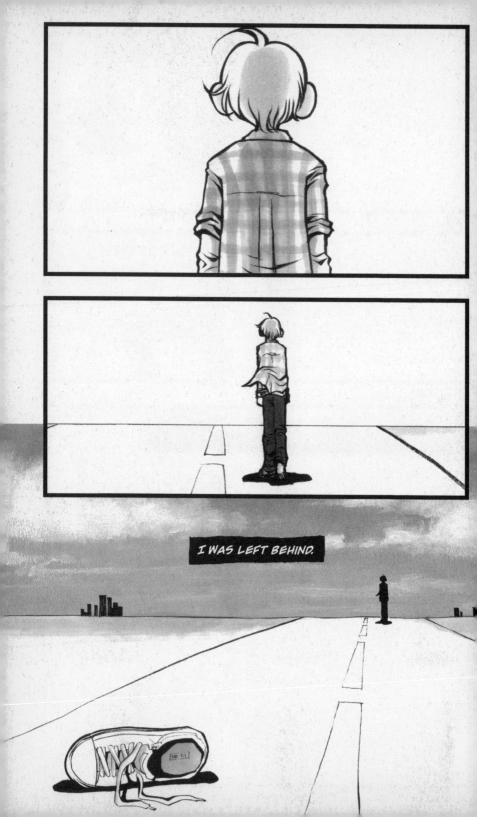

I WAS LEFT BEHIND.

Once upon a time ...

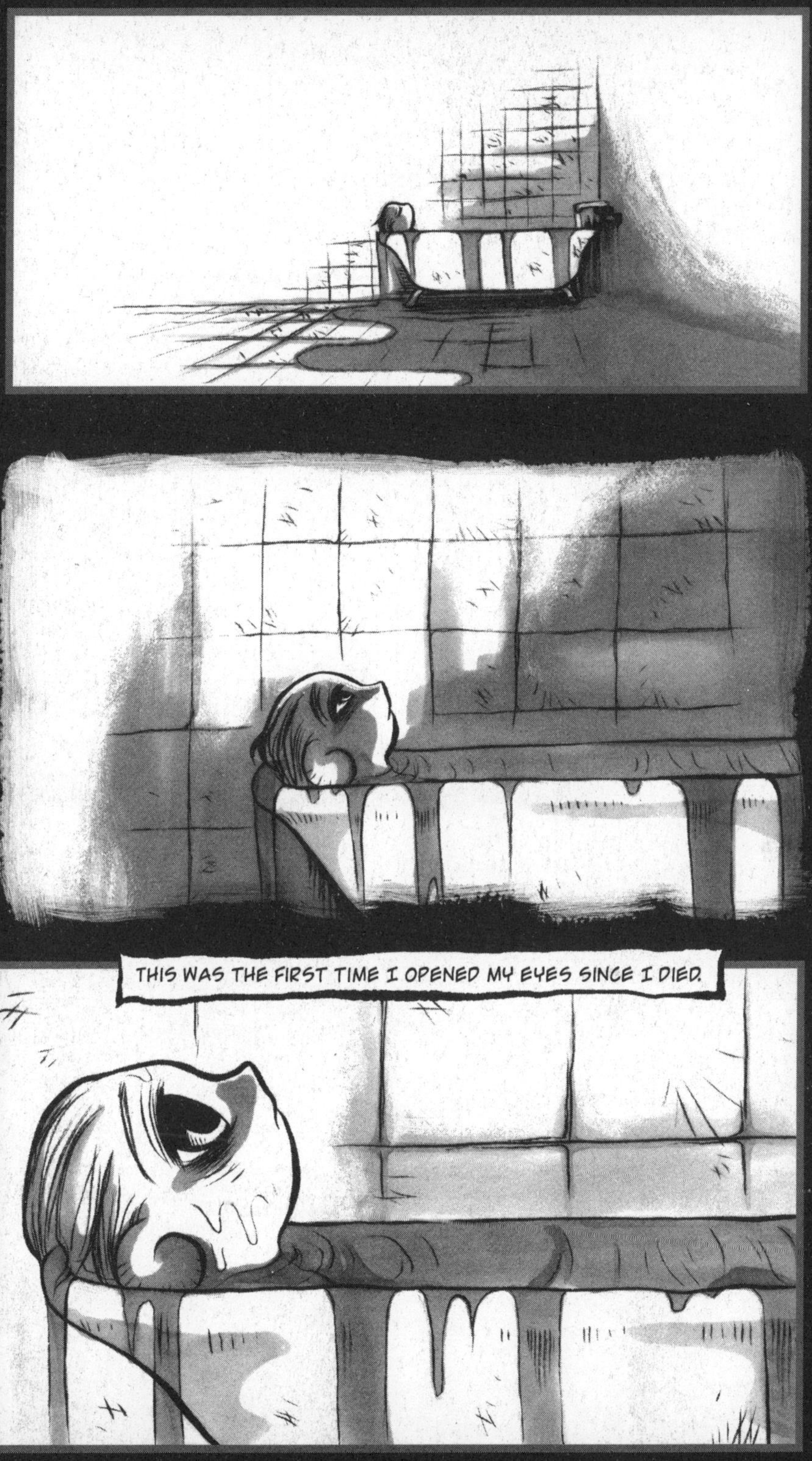
THIS WAS THE FIRST TIME I OPENED MY EYES SINCE I DIED.

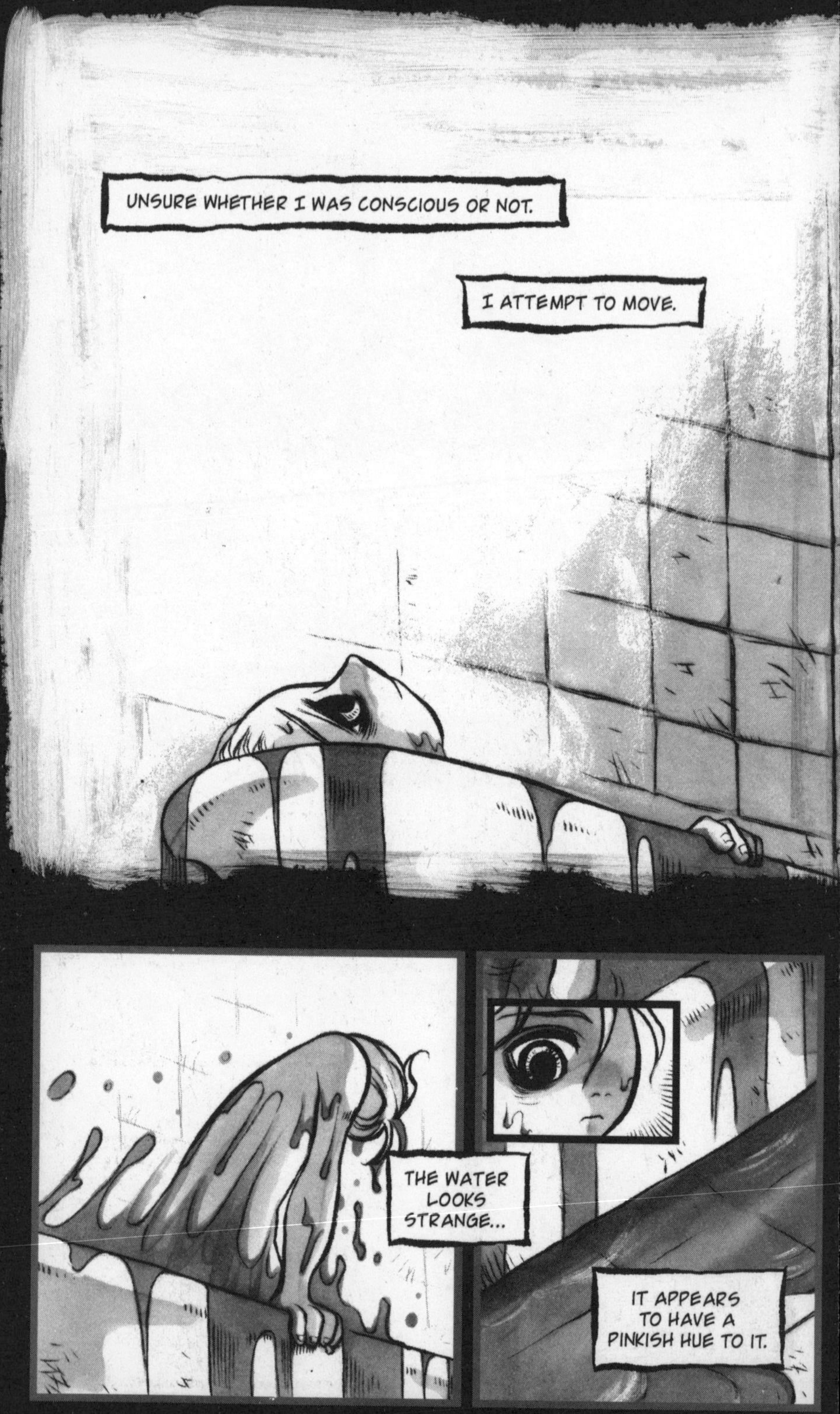
UNSURE WHETHER I WAS CONSCIOUS OR NOT.
I ATTEMPT TO MOVE.
THE WATER LOOKS STRANGE...
IT APPEARS TO HAVE A PINKISH HUE TO IT.

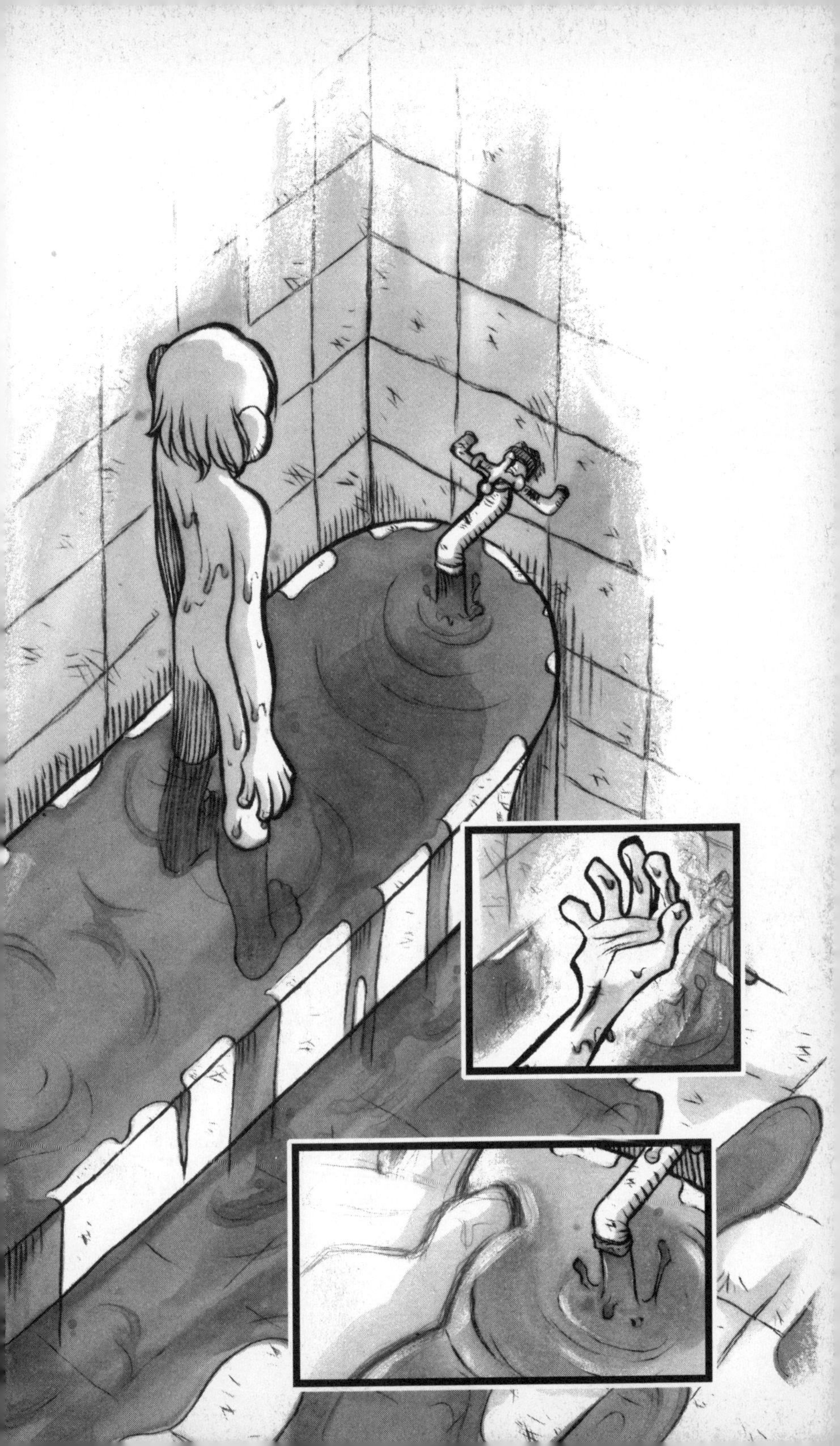

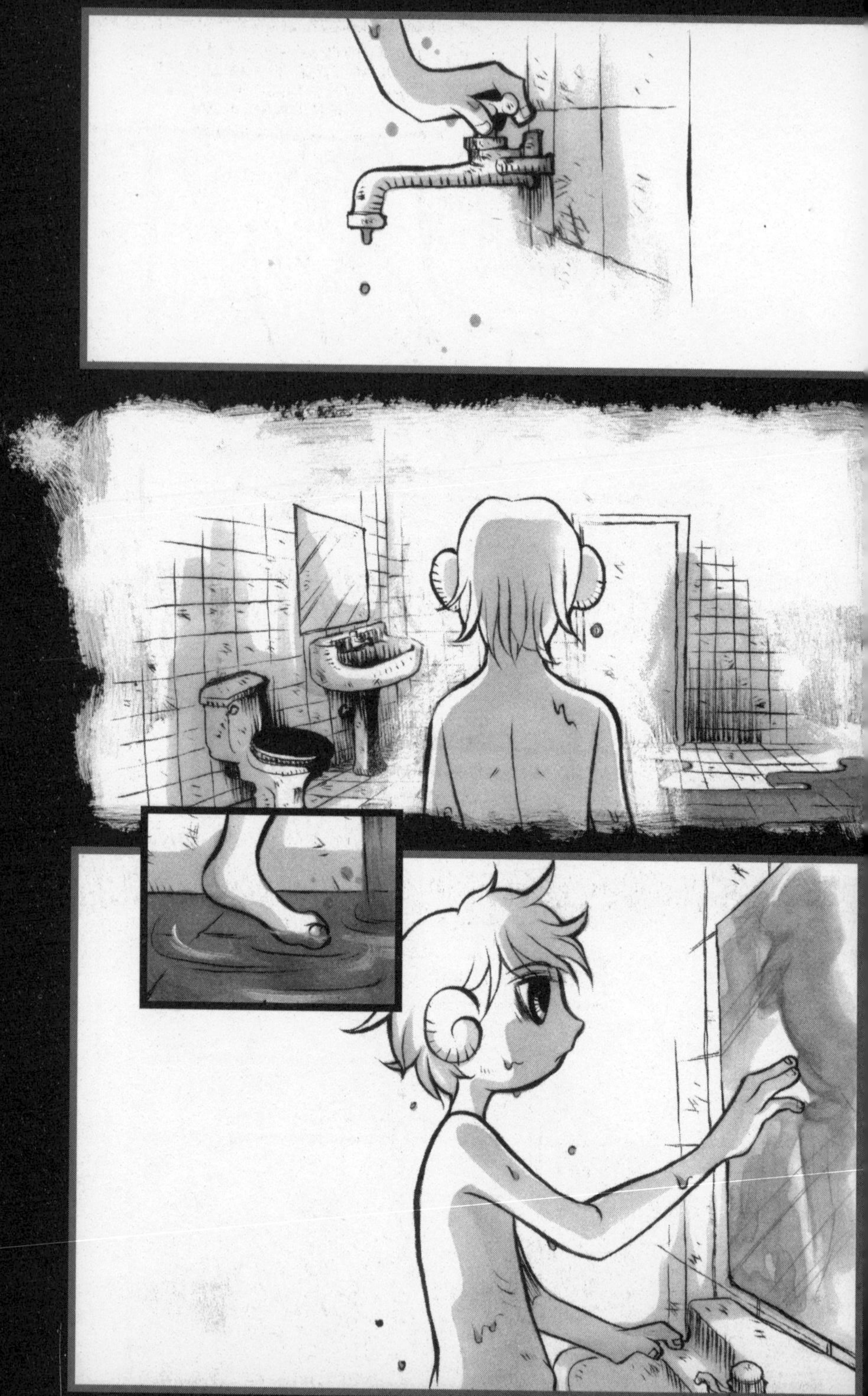

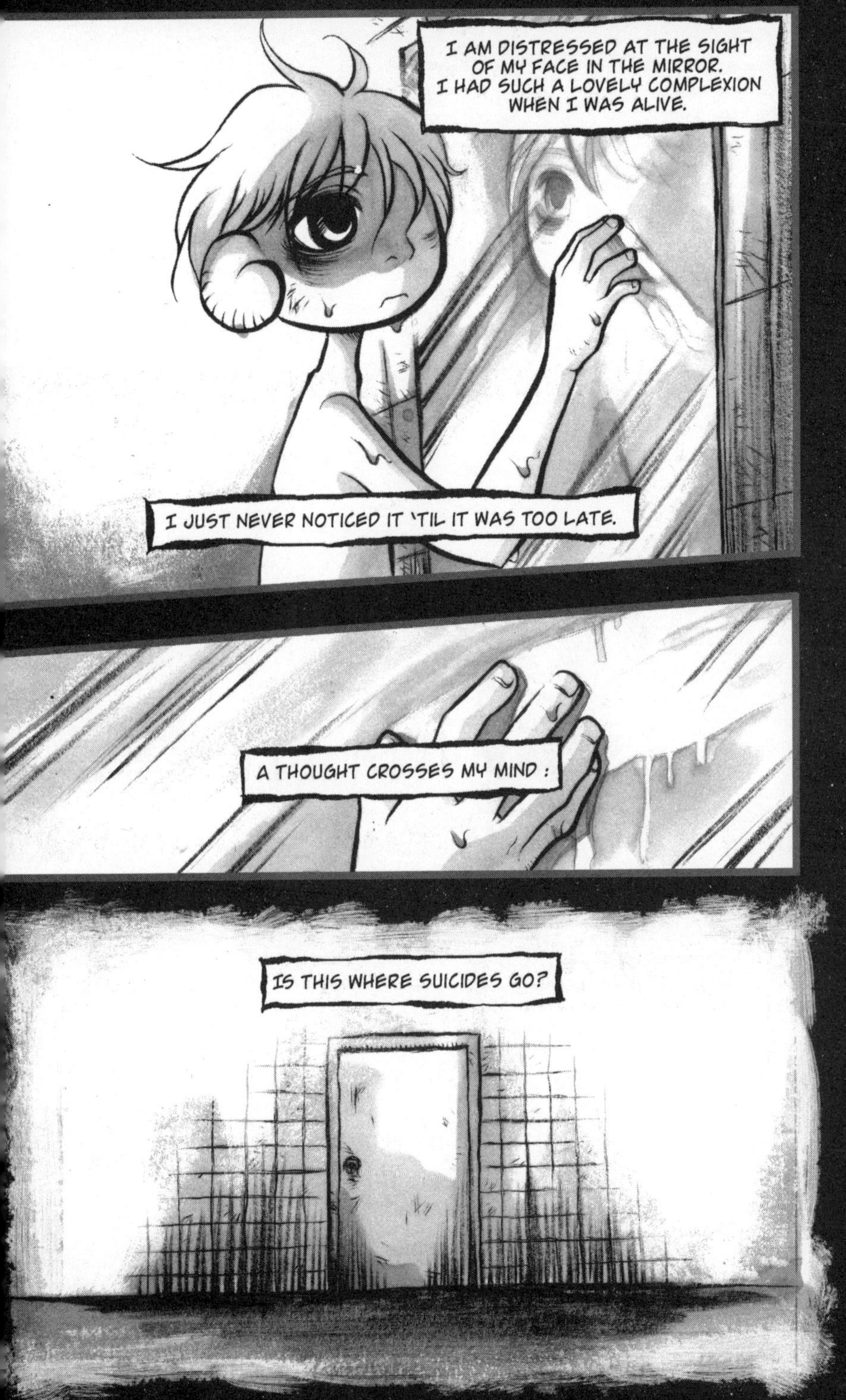
I AM DISTRESSED AT THE SIGHT OF MY FACE IN THE MIRROR. I HAD SUCH A LOVELY COMPLEXION WHEN I WAS ALIVE.
I JUST NEVER NOTICED IT 'TIL IT WAS TOO LATE.
A THOUGHT CROSSES MY MIND :
IS THIS WHERE SUICIDES GO?

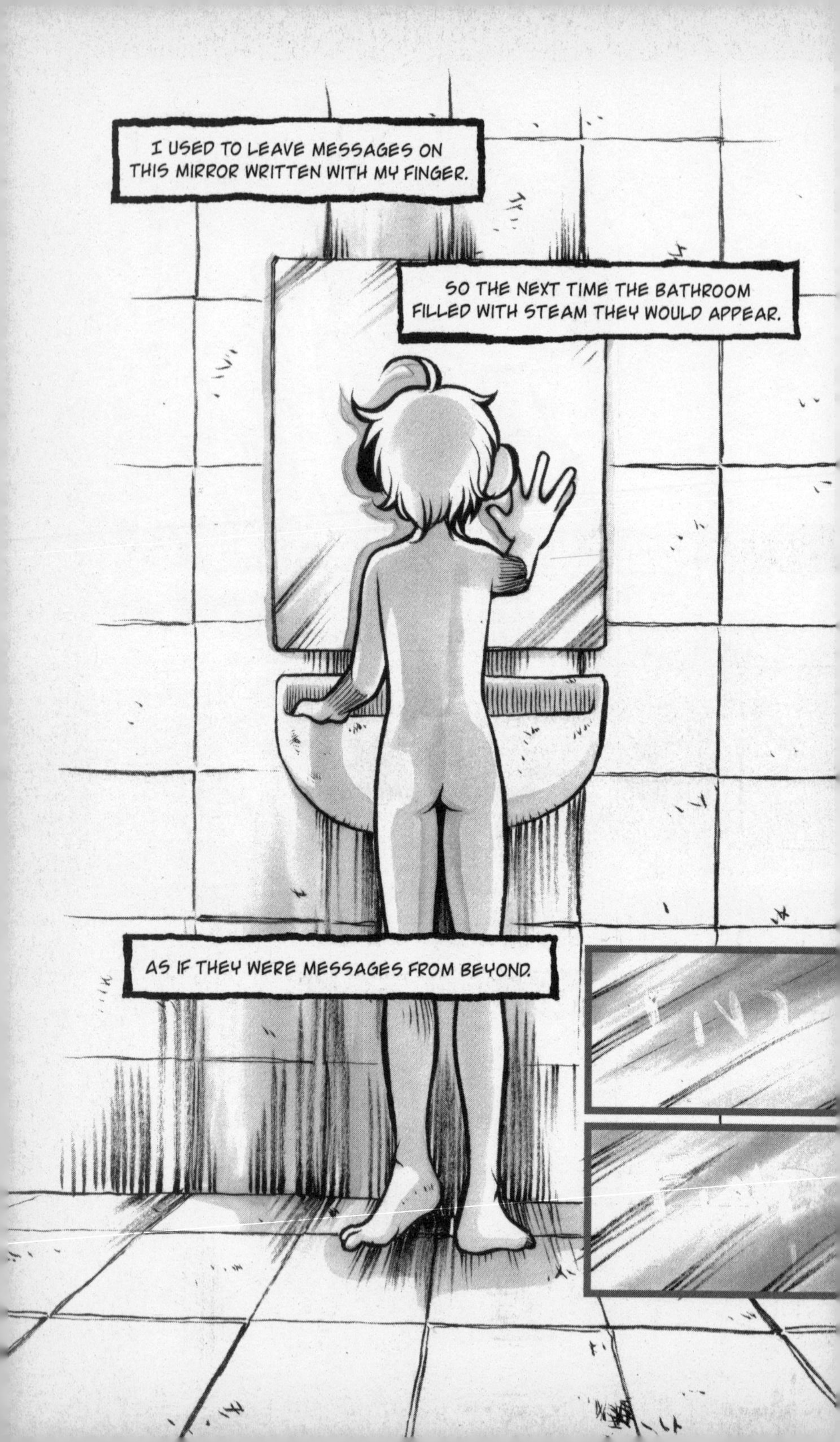
I USED TO LEAVE MESSAGES ON THIS MIRROR WRITTEN WITH MY FINGER.
SO THE NEXT TIME THE BATHROOM FILLED WITH STEAM THEY WOULD APPEAR.
AS IF THEY WERE MESSAGES FROM BEYOND.

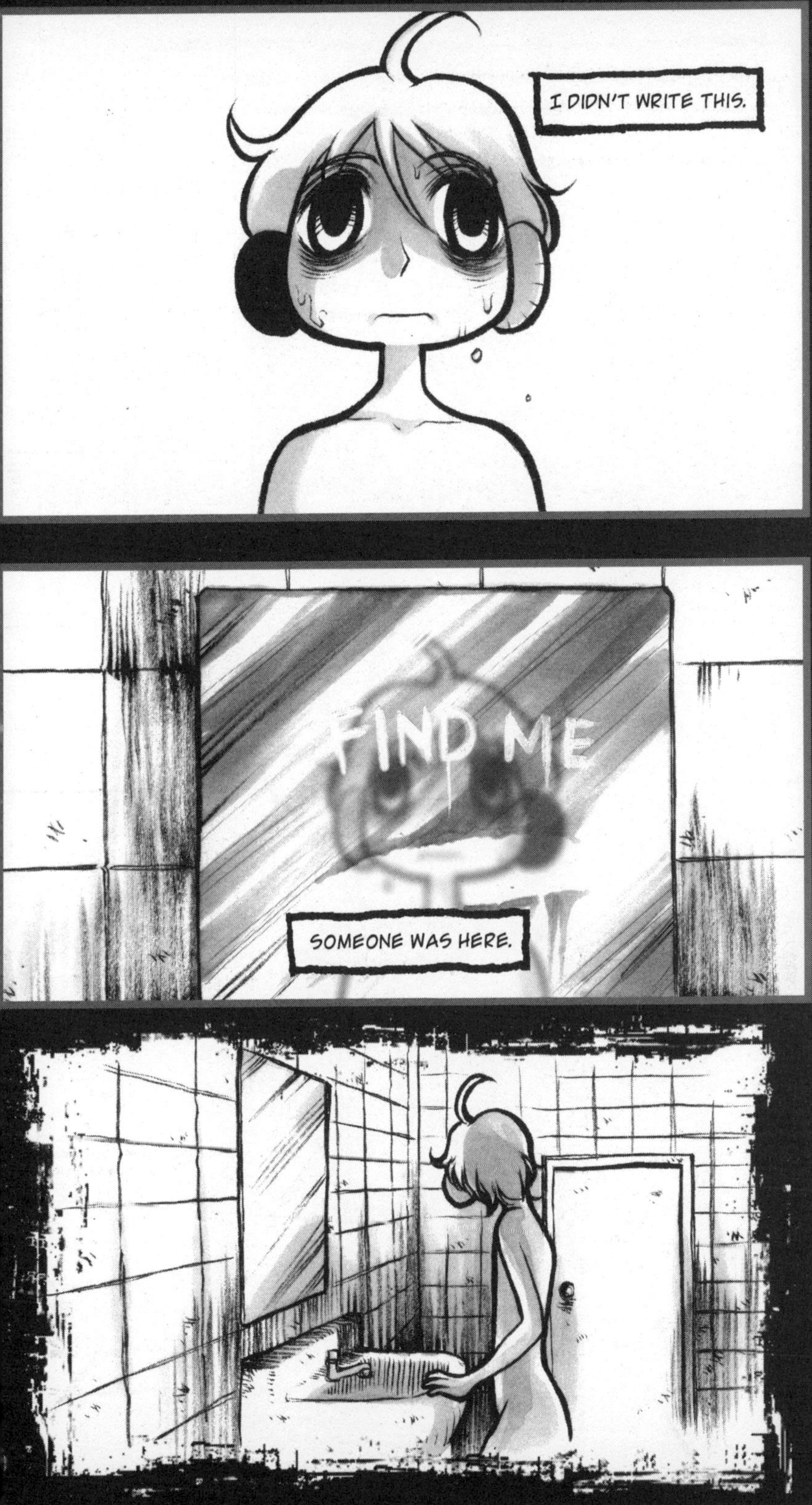
I DIDN'T WRITE THIS.
FIND ME
SOMEONE WAS HERE.

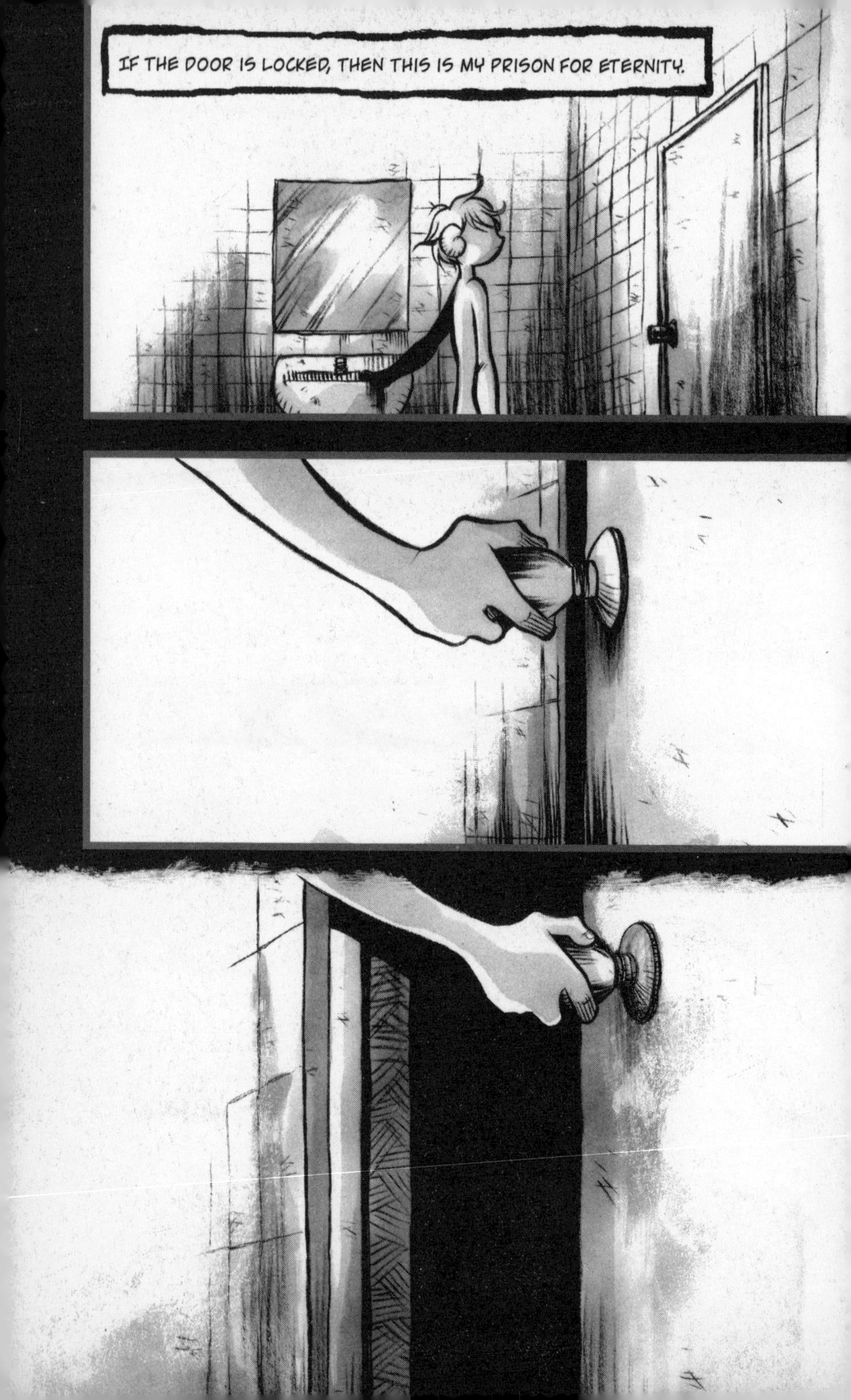
IF THE DOOR IS LOCKED, THEN THIS IS MY PRISON FOR ETERNITY.

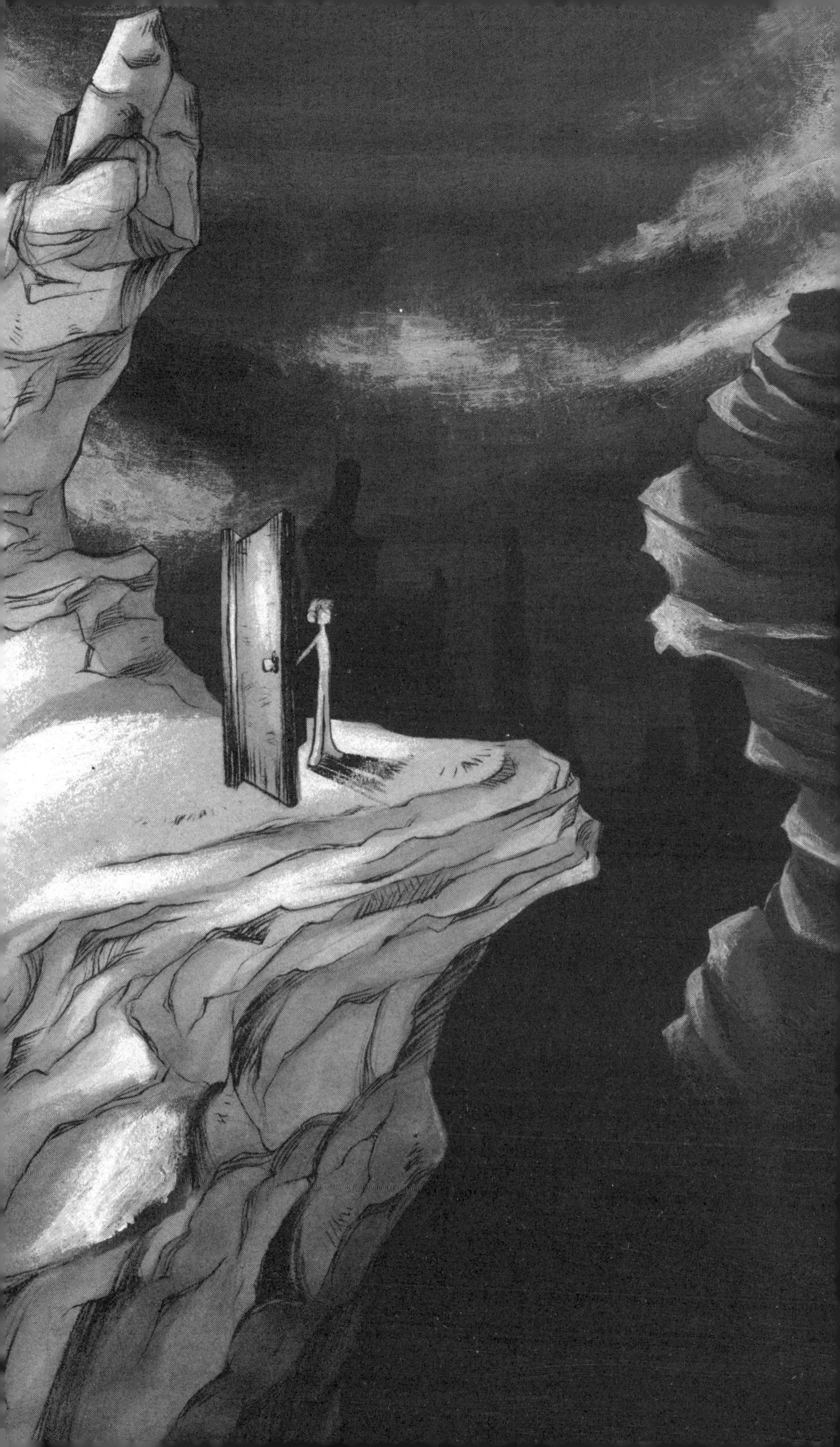

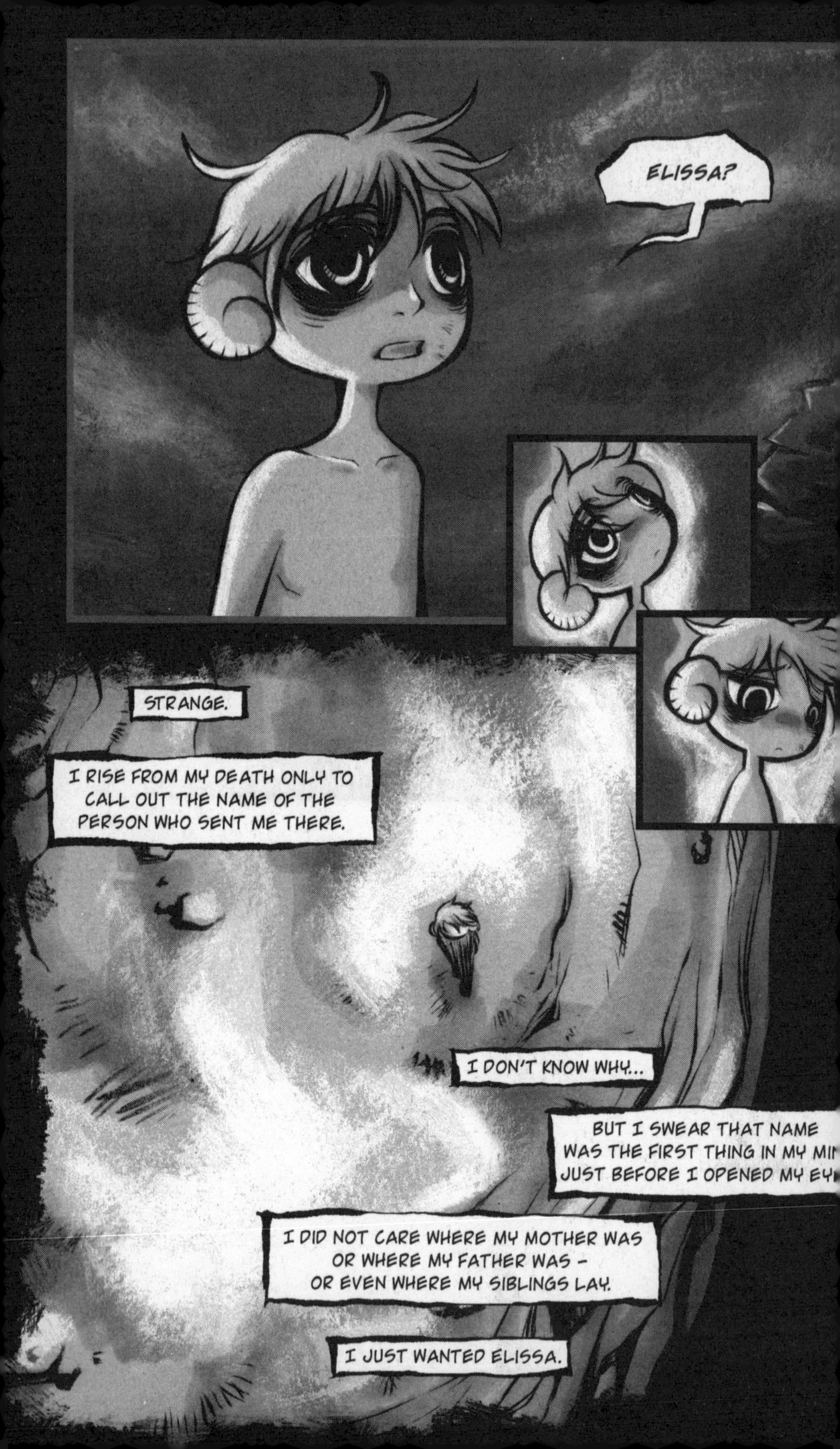
ELISSA?
STRANGE.
I RISE FROM MY DEATH ONLY TO CALL OUT THE NAME OF THE PERSON WHO SENT ME THERE.
I DON'T KNOW WHY...
BUT I SWEAR THAT NAME WAS THE FIRST THING IN MY MI
JUST BEFORE I OPENED MY EY
I DID NOT CARE WHERE MY MOTHER WAS OR WHERE MY FATHER WAS - OR EVEN WHERE MY SIBLINGS LAY.
I JUST WANTED ELISSA.

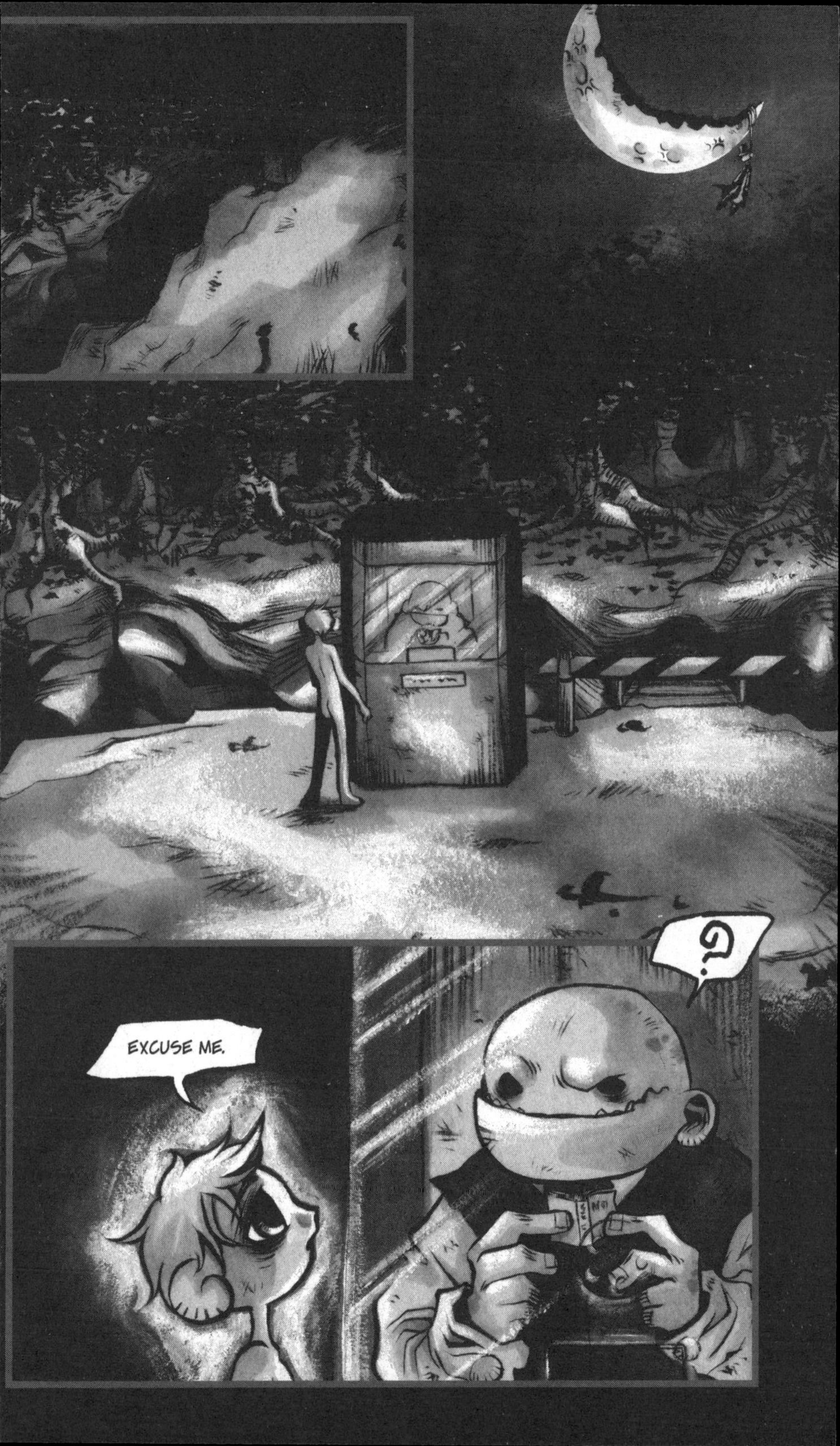
EXCUSE ME.
?

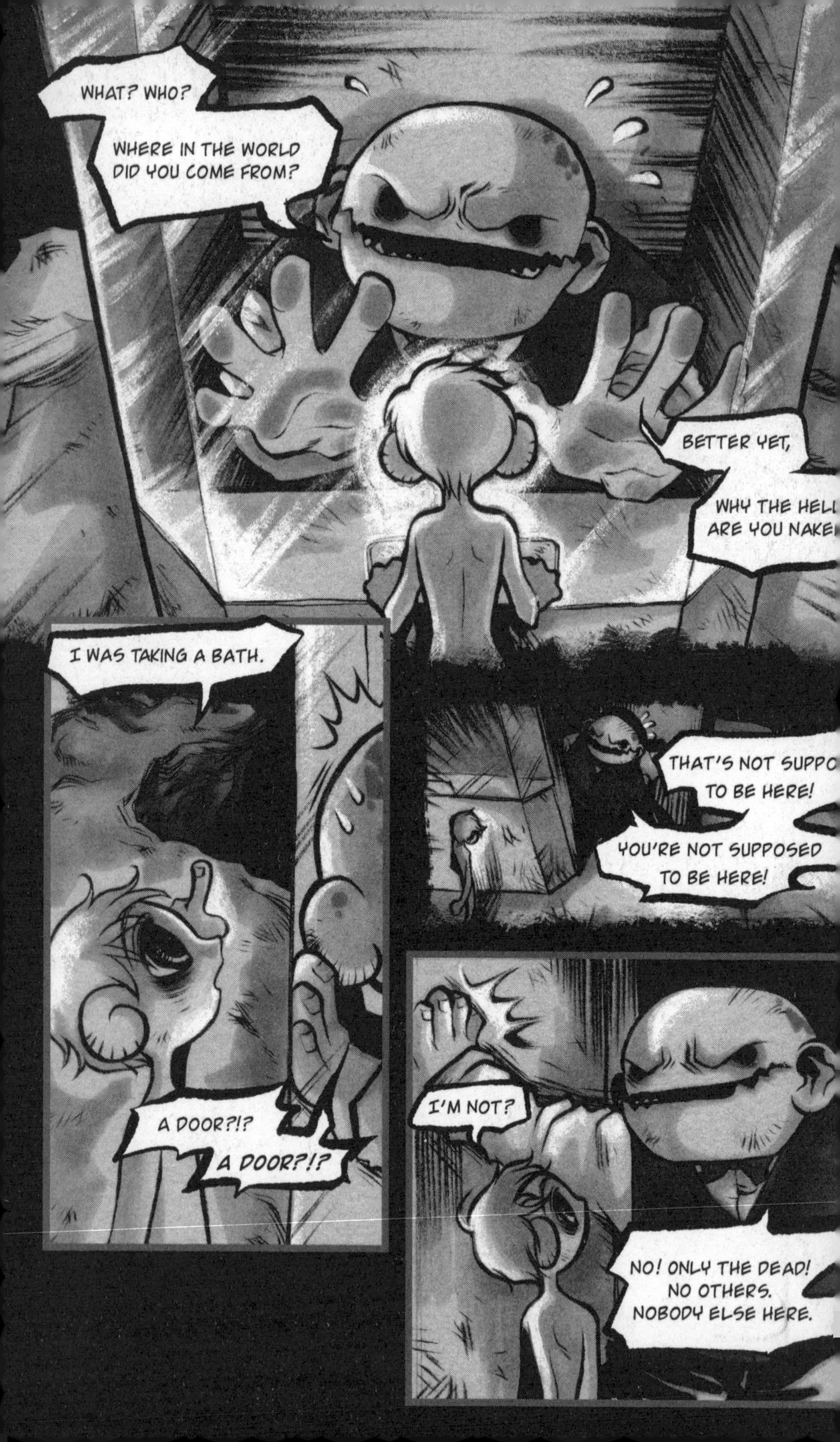
WHAT? WHO?
WHERE IN THE WORLD DID YOU COME FROM?
BETTER YET,
WHY THE HELL ARE YOU NAKE
I WAS TAKING A BATH.
A DOOR?!?
A DOOR?!?
THAT'S NOT SUPPO TO BE HERE!
YOU'RE NOT SUPPOSED TO BE HERE!
I'M NOT?
NO! ONLY THE DEAD! NO OTHERS. NOBODY ELSE HERE.

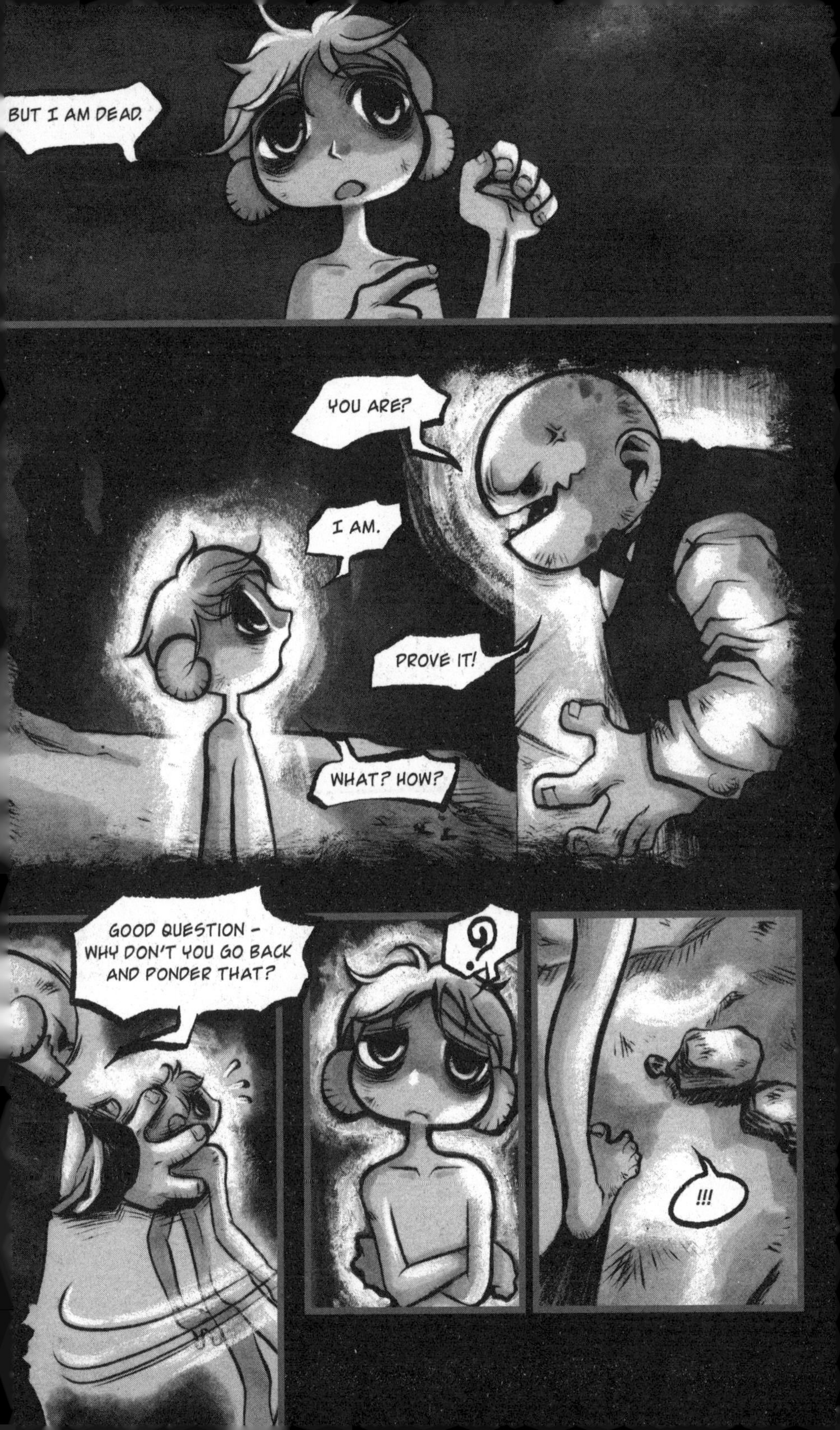
BUT I AM DEAD.
YOU ARE?
I AM.
PROVE IT!
WHAT? HOW?
GOOD QUESTION - WHY DON'T YOU GO BACK AND PONDER THAT?
?
!!!

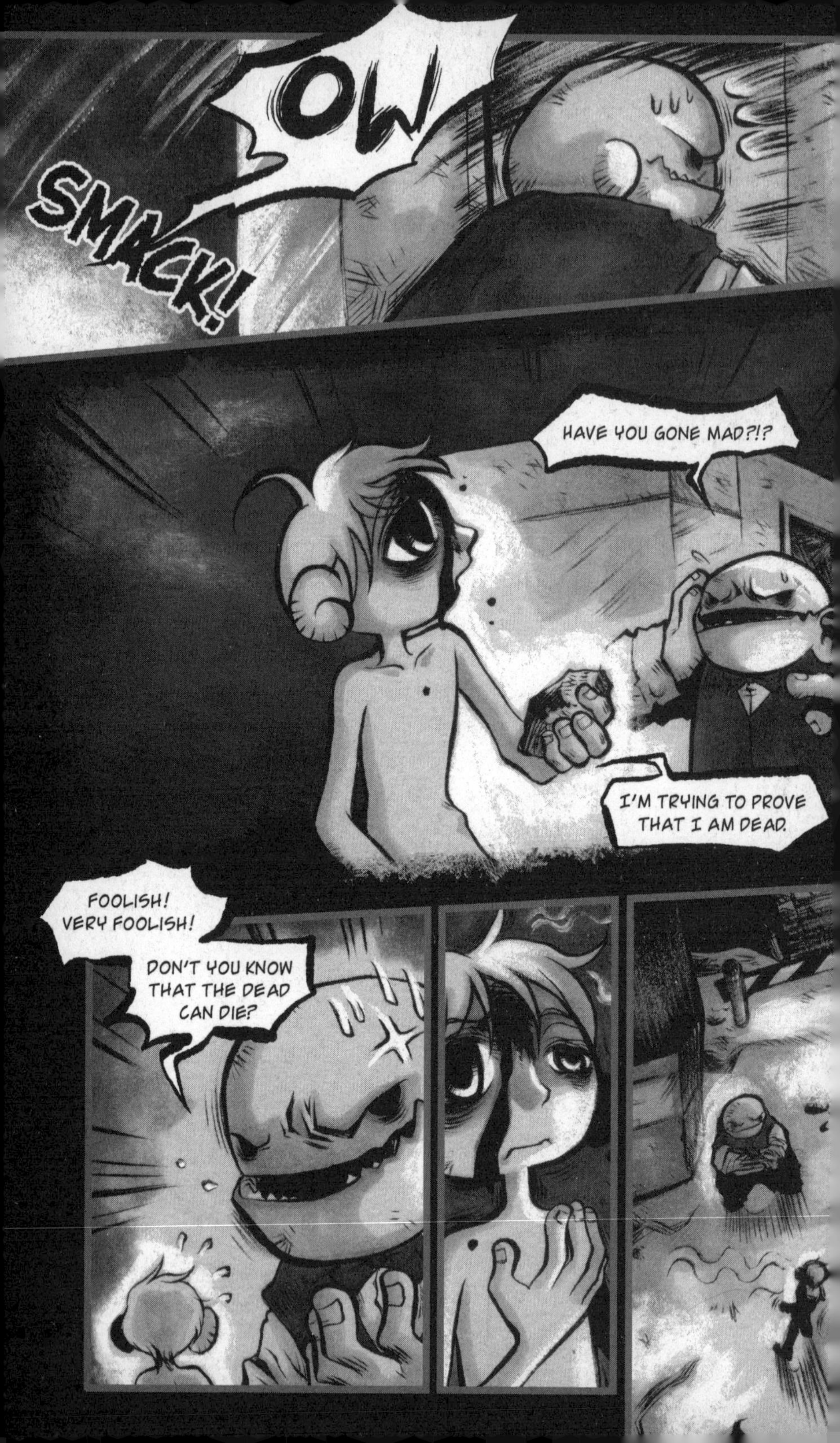
OW
SMACK!
HAVE YOU GONE MAD?!?
I'M TRYING TO PROVE THAT I AM DEAD.
FOOLISH! VERY FOOLISH!
DON'T YOU KNOW THAT THE DEAD CAN DIE?

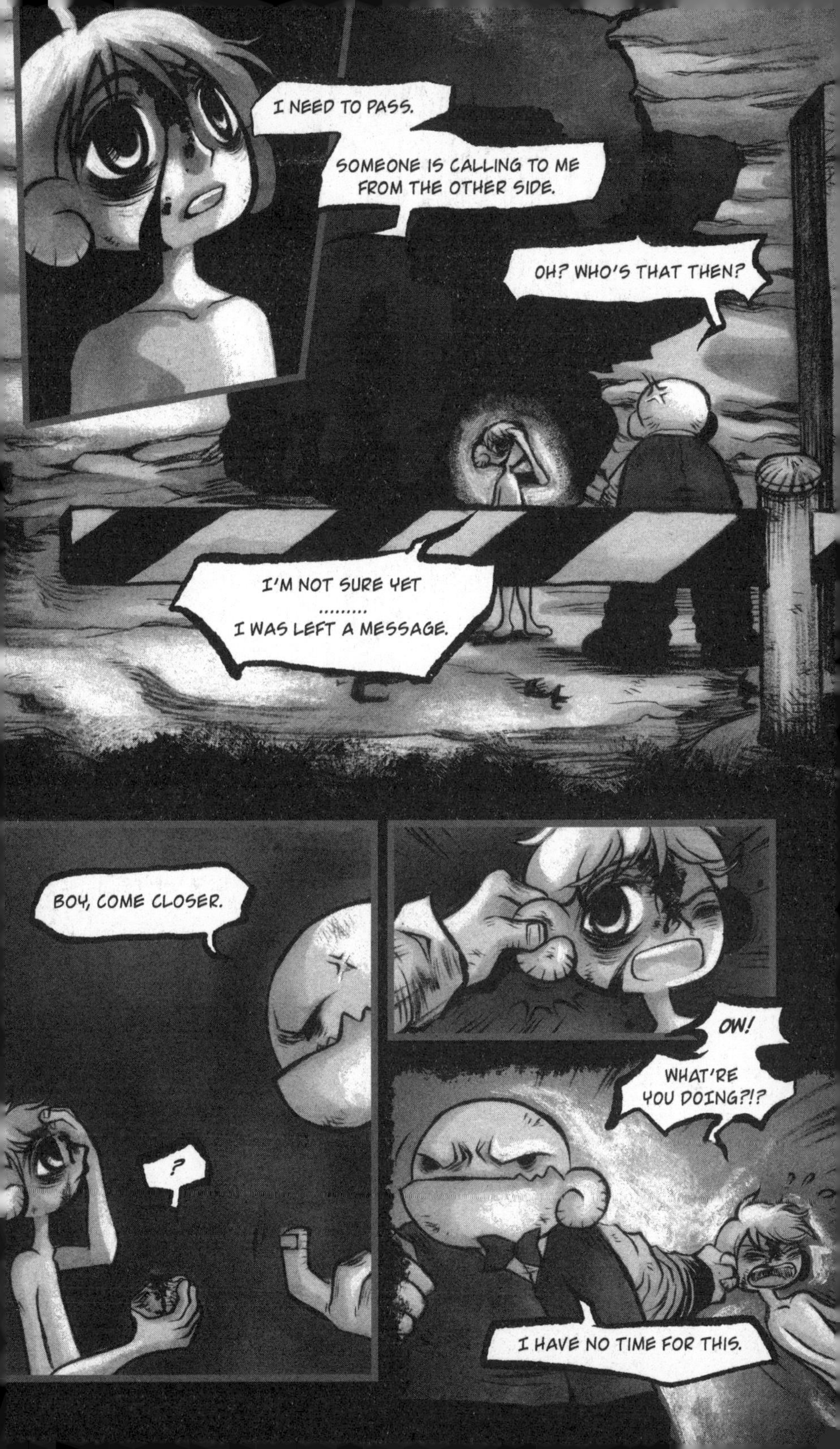
I NEED TO PASS.
SOMEONE IS CALLING TO ME FROM THE OTHER SIDE.
OH? WHO'S THAT THEN?
I'M NOT SURE YET .... I WAS LEFT A MESSAGE.
BOY, COME CLOSER.
?
OW!
WHAT'RE YOU DOING?!?
I HAVE NO TIME FOR THIS.

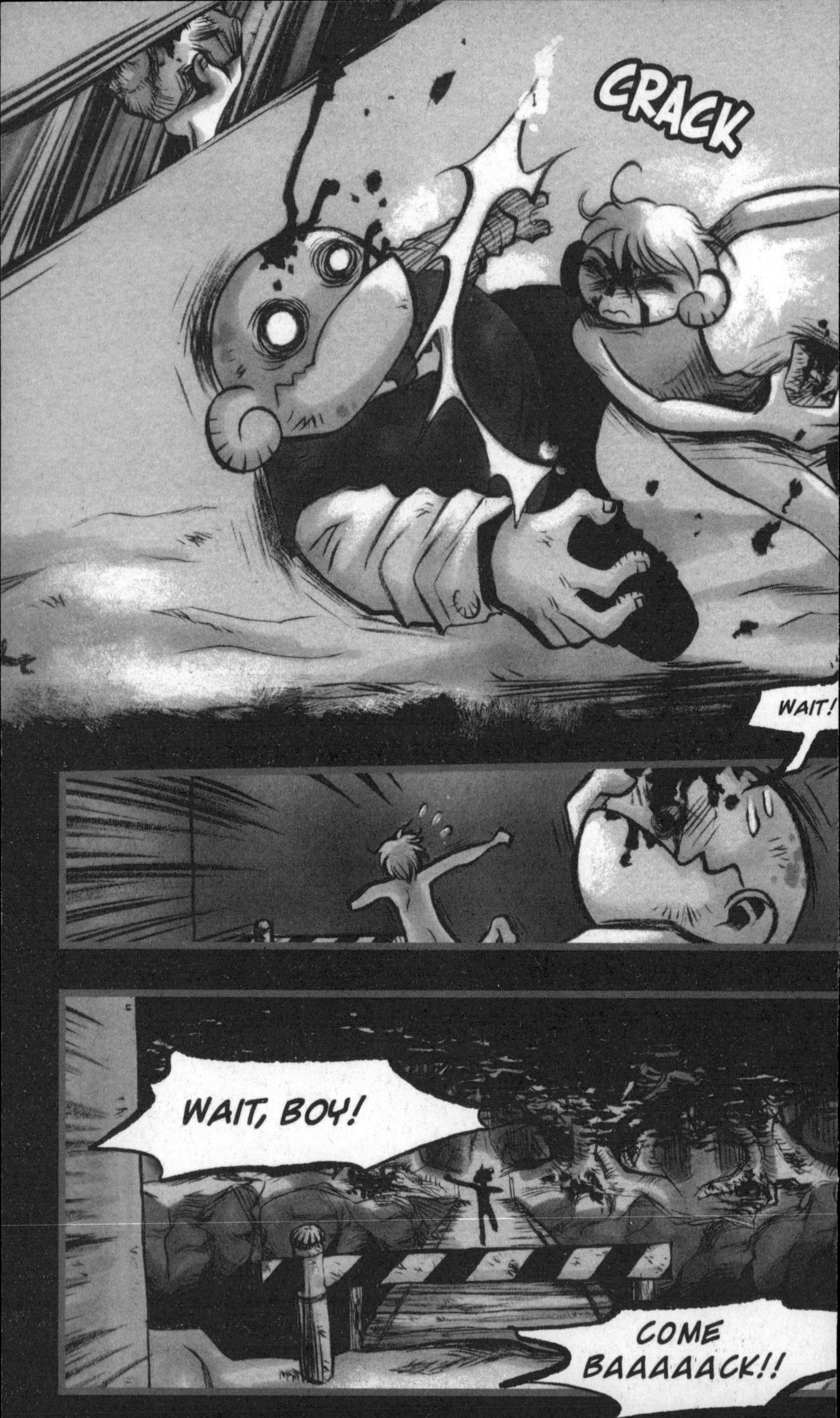
CRACK
WAIT!
WAIT, BOY!
COME BAAAAACK!!

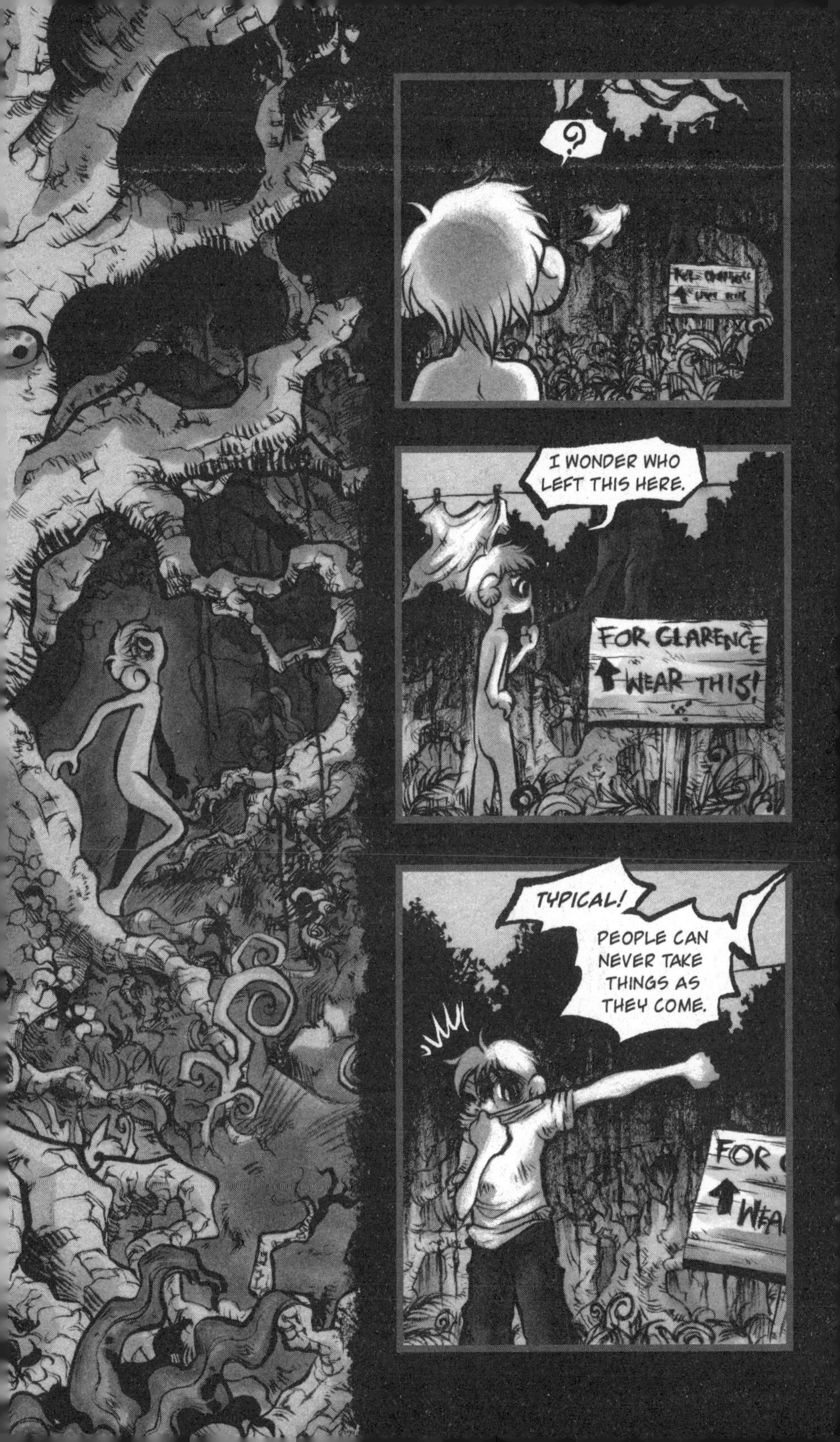
?
I WONDER WHO LEFT THIS HERE.
FOR CLARENCE
WEAR THIS!
TYPICAL!
PEOPLE CAN NEVER TAKE THINGS AS THEY COME.

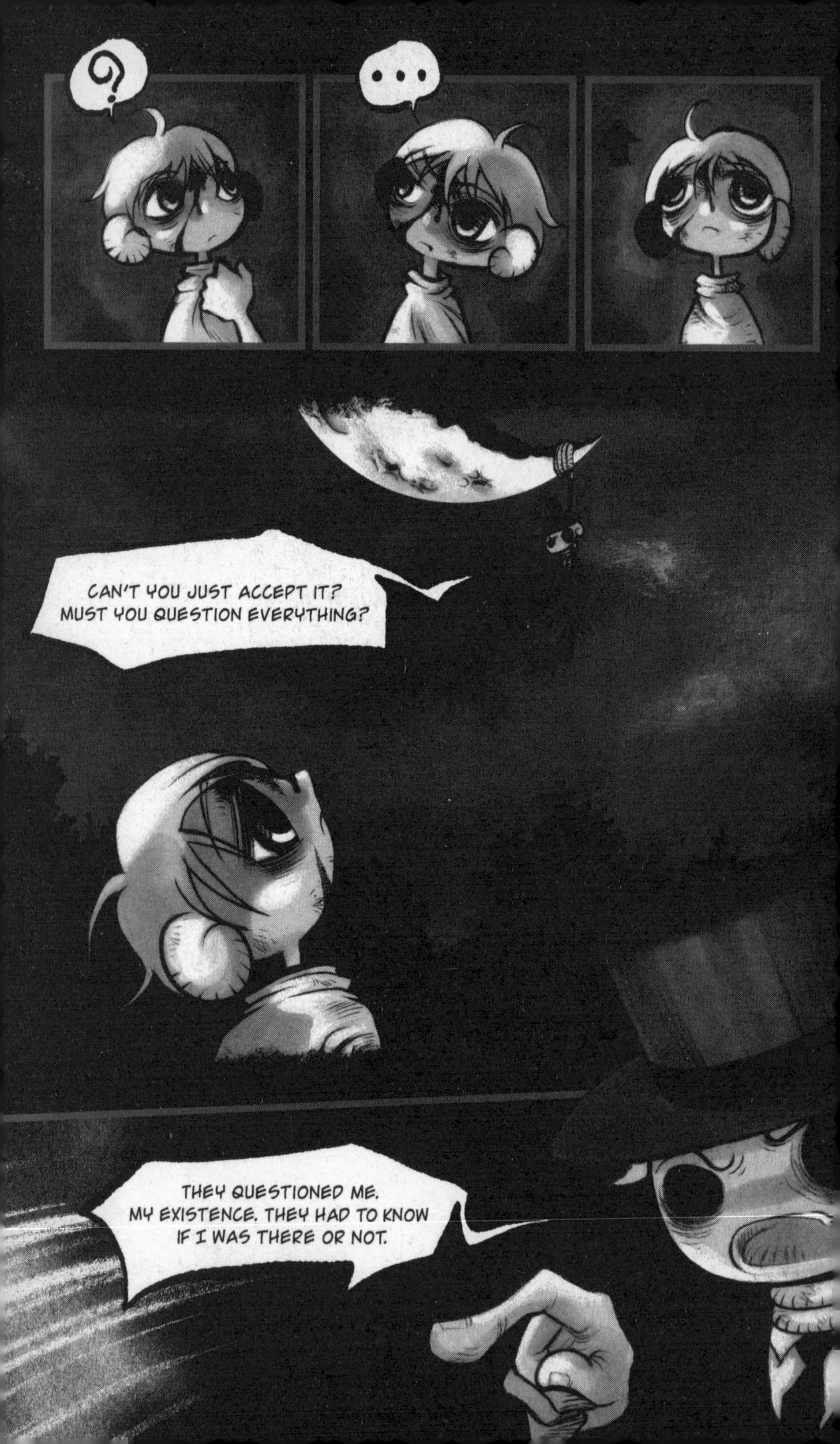
?
...
CAN'T YOU JUST ACCEPT IT? MUST YOU QUESTION EVERYTHING?
THEY QUESTIONED ME. MY EXISTENCE. THEY HAD TO KNOW IF I WAS THERE OR NOT.

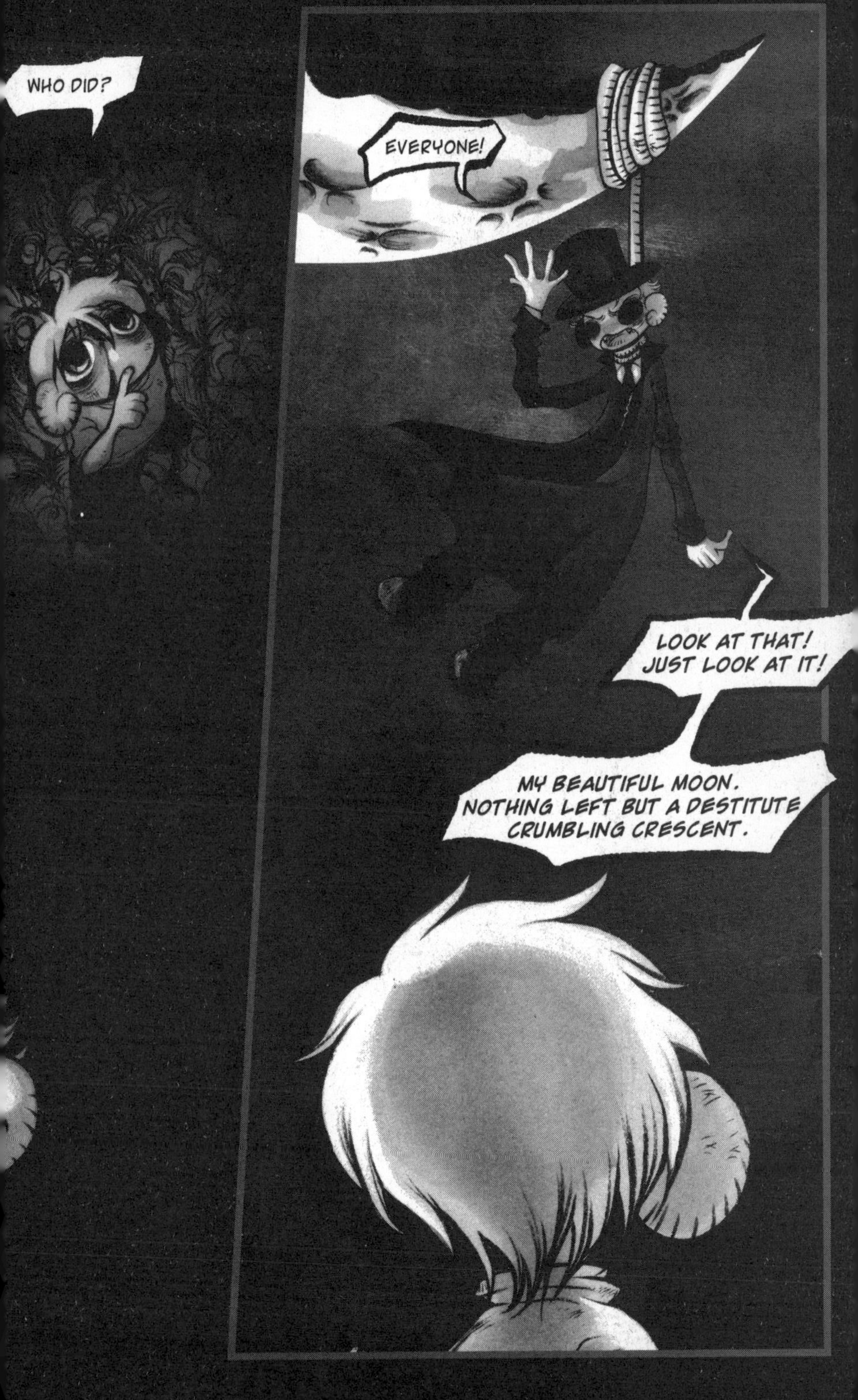
WHO DID?
EVERYONE!
LOOK AT THAT! JUST LOOK AT IT!
MY BEAUTIFUL MOON. NOTHING LEFT BUT A DESTITUTE CRUMBLING CRESCENT.

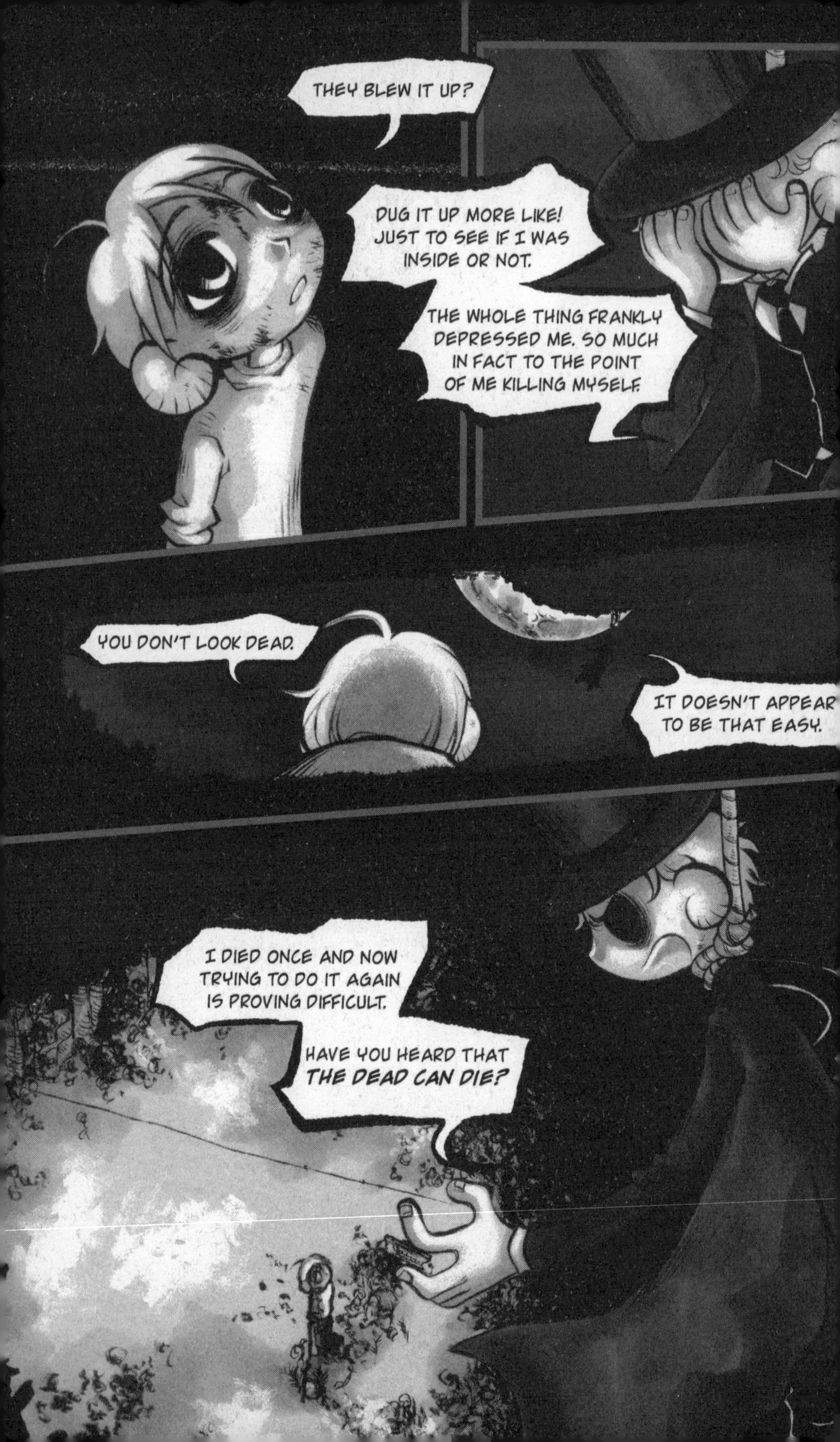
THEY BLEW IT UP?
DUG IT UP MORE LIKE! JUST TO SEE IF I WAS INSIDE OR NOT.
THE WHOLE THING FRANKLY DEPRESSED ME. SO MUCH IN FACT TO THE POINT OF ME KILLING MYSELF.
YOU DON'T LOOK DEAD.
IT DOESN'T APPEAR TO BE THAT EASY.
I DIED ONCE AND NOW TRYING TO DO IT AGAIN IS PROVING DIFFICULT.
HAVE YOU HEARD THAT *THE DEAD CAN DIE?*

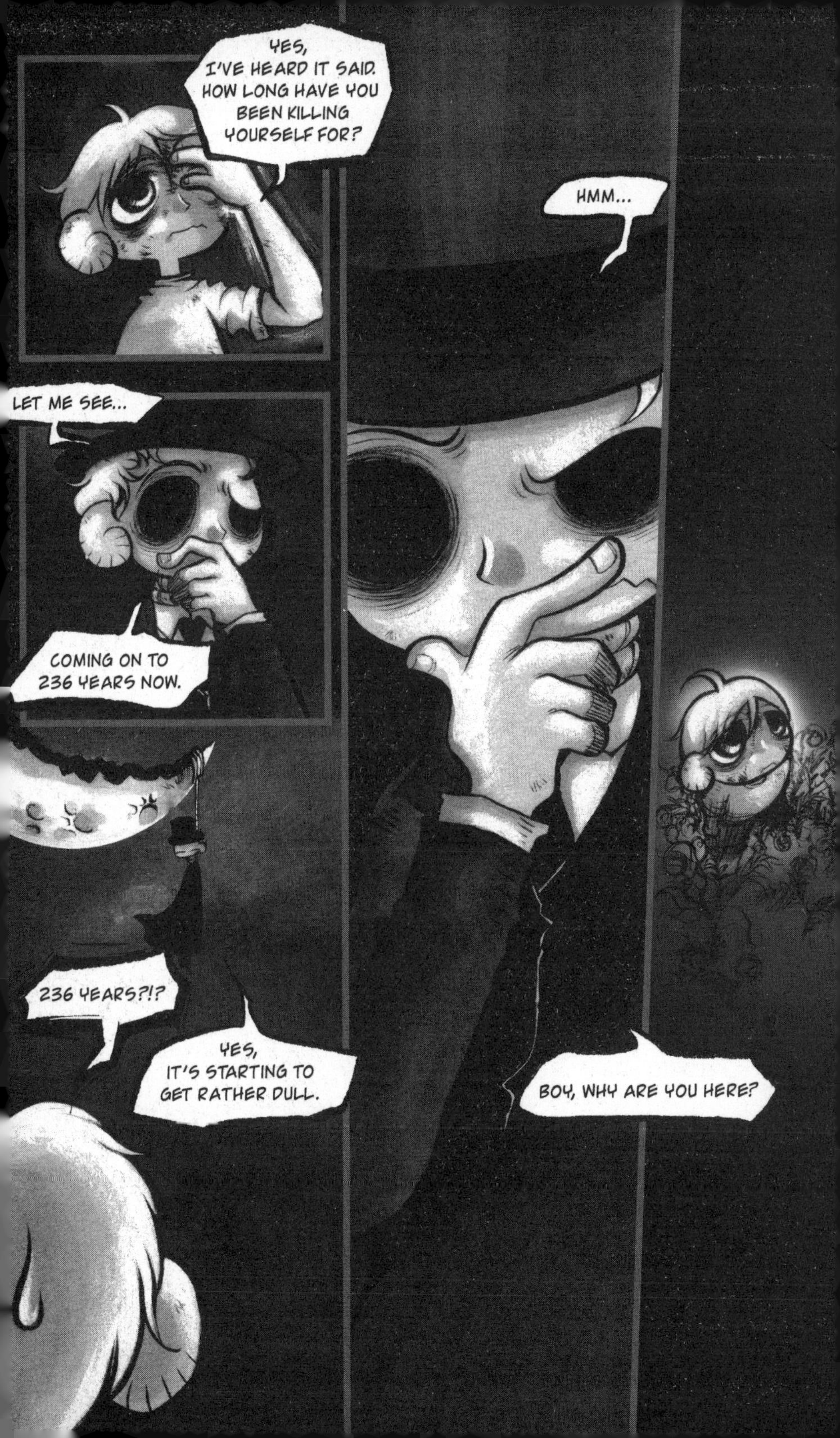

YES,
I'VE HEARD IT SAID.
HOW LONG HAVE YOU
BEEN KILLING
YOURSELF FOR?
LET ME SEE...
COMING ON TO
236 YEARS NOW.
HMM...
236 YEARS?!?
YES,
IT'S STARTING TO
GET RATHER DULL.
BOY, WHY ARE YOU HERE?

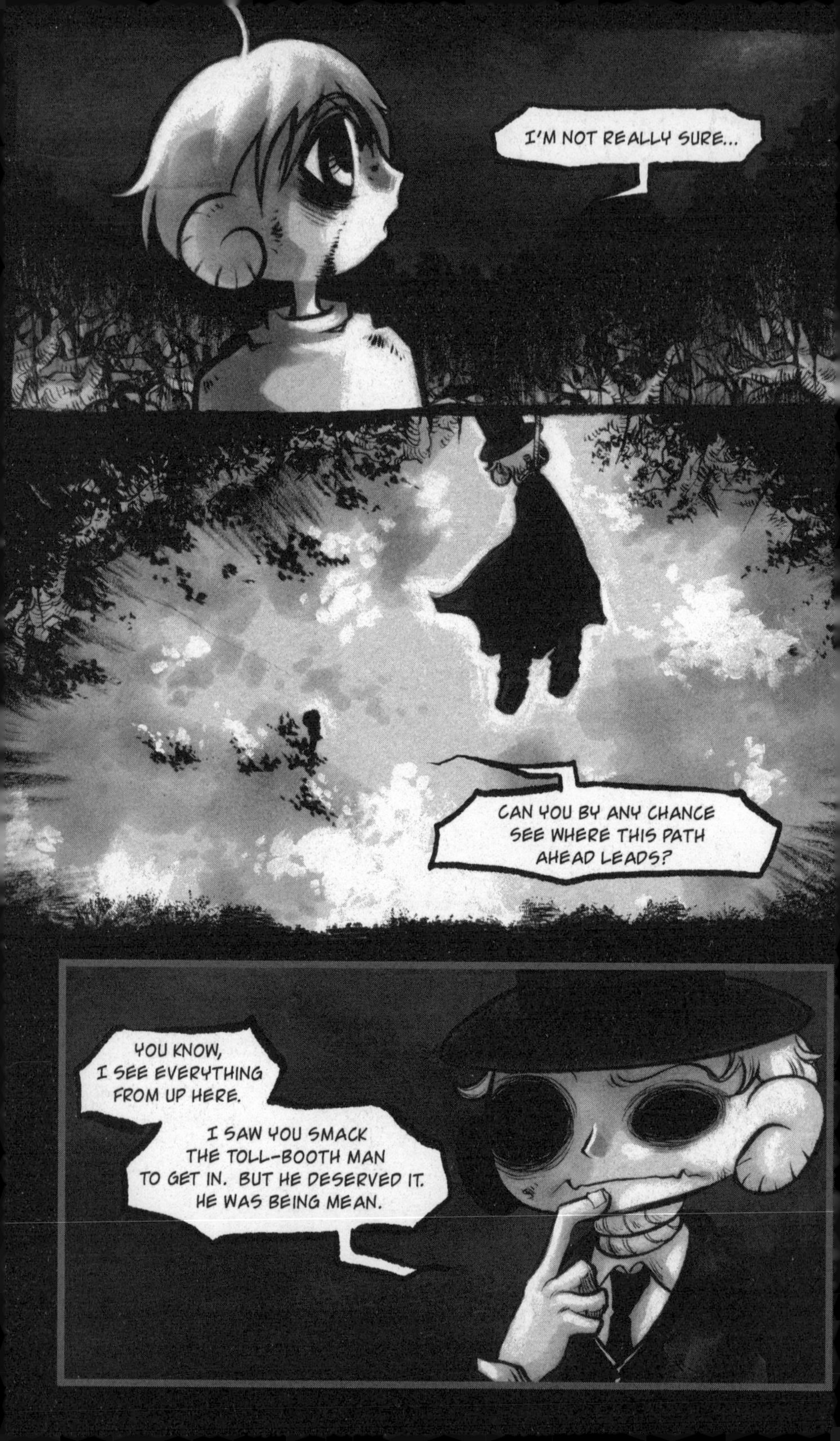
I'M NOT REALLY SURE...
CAN YOU BY ANY CHANCE SEE WHERE THIS PATH AHEAD LEADS?
YOU KNOW, I SEE EVERYTHING FROM UP HERE.
I SAW YOU SMACK THE TOLL-BOOTH MAN TO GET IN. BUT HE DESERVED IT. HE WAS BEING MEAN.

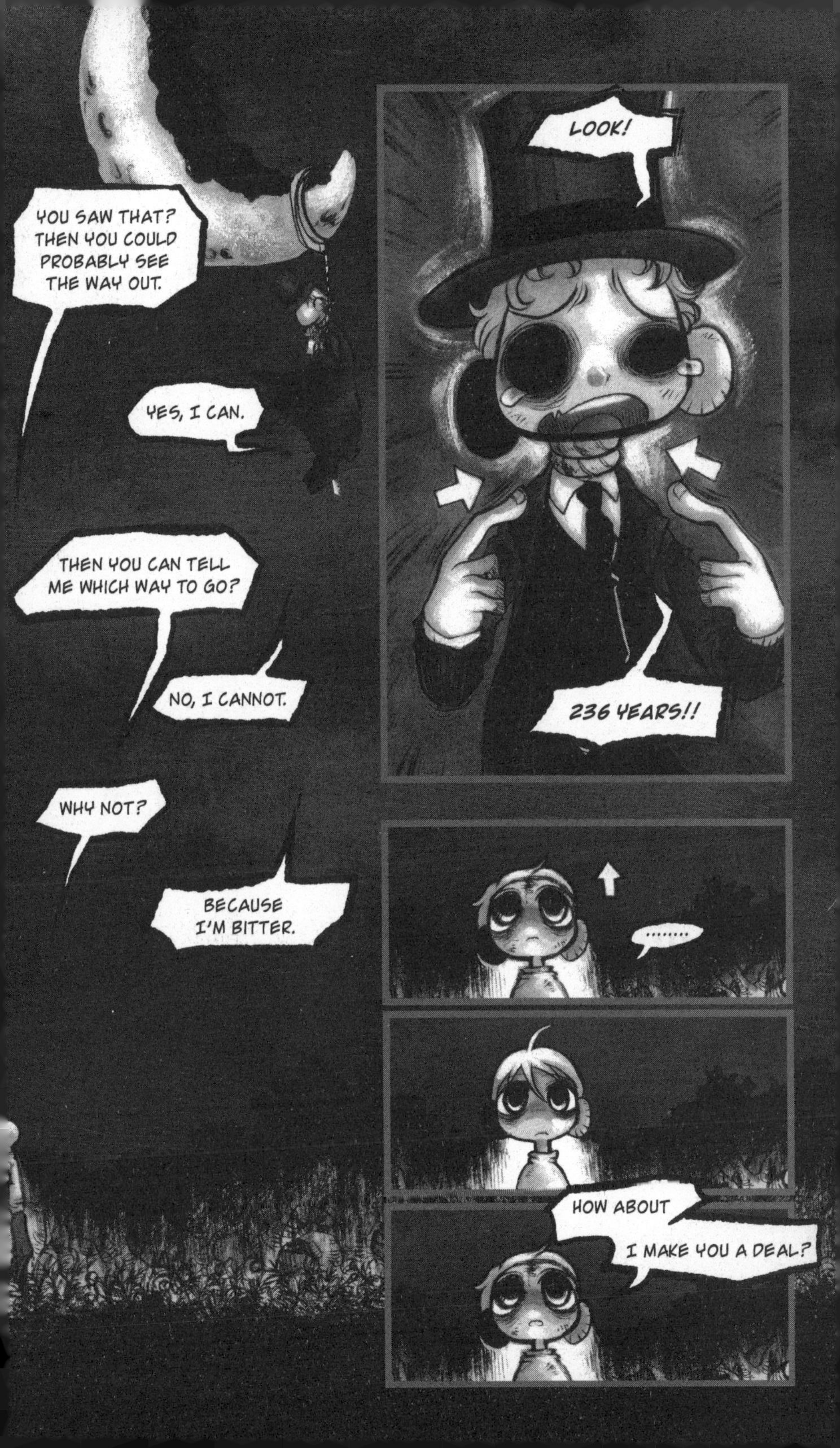
YOU SAW THAT? THEN YOU COULD PROBABLY SEE THE WAY OUT.
YES, I CAN.
THEN YOU CAN TELL ME WHICH WAY TO GO?
NO, I CANNOT.
WHY NOT?
BECAUSE I'M BITTER.
LOOK!
236 YEARS!!
....
HOW ABOUT
I MAKE YOU A DEAL?

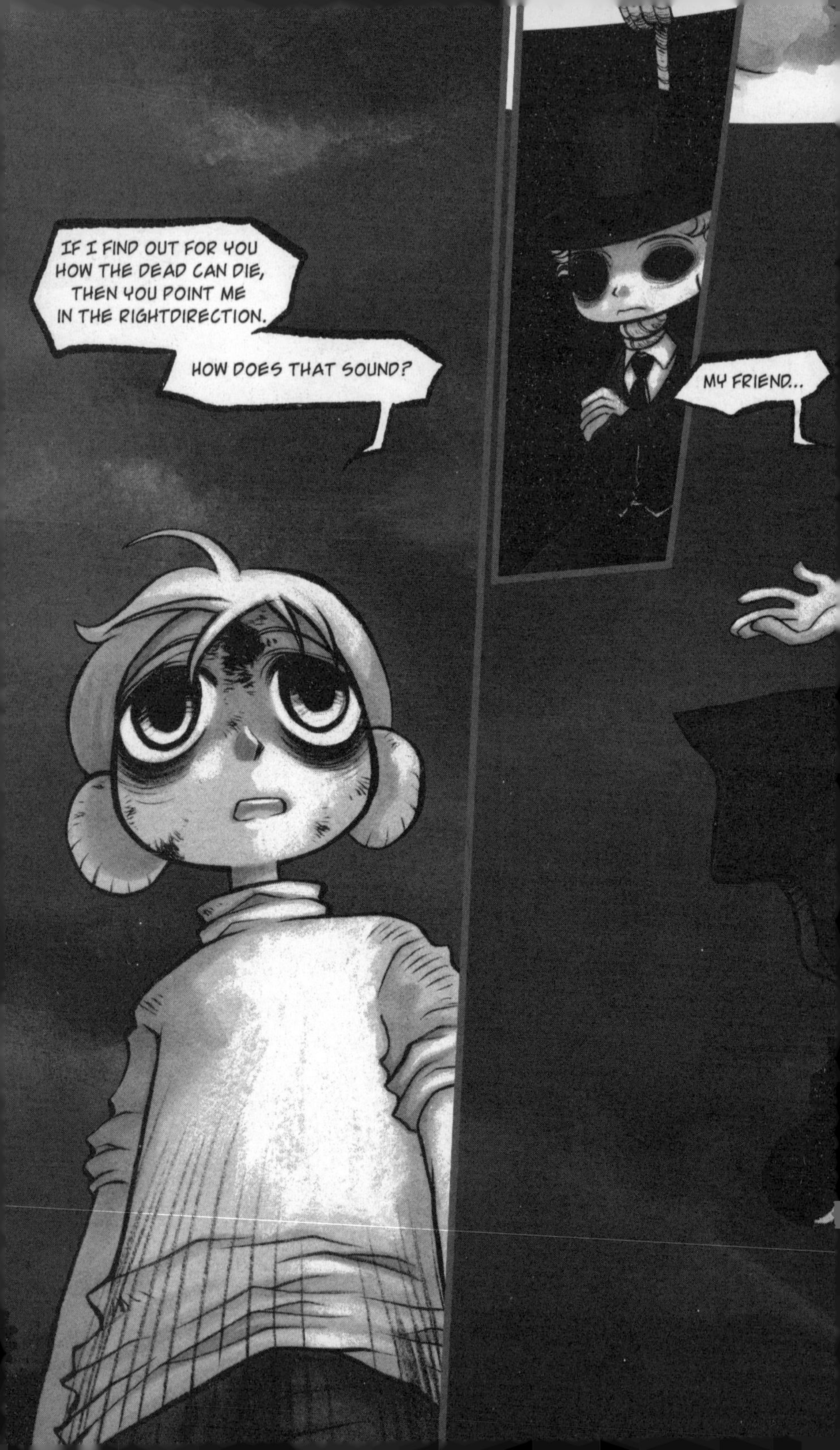
IF I FIND OUT FOR YOU HOW THE DEAD CAN DIE, THEN YOU POINT ME IN THE RIGHTDIRECTION.
HOW DOES THAT SOUND?
MY FRIEND...

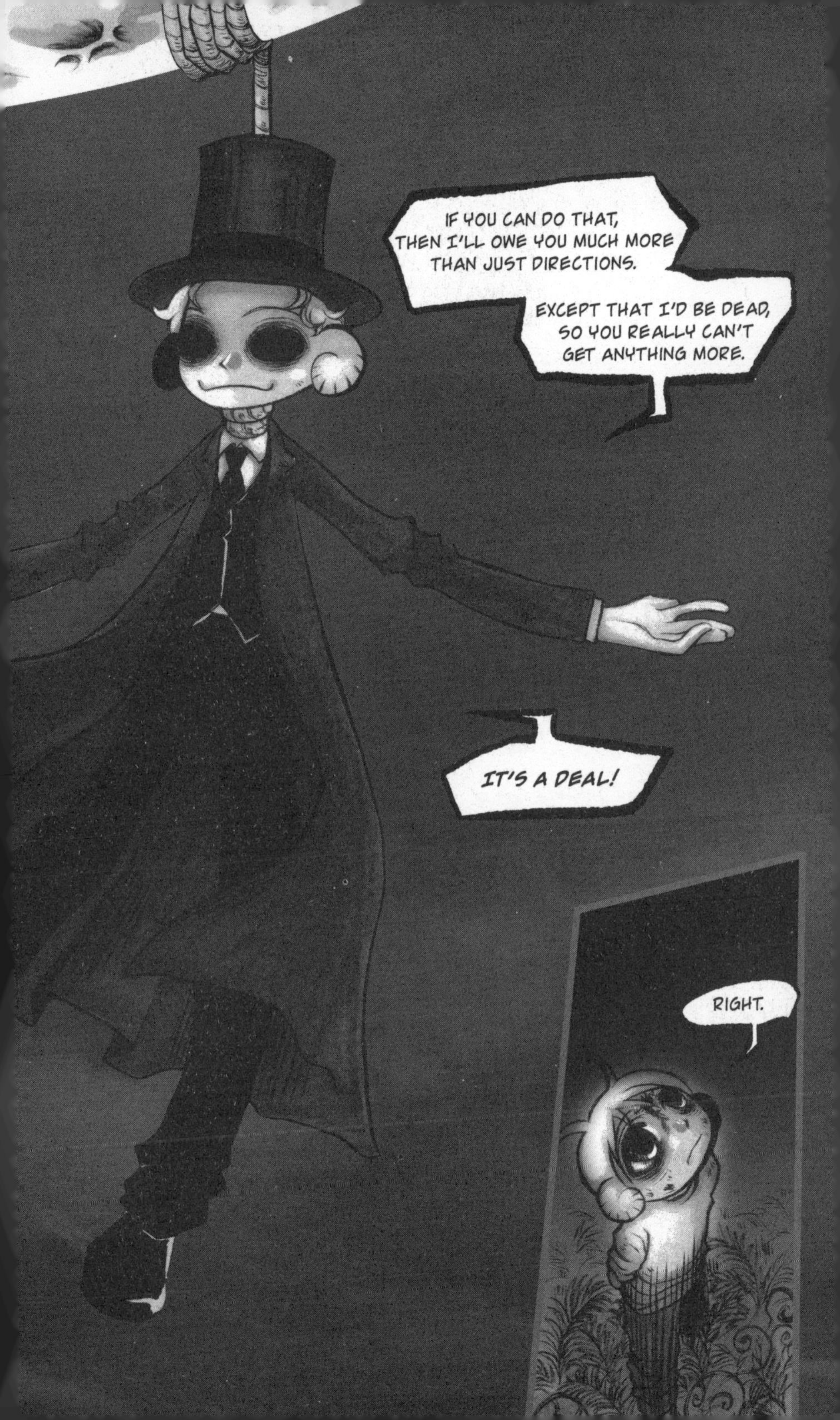
IF YOU CAN DO THAT, THEN I'LL OWE YOU MUCH MORE THAN JUST DIRECTIONS.
EXCEPT THAT I'D BE DEAD, SO YOU REALLY CAN'T GET ANYTHING MORE.
IT'S A DEAL!
RIGHT.

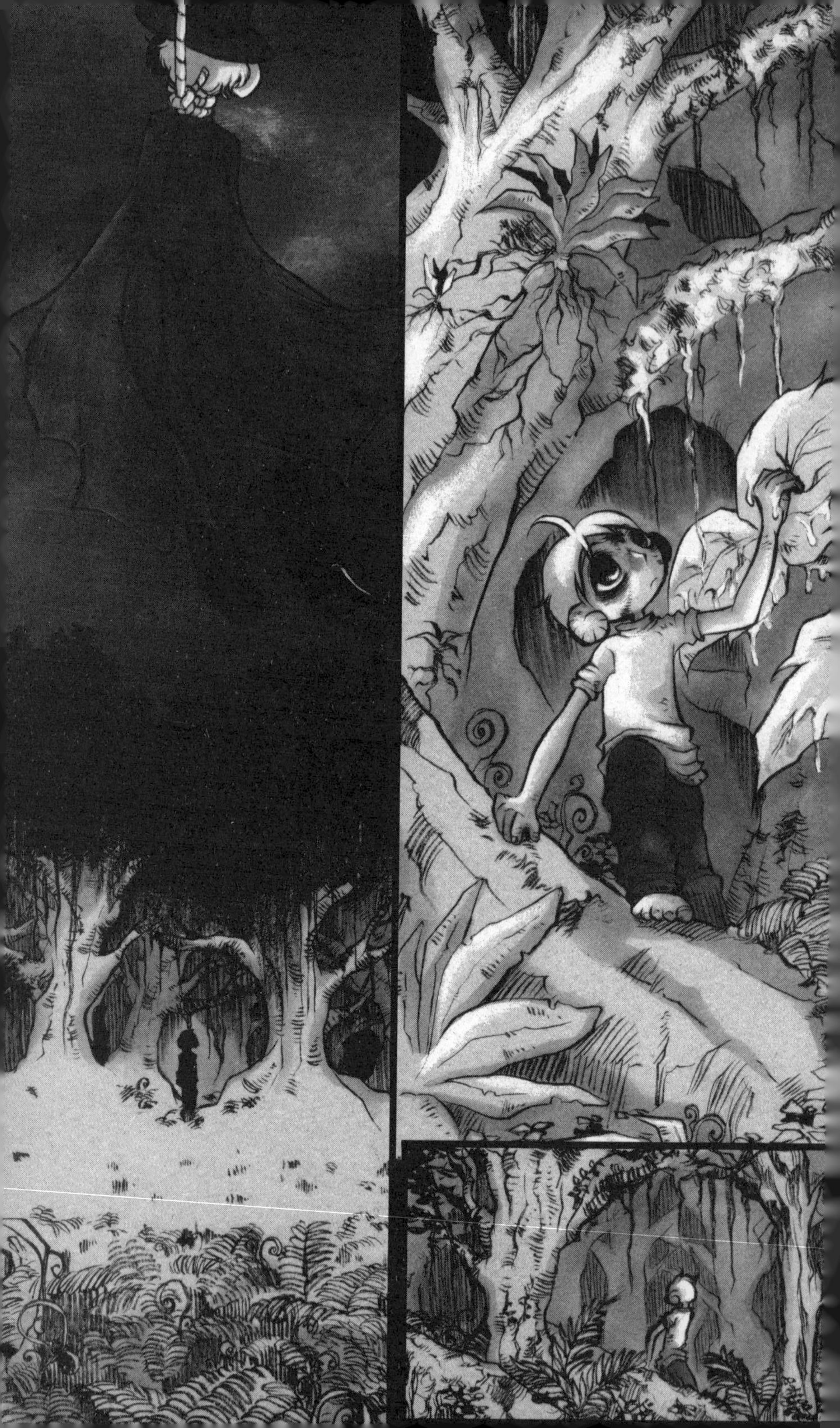

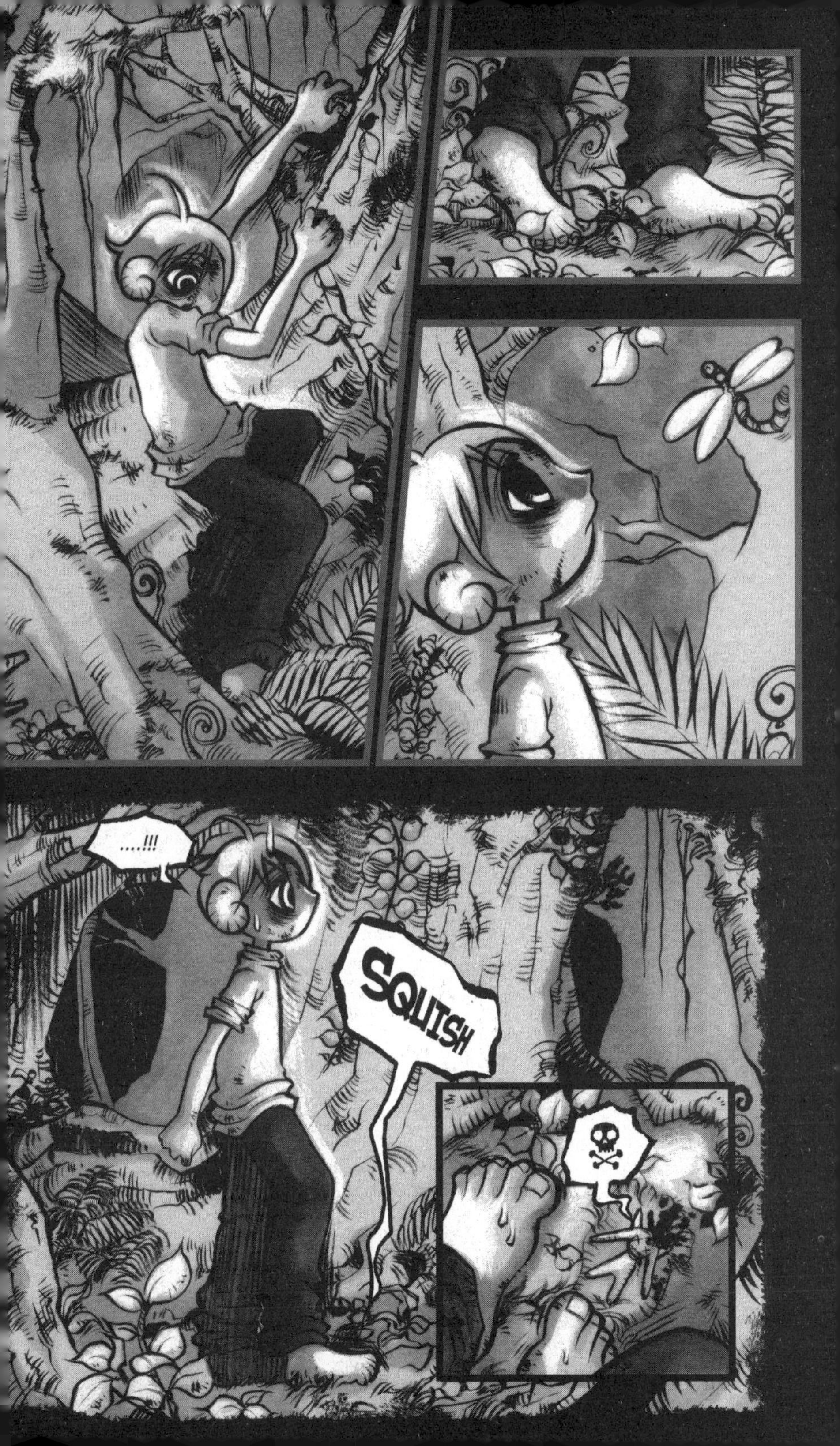

.....!!!
SQUISH

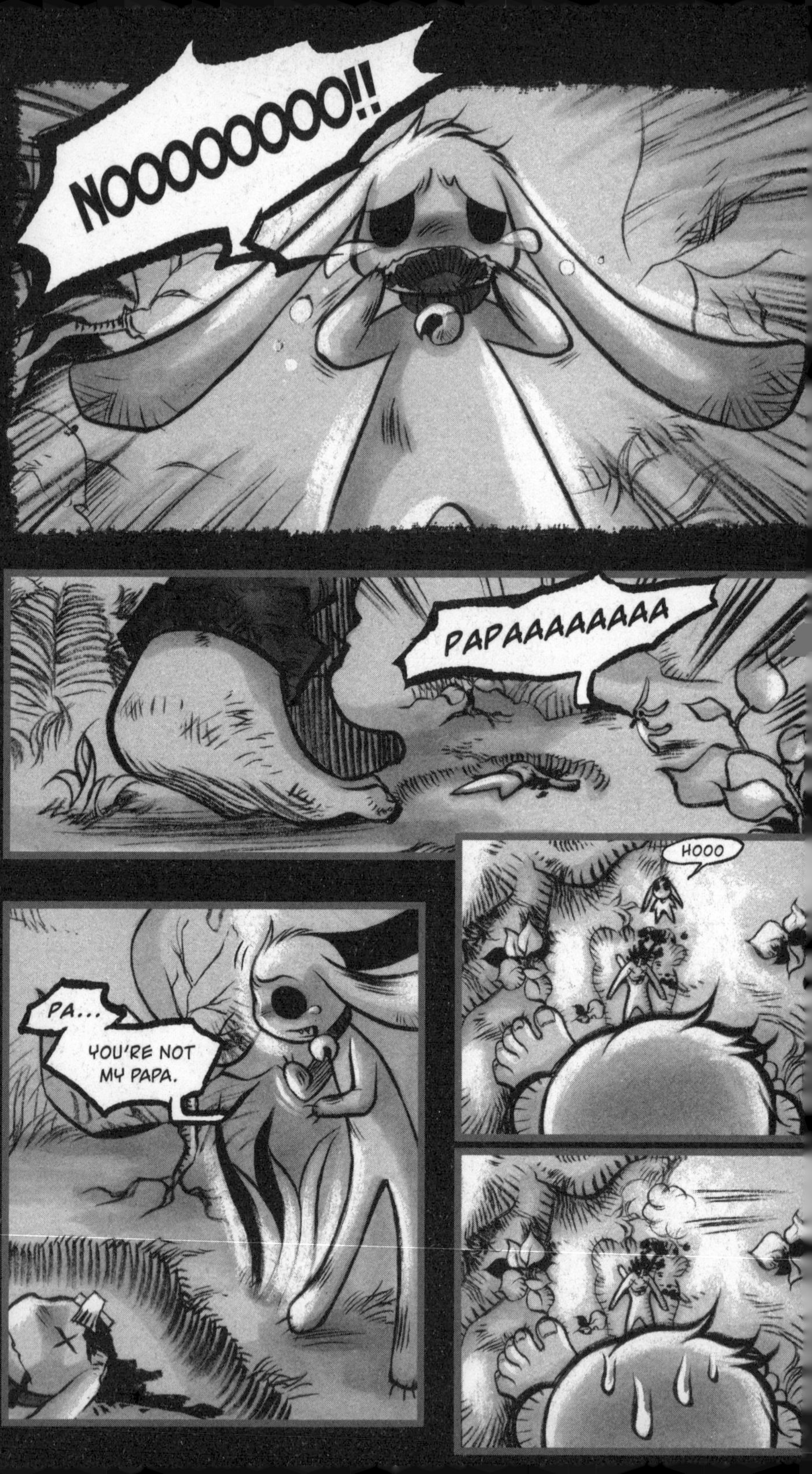
NOOOOOOOO!!
PAPAAAAAAAA
PA...
YOU'RE NOT MY PAPA.
HOOO

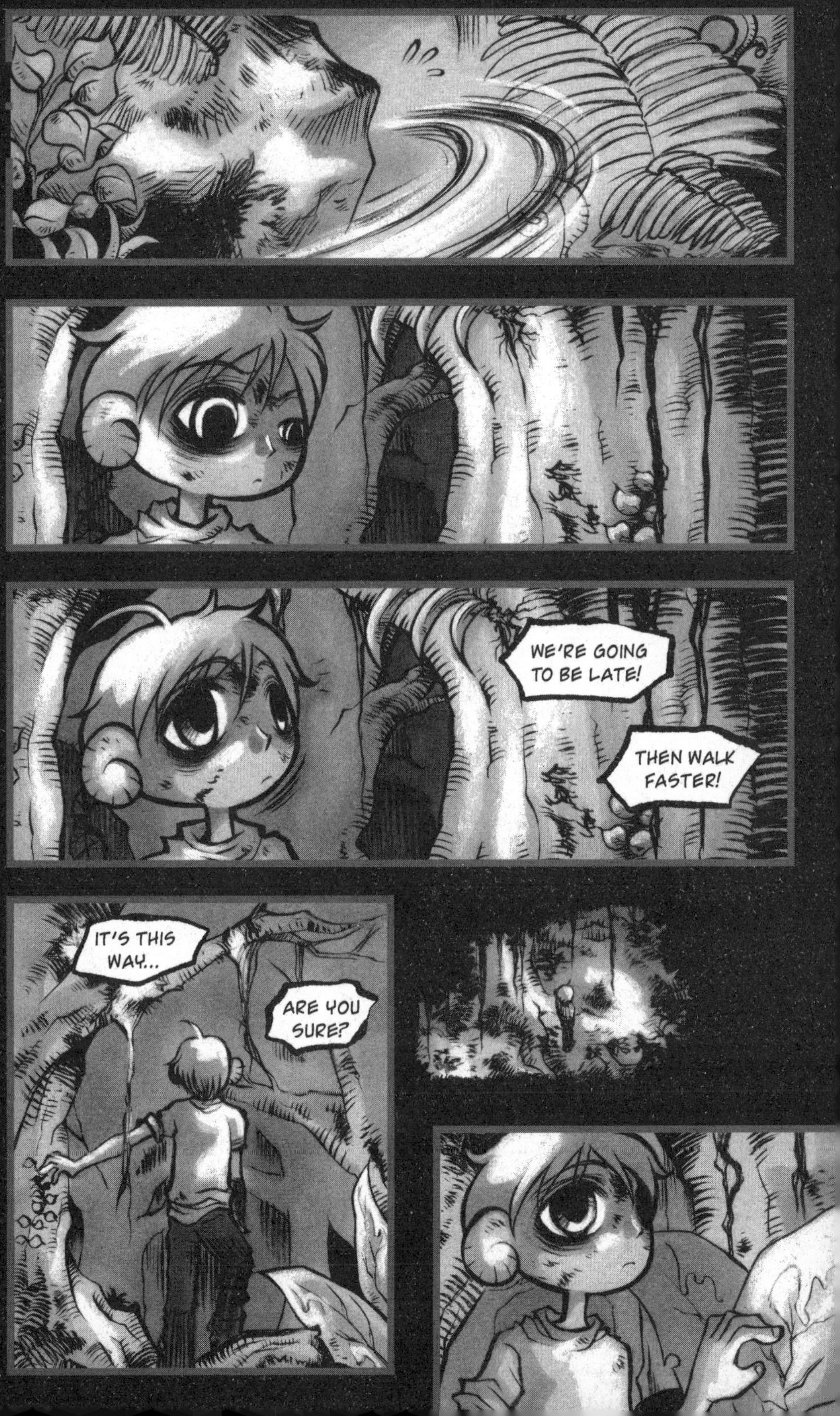
WE'RE GOING TO BE LATE!
THEN WALK FASTER!
IT'S THIS WAY...
ARE YOU SURE?

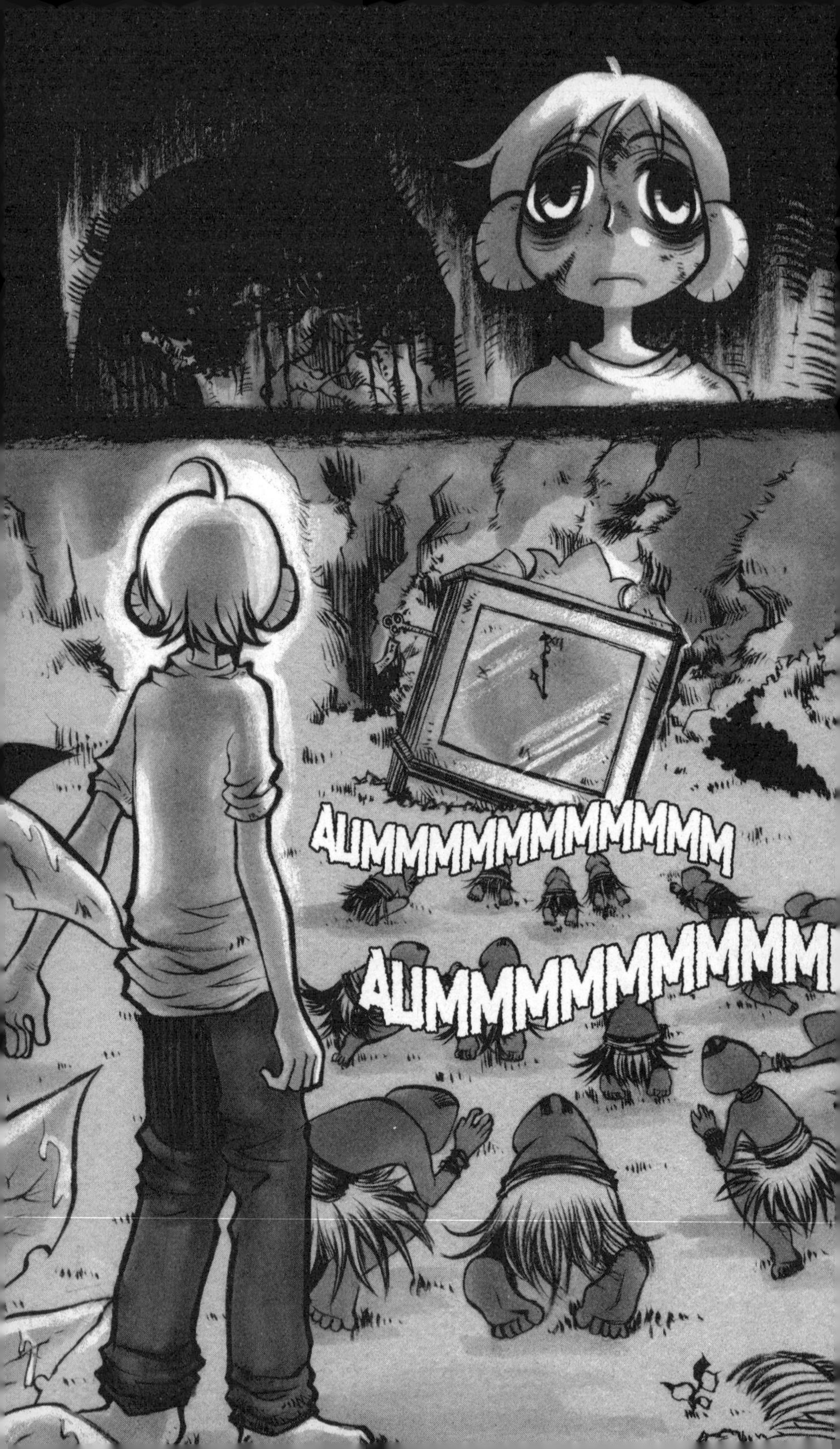
AUMMMMMMMMMMM
AUMMMMMMMMMMM

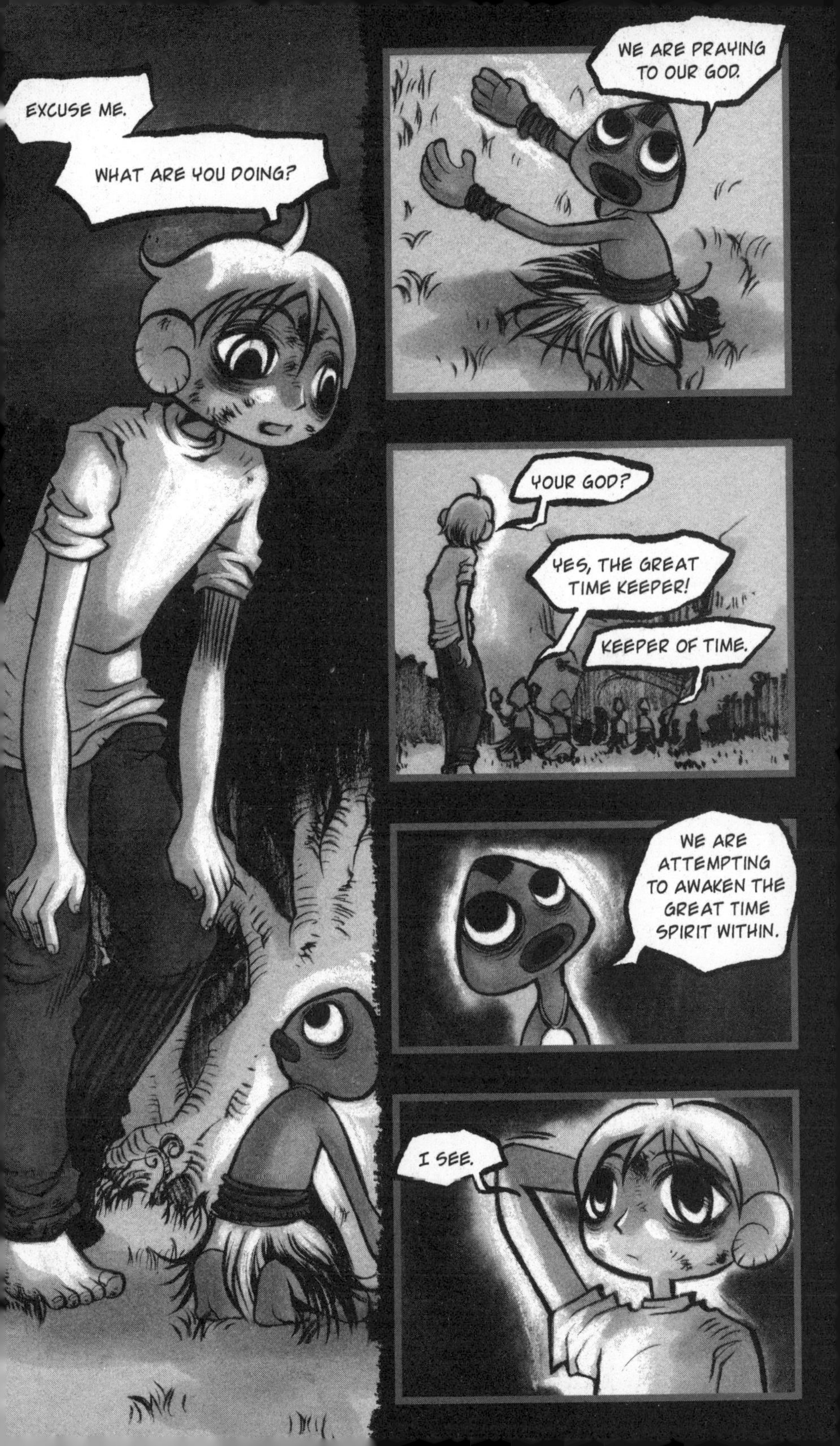
EXCUSE ME.
WHAT ARE YOU DOING?
WE ARE PRAYING TO OUR GOD.
YOUR GOD?
YES, THE GREAT TIME KEEPER!
KEEPER OF TIME.
WE ARE ATTEMPTING TO AWAKEN THE GREAT TIME SPIRIT WITHIN.
I SEE.

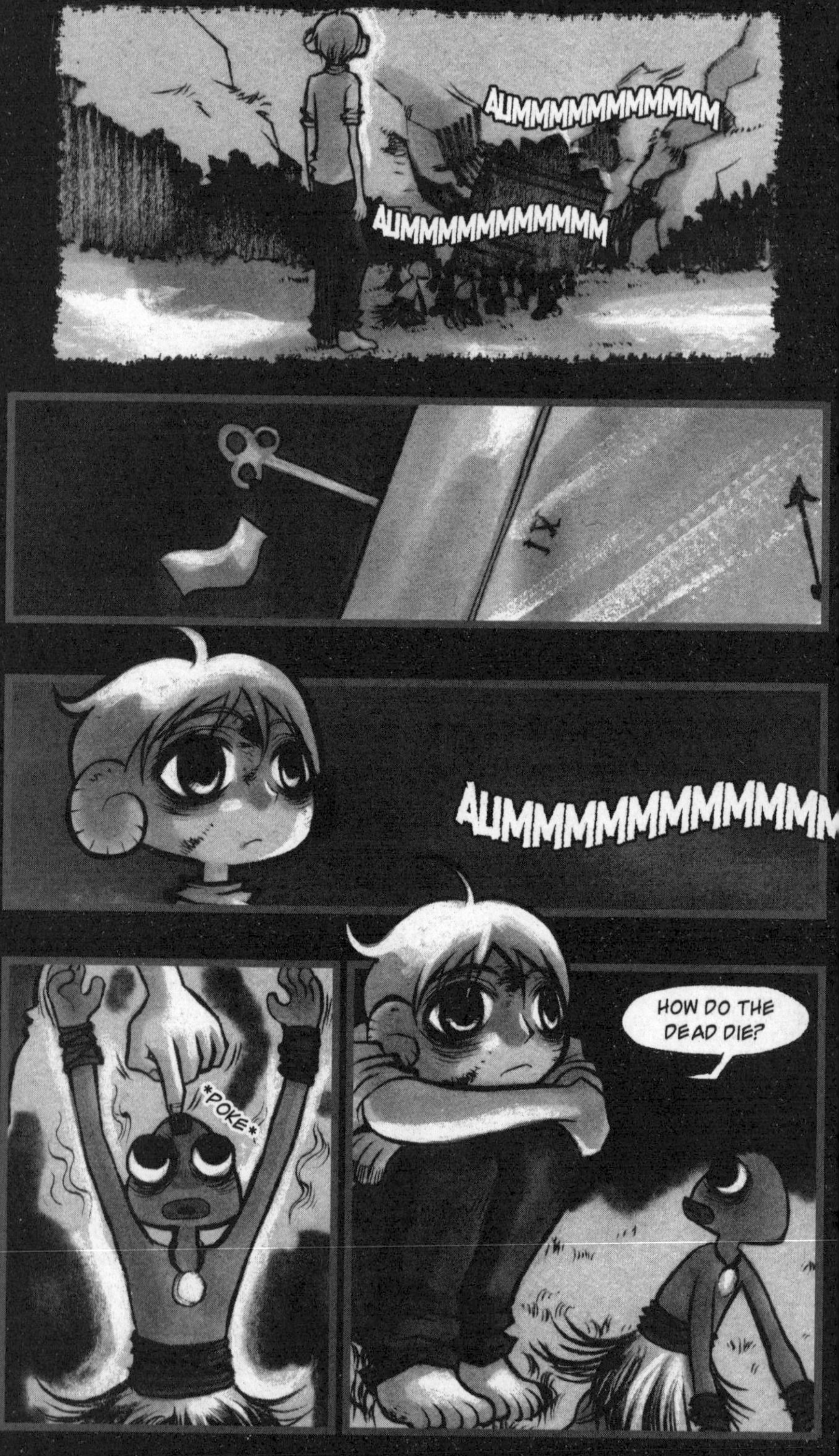
AUMMMMMMMMMMM
AUMMMMMMMMMMMM
AUMMMMMMMMMMMM
POKE
HOW DO THE DEAD DIE?

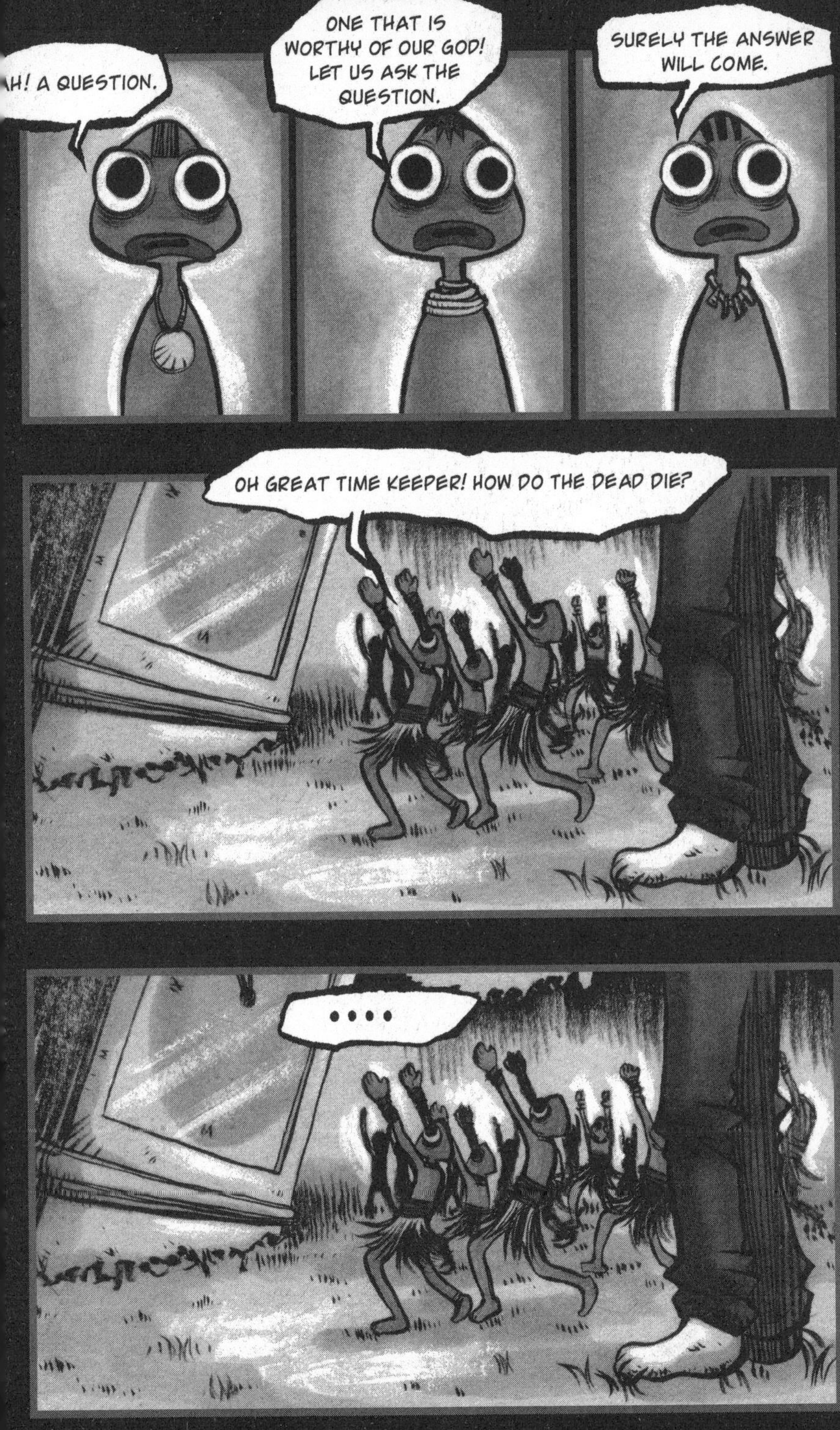
AH! A QUESTION.
ONE THAT IS WORTHY OF OUR GOD! LET US ASK THE QUESTION.
SURELY THE ANSWER WILL COME.
OH GREAT TIME KEEPER! HOW DO THE DEAD DIE?
....

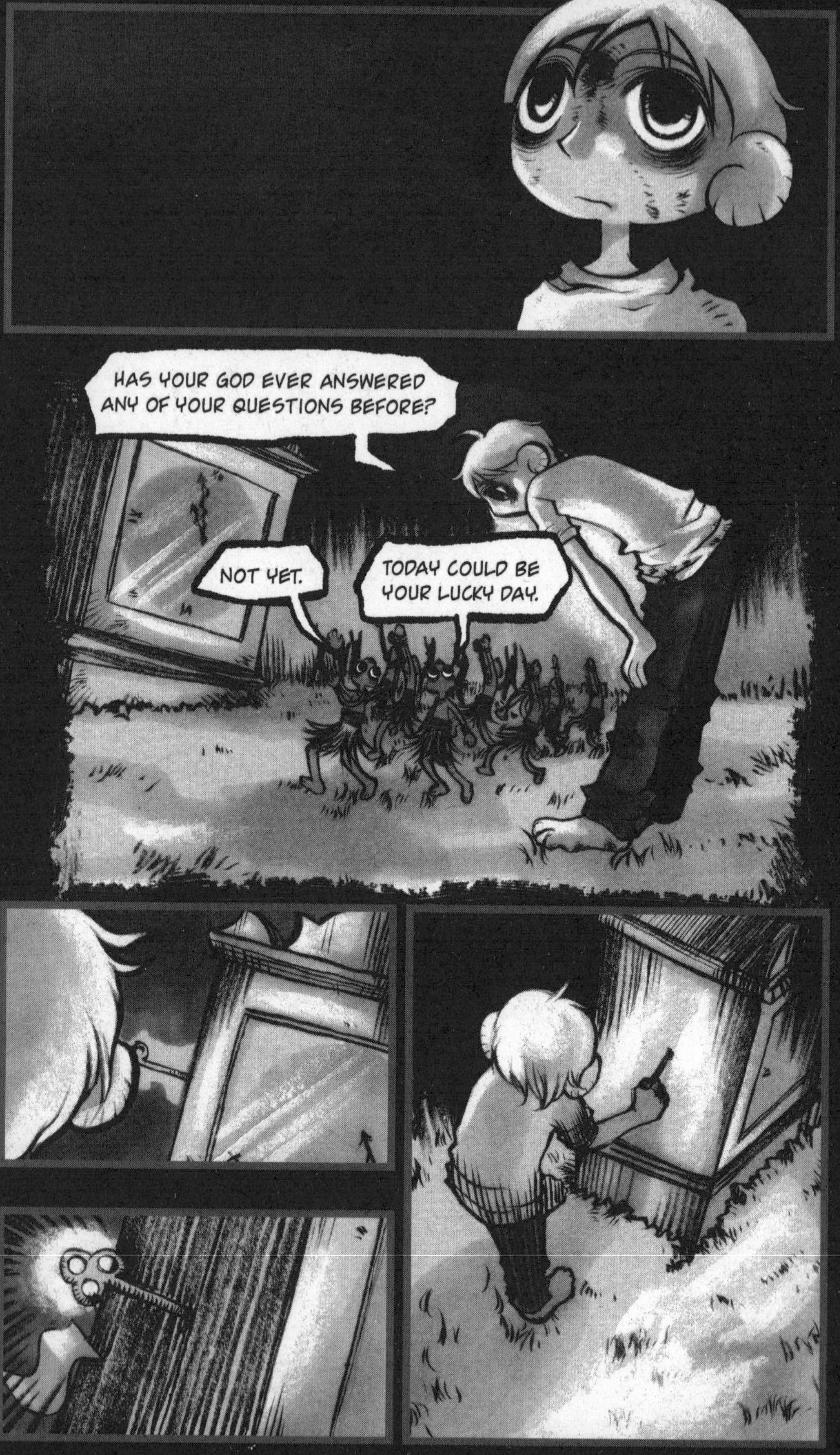
HAS YOUR GOD EVER ANSWERED ANY OF YOUR QUESTIONS BEFORE?
NOT YET.
TODAY COULD BE YOUR LUCKY DAY.

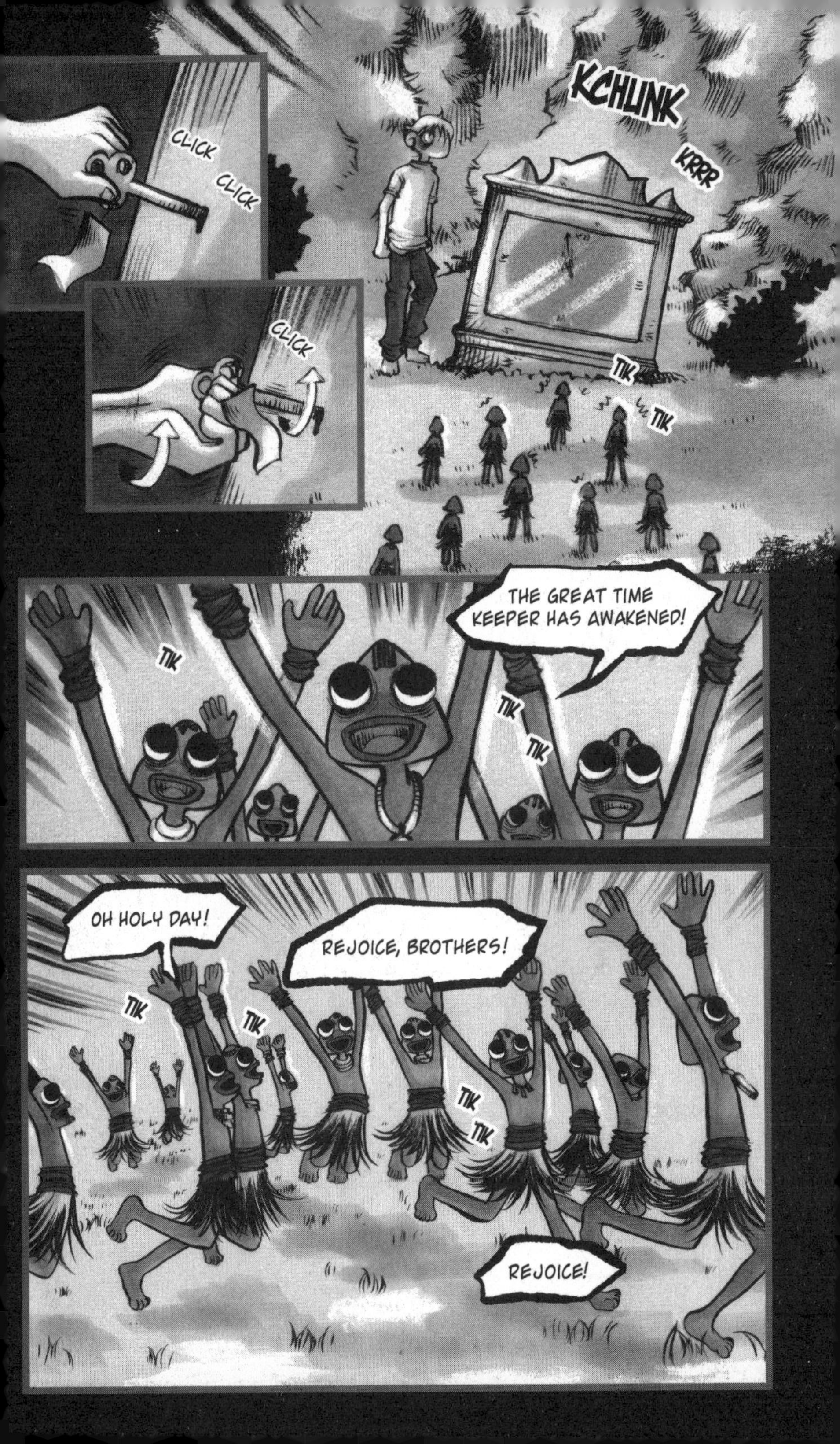
CLICK
CLICK
CLICK
KCHUNK
KRRR
TIK
TIK
TIK
THE GREAT TIME KEEPER HAS AWAKENED!
TIK
TIK
OH HOLY DAY!
REJOICE, BROTHERS!
TIK
TIK
TIK
TIK
REJOICE!

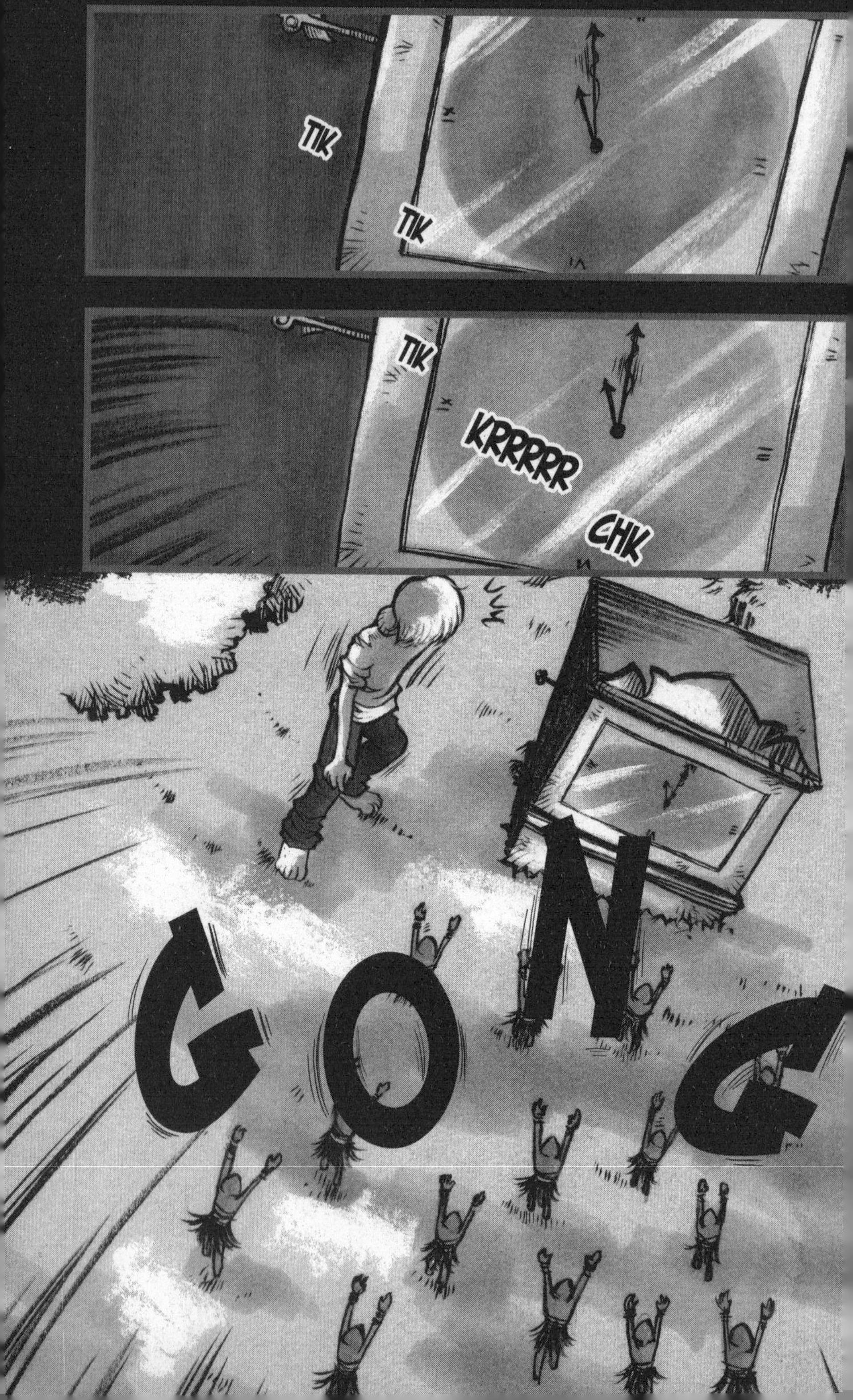
TIK
TIK
TIK
KRRRRR
CHK
GONG

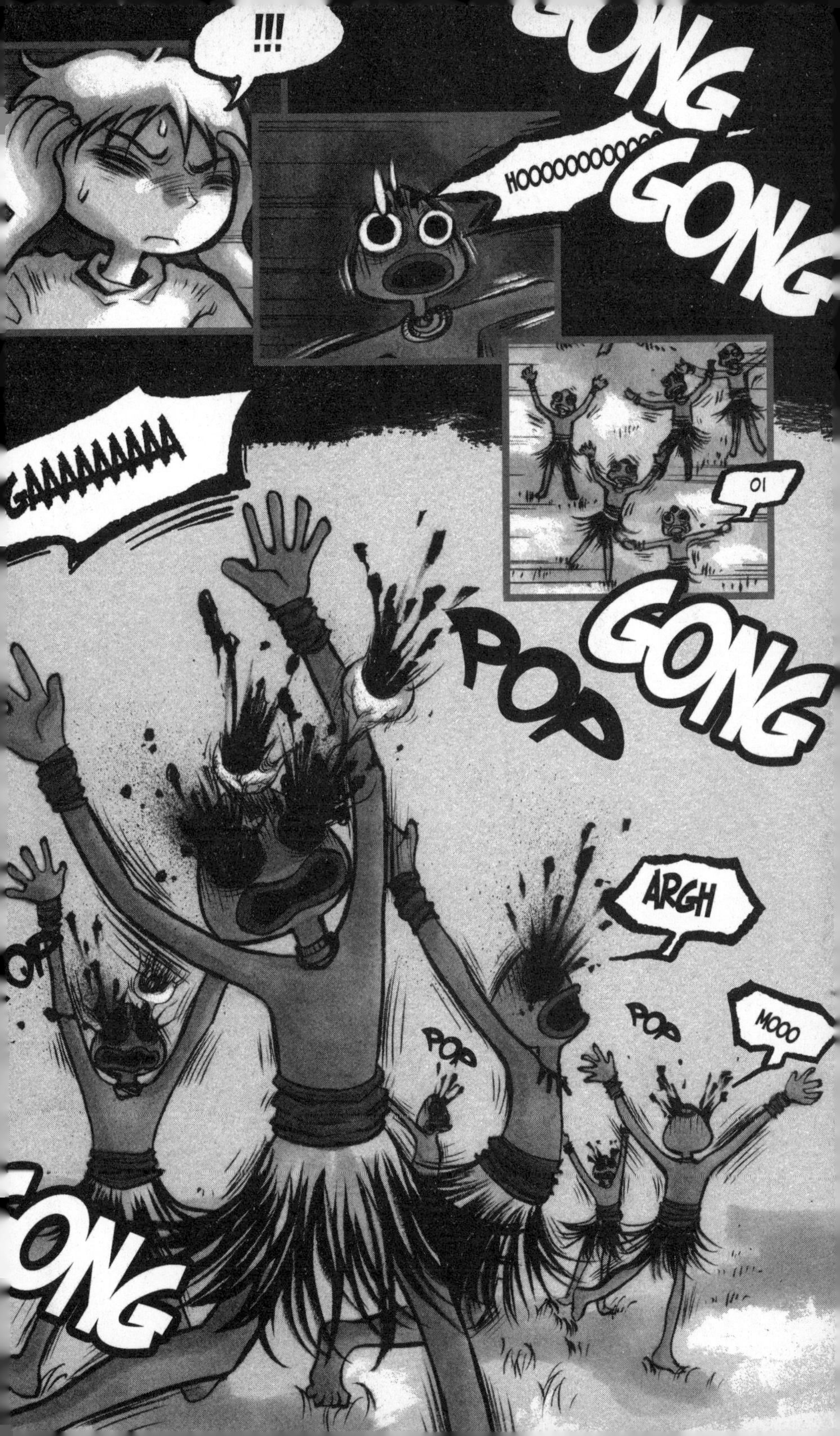
!!!
GONG
HOOOOOOOOOOOO
GONG
GONG
GAAAAAAAAA
OI
GONG
POP
ARGH
POP
POP
MOOO
GONG

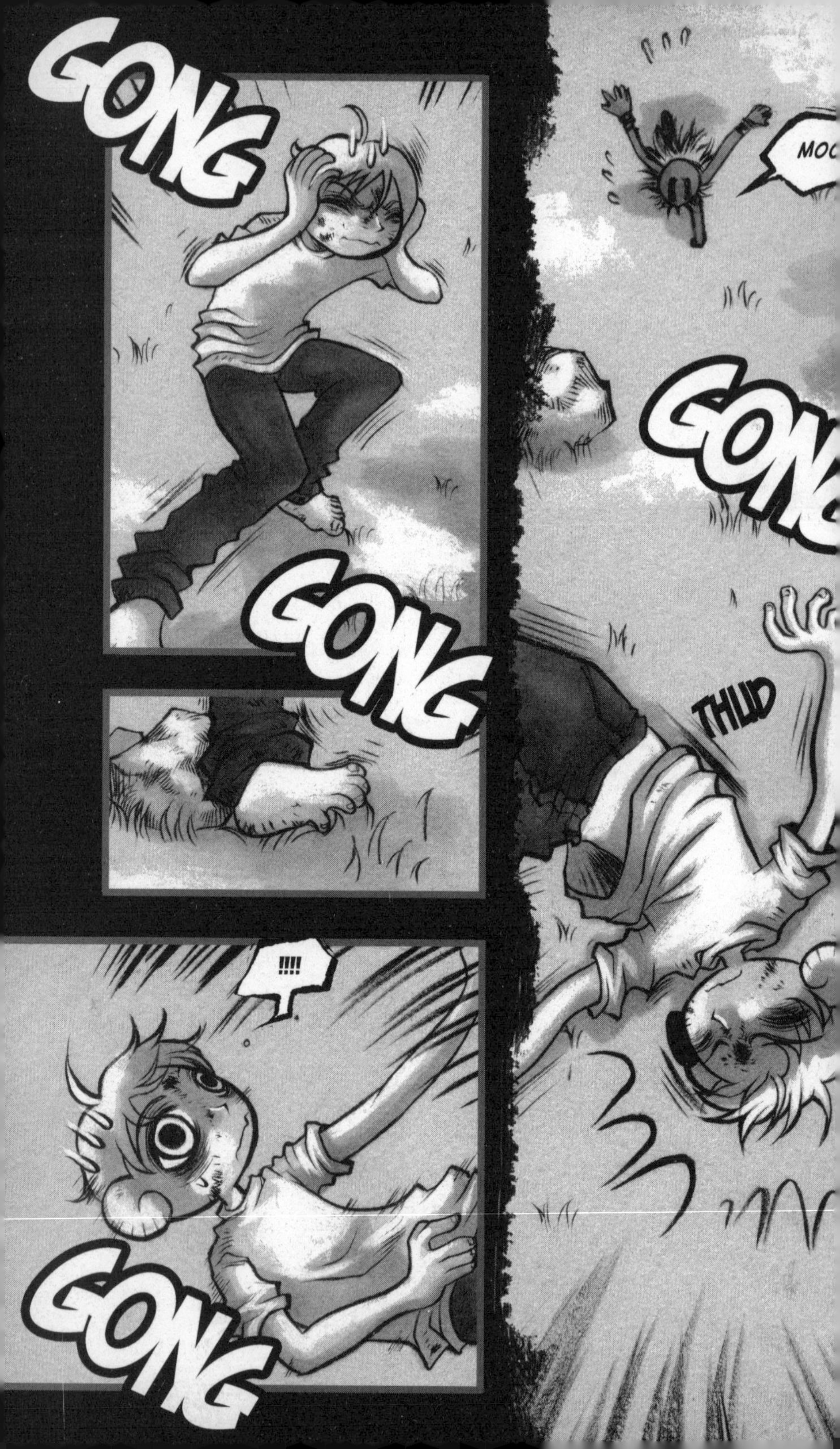
MOC
GON
THUD
GONG
GONG
!!!!
GONG

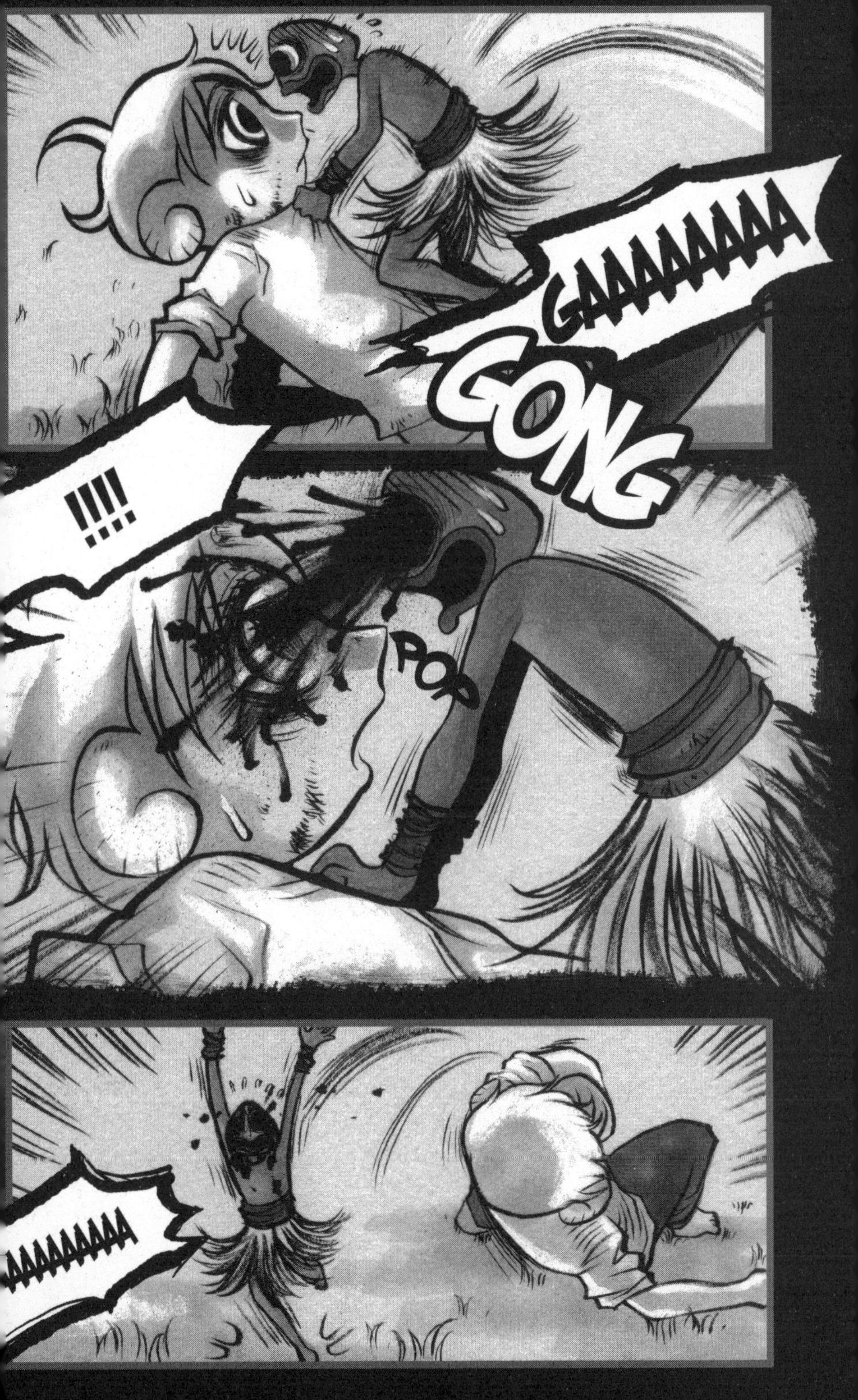
GAAAAAAAA
GONG
!!!!
POP
AAAAAAAA

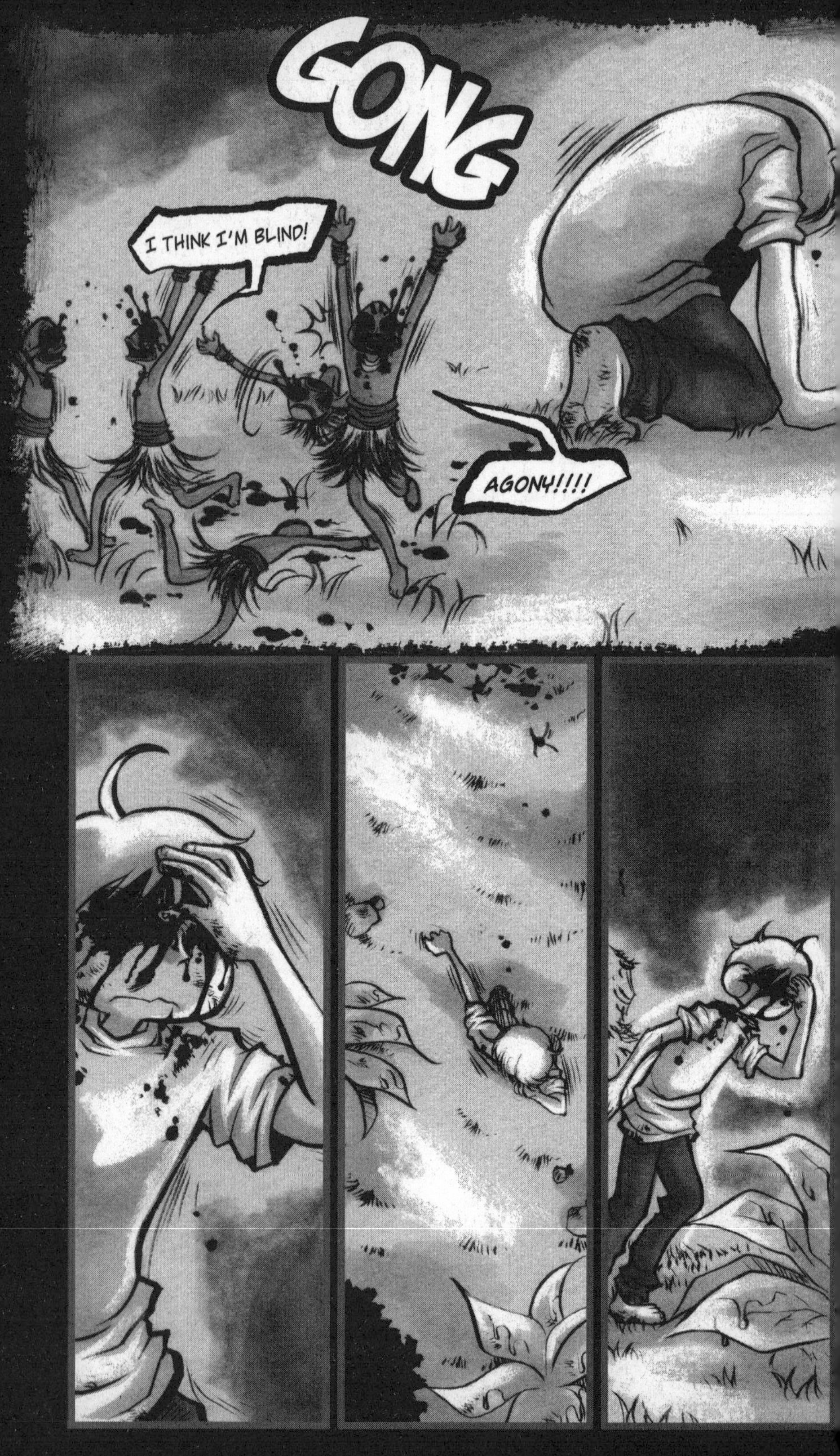
GONG
I THINK I'M BLIND!
AGONY!!!!!

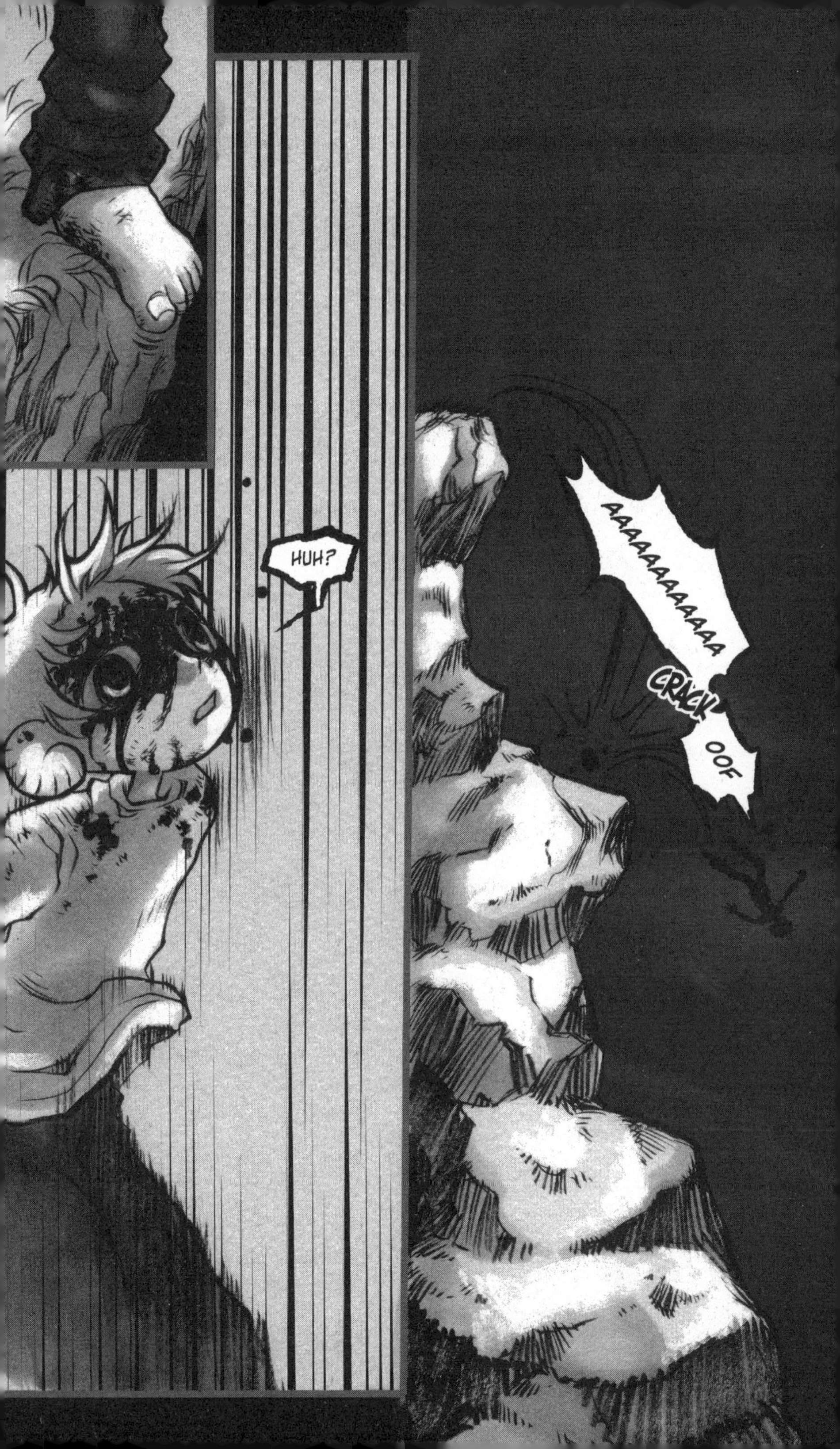
HUH?
AAAAAAAAAAAA
CRACK
OOF

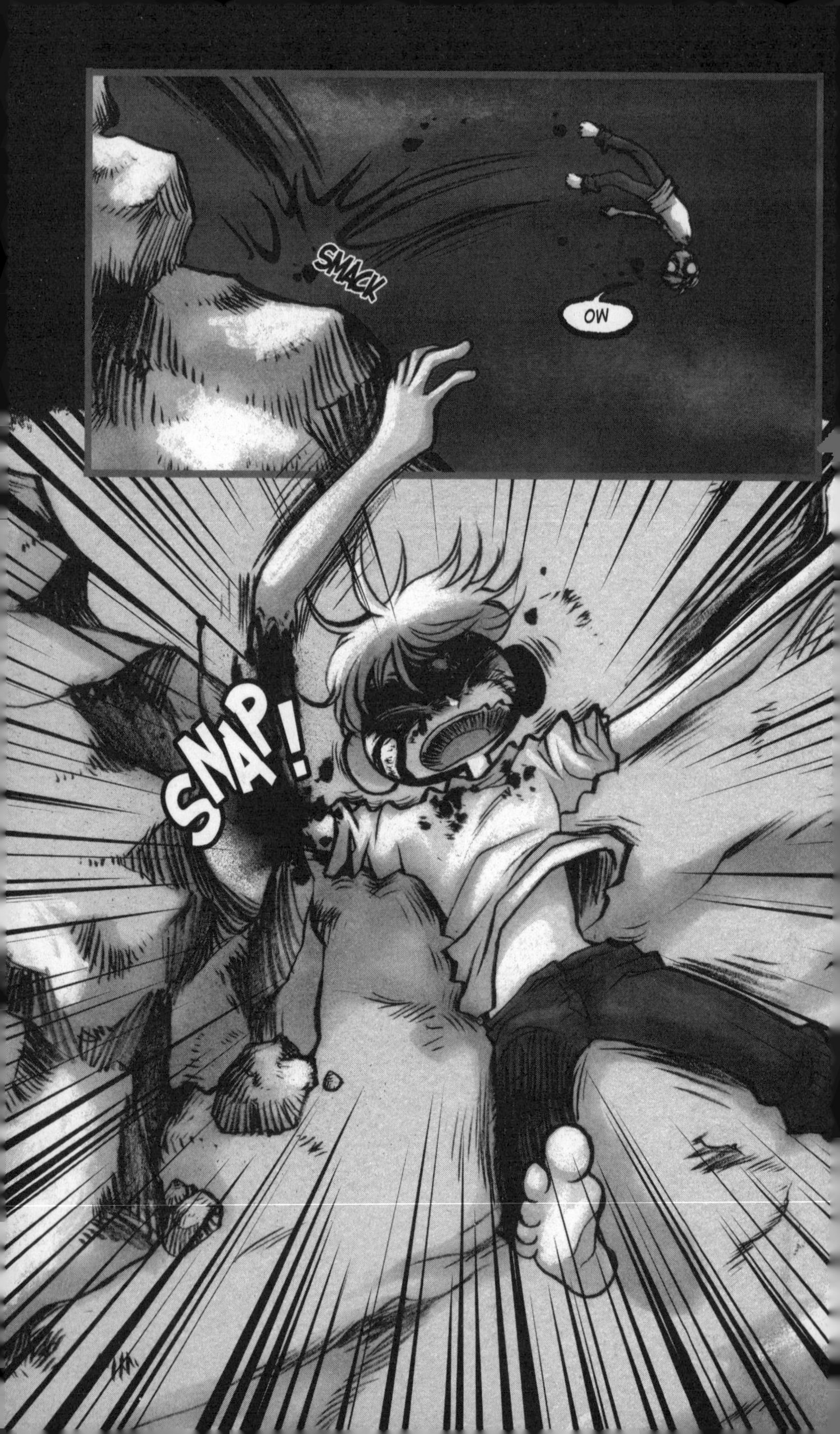
SMACK
OW
SNAP!

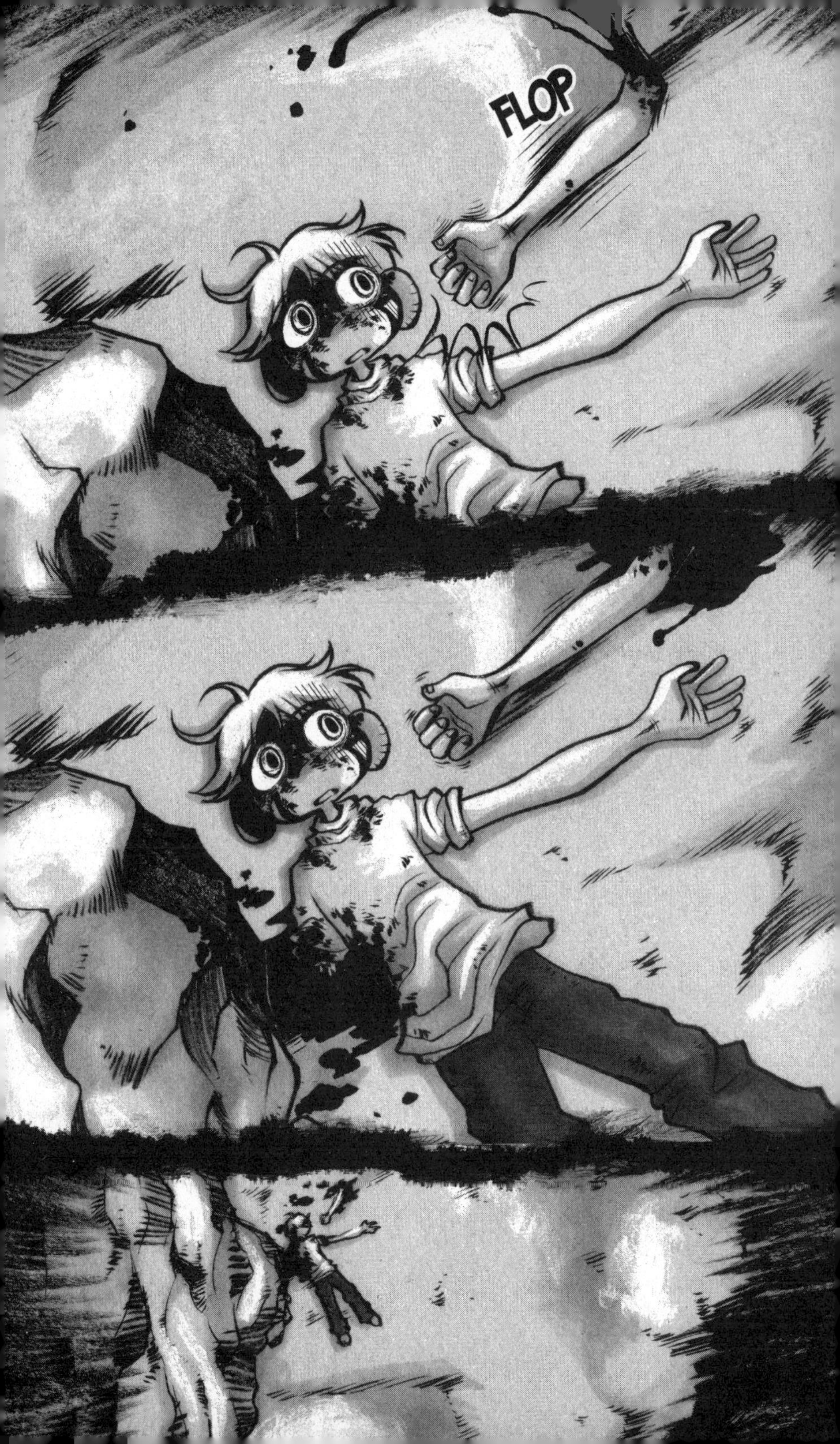
FLOP

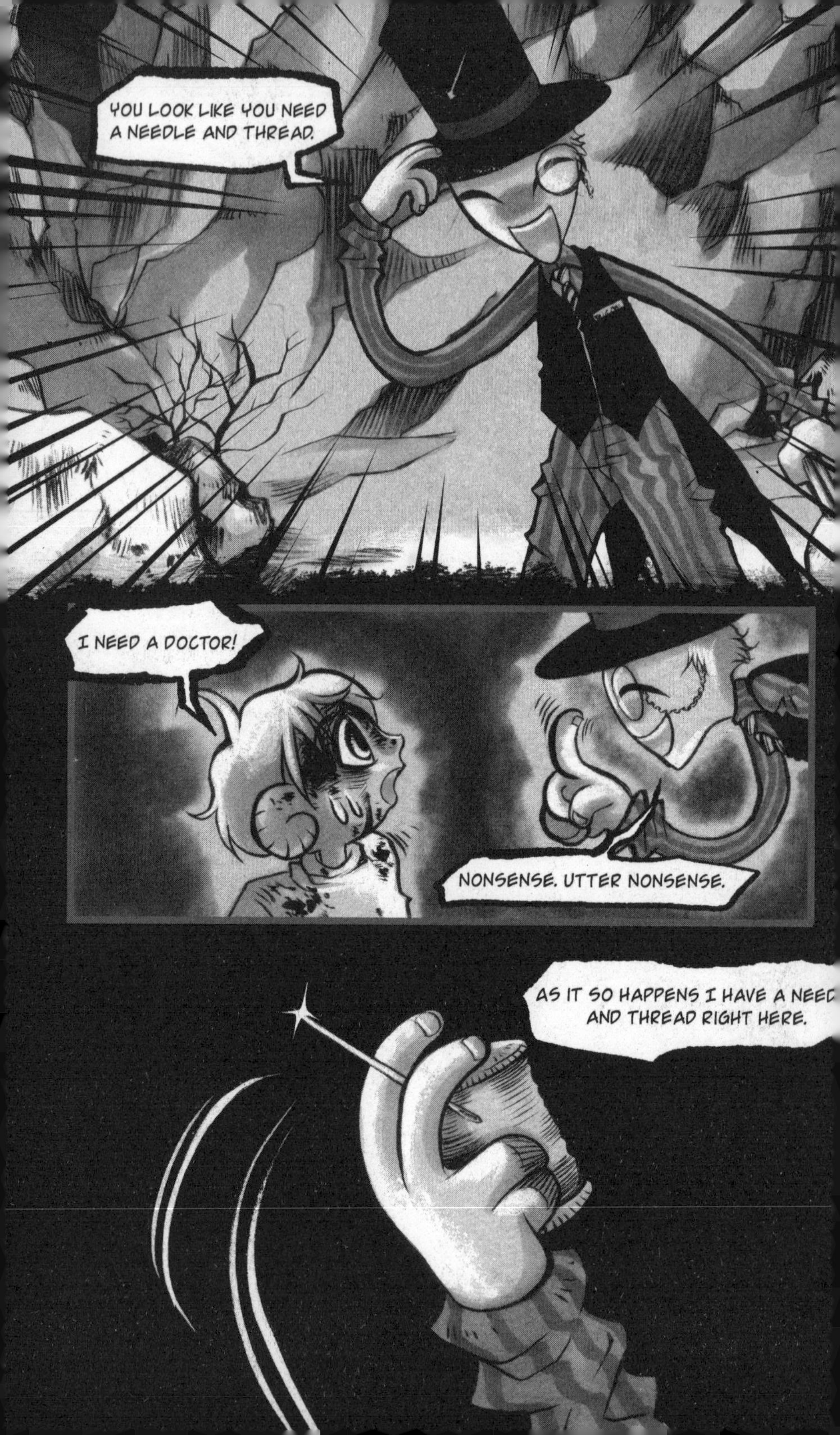
YOU LOOK LIKE YOU NEED A NEEDLE AND THREAD.
I NEED A DOCTOR!
NONSENSE. UTTER NONSENSE.
AS IT SO HAPPENS I HAVE A NEEE AND THREAD RIGHT HERE.

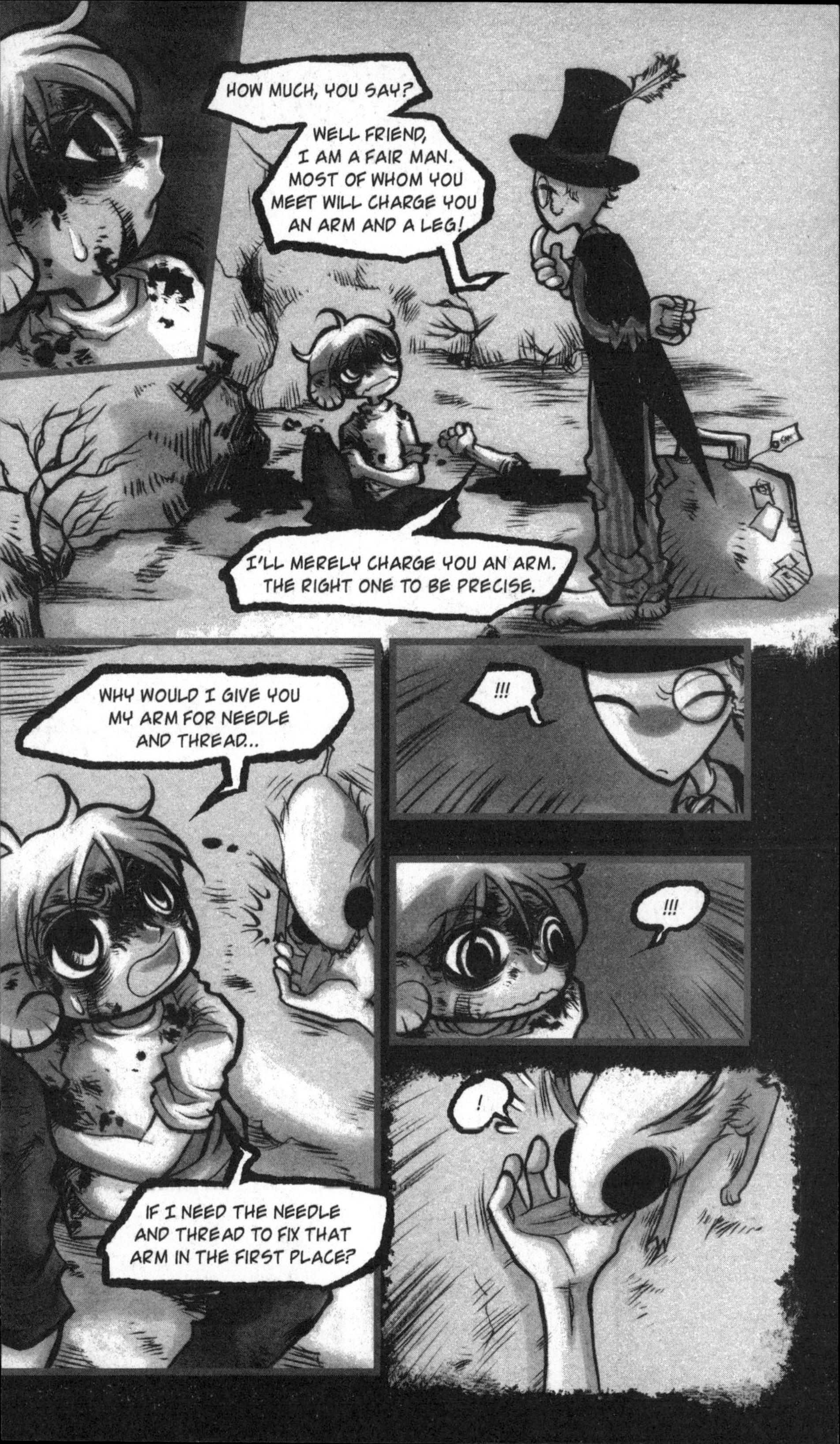
HOW MUCH, YOU SAY?
WELL FRIEND, I AM A FAIR MAN. MOST OF WHOM YOU MEET WILL CHARGE YOU AN ARM AND A LEG!
I'LL MERELY CHARGE YOU AN ARM. THE RIGHT ONE TO BE PRECISE.
WHY WOULD I GIVE YOU MY ARM FOR NEEDLE AND THREAD...
!!!
!!!
IF I NEED THE NEEDLE AND THREAD TO FIX THAT ARM IN THE FIRST PLACE?
!

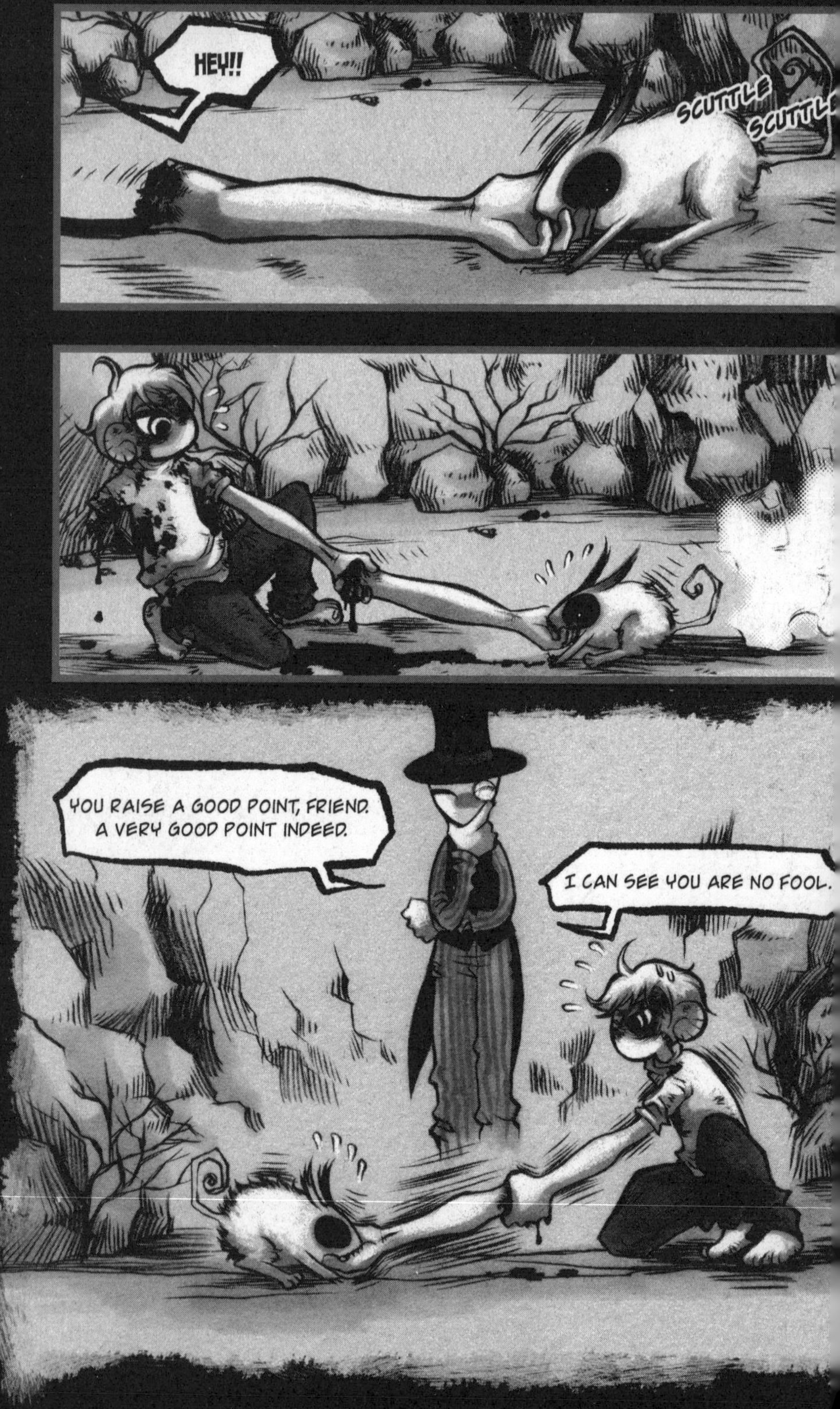
HEY!!
SCUTTLE
SCUTTLE
YOU RAISE A GOOD POINT, FRIEND. A VERY GOOD POINT INDEED.
I CAN SEE YOU ARE NO FOOL.

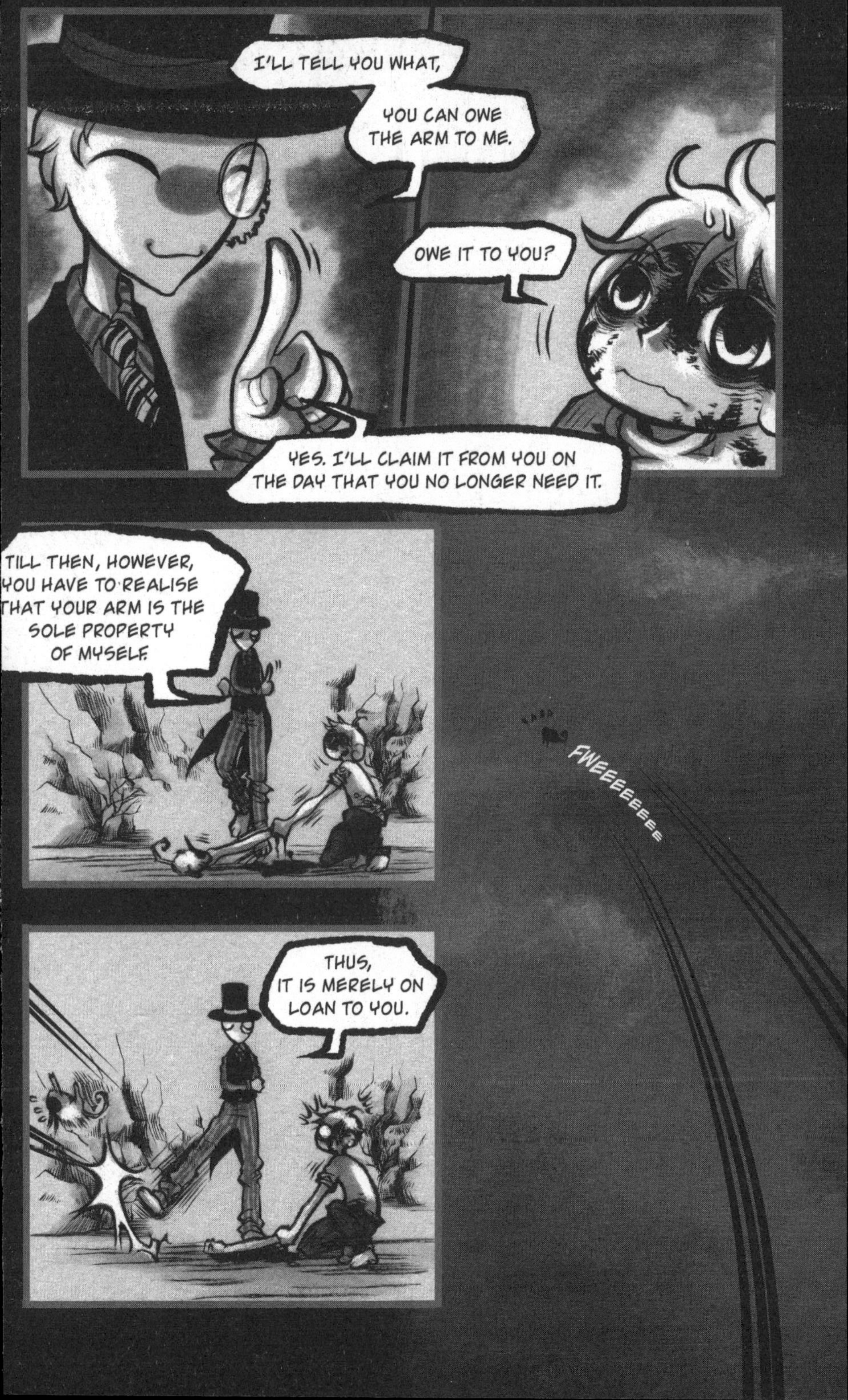
I'LL TELL YOU WHAT,
YOU CAN OWE THE ARM TO ME.
OWE IT TO YOU?
YES. I'LL CLAIM IT FROM YOU ON THE DAY THAT YOU NO LONGER NEED IT.
TILL THEN, HOWEVER, YOU HAVE TO REALISE THAT YOUR ARM IS THE SOLE PROPERTY OF MYSELF.
FWEEEEEEEE
THUS, IT IS MERELY ON LOAN TO YOU.

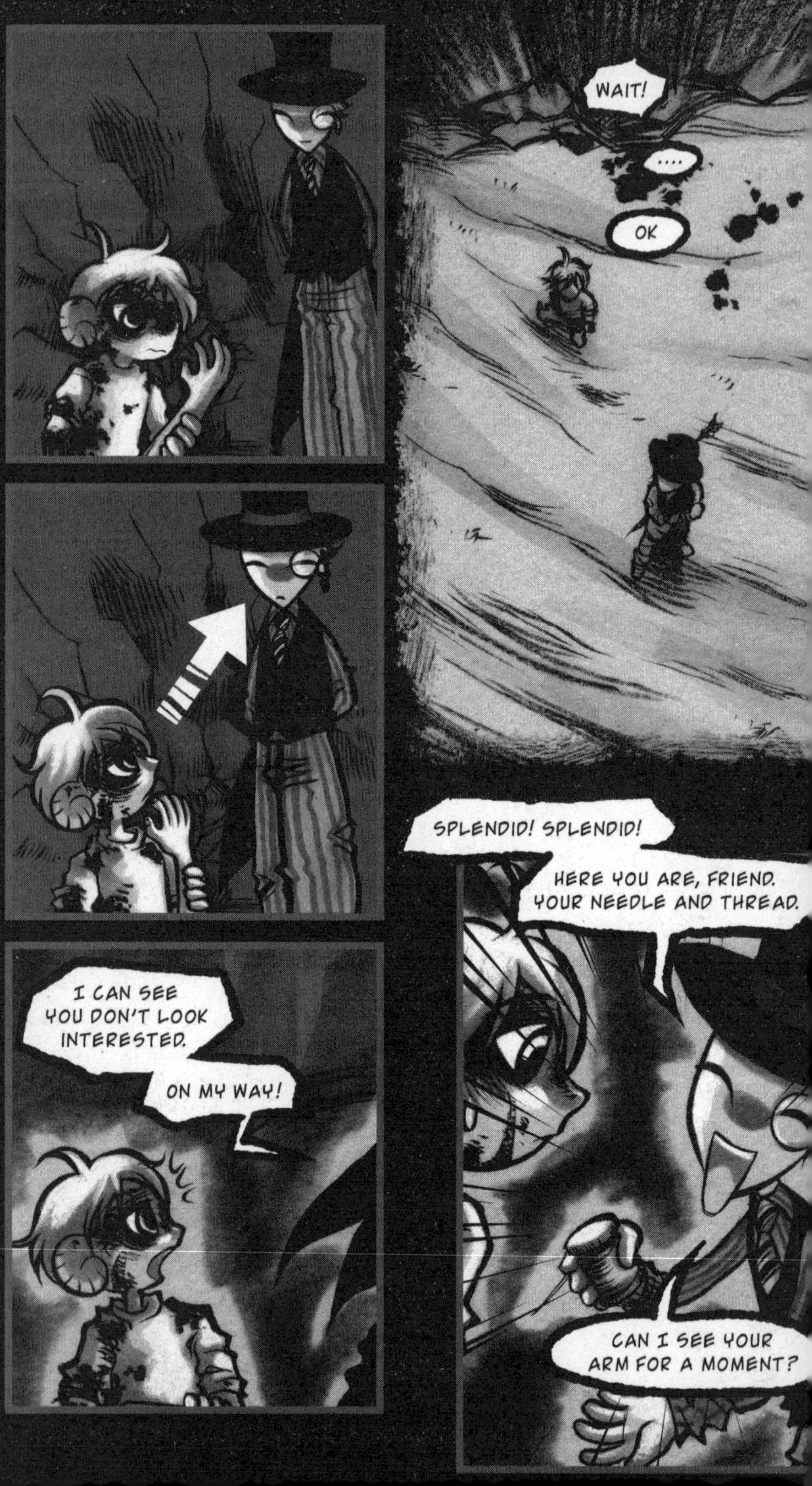
WAIT!
....
OK
I CAN SEE YOU DON'T LOOK INTERESTED.
ON MY WAY!
SPLENDID! SPLENDID!
HERE YOU ARE, FRIEND. YOUR NEEDLE AND THREAD.
CAN I SEE YOUR ARM FOR A MOMENT?

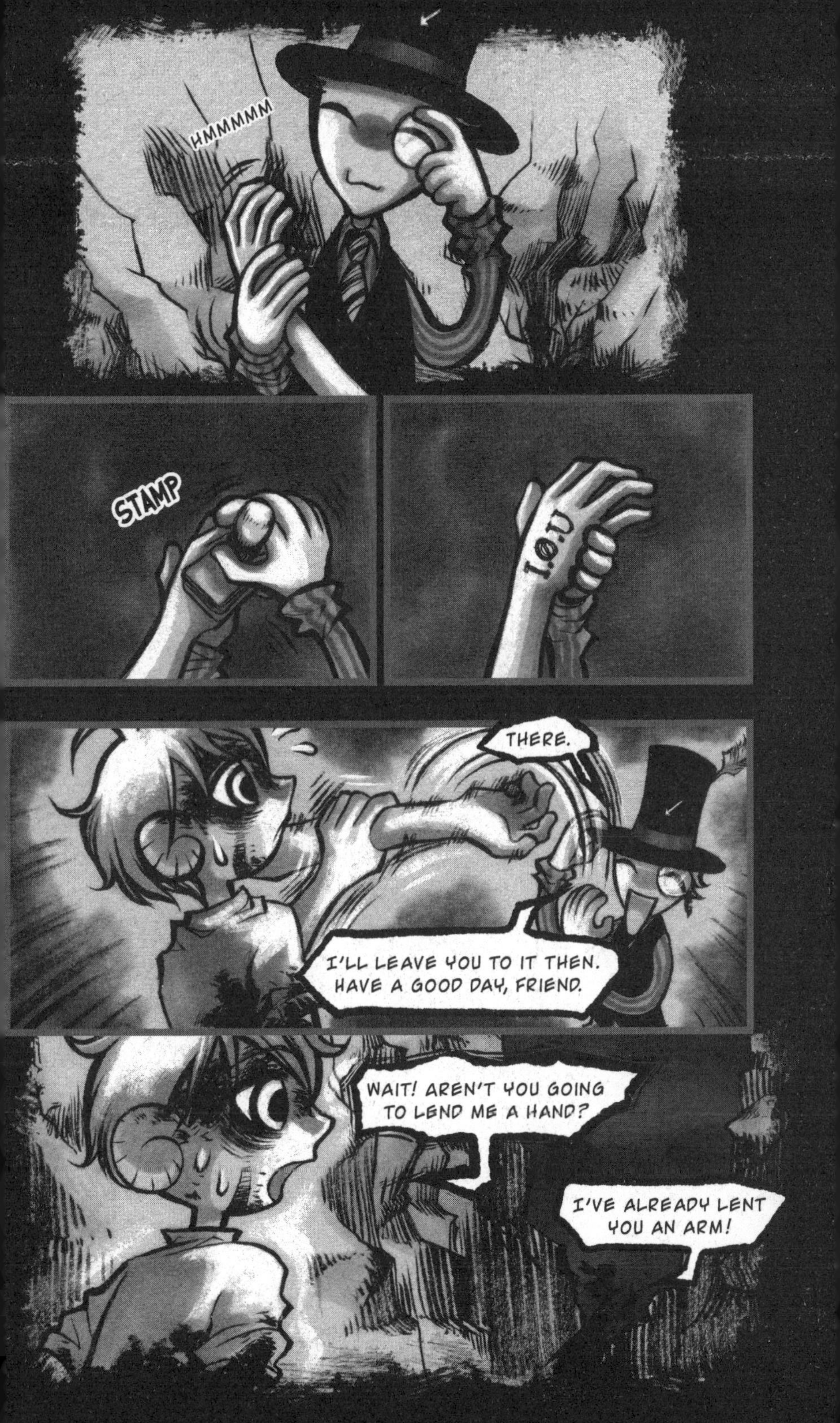
HMMMMM
STAMP
I.O.U
THERE.
I'LL LEAVE YOU TO IT THEN. HAVE A GOOD DAY, FRIEND.
WAIT! AREN'T YOU GOING TO LEND ME A HAND?
I'VE ALREADY LENT YOU AN ARM!

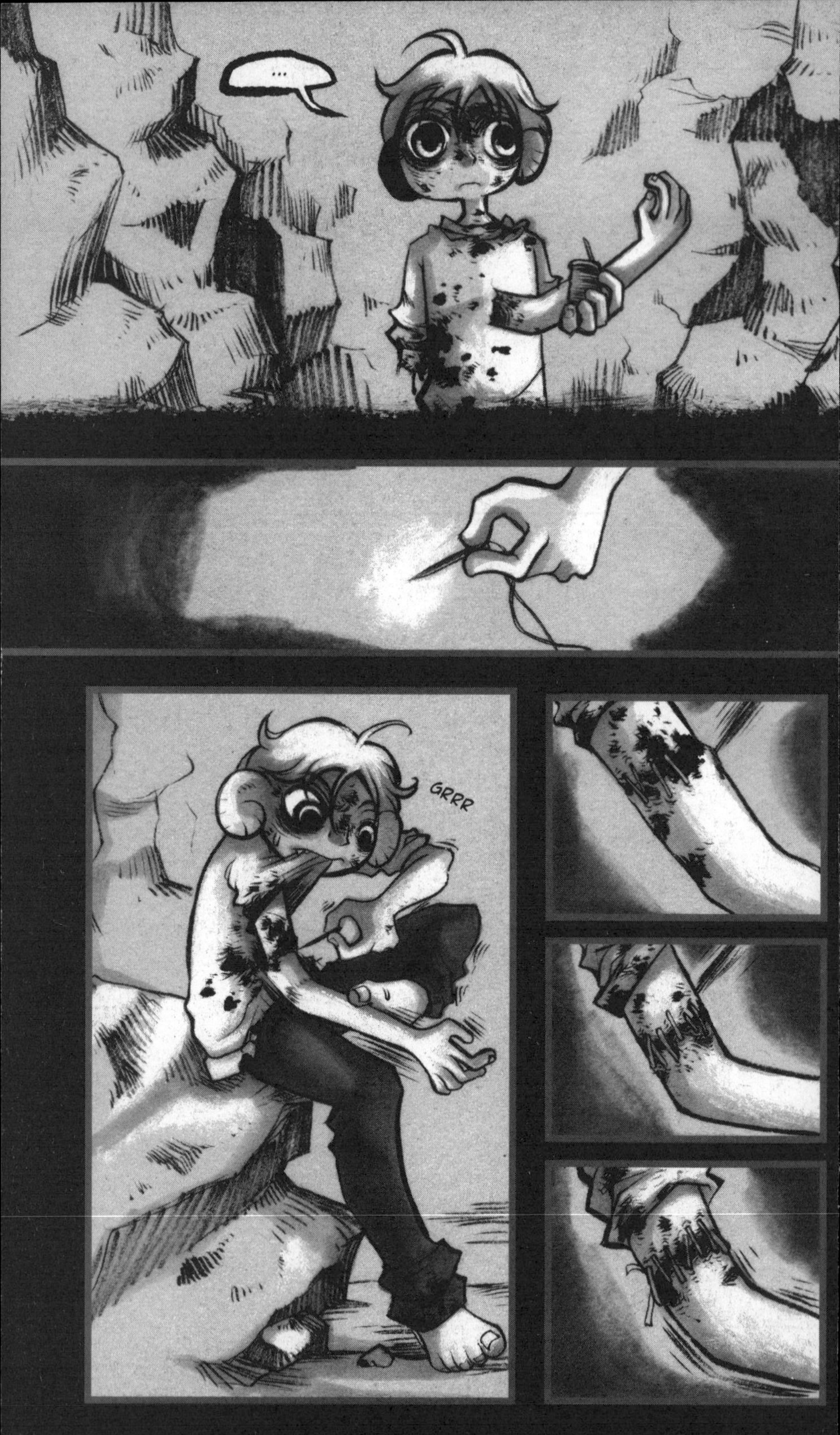
...
GRRR

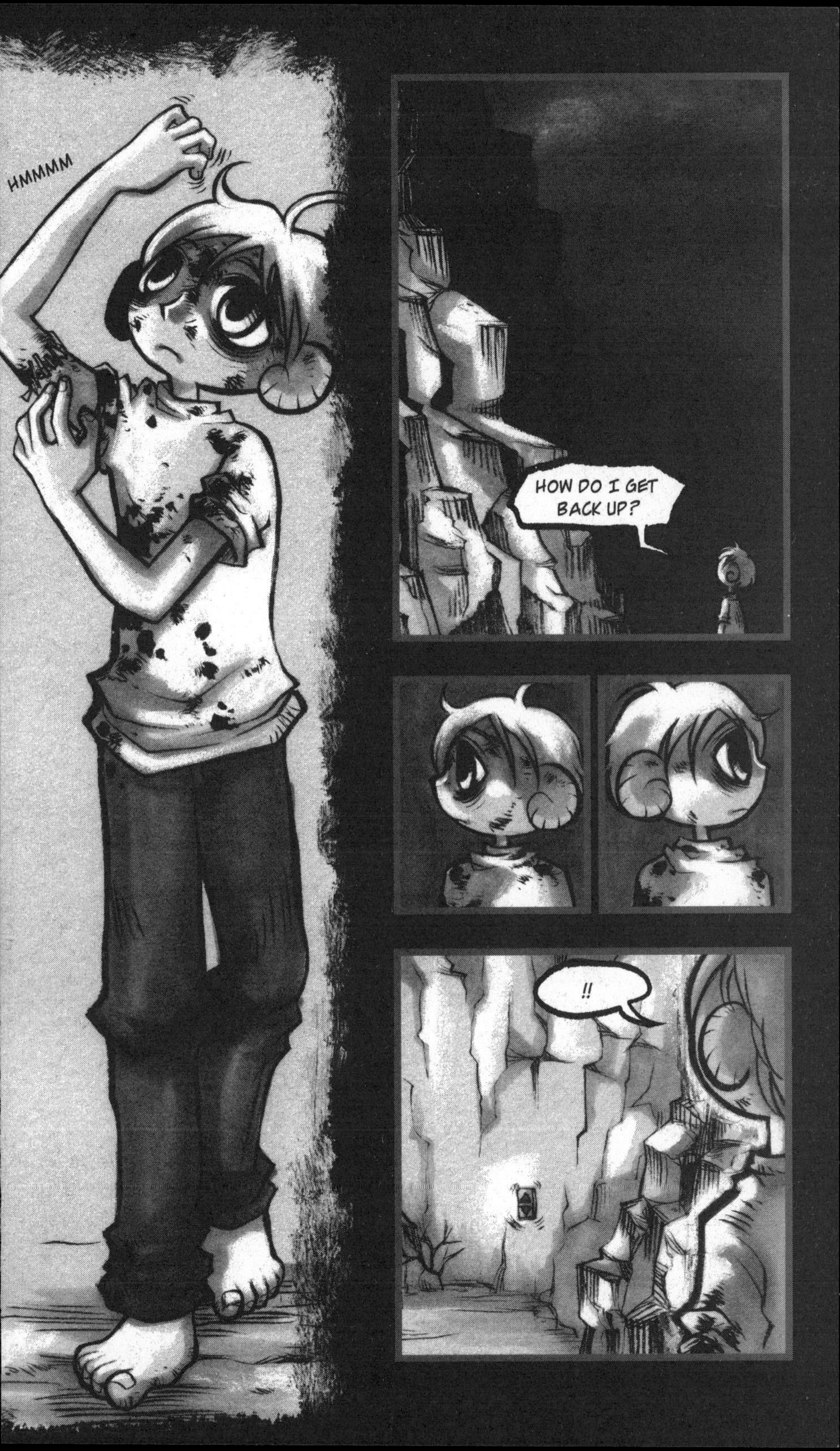
HMMMM
HOW DO I GET BACK UP?
!!

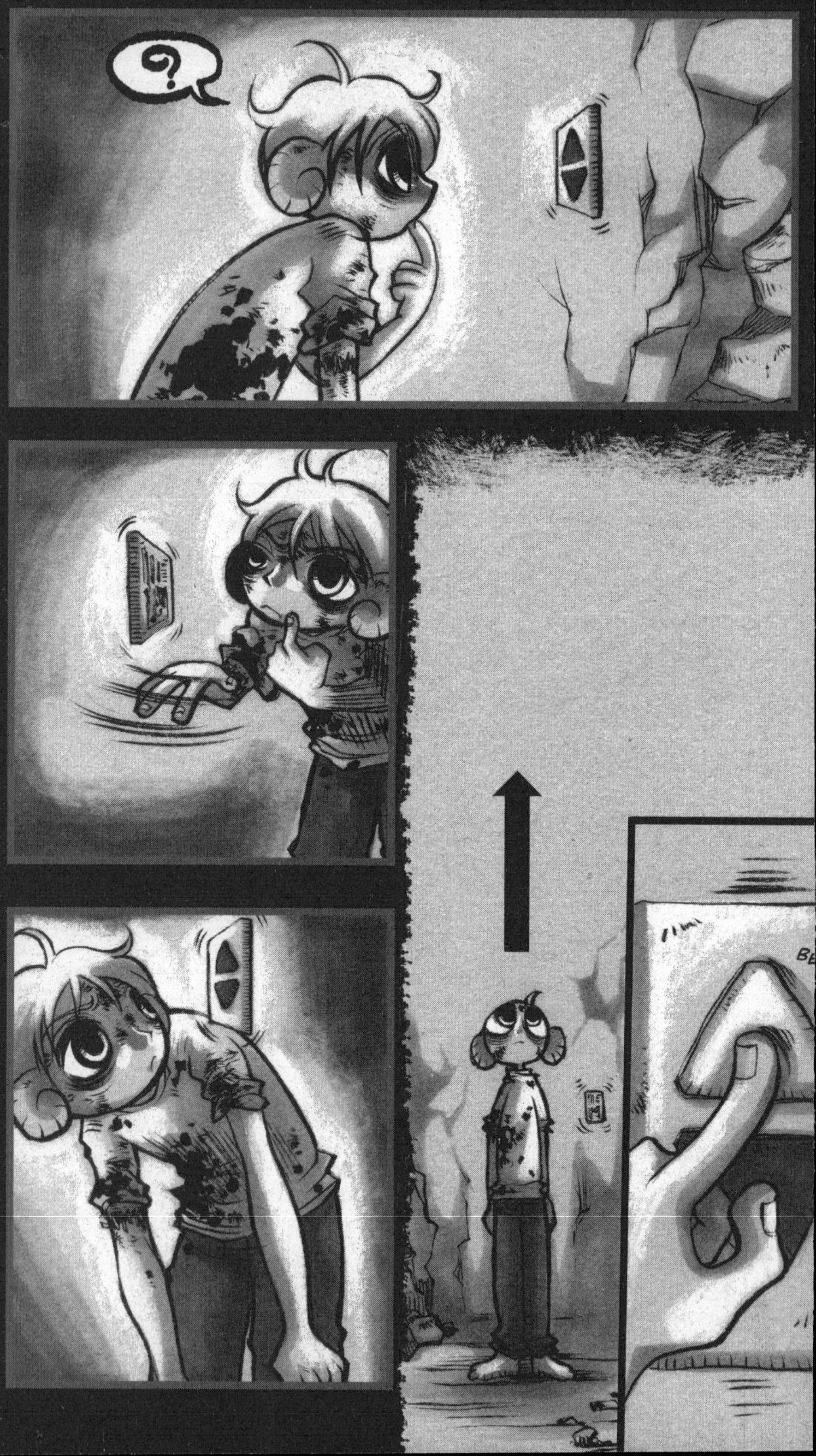
?

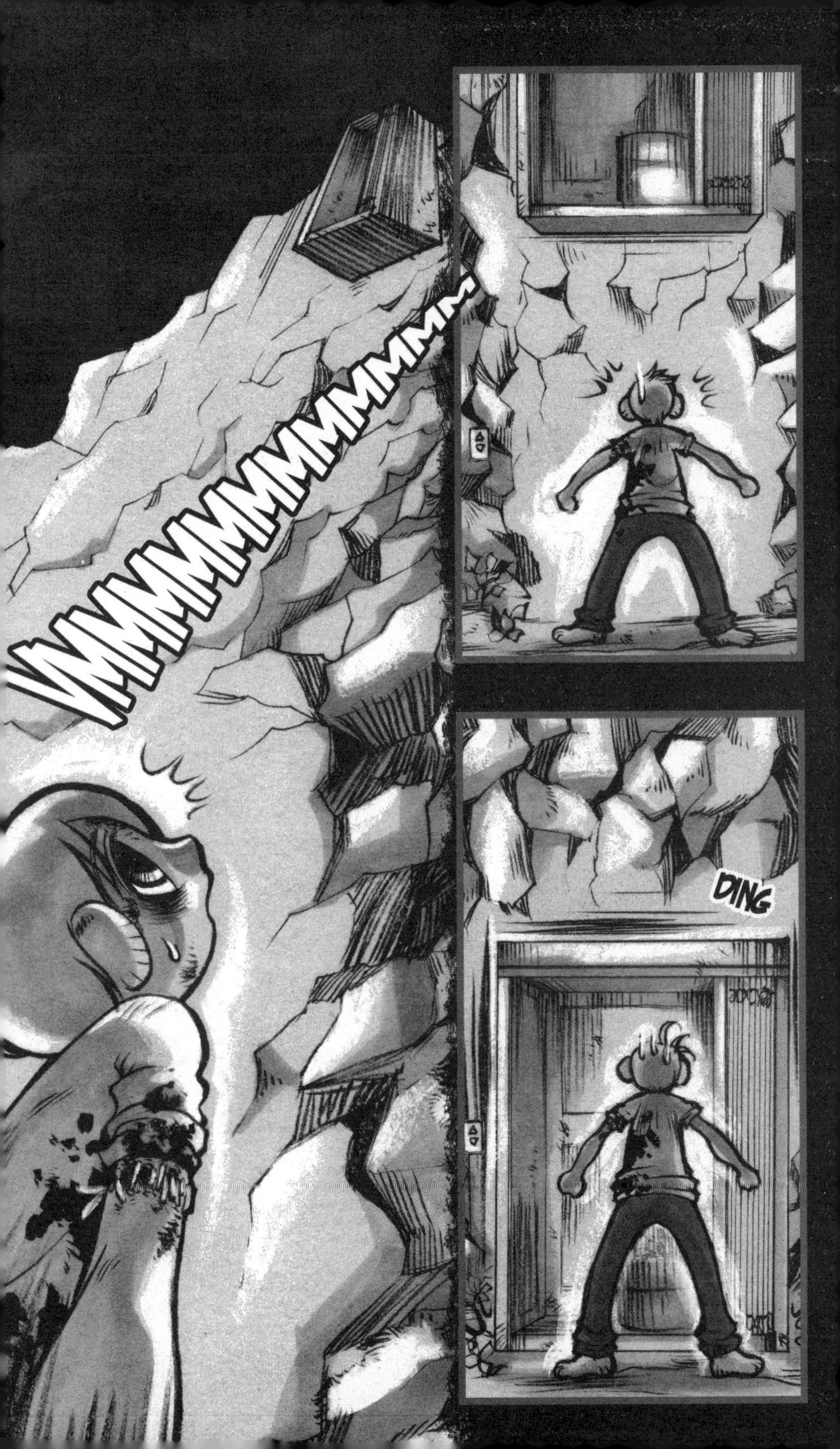
VMMMMMMMMMMMMMM
DING

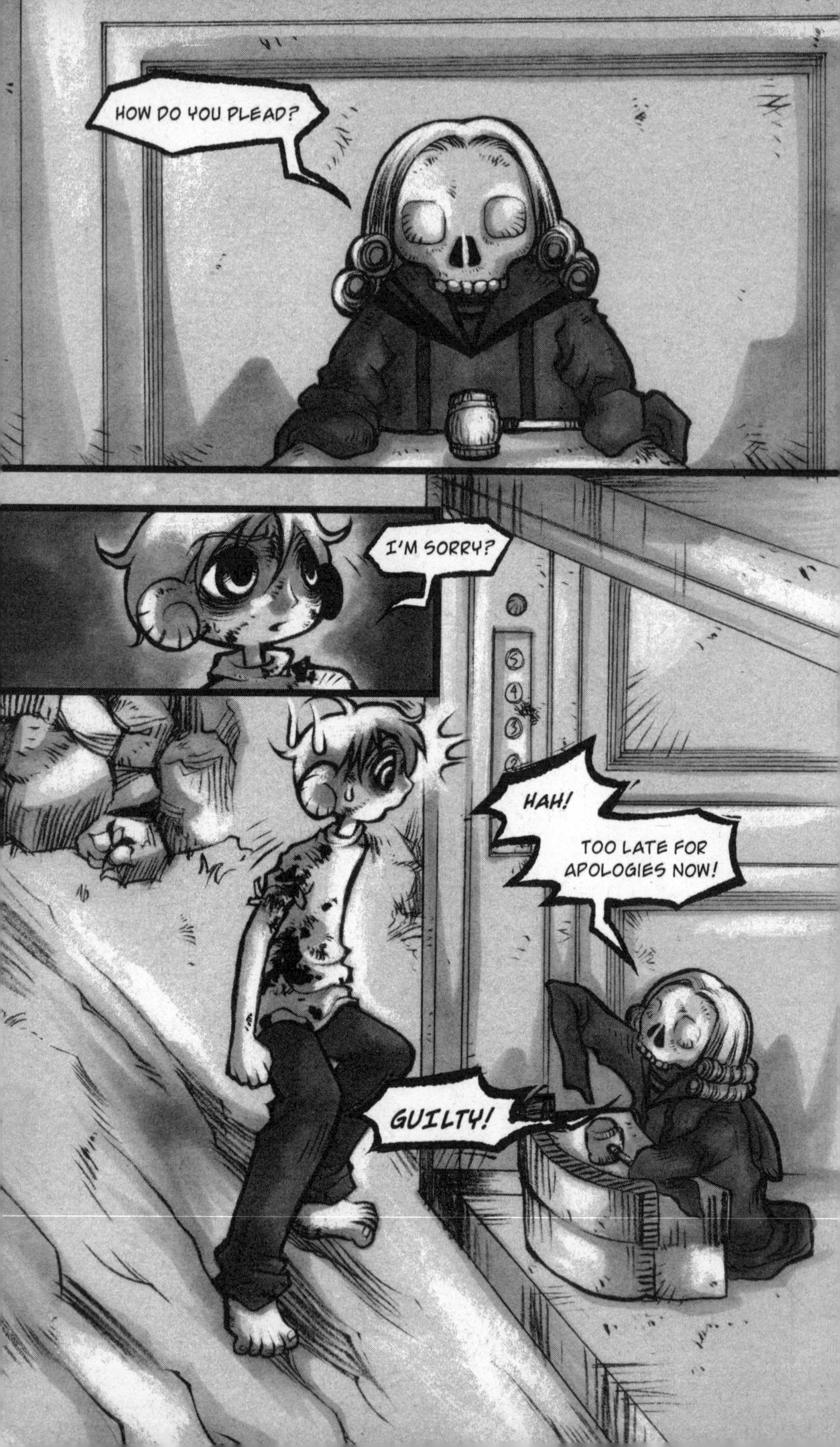
HOW DO YOU PLEAD?
I'M SORRY?
HAH!
TOO LATE FOR APOLOGIES NOW!
GUILTY!

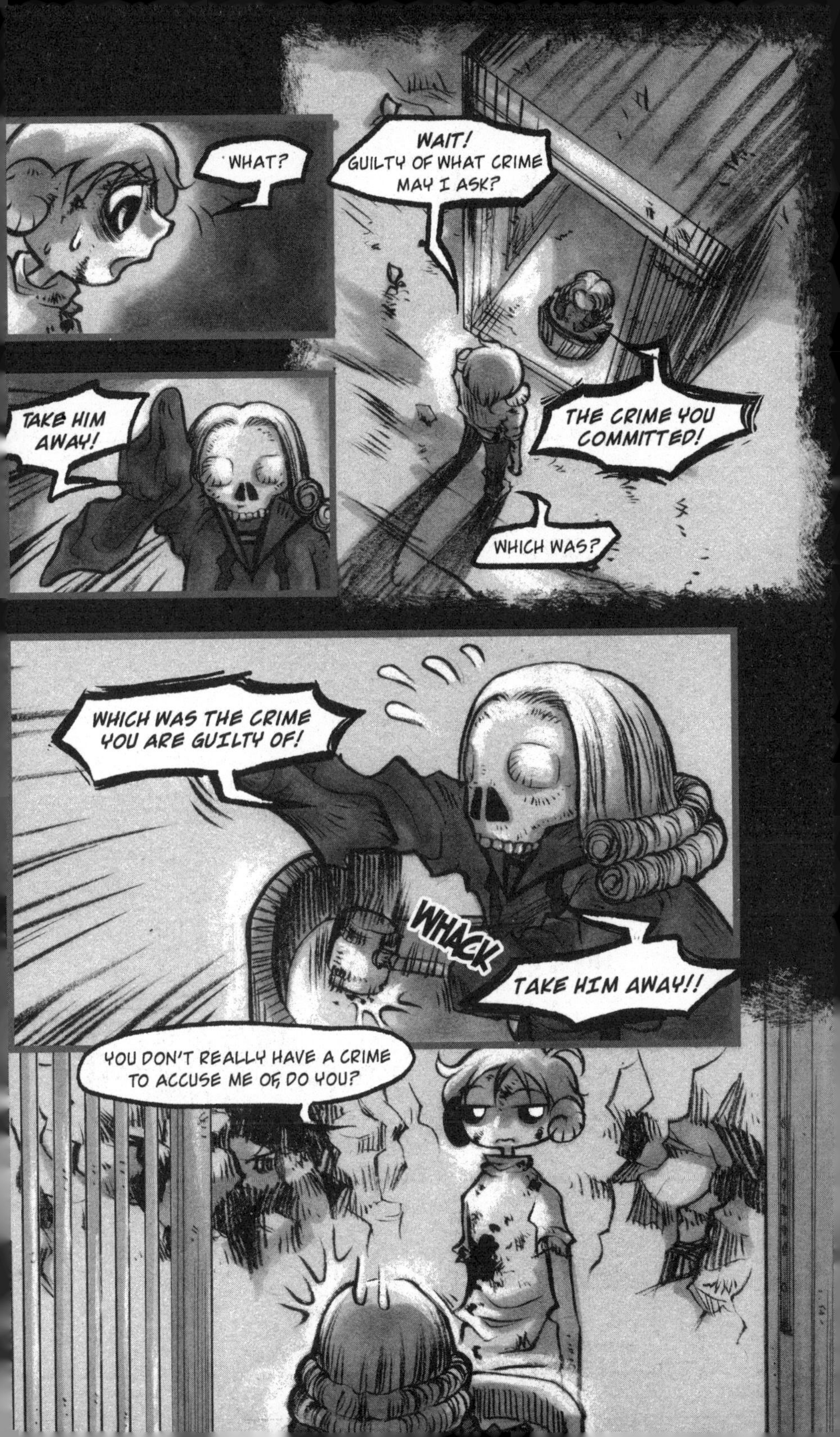
WHAT?
WAIT! GUILTY OF WHAT CRIME MAY I ASK?
TAKE HIM AWAY!
THE CRIME YOU COMMITTED!
WHICH WAS?
WHICH WAS THE CRIME YOU ARE GUILTY OF!
WHACK
TAKE HIM AWAY!!
YOU DON'T REALLY HAVE A CRIME TO ACCUSE ME OF, DO YOU?

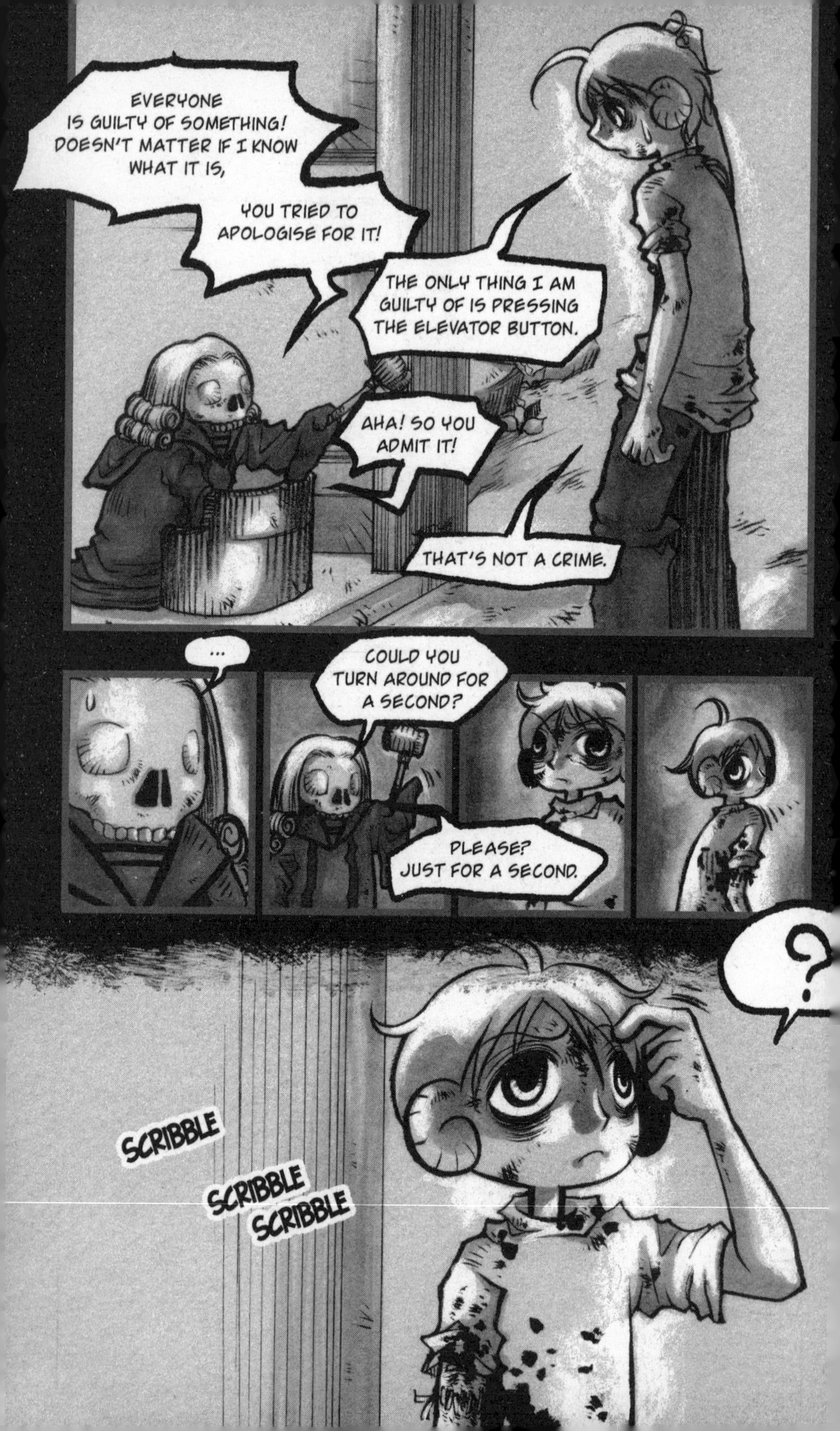
EVERYONE IS GUILTY OF SOMETHING! DOESN'T MATTER IF I KNOW WHAT IT IS,
YOU TRIED TO APOLOGISE FOR IT!
THE ONLY THING I AM GUILTY OF IS PRESSING THE ELEVATOR BUTTON.
AHA! SO YOU ADMIT IT!
THAT'S NOT A CRIME.
...
COULD YOU TURN AROUND FOR A SECOND?
PLEASE? JUST FOR A SECOND.
?
SCRIBBLE
SCRIBBLE
SCRIBBLE

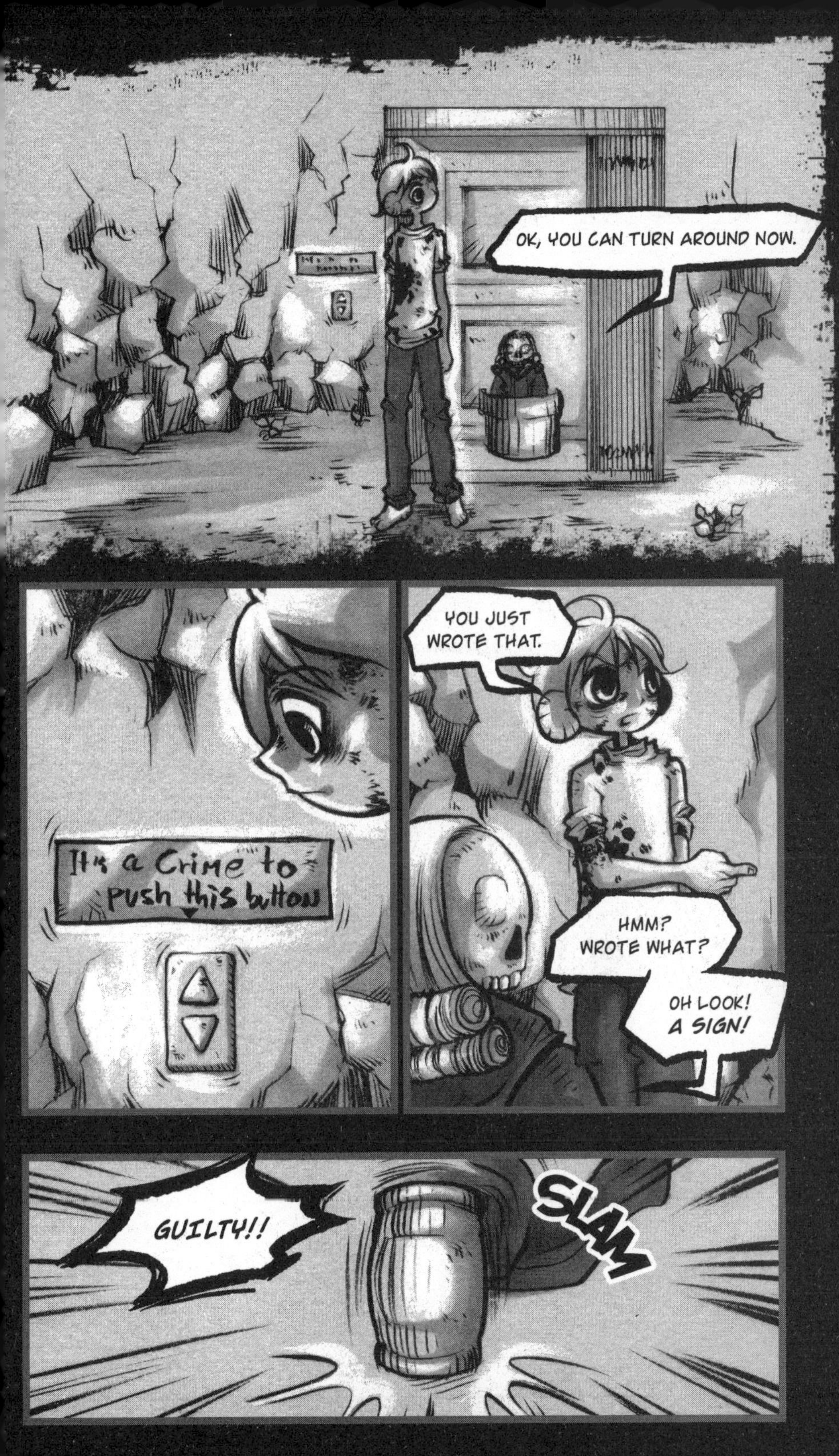
OK, YOU CAN TURN AROUND NOW.
It's a Crime to push this button
YOU JUST WROTE THAT.
HMM? WROTE WHAT?
OH LOOK! A SIGN!
GUILTY!!
SLAM

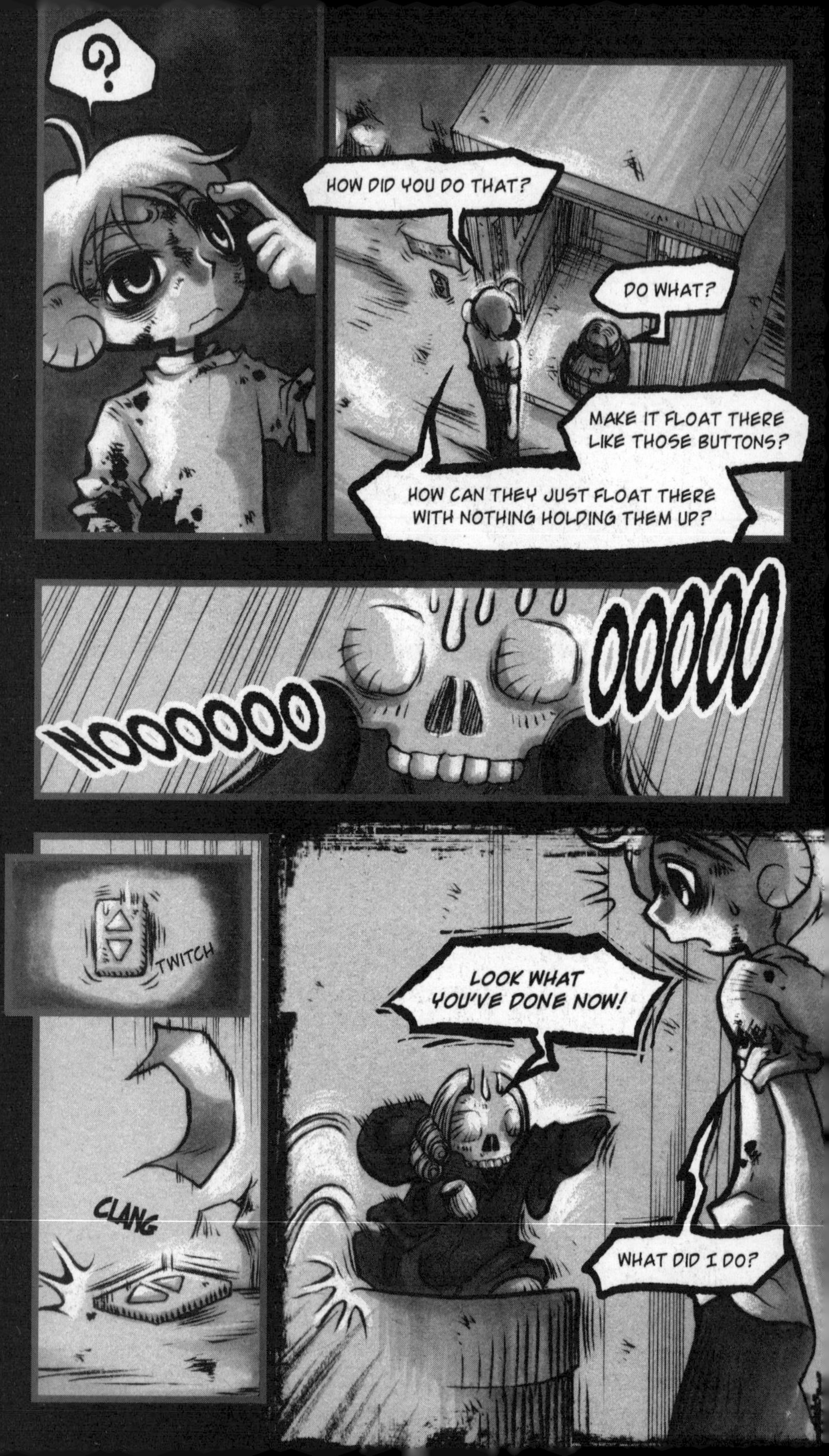
?
HOW DID YOU DO THAT?
DO WHAT?
MAKE IT FLOAT THERE LIKE THOSE BUTTONS?
HOW CAN THEY JUST FLOAT THERE WITH NOTHING HOLDING THEM UP?
NOOOOOOOOOOOO
TWITCH
CLANG
LOOK WHAT YOU'VE DONE NOW!
WHAT DID I DO?

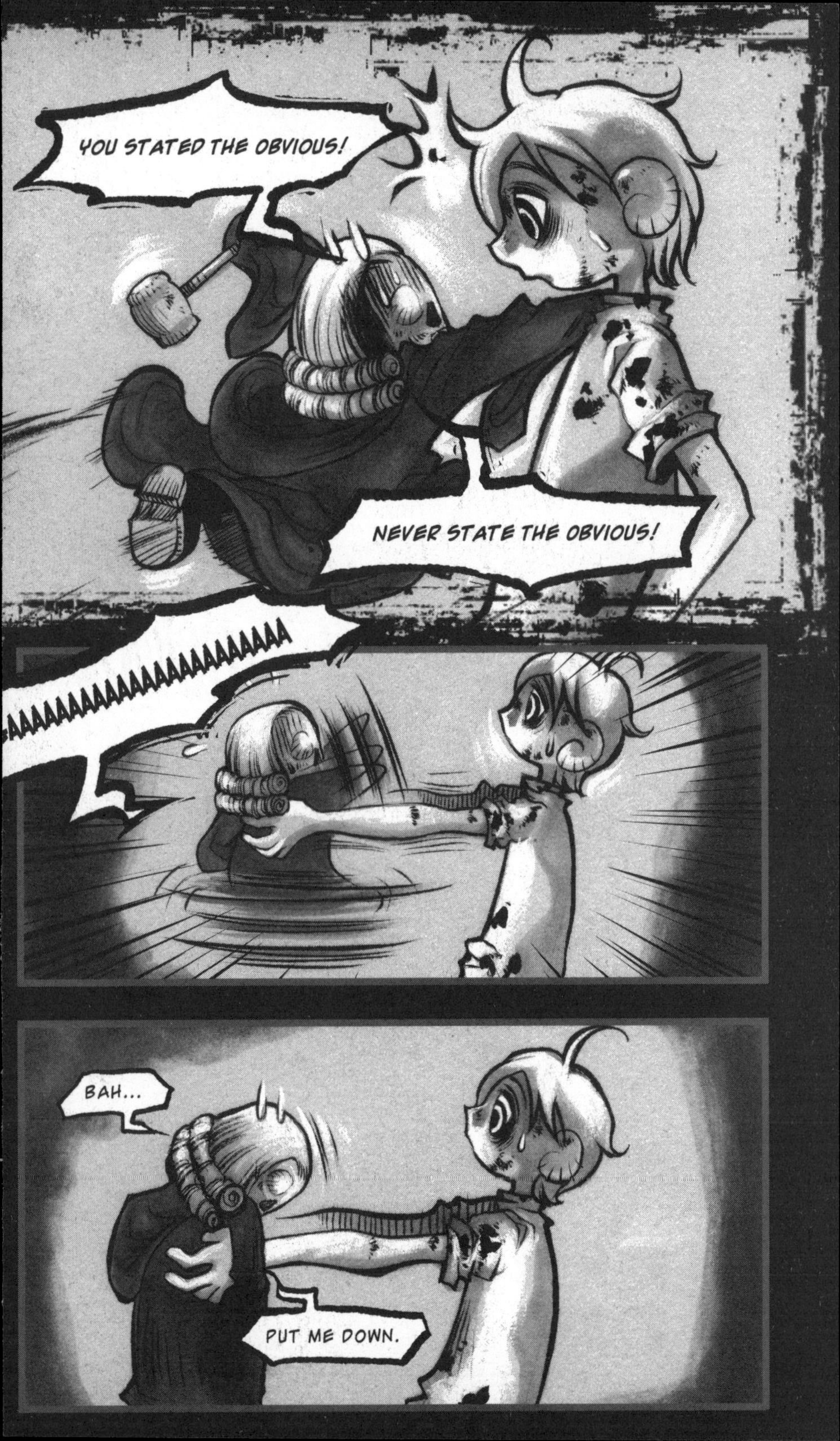
YOU STATED THE OBVIOUS!
NEVER STATE THE OBVIOUS!
AAAAAAAAAAAAAAAAAAAAAAAAAAAAAAAAAAAA
BAH...
PUT ME DOWN.

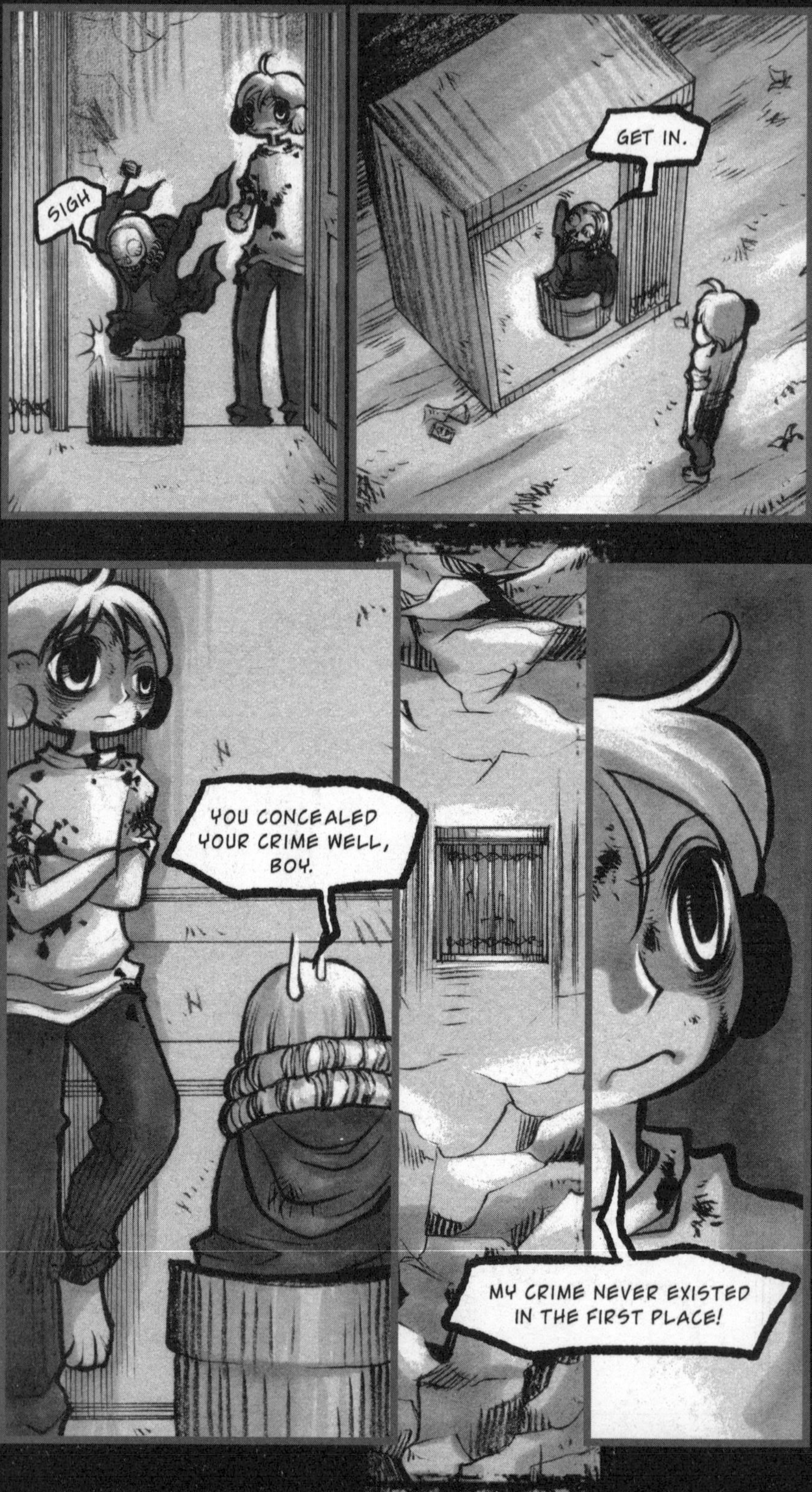
SIGH
GET IN.
YOU CONCEALED YOUR CRIME WELL, BOY.
MY CRIME NEVER EXISTED IN THE FIRST PLACE!

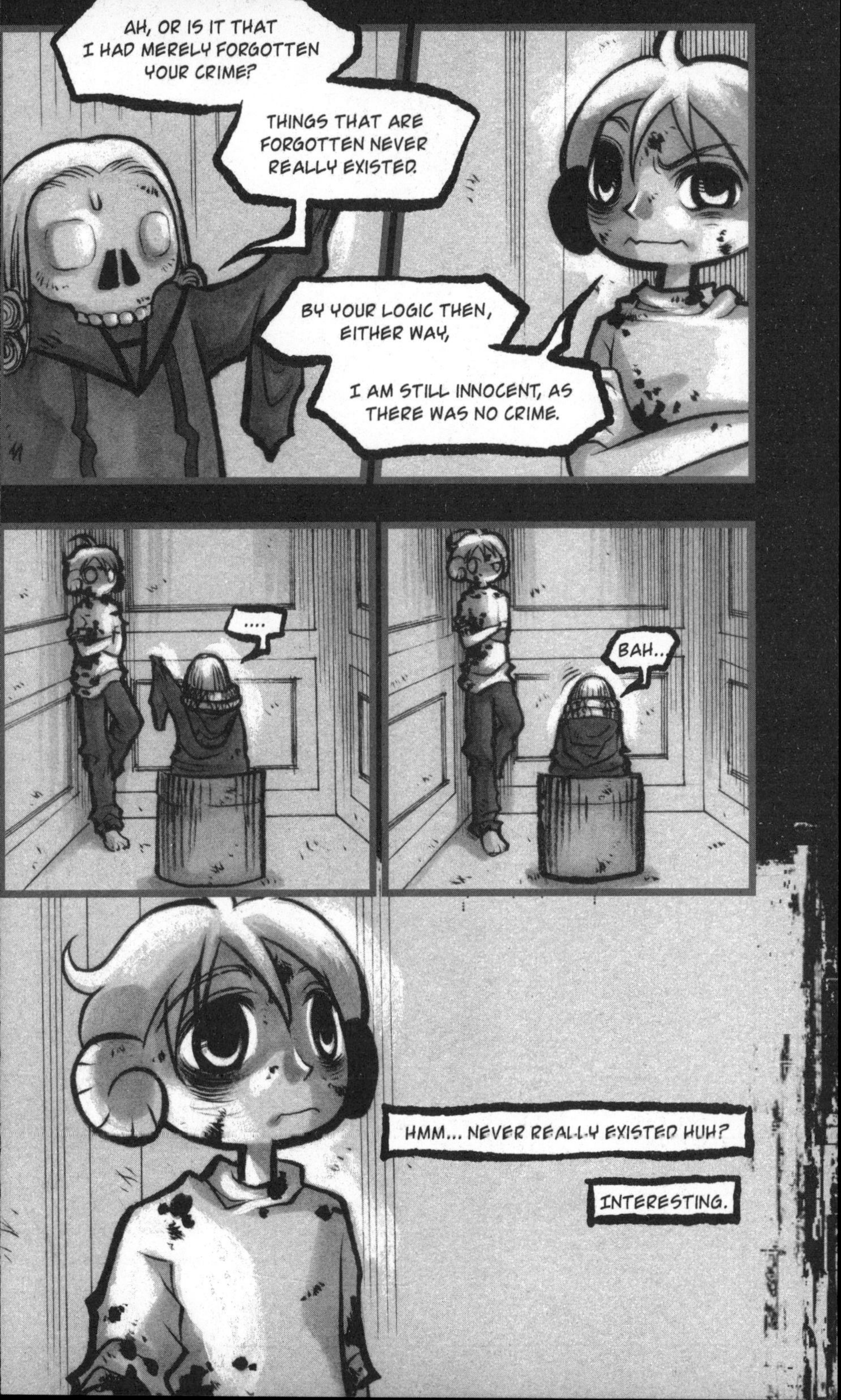

AH, OR IS IT THAT I HAD MERELY FORGOTTEN YOUR CRIME?
THINGS THAT ARE FORGOTTEN NEVER REALLY EXISTED.
BY YOUR LOGIC THEN, EITHER WAY,
I AM STILL INNOCENT, AS THERE WAS NO CRIME.
....
BAH...
HMM... NEVER REALLY EXISTED HUH?
INTERESTING.

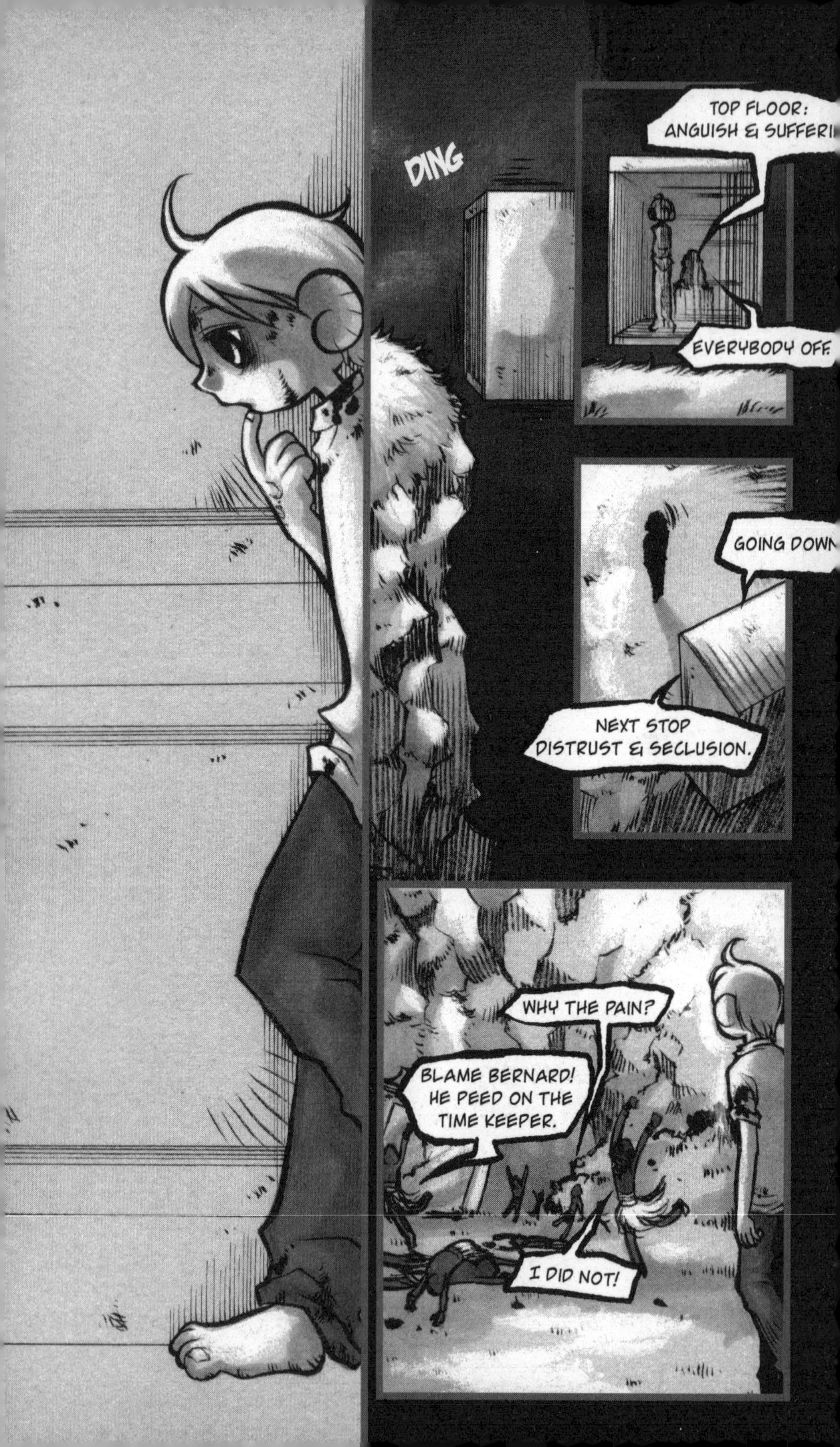
DING
TOP FLOOR: ANGUISH & SUFFERI
EVERYBODY OFF.
GOING DOWN
NEXT STOP DISTRUST & SECLUSION.
WHY THE PAIN?
BLAME BERNARD! HE PEED ON THE TIME KEEPER.
I DID NOT!

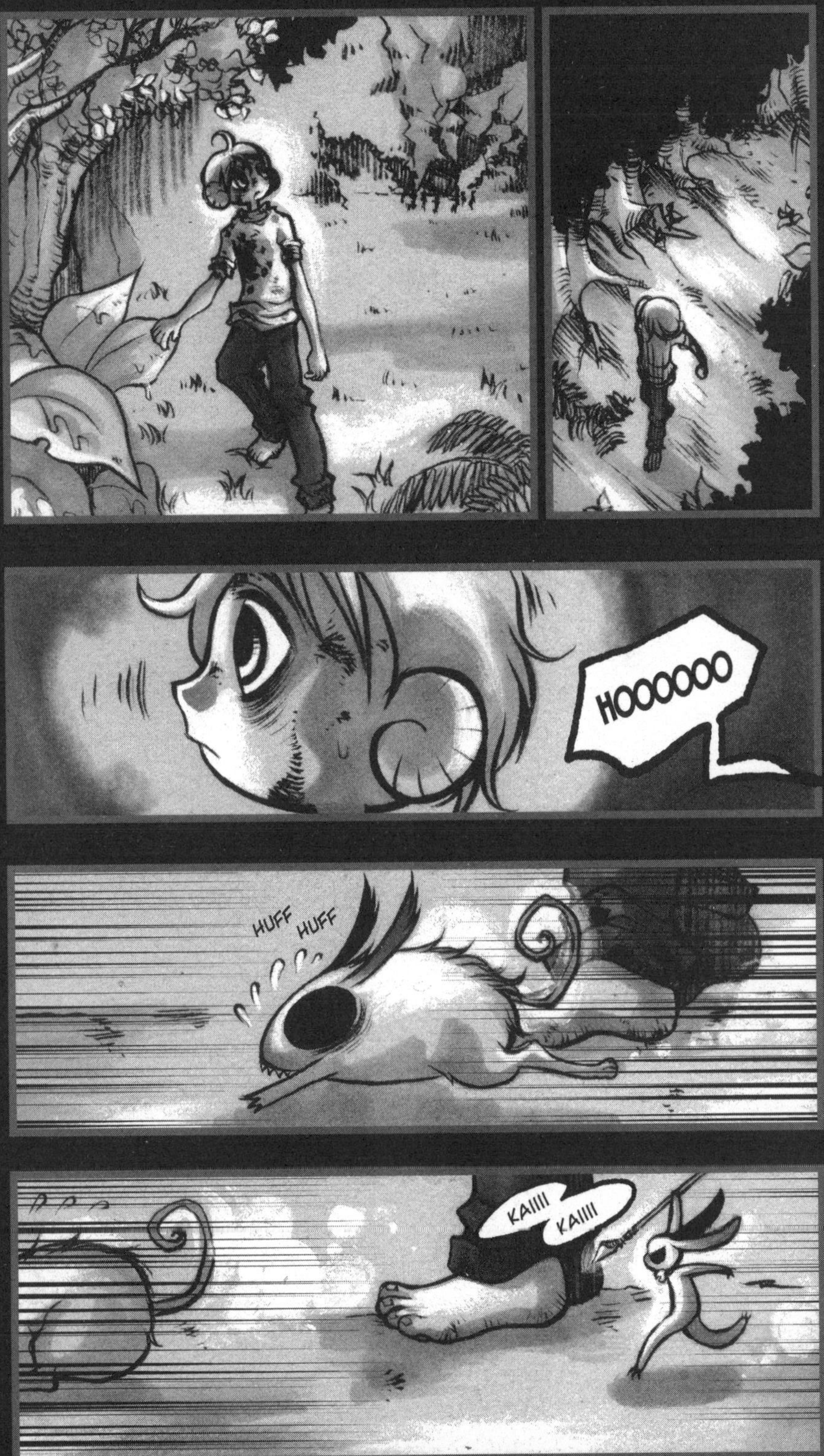
HOOOOOO
HUFF
HUFF
KAIIII
KAIIII

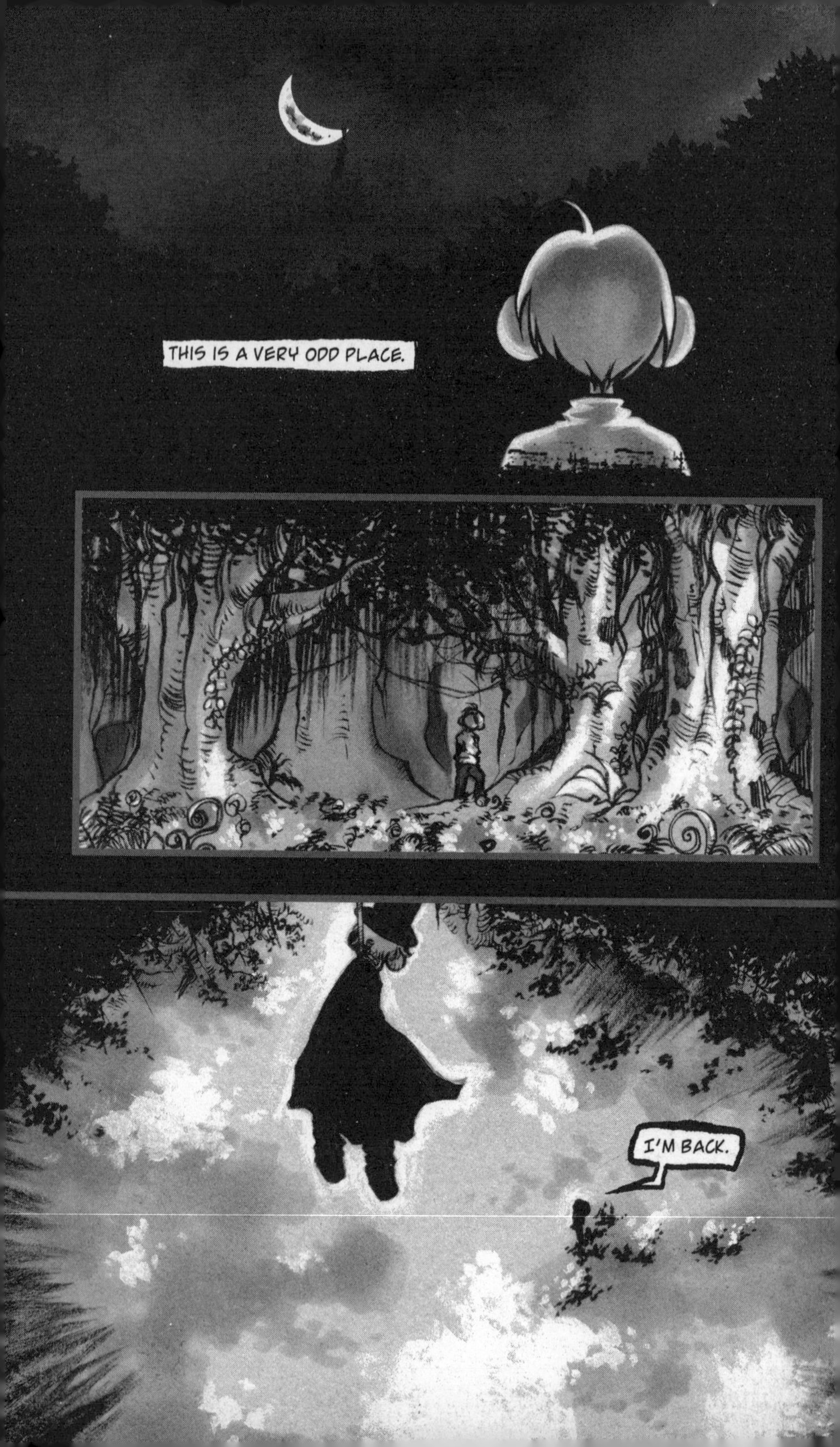
THIS IS A VERY ODD PLACE.
I'M BACK.

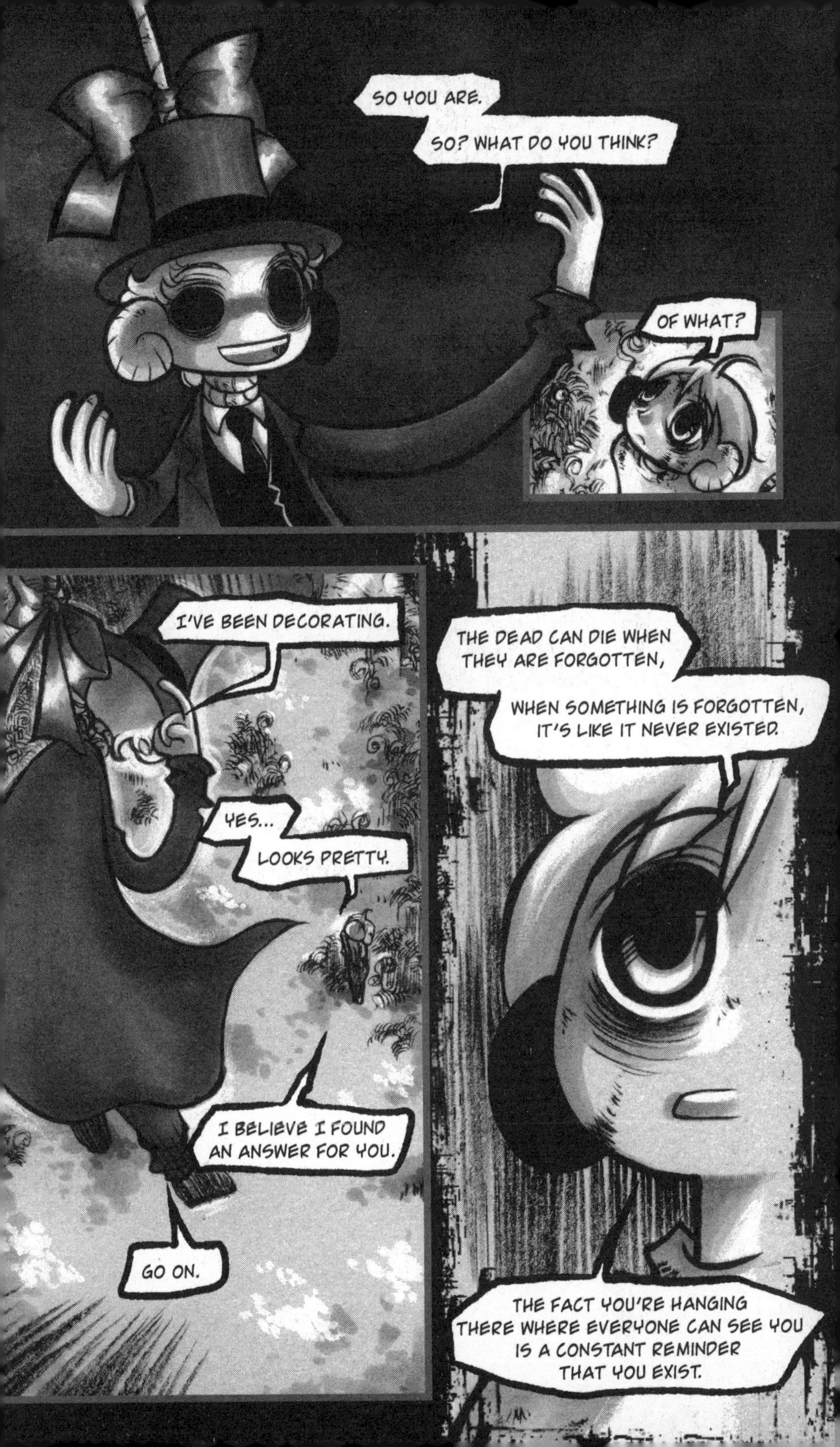
SO YOU ARE.
SO? WHAT DO YOU THINK?
OF WHAT?
I'VE BEEN DECORATING.
YES...
LOOKS PRETTY.
I BELIEVE I FOUND AN ANSWER FOR YOU.
GO ON.
THE DEAD CAN DIE WHEN THEY ARE FORGOTTEN,
WHEN SOMETHING IS FORGOTTEN, IT'S LIKE IT NEVER EXISTED.
THE FACT YOU'RE HANGING THERE WHERE EVERYONE CAN SEE YOU IS A CONSTANT REMINDER THAT YOU EXIST.

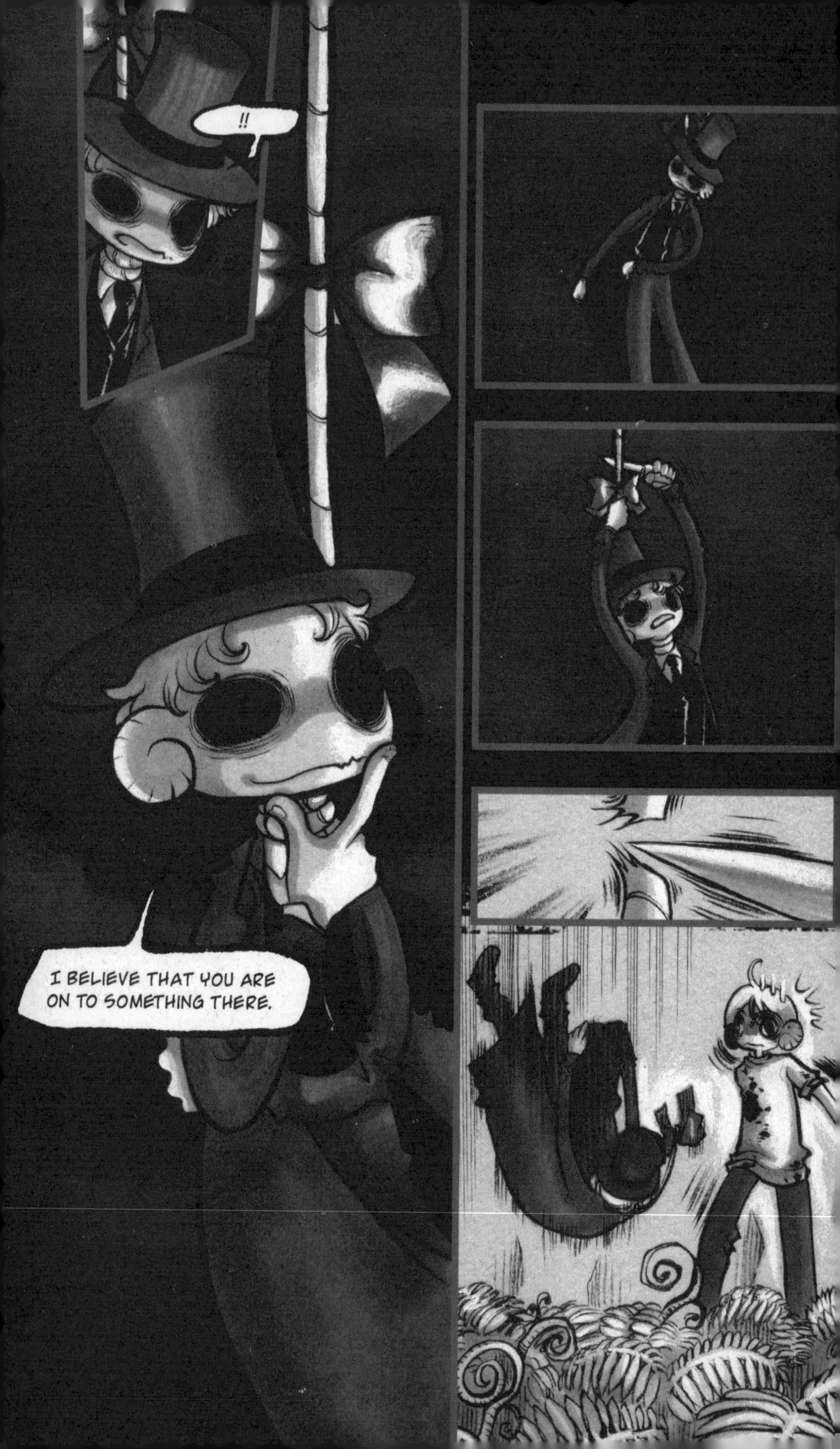
!!
I BELIEVE THAT YOU ARE ON TO SOMETHING THERE.

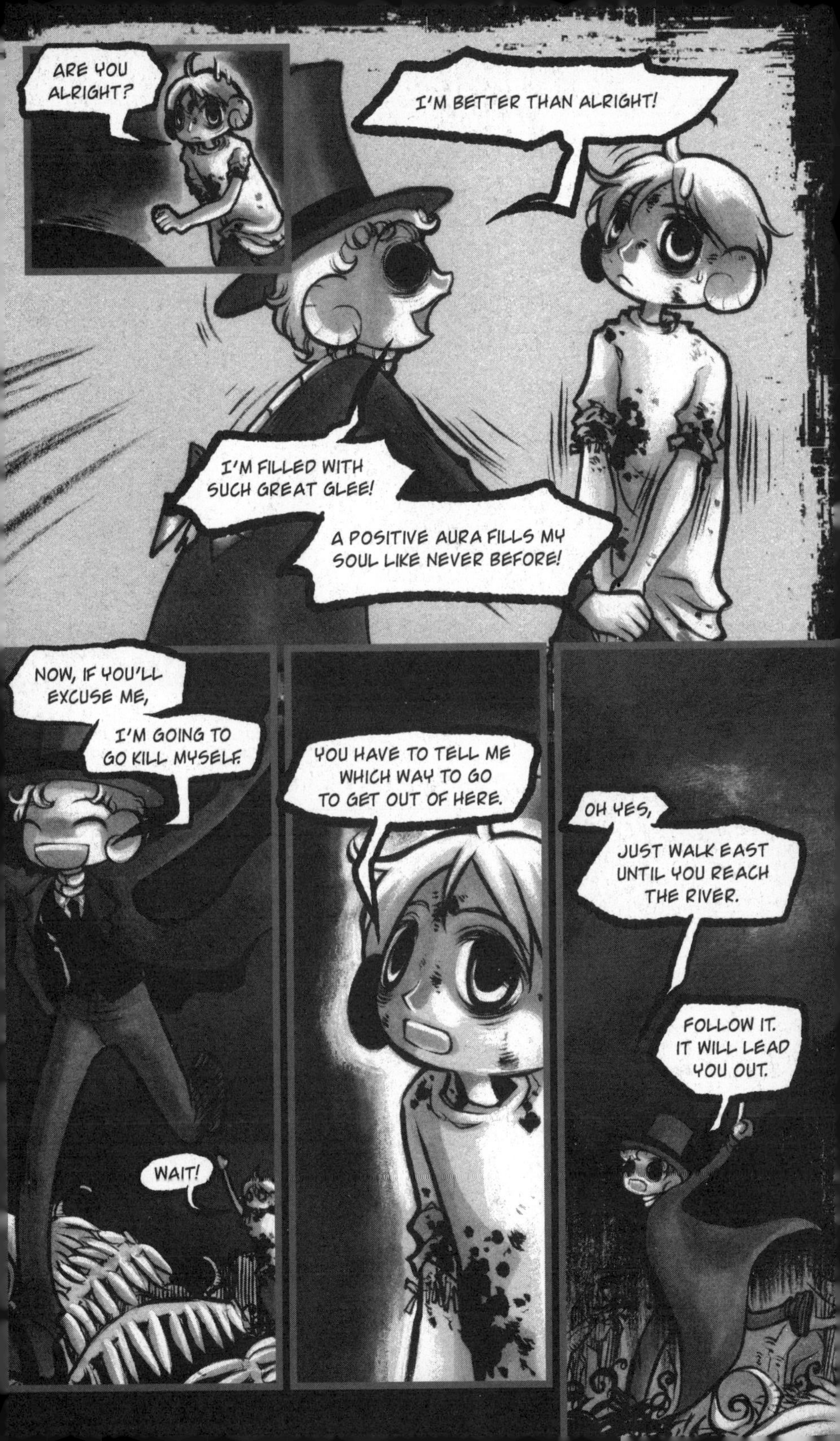
ARE YOU ALRIGHT?
I'M BETTER THAN ALRIGHT!
I'M FILLED WITH SUCH GREAT GLEE!
A POSITIVE AURA FILLS MY SOUL LIKE NEVER BEFORE!
NOW, IF YOU'LL EXCUSE ME,
I'M GOING TO GO KILL MYSELF.
WAIT!
YOU HAVE TO TELL ME WHICH WAY TO GO TO GET OUT OF HERE.
OH YES,
JUST WALK EAST UNTIL YOU REACH THE RIVER.
FOLLOW IT. IT WILL LEAD YOU OUT.

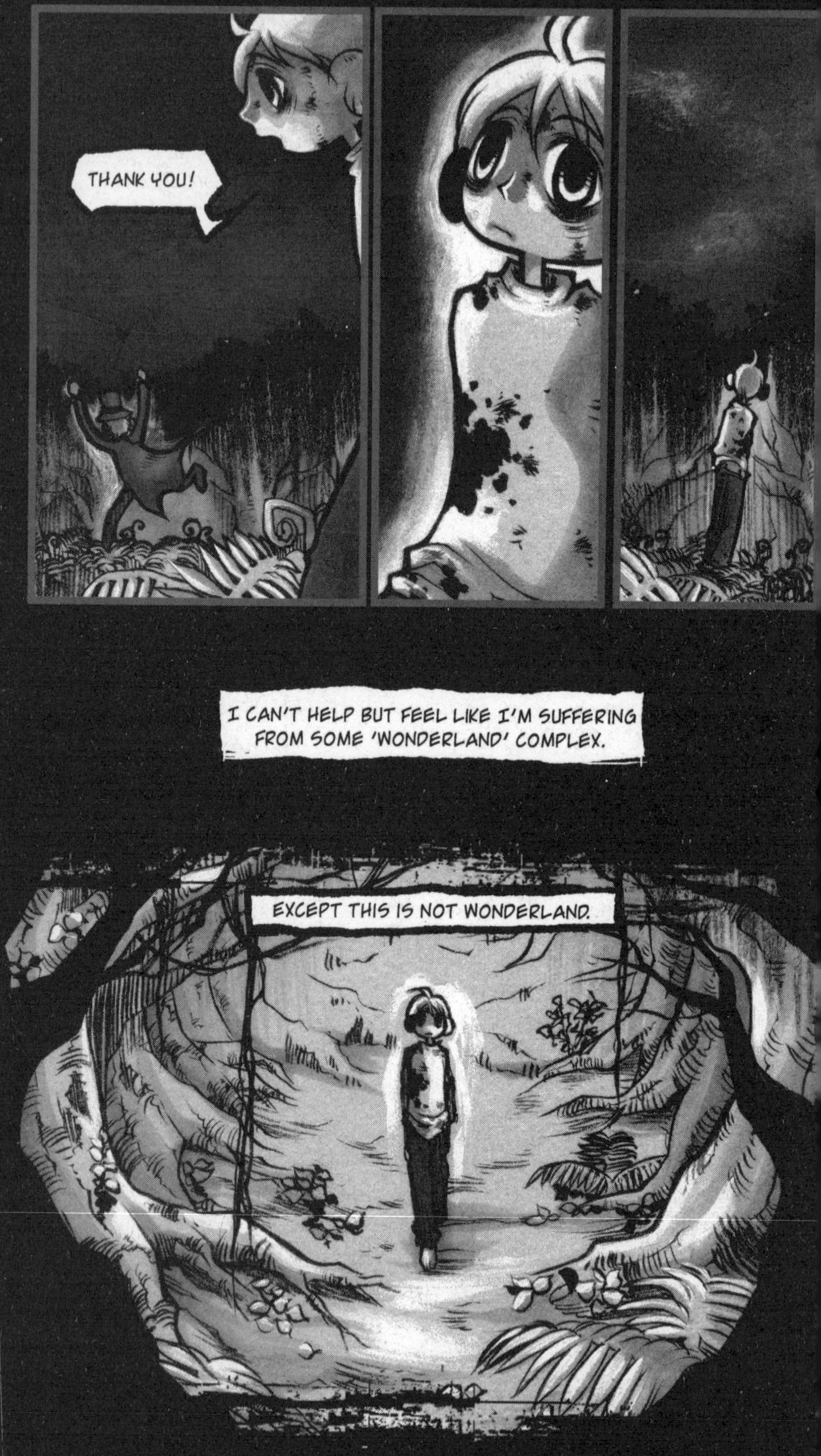
THANK YOU!
I CAN'T HELP BUT FEEL LIKE I'M SUFFERING FROM SOME 'WONDERLAND' COMPLEX.
EXCEPT THIS IS NOT WONDERLAND.

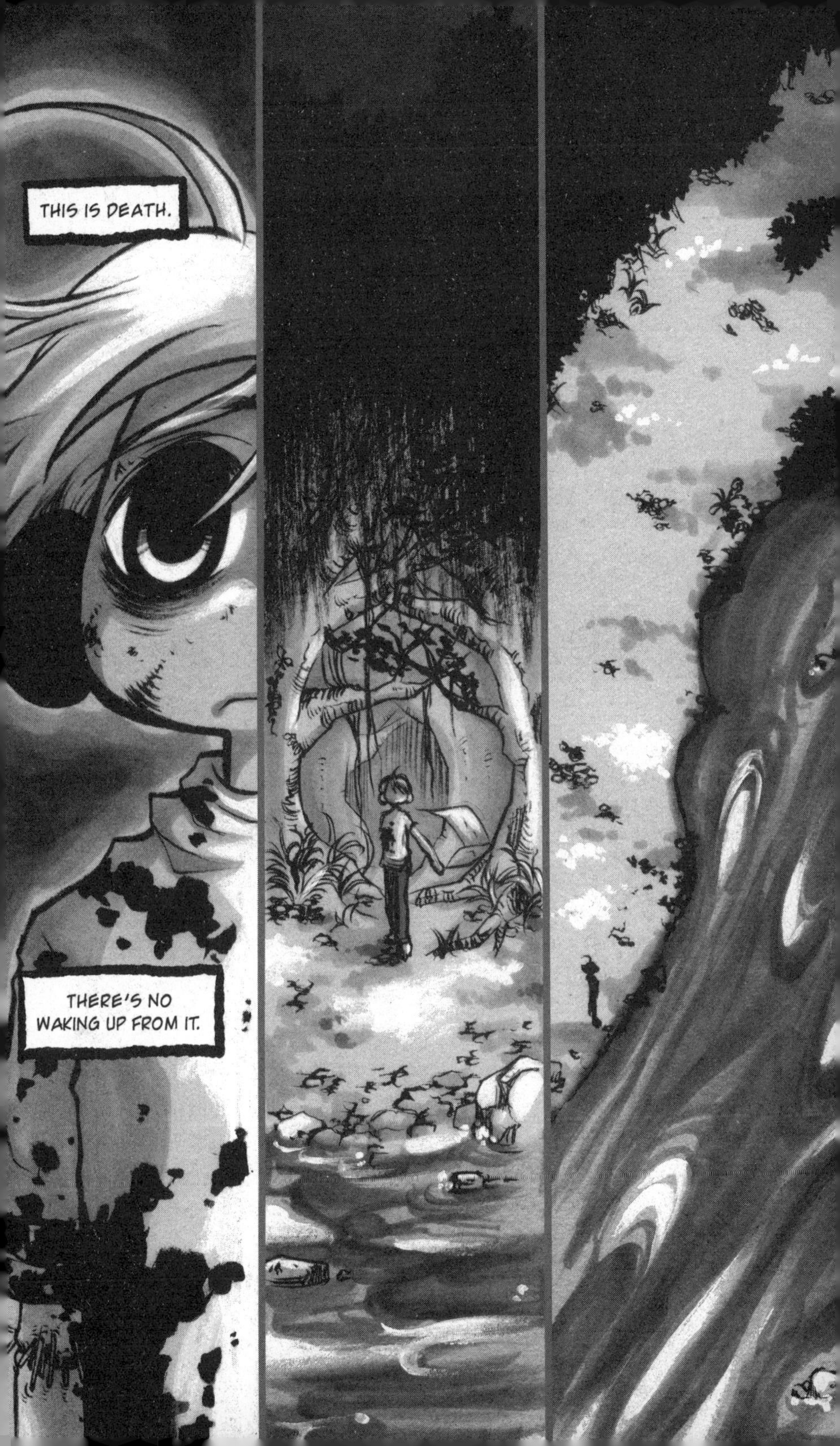
THIS IS DEATH.
THERE'S NO WAKING UP FROM IT.

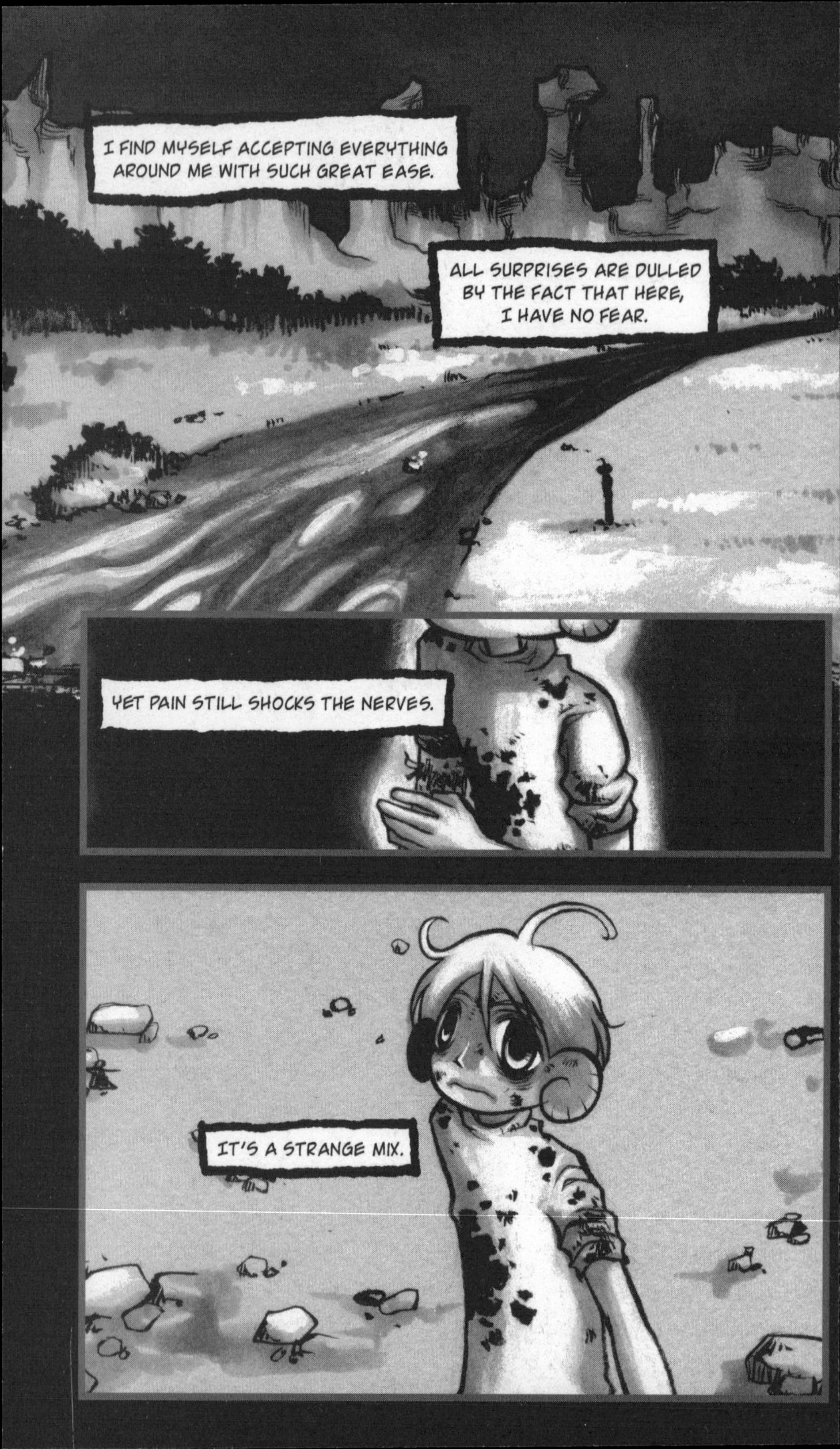
I FIND MYSELF ACCEPTING EVERYTHING AROUND ME WITH SUCH GREAT EASE.
ALL SURPRISES ARE DULLED BY THE FACT THAT HERE, I HAVE NO FEAR.
YET PAIN STILL SHOCKS THE NERVES.
IT'S A STRANGE MIX.

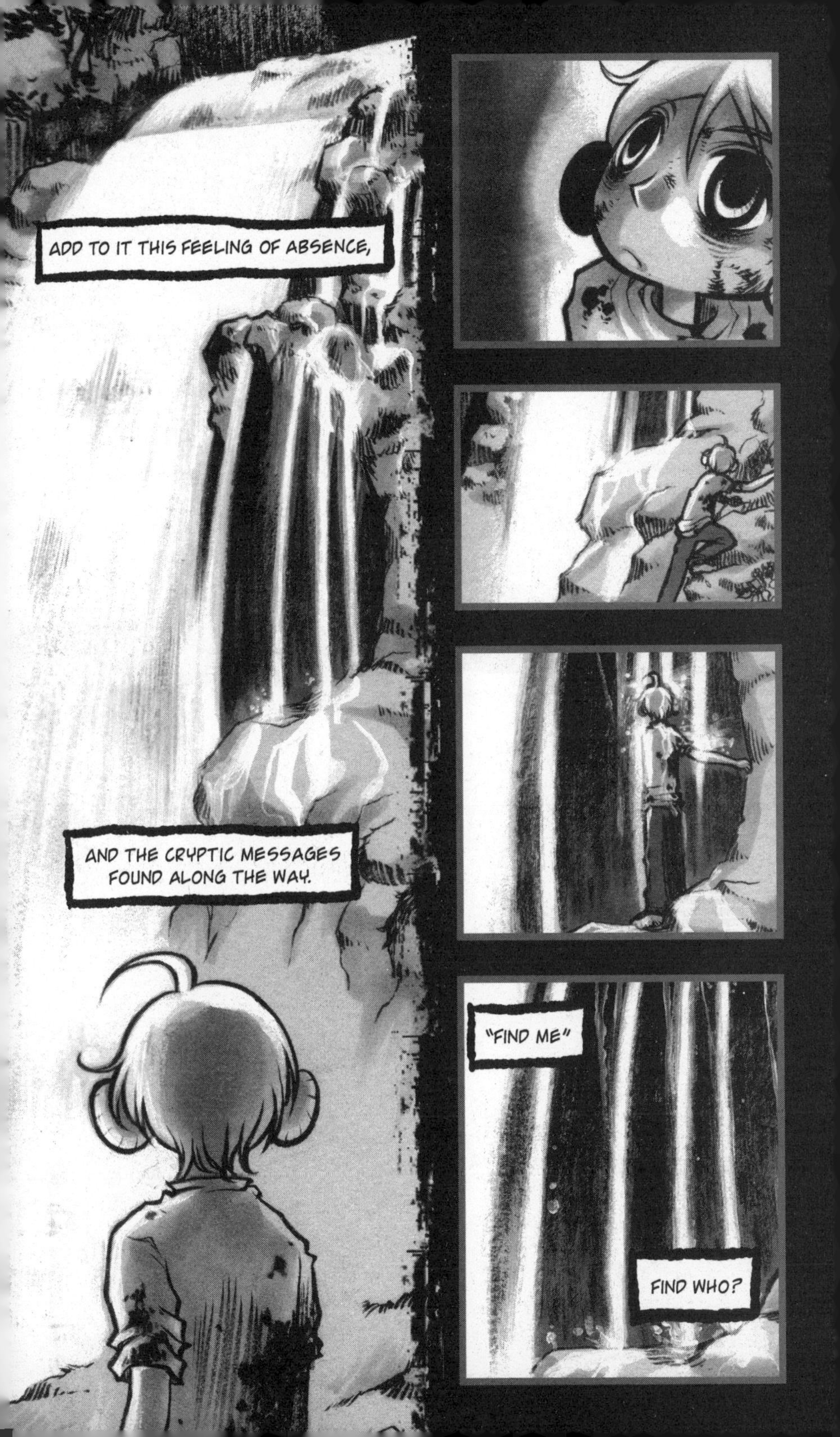
ADD TO IT THIS FEELING OF ABSENCE,
AND THE CRYPTIC MESSAGES FOUND ALONG THE WAY.
"FIND ME"
FIND WHO?

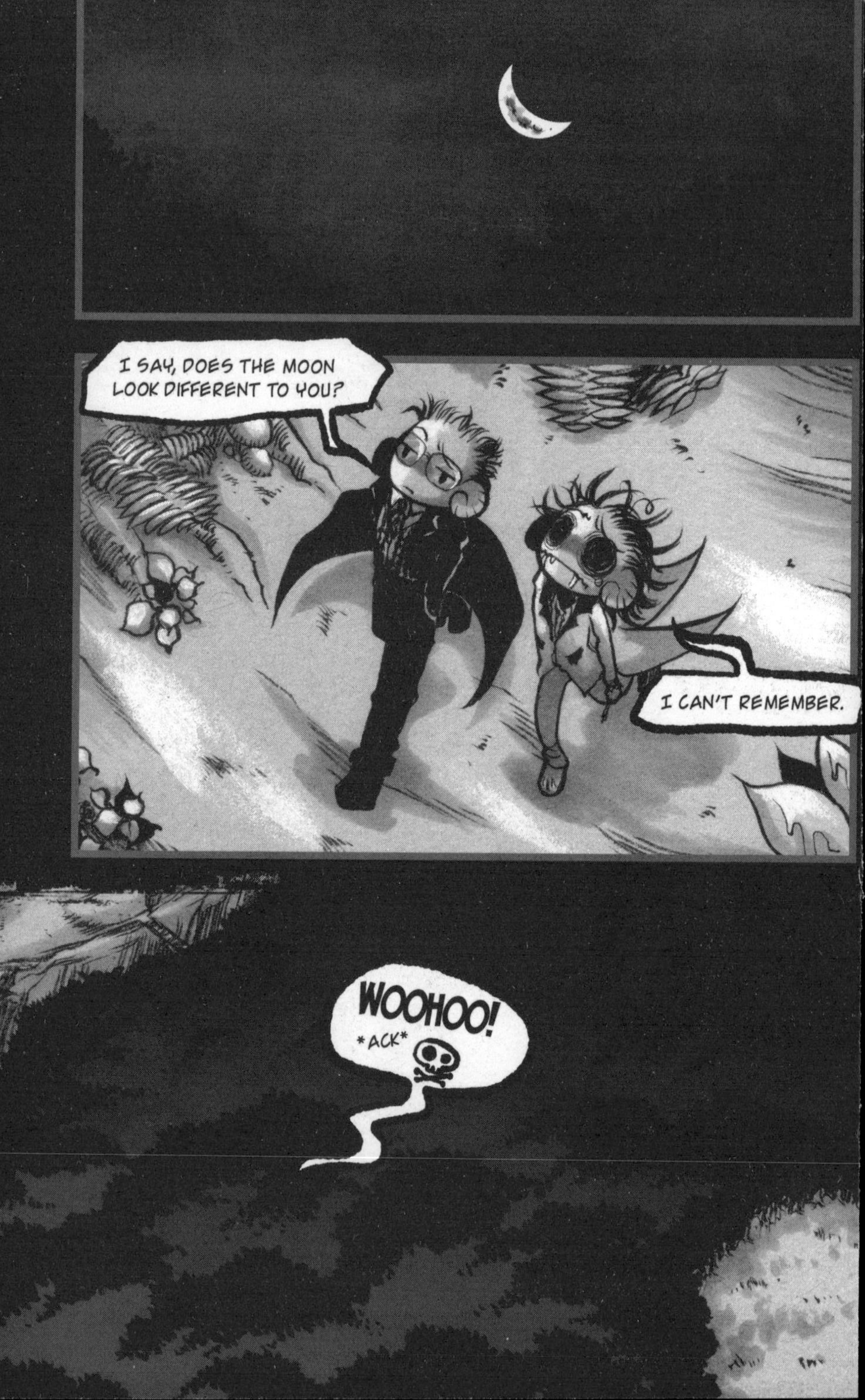
I SAY, DOES THE MOON LOOK DIFFERENT TO YOU?
I CAN'T REMEMBER.
WOOHOO!
ACK

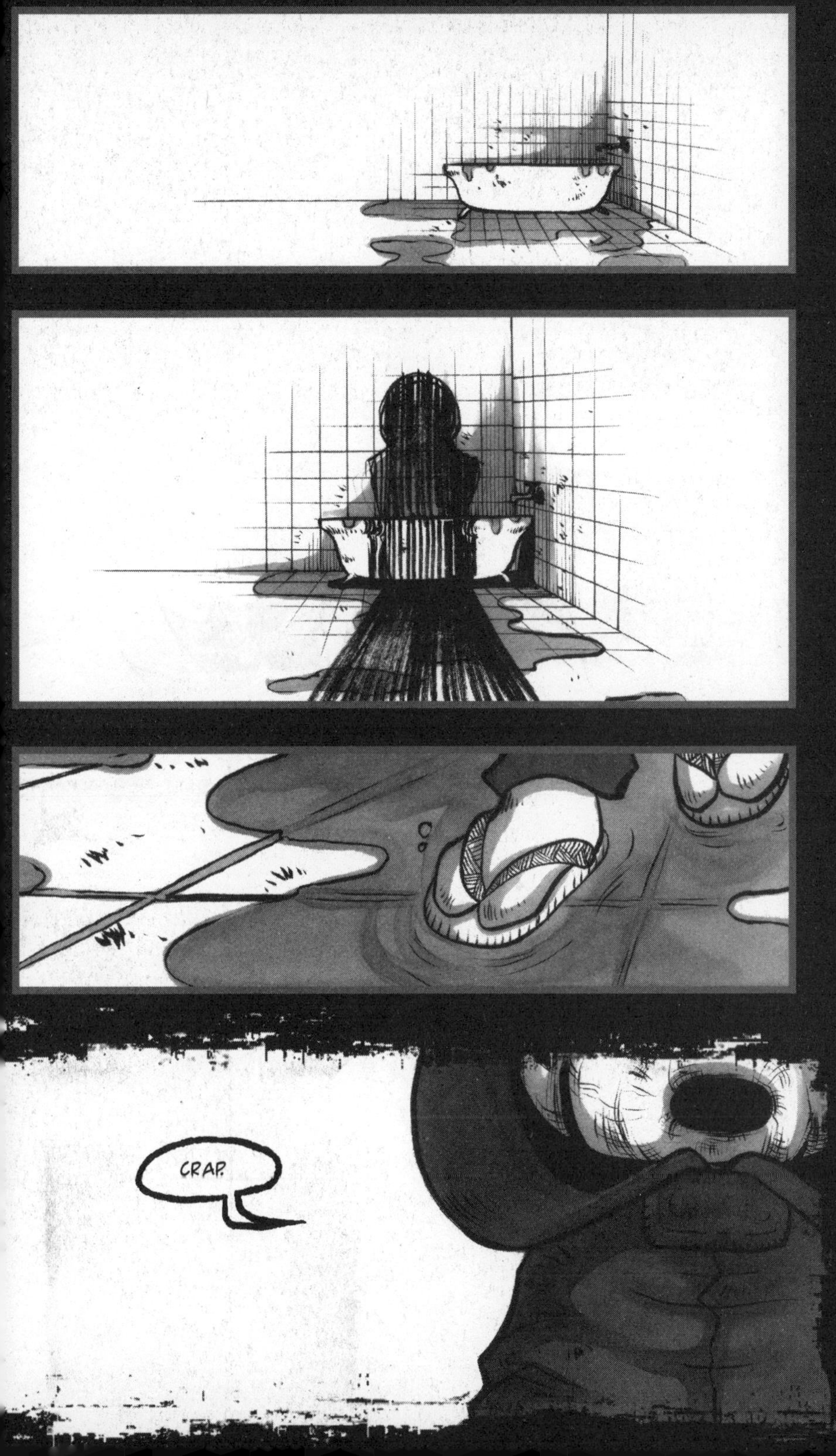
CRAP.

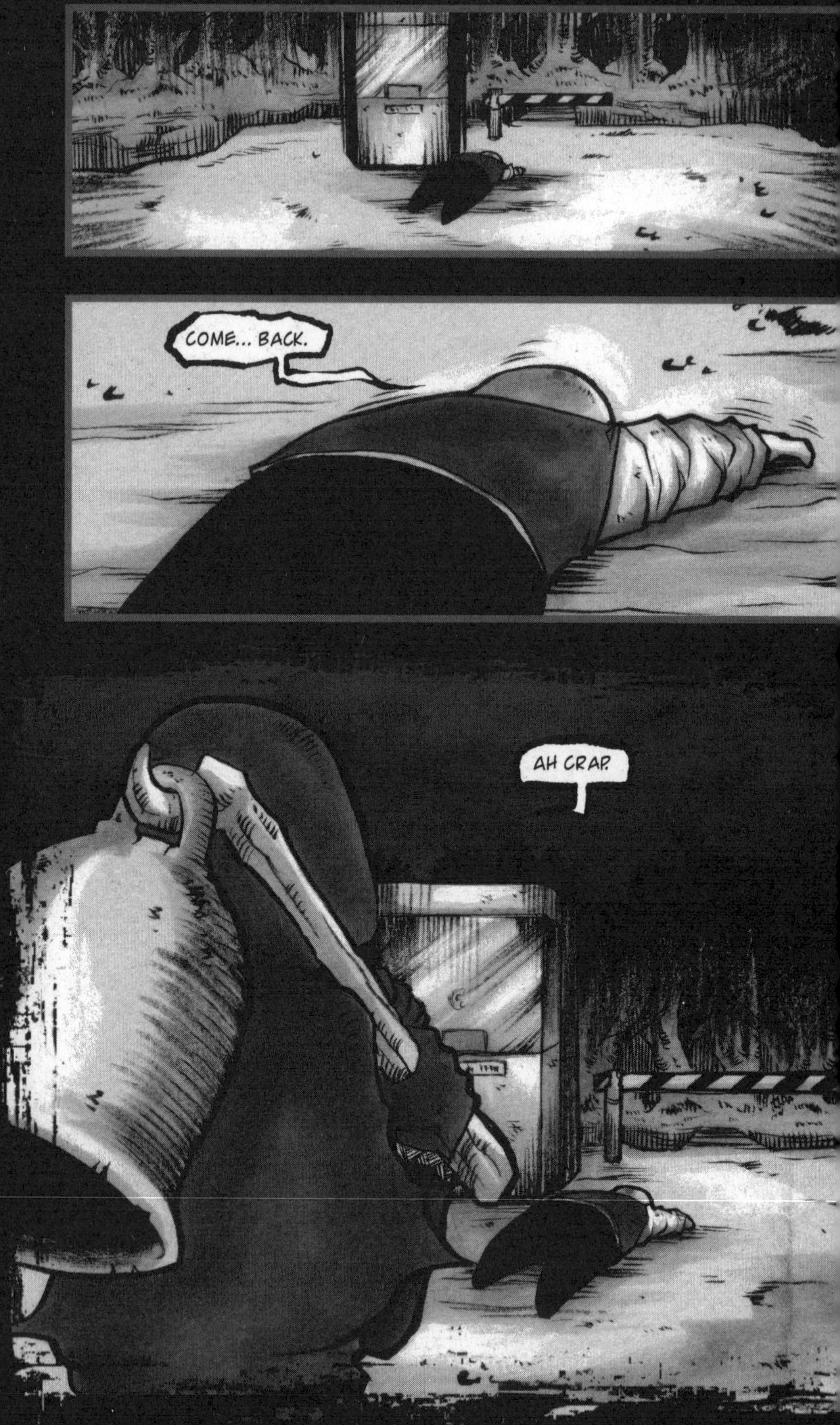
COME... BACK.
AH CRAP.

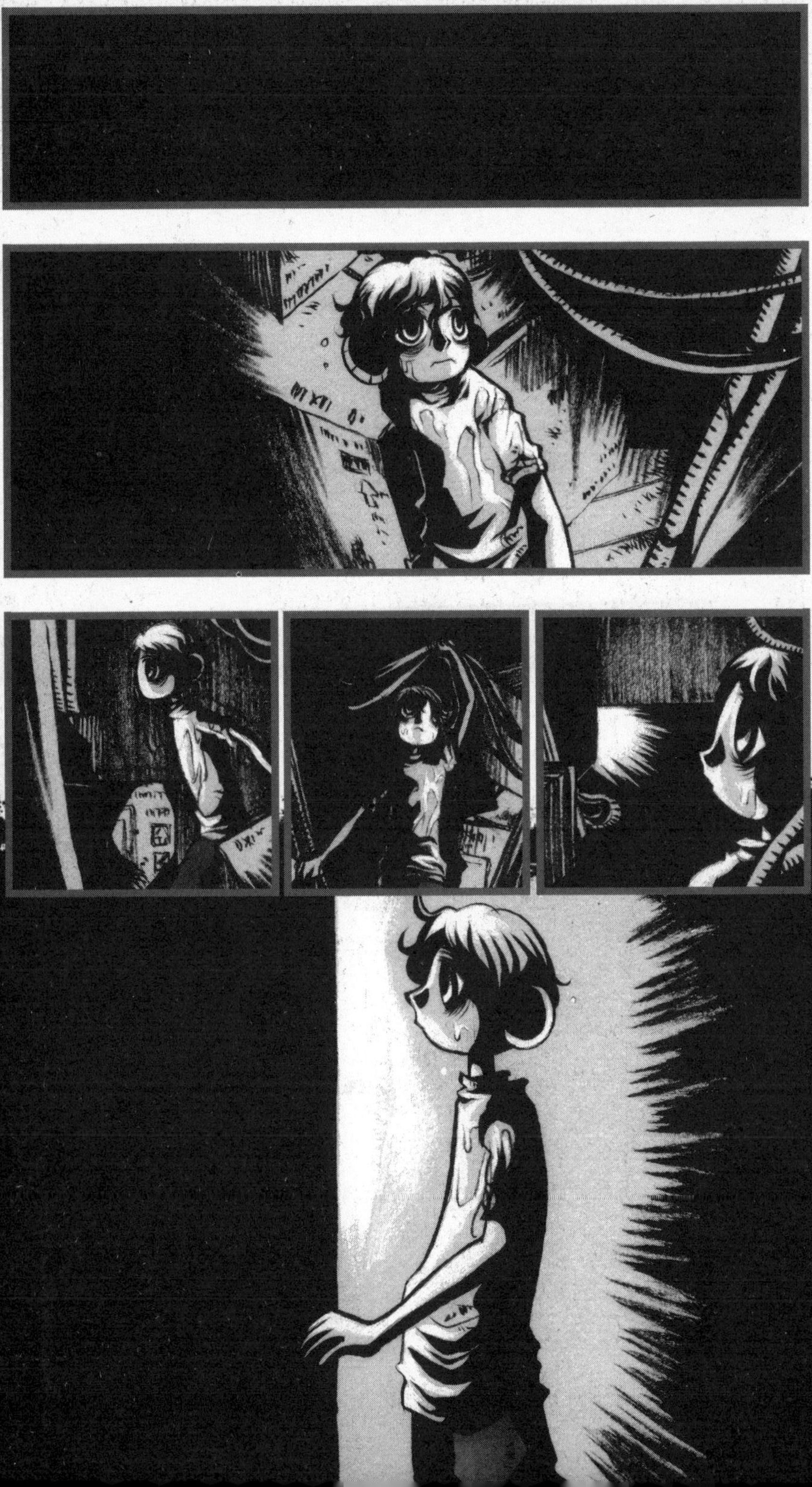

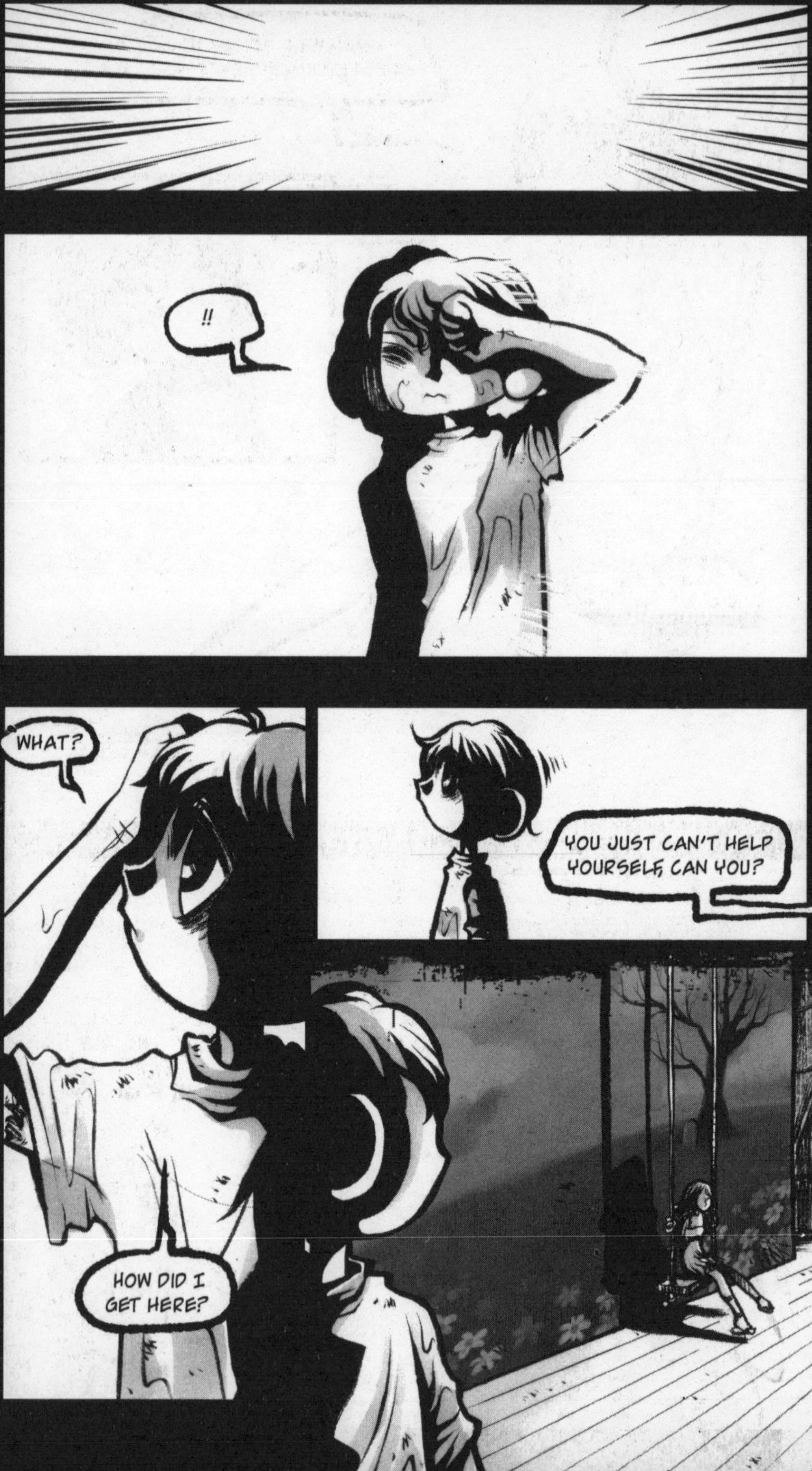

!!
WHAT?
YOU JUST CAN'T HELP YOURSELF, CAN YOU?
HOW DID I GET HERE?

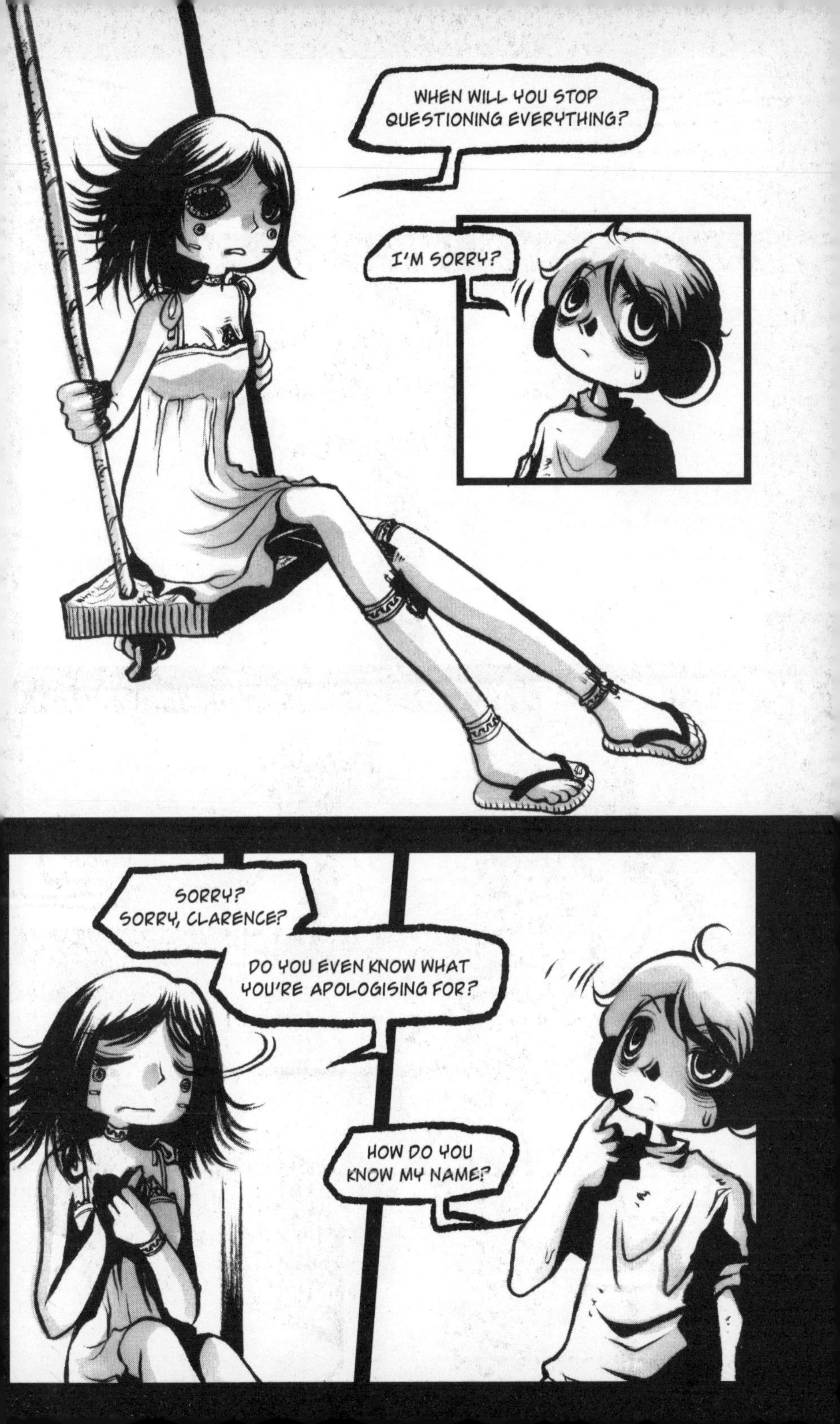
WHEN WILL YOU STOP QUESTIONING EVERYTHING?
I'M SORRY?
SORRY? SORRY, CLARENCE?
DO YOU EVEN KNOW WHAT YOU'RE APOLOGISING FOR?
HOW DO YOU KNOW MY NAME?

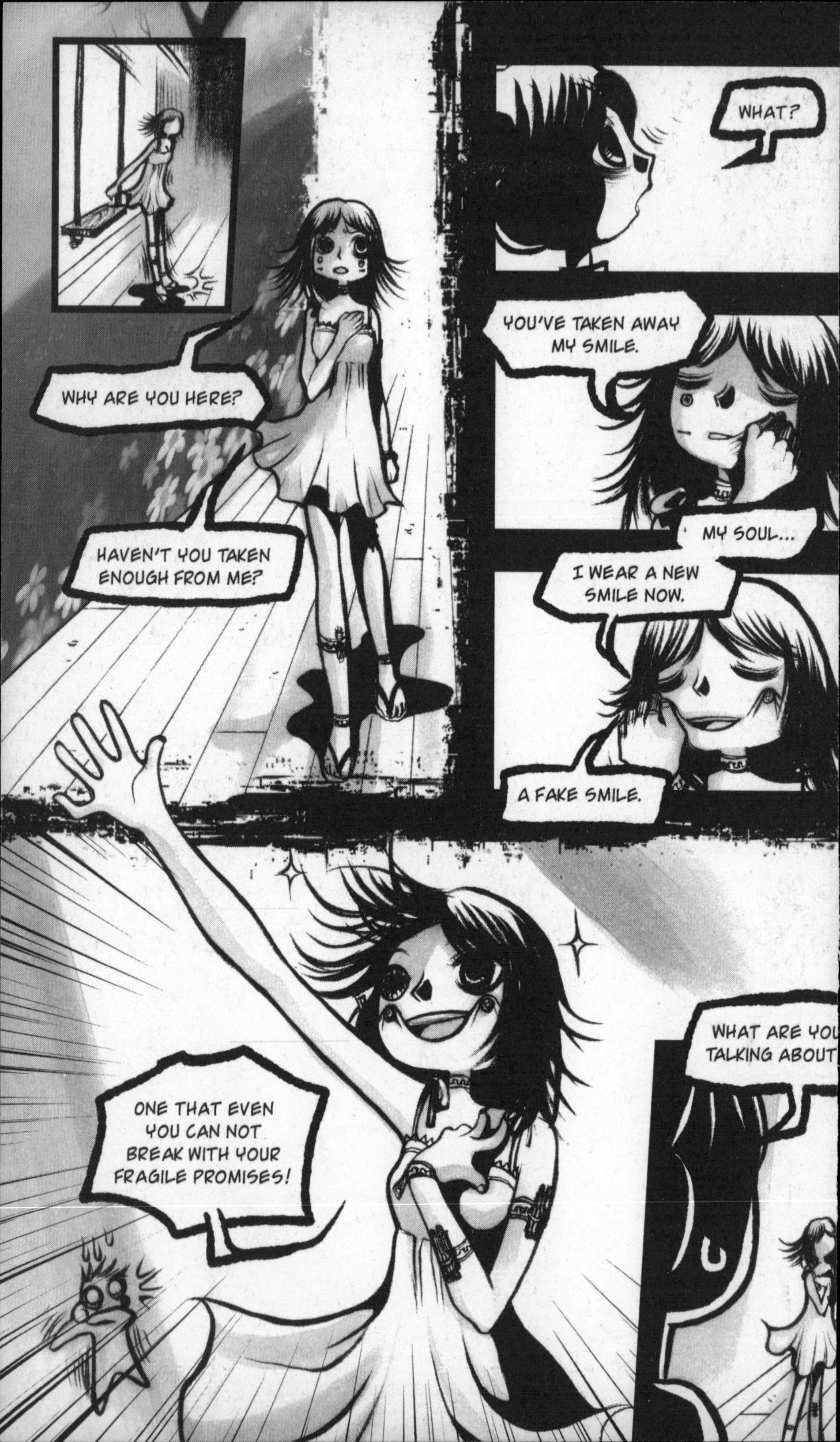
WHY ARE YOU HERE?
HAVEN'T YOU TAKEN ENOUGH FROM ME?
WHAT?
YOU'VE TAKEN AWAY MY SMILE.
MY SOUL...
I WEAR A NEW SMILE NOW.
A FAKE SMILE.
WHAT ARE YOU TALKING ABOUT
ONE THAT EVEN YOU CAN NOT BREAK WITH YOUR FRAGILE PROMISES!

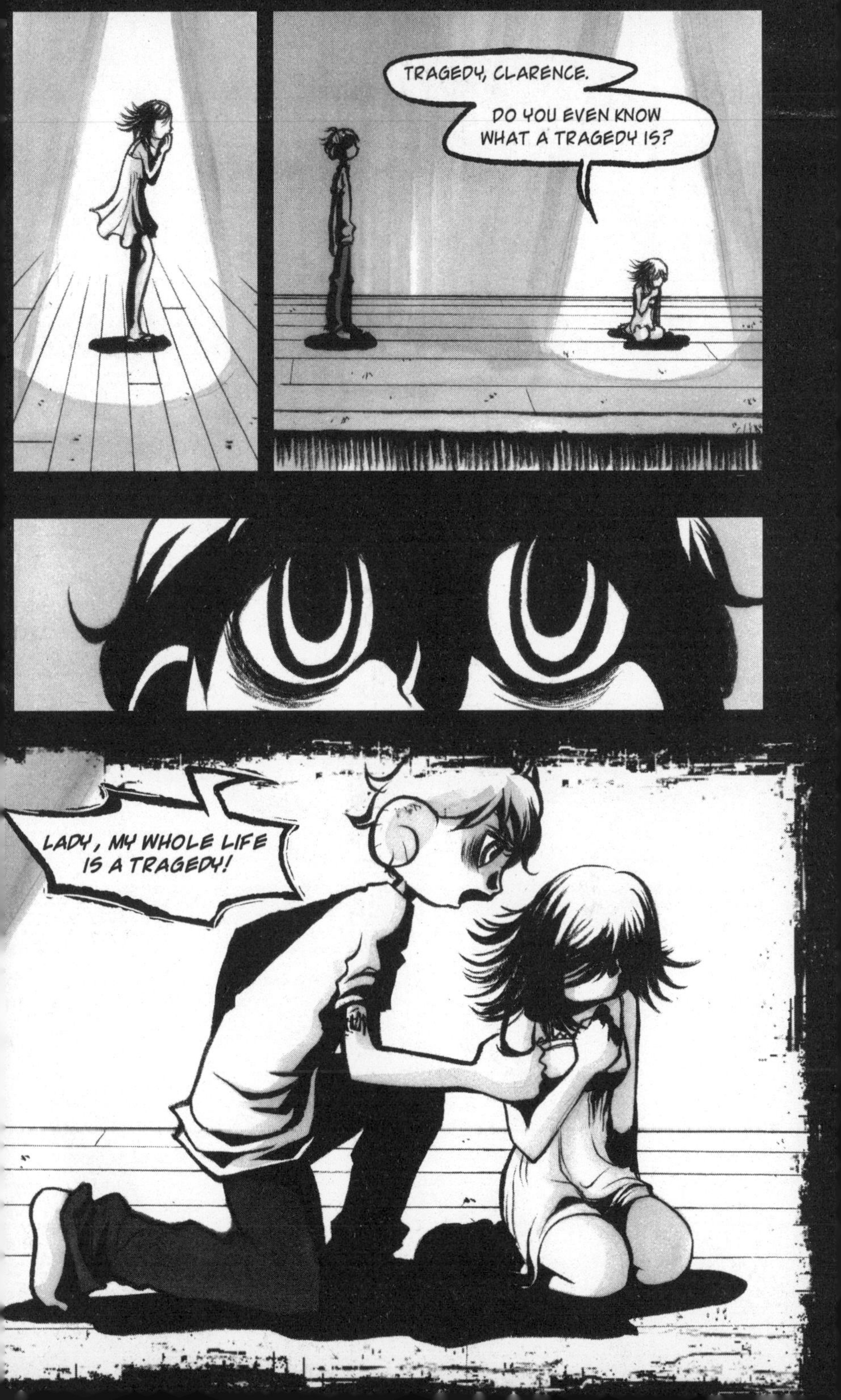
TRAGEDY, CLARENCE.
DO YOU EVEN KNOW WHAT A TRAGEDY IS?
LADY, MY WHOLE LIFE IS A TRAGEDY!

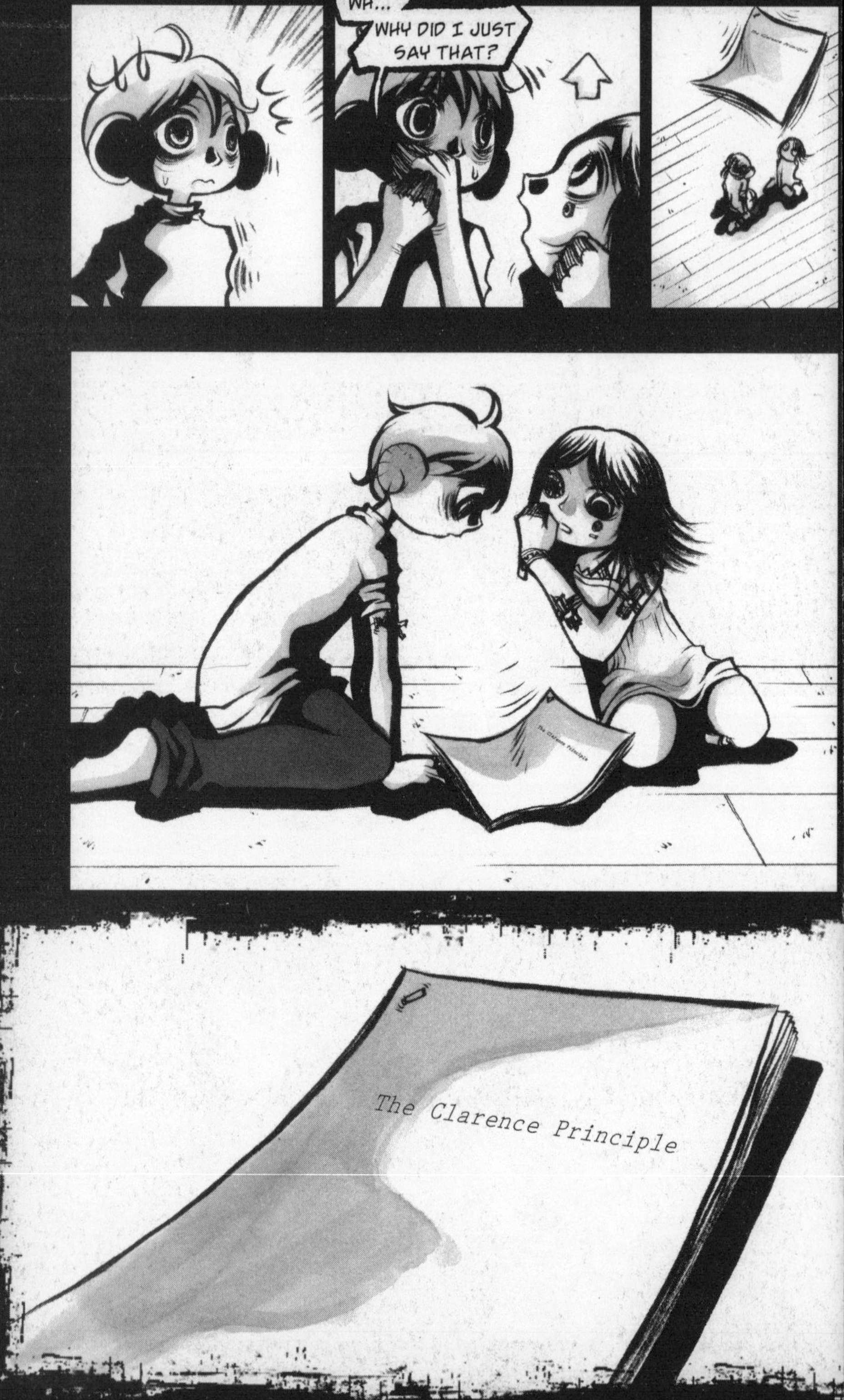
WH...
WHY DID I JUST SAY THAT?
The Clarence Principle

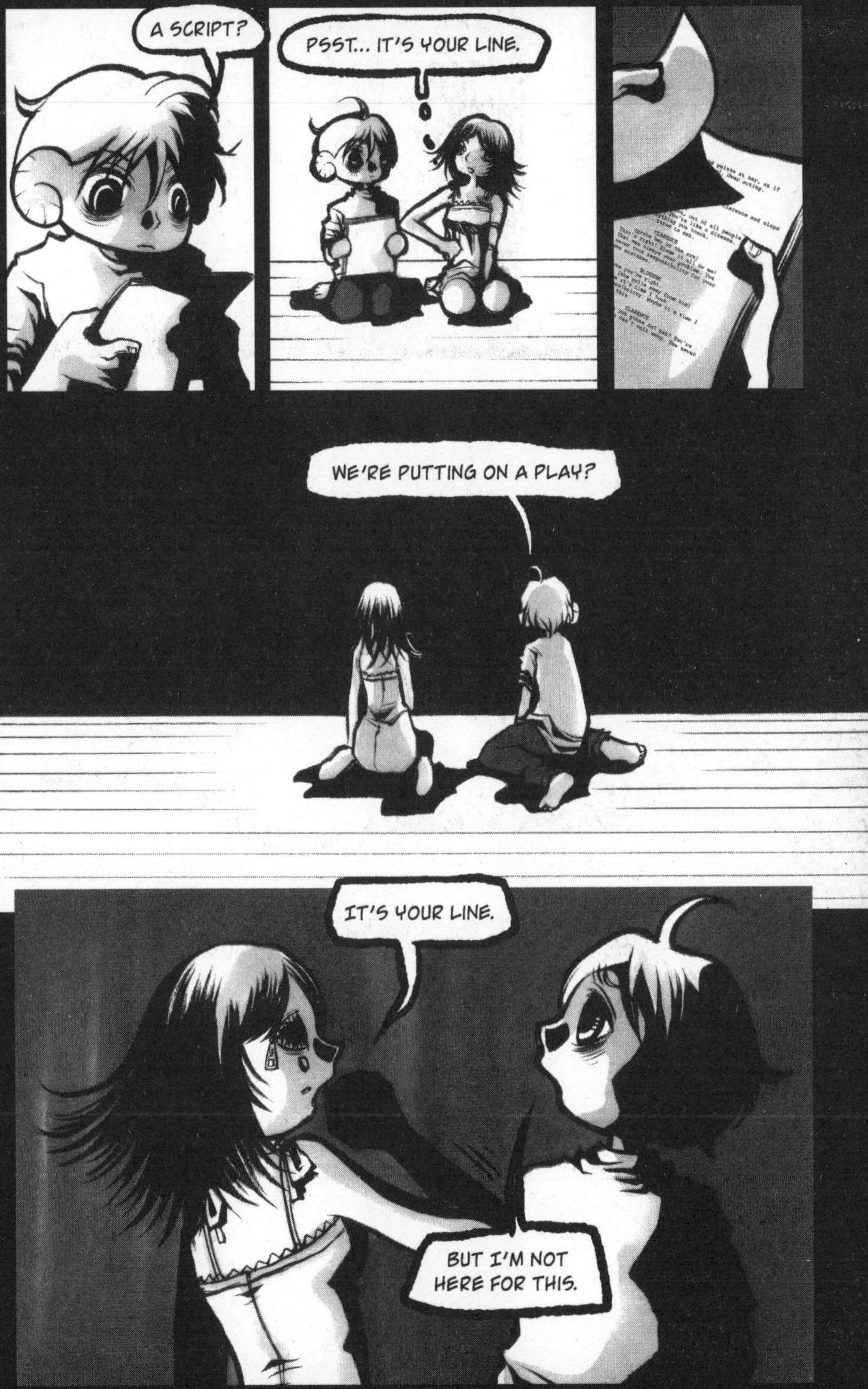
A SCRIPT?
PSST... IT'S YOUR LINE.
WE'RE PUTTING ON A PLAY?
IT'S YOUR LINE.
BUT I'M NOT HERE FOR THIS.

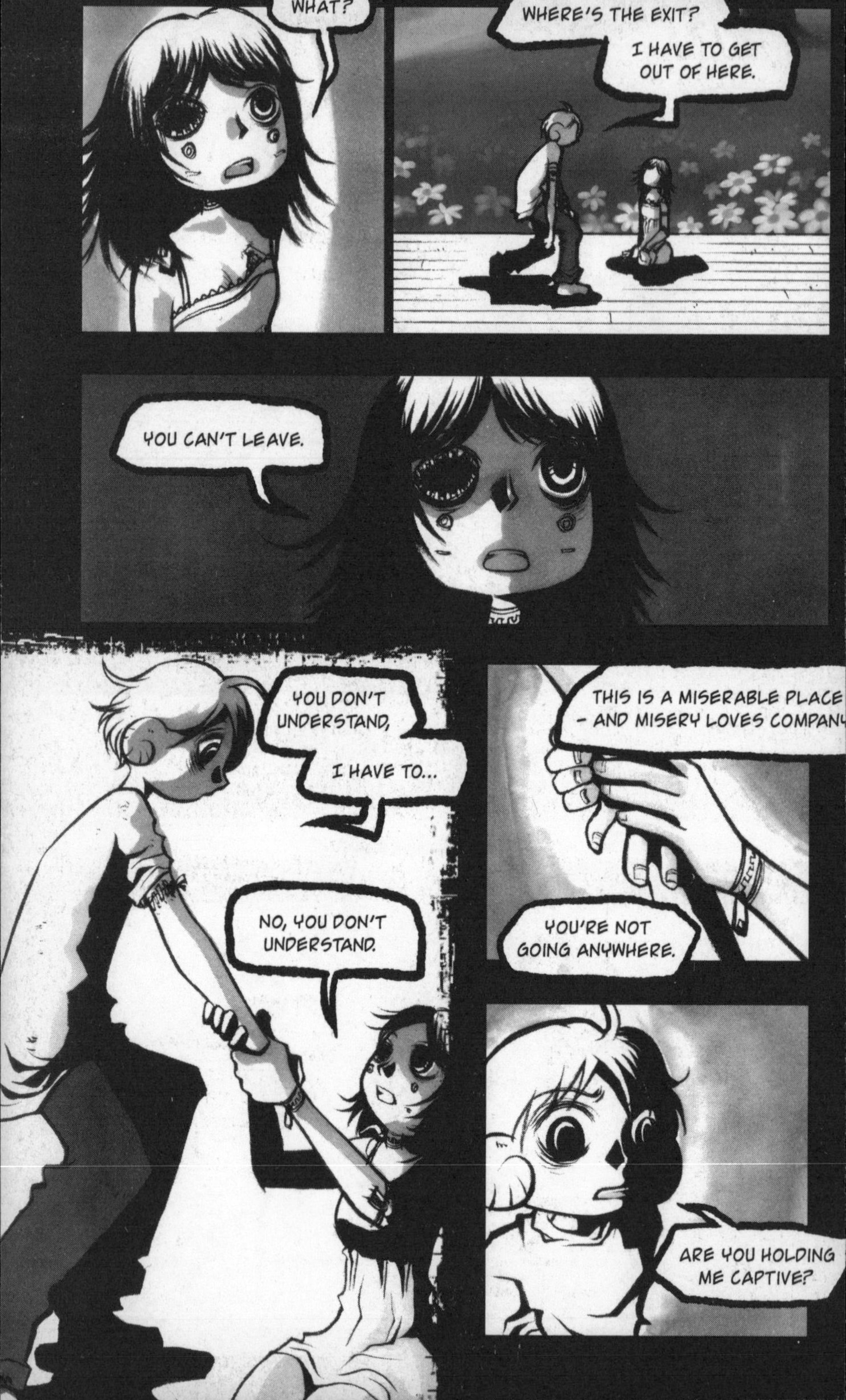
WHAT?
WHERE'S THE EXIT?
I HAVE TO GET OUT OF HERE.
YOU CAN'T LEAVE.
YOU DON'T UNDERSTAND,
I HAVE TO...
NO, YOU DON'T UNDERSTAND.
THIS IS A MISERABLE PLACE - AND MISERY LOVES COMPANY
YOU'RE NOT GOING ANYWHERE.
ARE YOU HOLDING ME CAPTIVE?

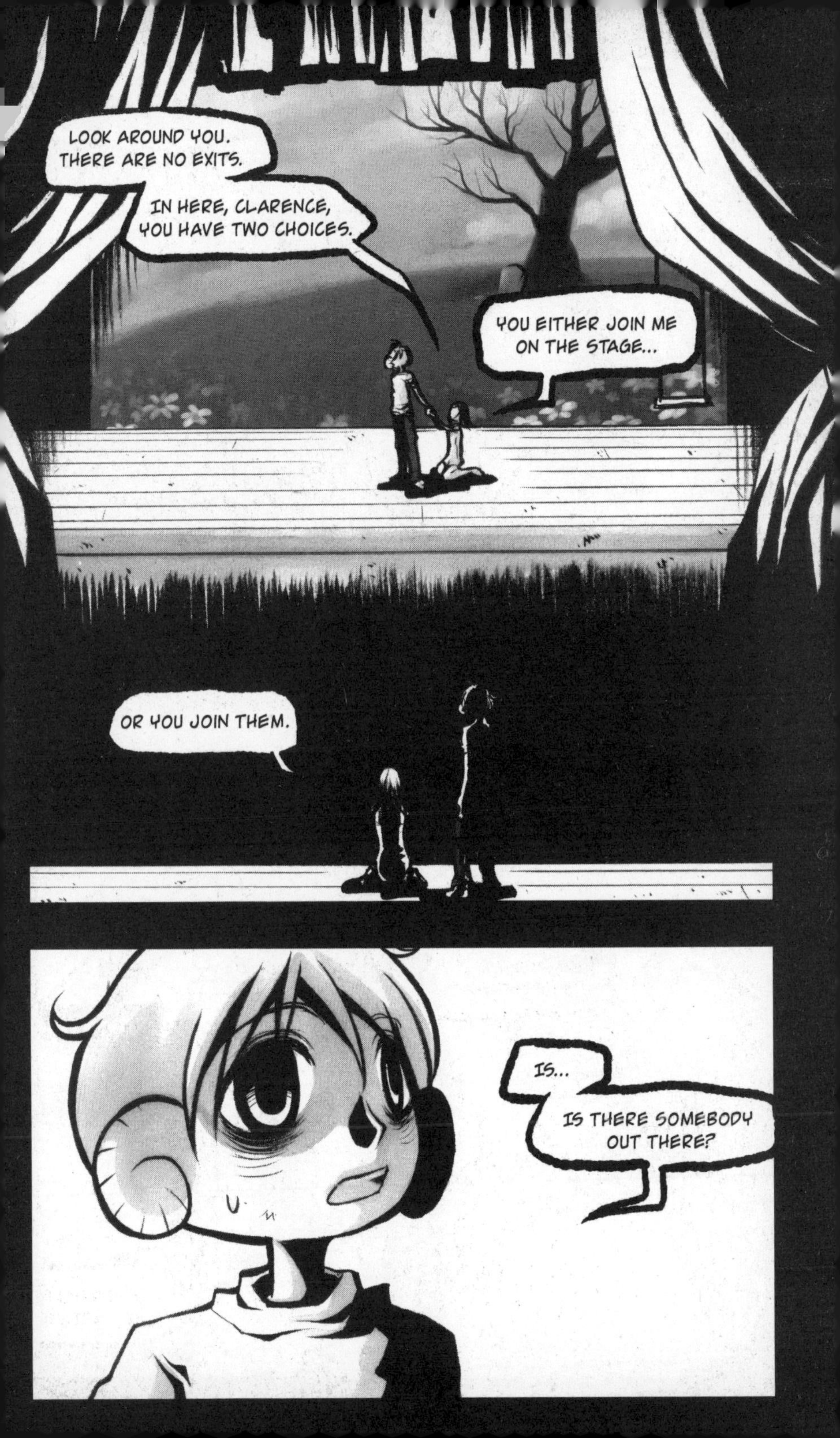
LOOK AROUND YOU. THERE ARE NO EXITS.
IN HERE, CLARENCE, YOU HAVE TWO CHOICES.
YOU EITHER JOIN ME ON THE STAGE...
OR YOU JOIN THEM.
IS...
IS THERE SOMEBODY OUT THERE?

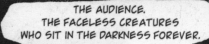

THE AUDIENCE.
THE FACELESS CREATURES
WHO SIT IN THE DARKNESS FOREVER.

UNHEARD, UNFEELING,
SPIRITLESS...

STILL.

IT'S YOUR CHOICE.

the clar

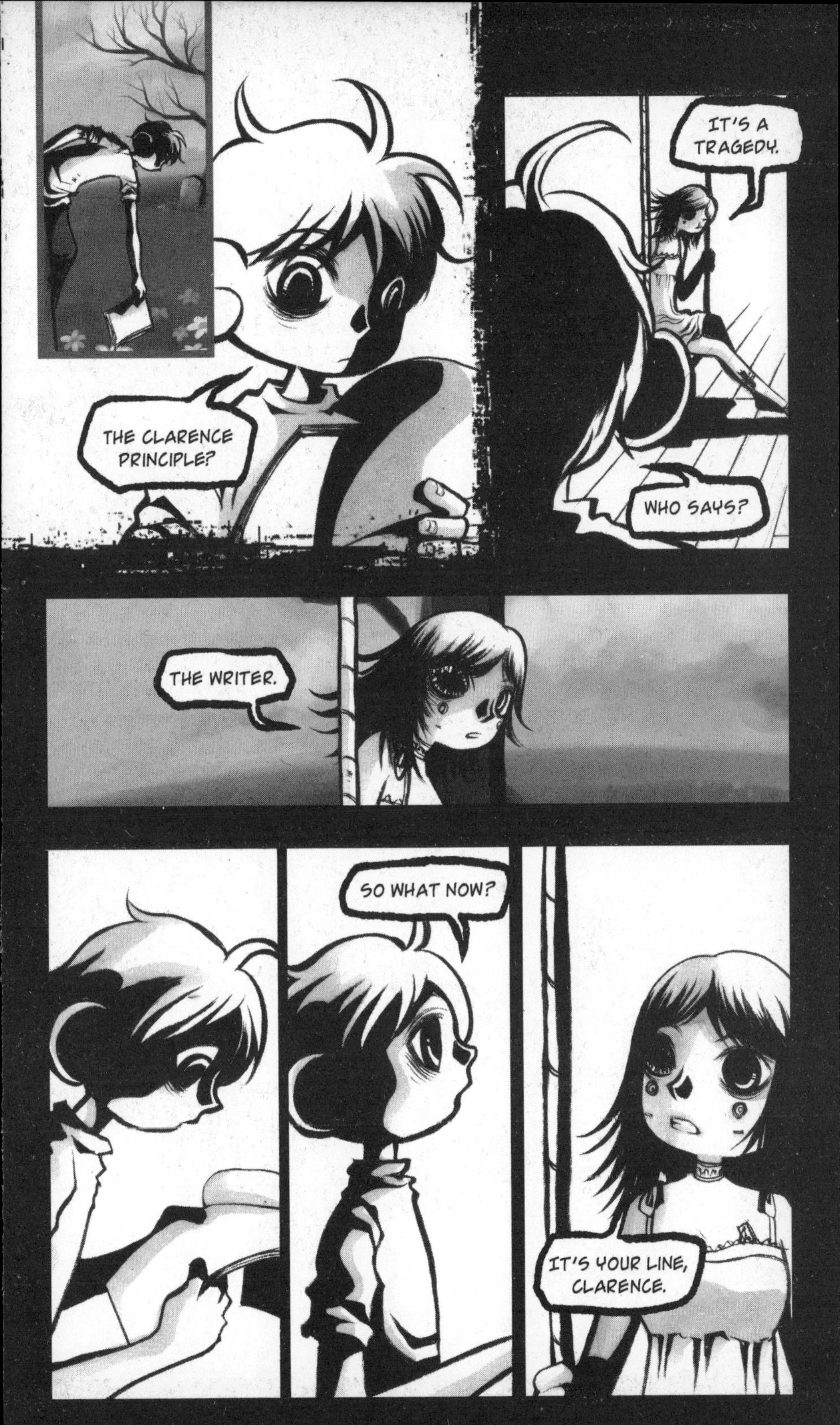
THE CLARENCE PRINCIPLE?
IT'S A TRAGEDY.
WHO SAYS?
THE WRITER.
SO WHAT NOW?
IT'S YOUR LINE, CLARENCE.

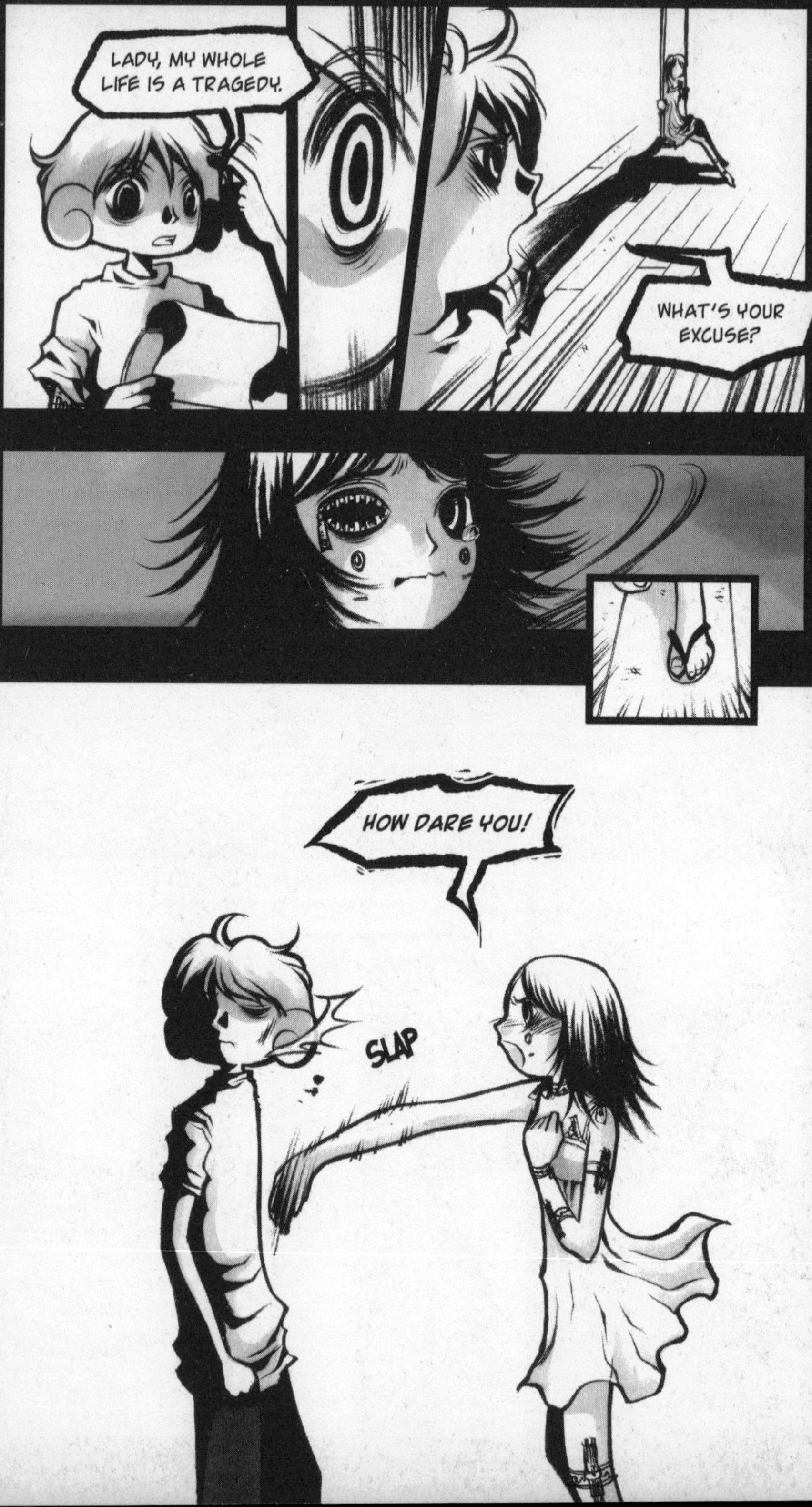
LADY, MY WHOLE LIFE IS A TRAGEDY.
WHAT'S YOUR EXCUSE?
HOW DARE YOU!
SLAP

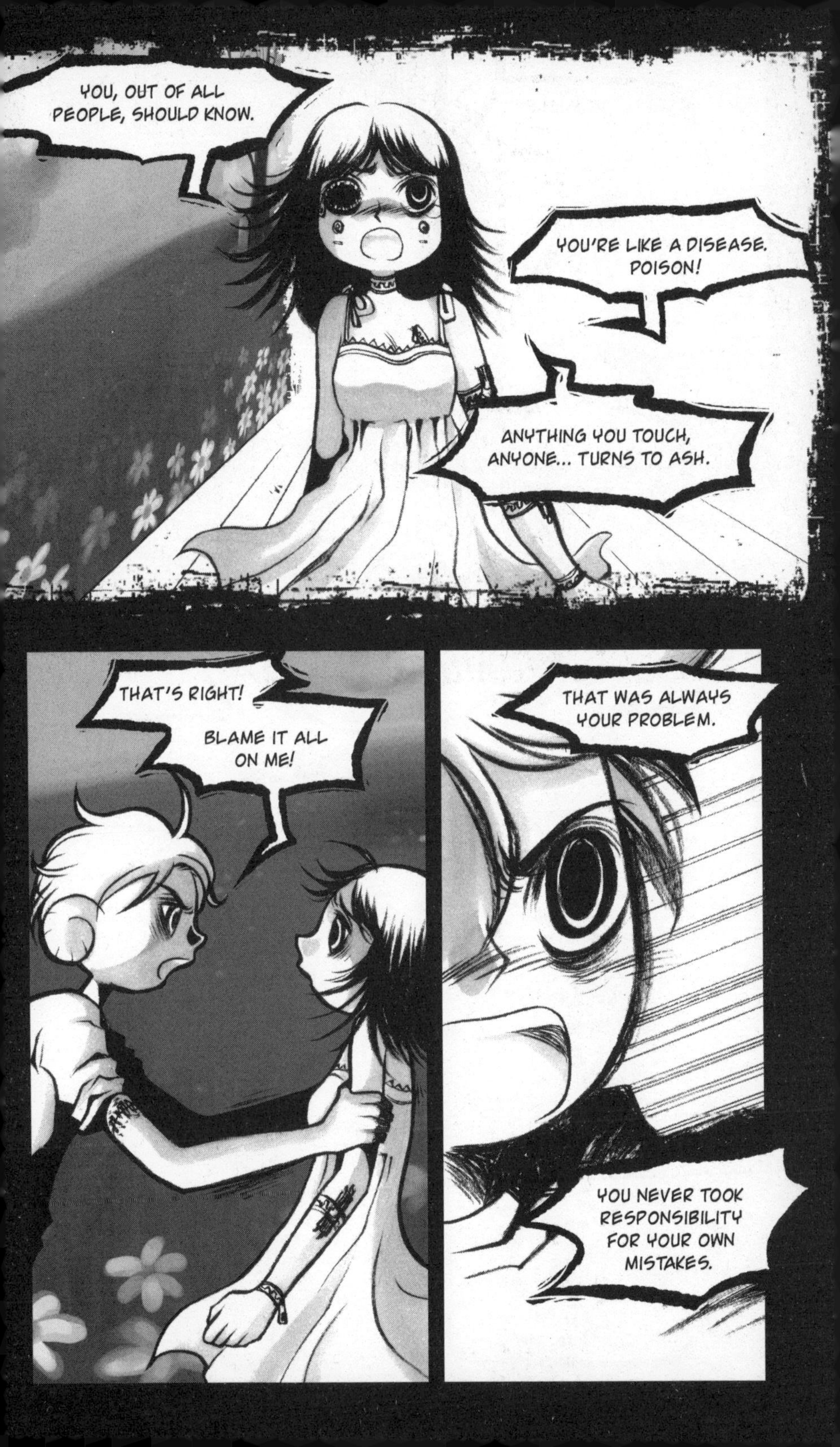
YOU, OUT OF ALL PEOPLE, SHOULD KNOW.
YOU'RE LIKE A DISEASE. POISON!
ANYTHING YOU TOUCH, ANYONE... TURNS TO ASH.
THAT'S RIGHT!
BLAME IT ALL ON ME!
THAT WAS ALWAYS YOUR PROBLEM.
YOU NEVER TOOK RESPONSIBILITY FOR YOUR OWN MISTAKES.

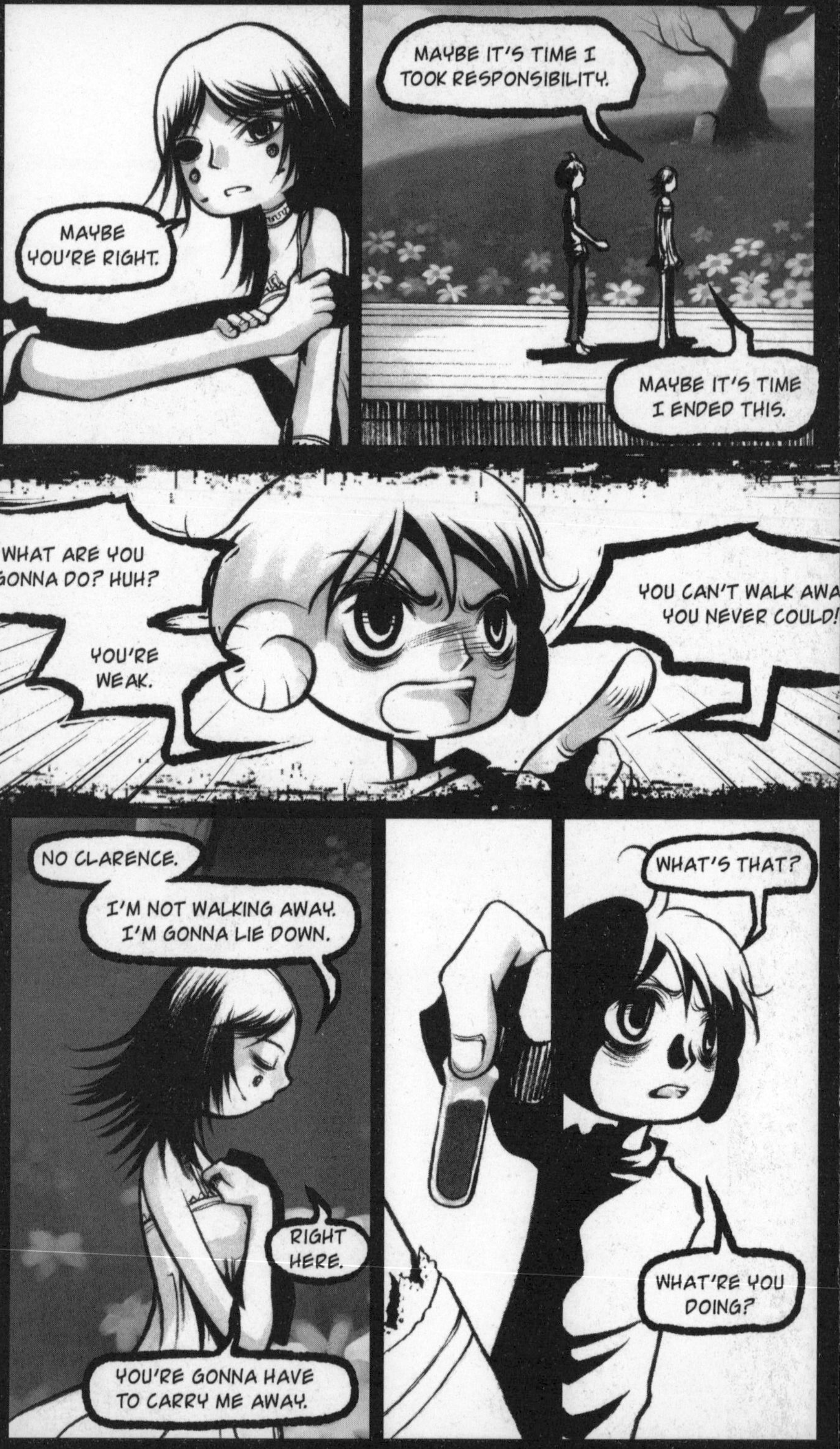
MAYBE YOU'RE RIGHT.
MAYBE IT'S TIME I TOOK RESPONSIBILITY.
MAYBE IT'S TIME I ENDED THIS.
WHAT ARE YOU GONNA DO? HUH?
YOU'RE WEAK.
YOU CAN'T WALK AWA
YOU NEVER COULD!
NO CLARENCE.
I'M NOT WALKING AWAY. I'M GONNA LIE DOWN.
RIGHT HERE.
YOU'RE GONNA HAVE TO CARRY ME AWAY.
WHAT'S THAT?
WHAT'RE YOU DOING?

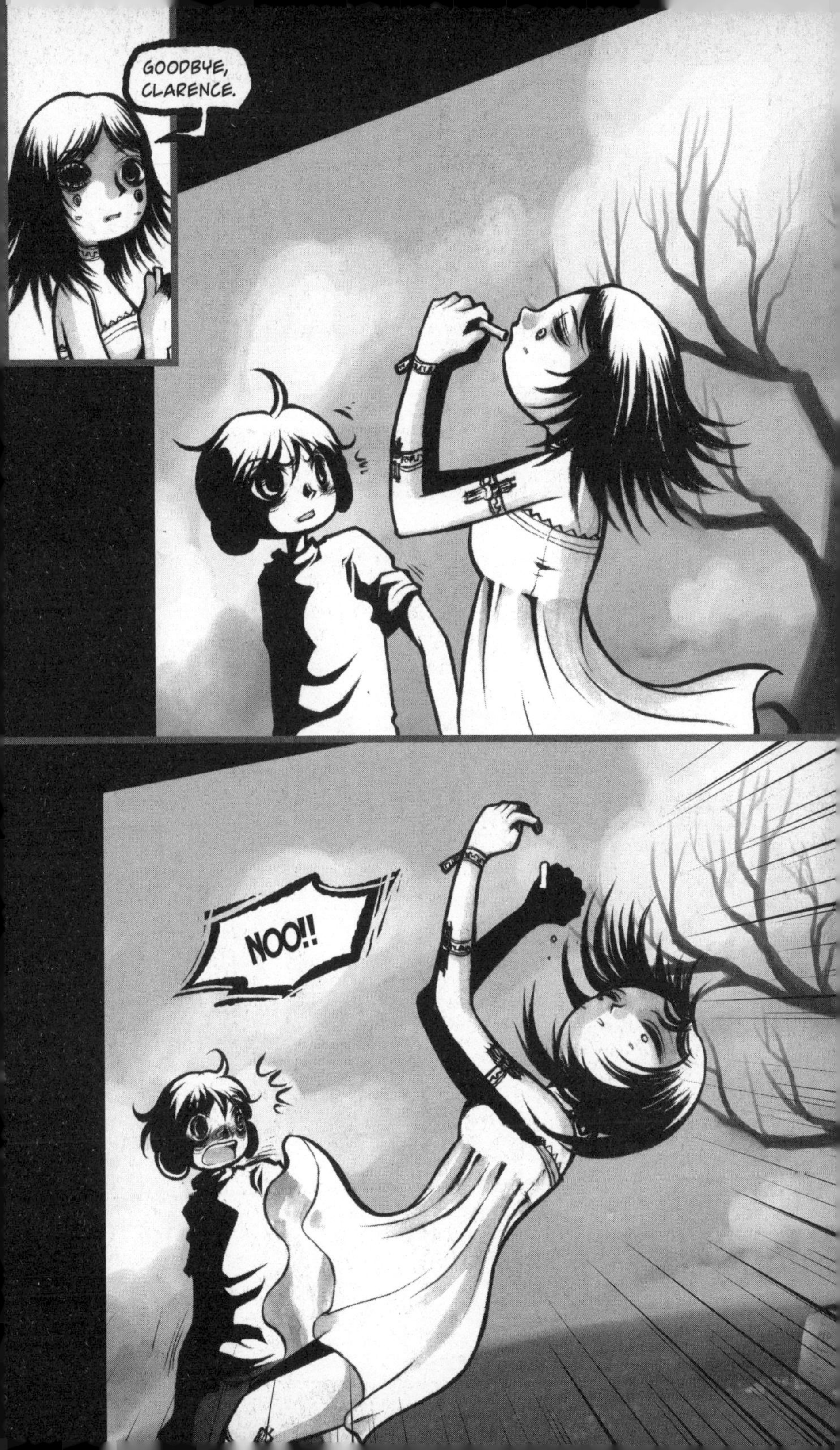
GOODBYE, CLARENCE.
NOO!!

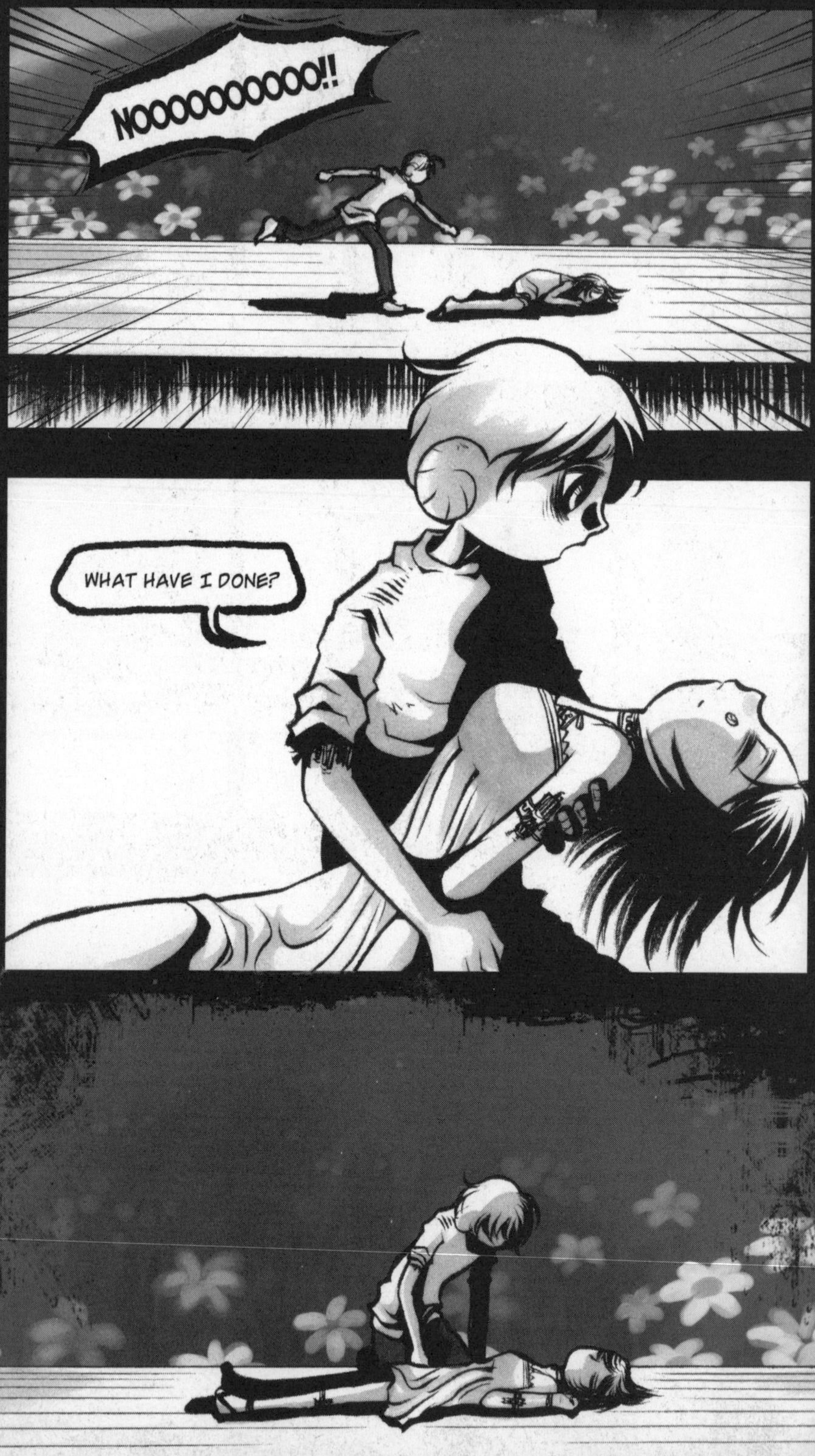
NOOOOOOOOOO!!
WHAT HAVE I DONE?

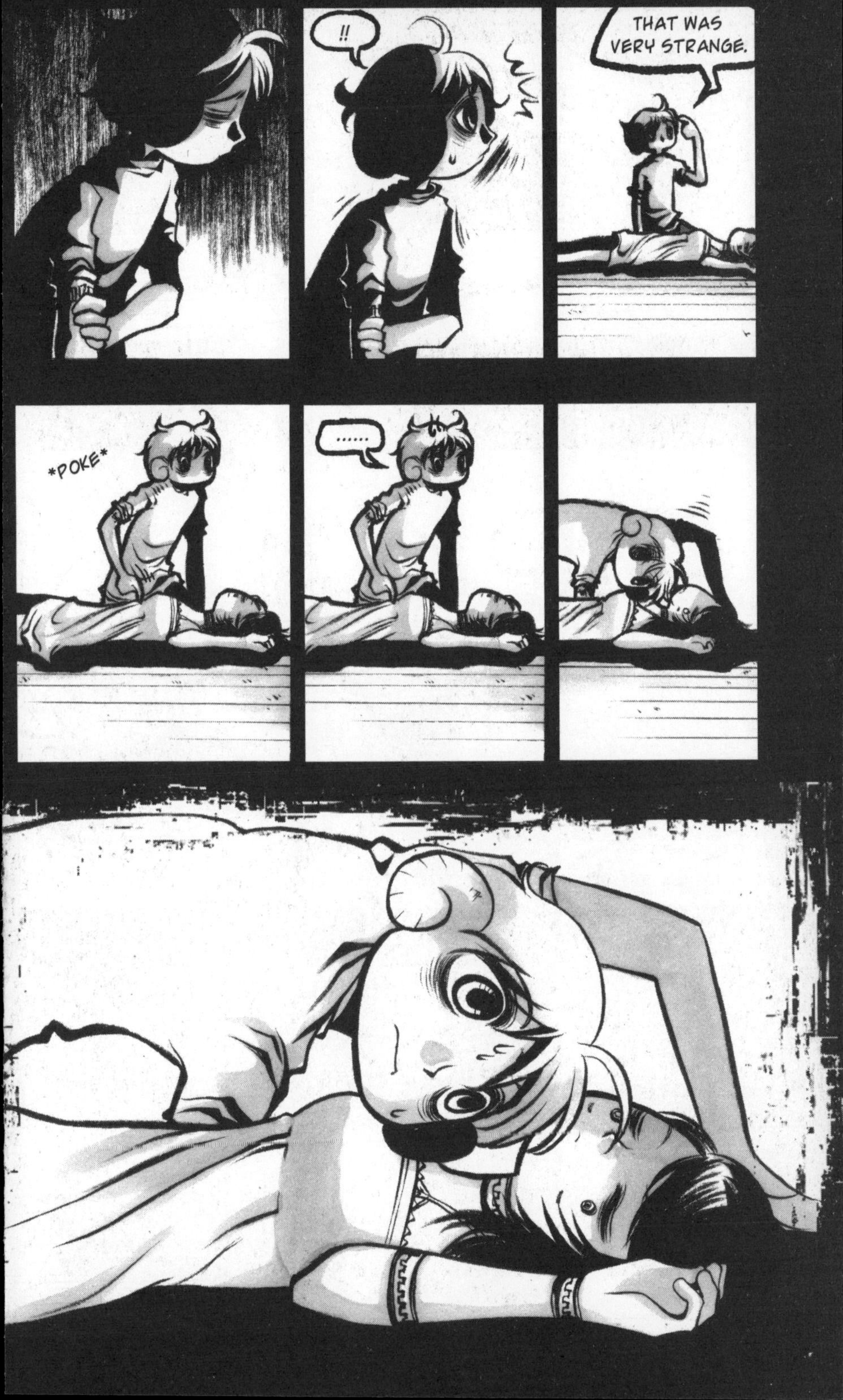
!!
THAT WAS VERY STRANGE.
POKE
....

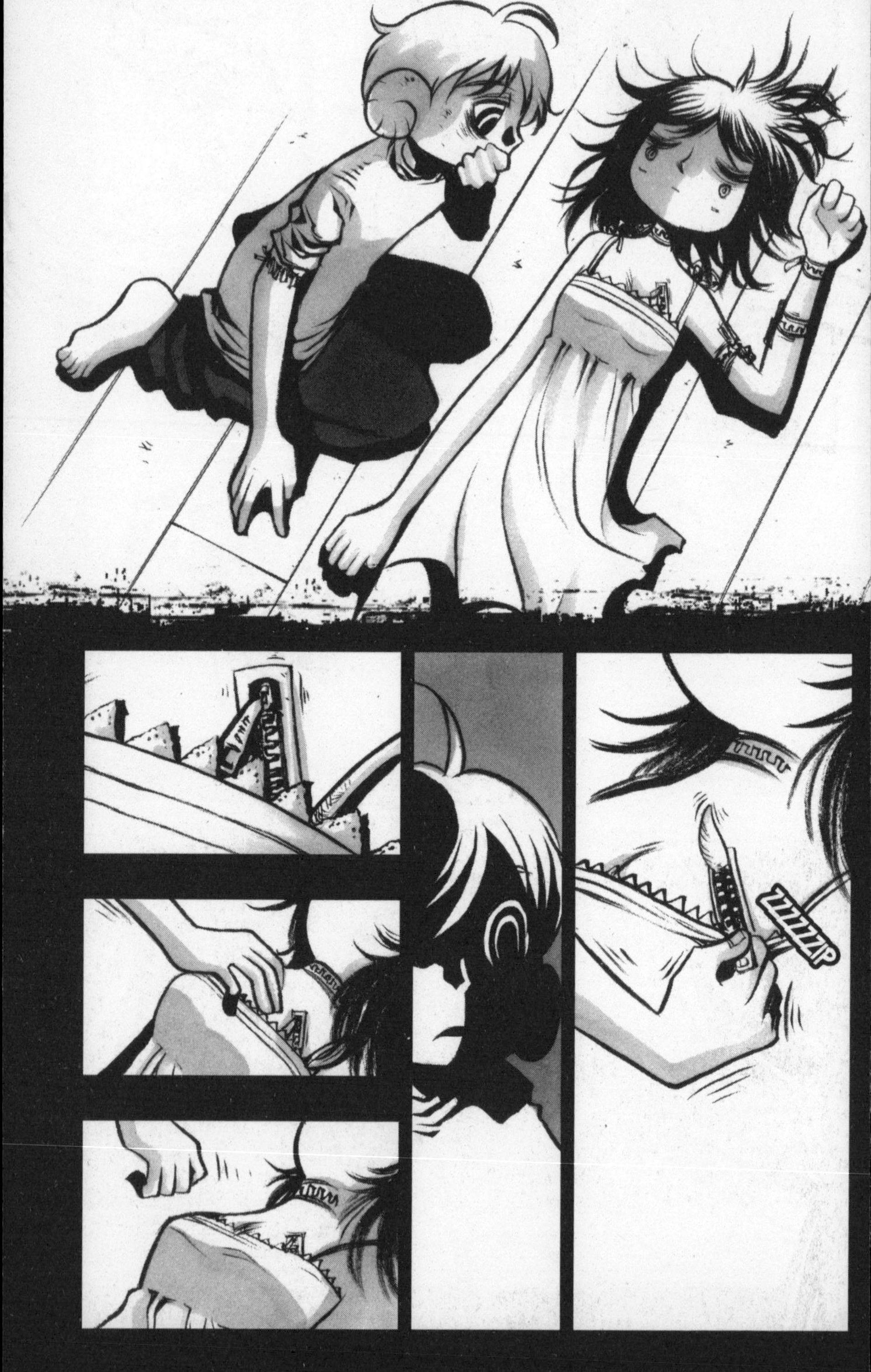

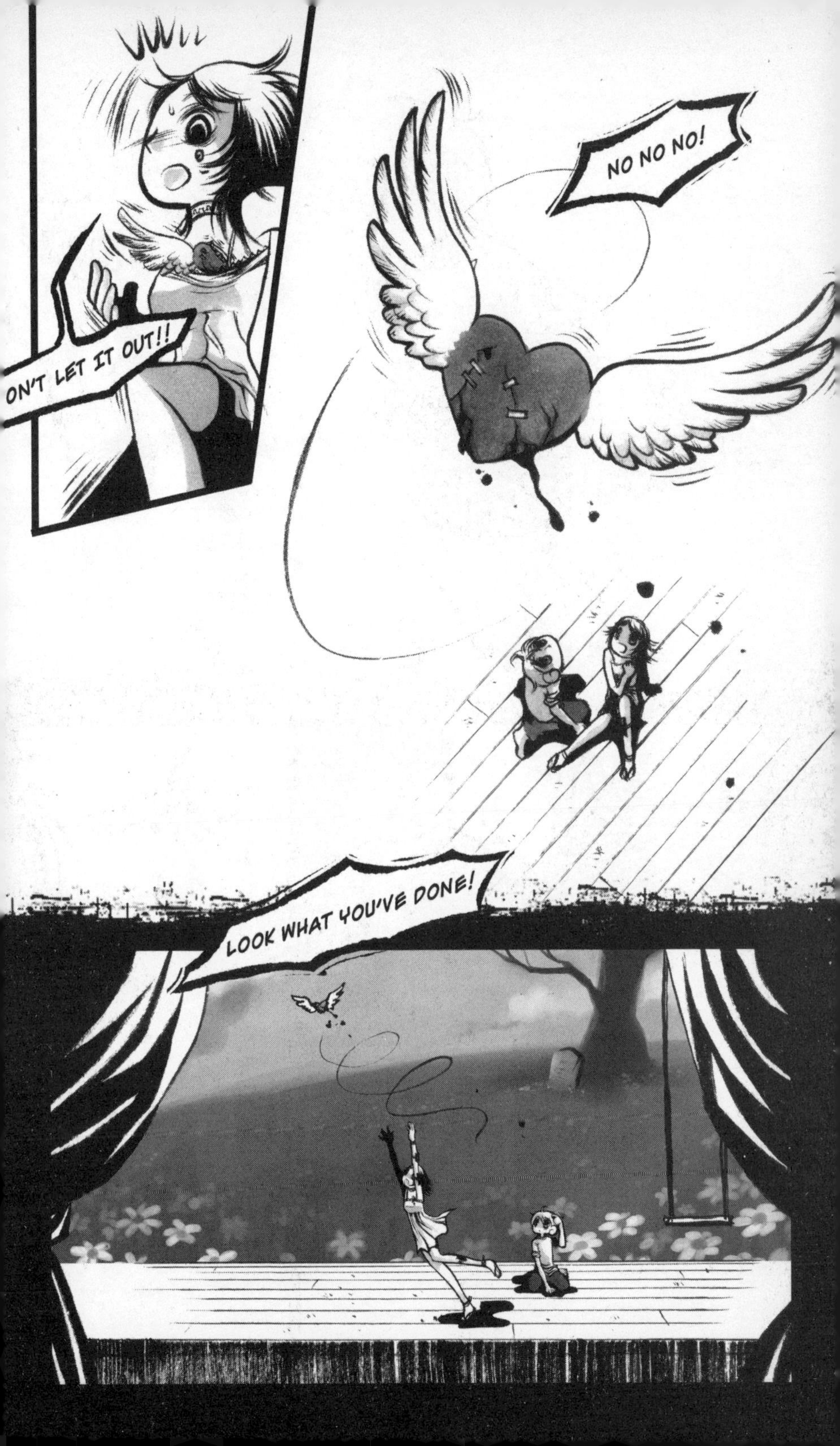
ON'T LET IT OUT!!
NO NO NO!
LOOK WHAT YOU'VE DONE!

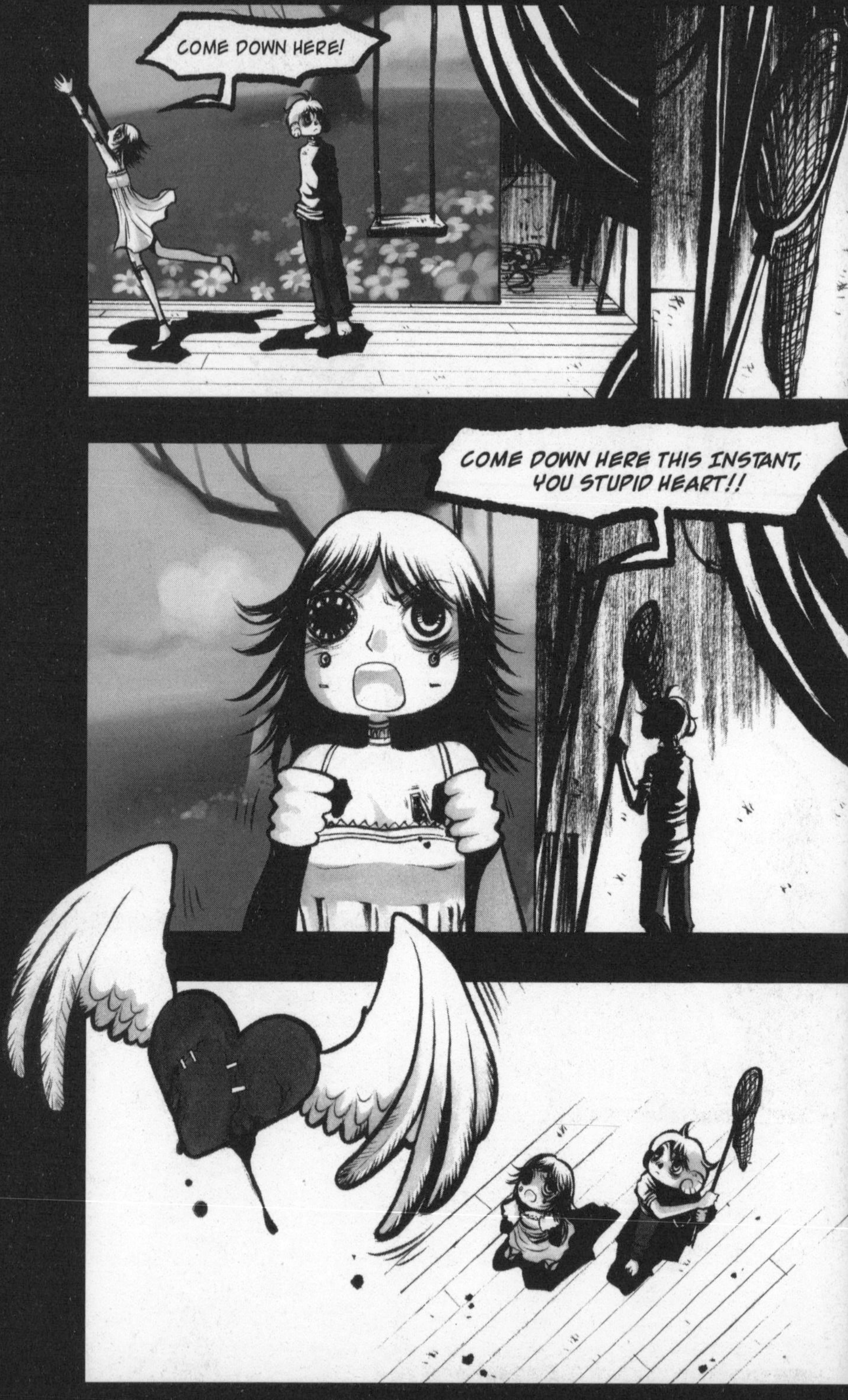
COME DOWN HERE!
COME DOWN HERE THIS INSTANT, YOU STUPID HEART!!

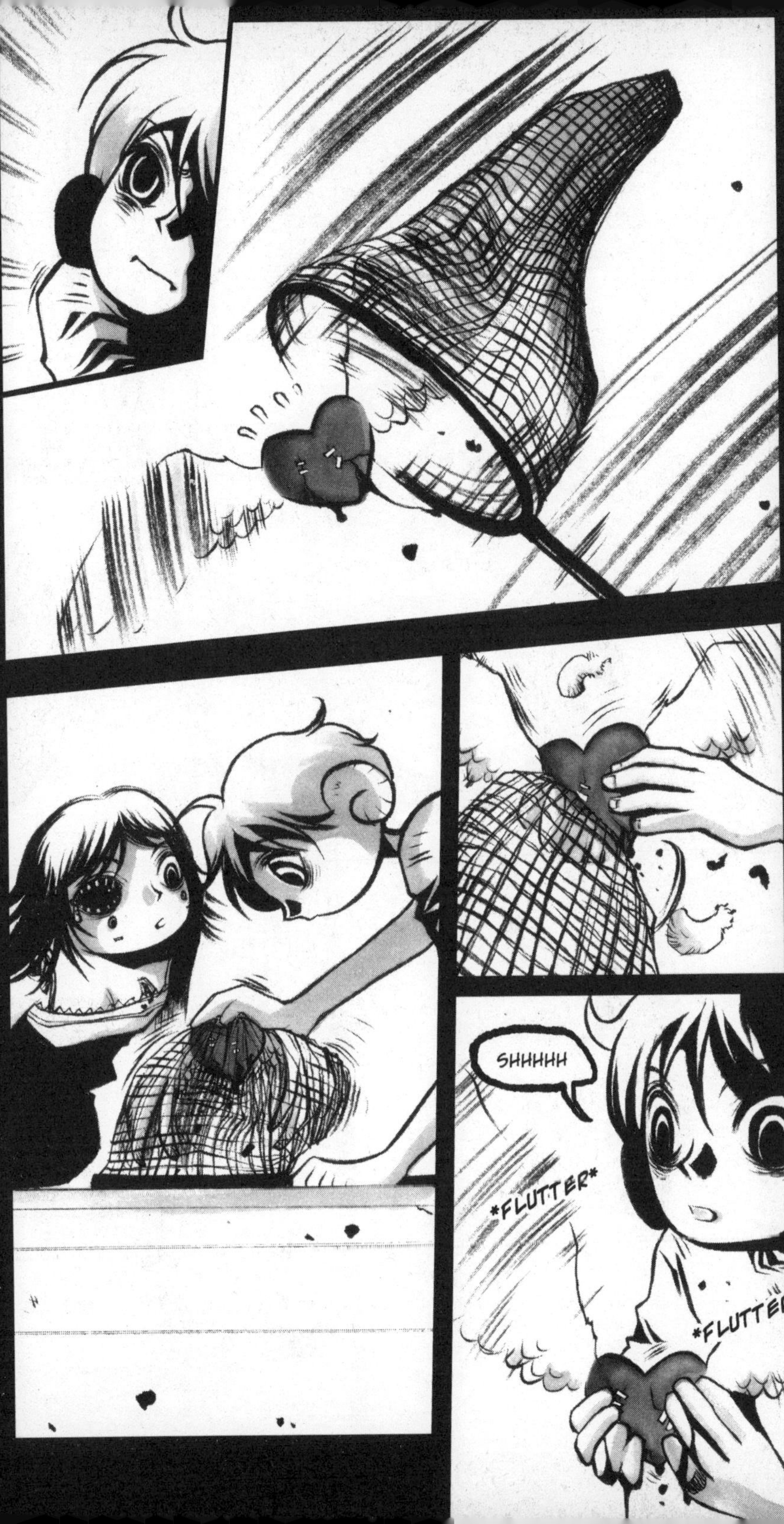
SHHHHH
FLUTTER
FLUTTER

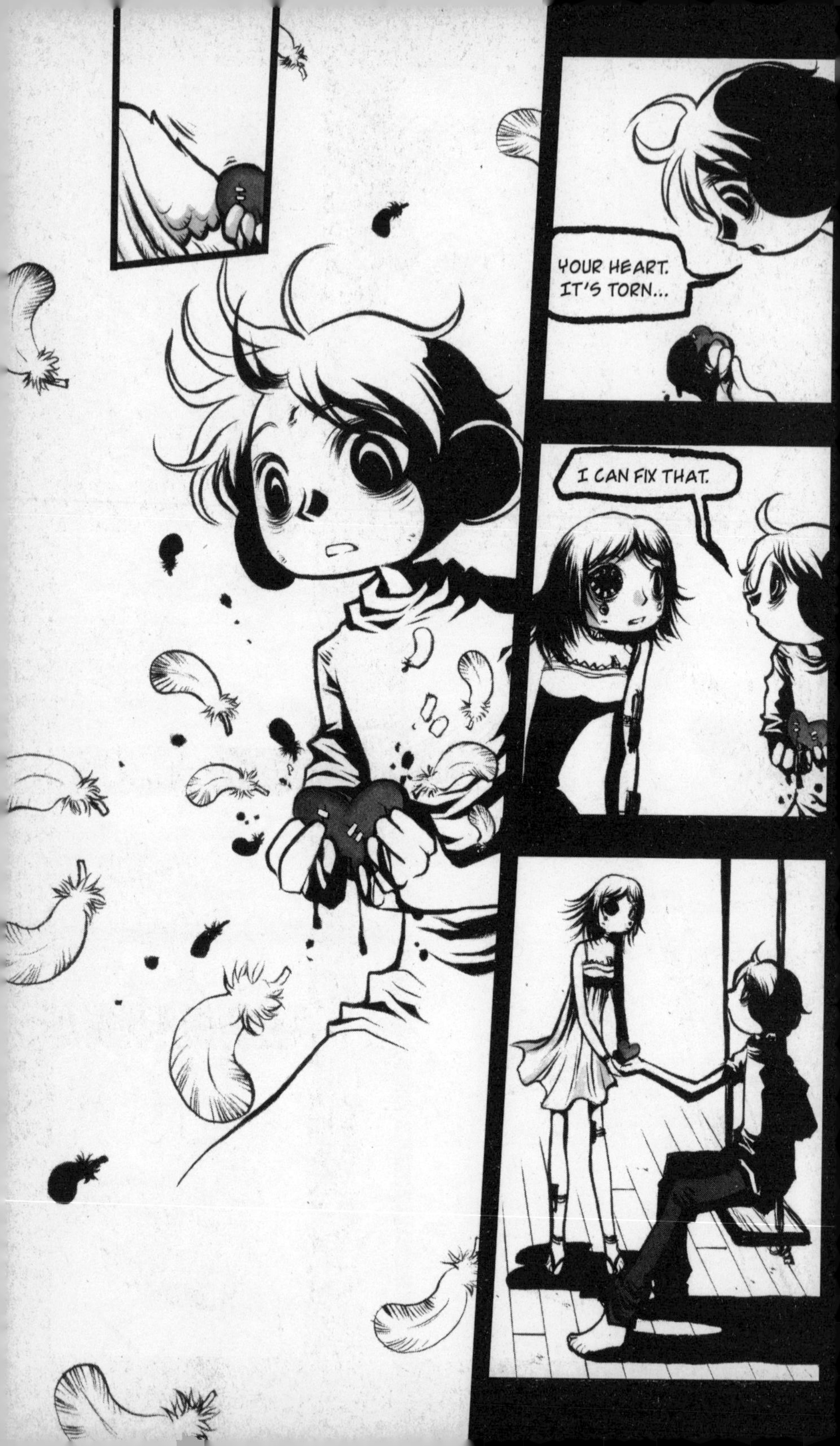
YOUR HEART.
IT'S TORN...
I CAN FIX THAT.

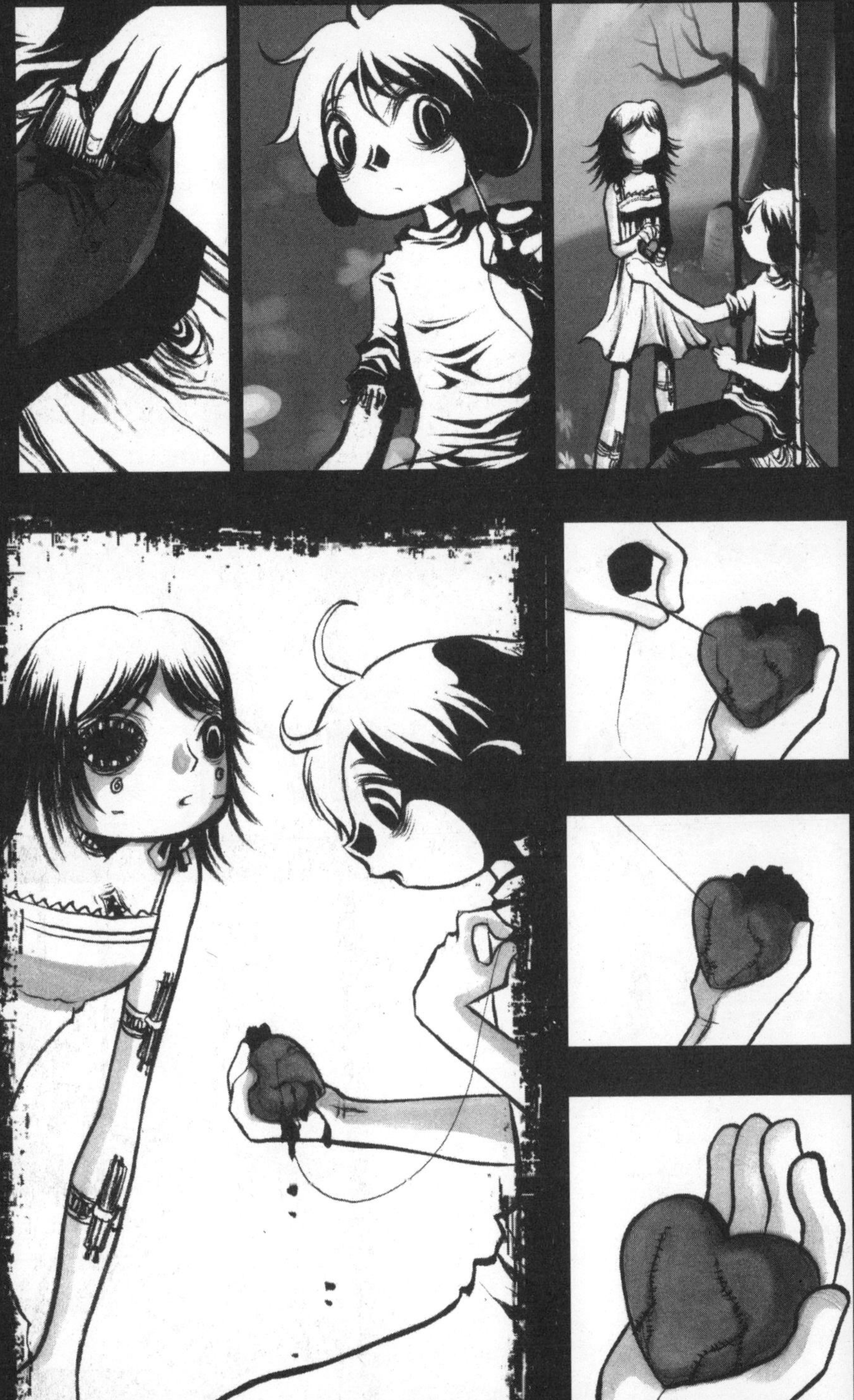

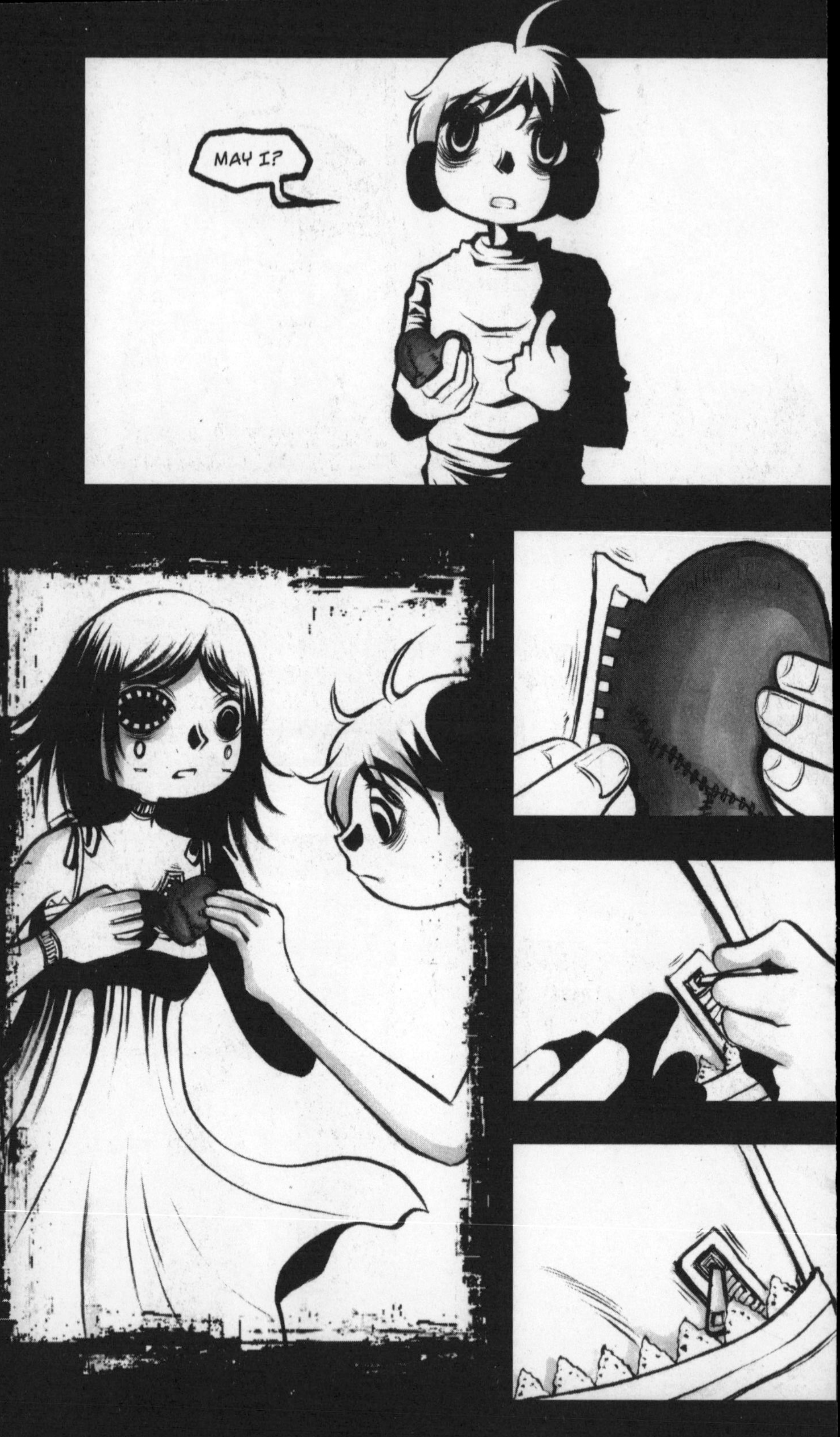
MAY I?

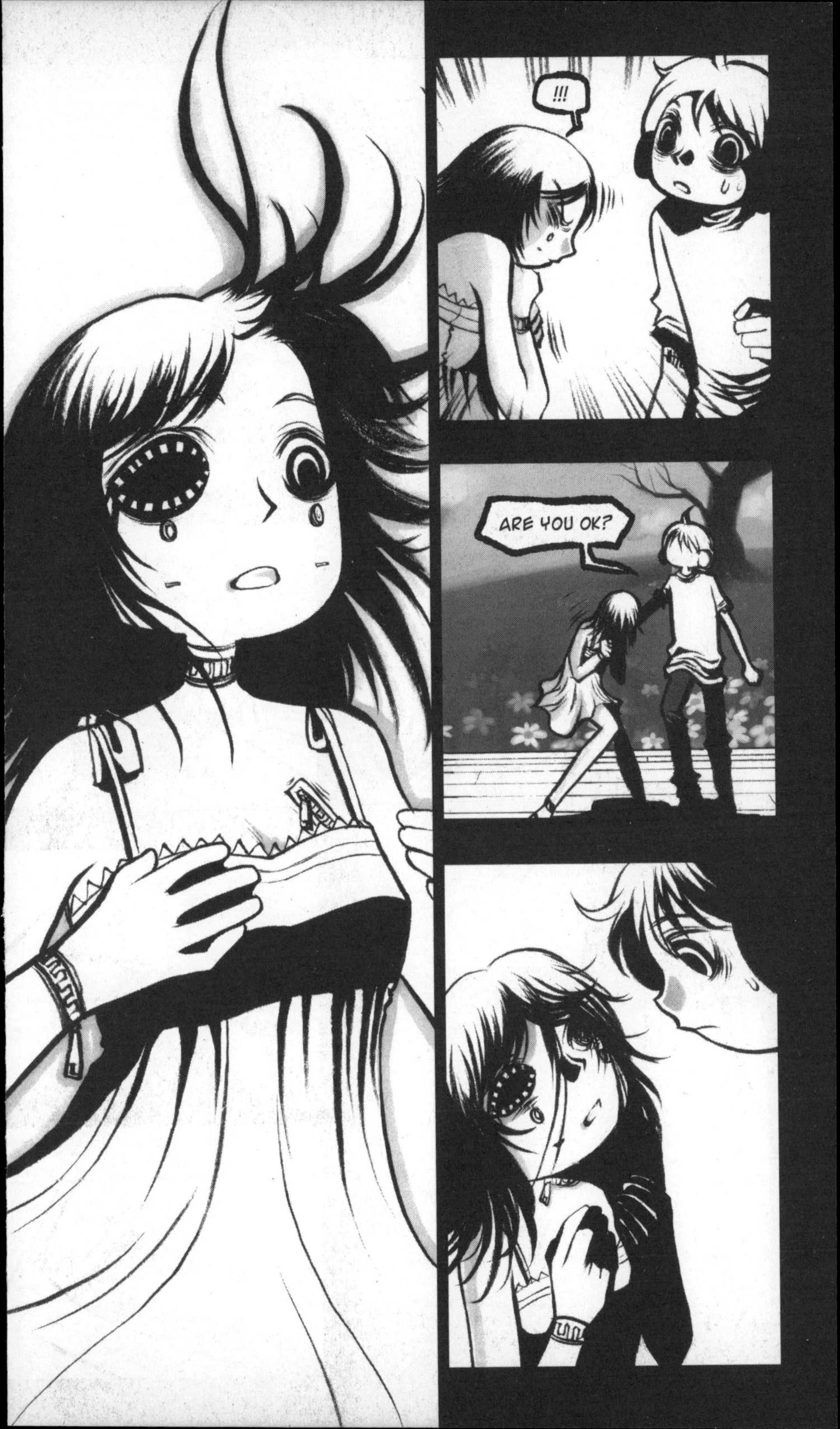
!!!
ARE YOU OK?

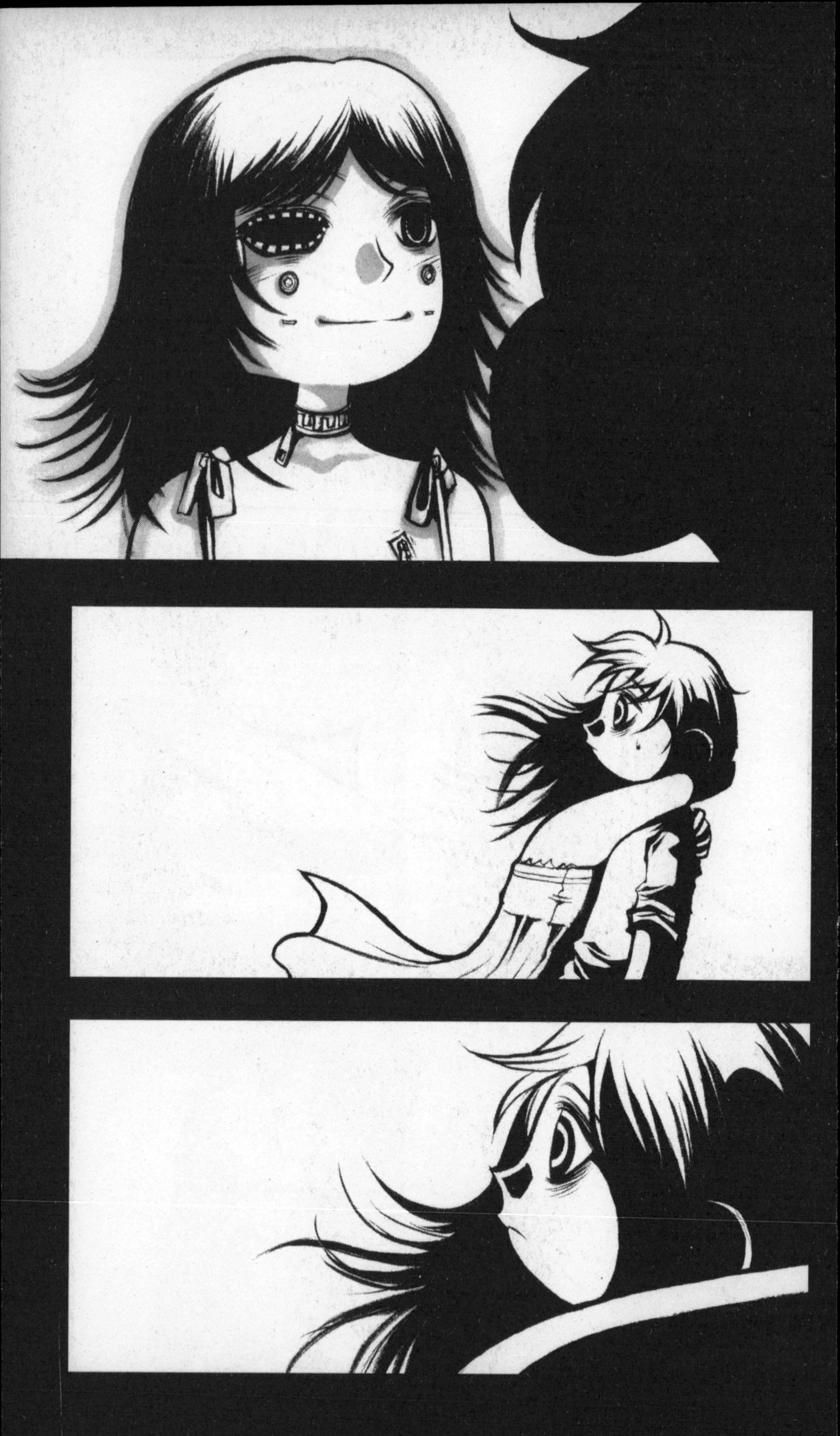

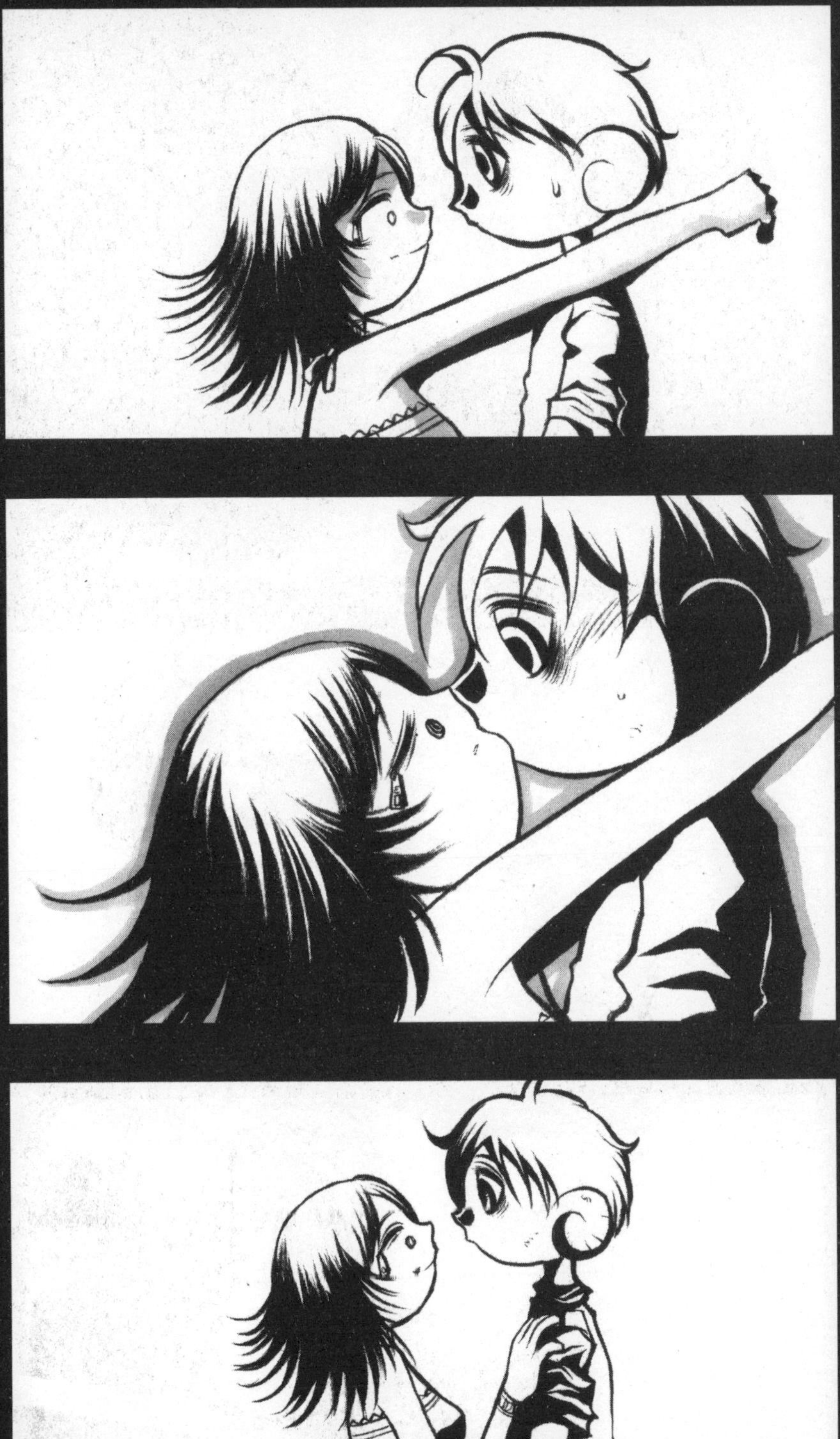

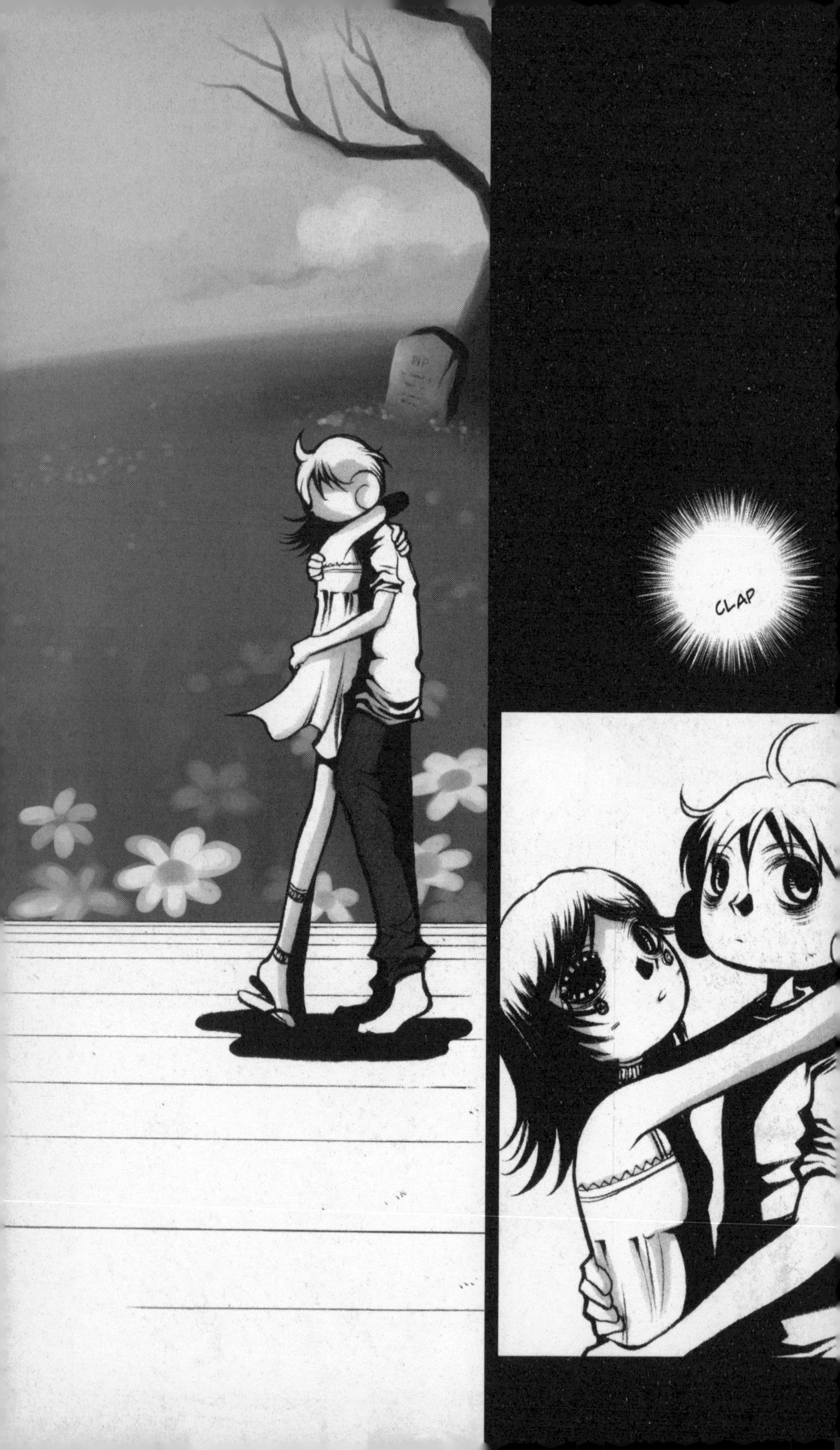
CLAP

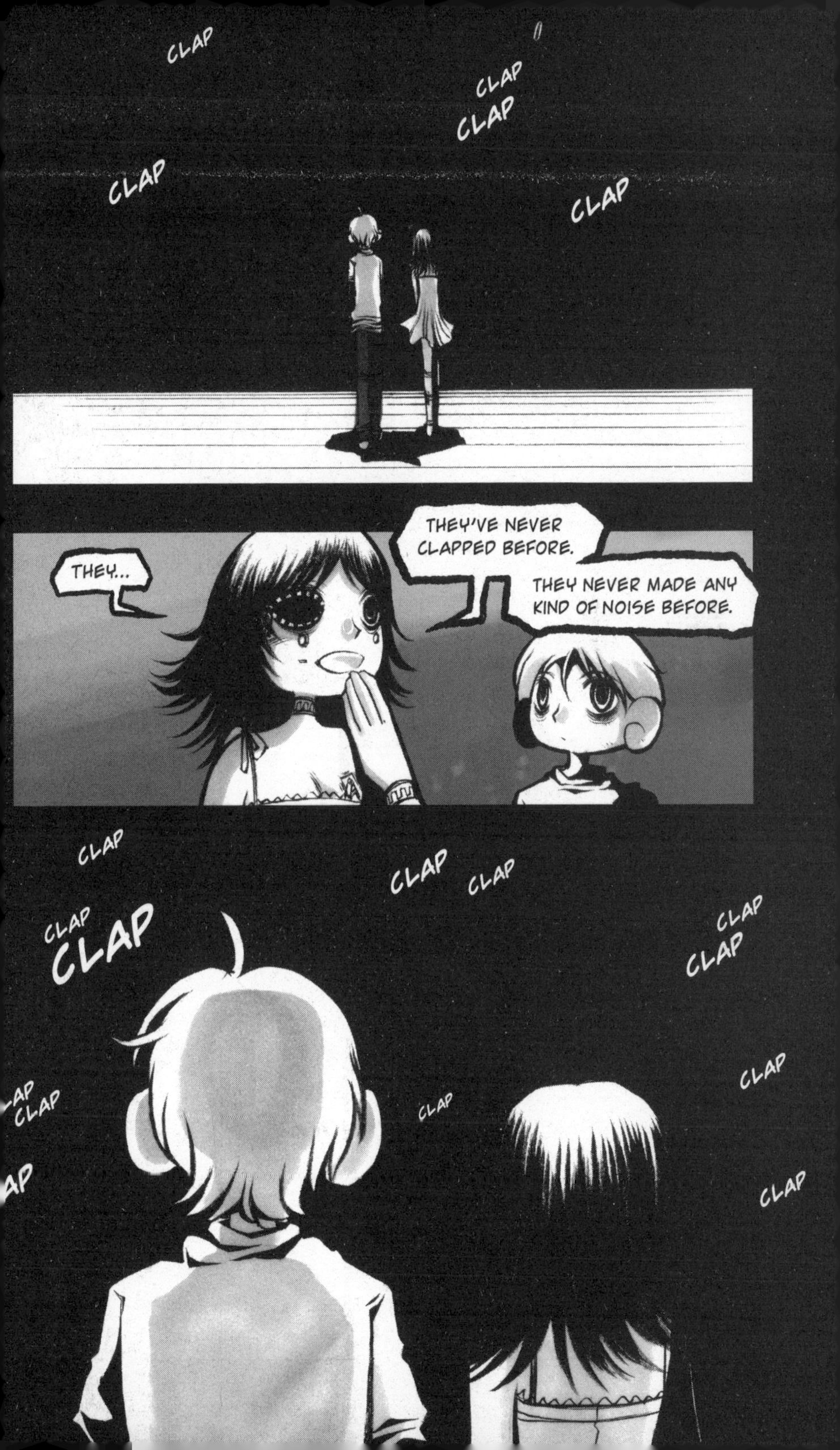
CLAP
CLAP
CLAP
CLAP
CLAP
THEY...
THEY'VE NEVER CLAPPED BEFORE.
THEY NEVER MADE ANY KIND OF NOISE BEFORE.
CLAP
CLAP
CLAP
CLAP
CLAP
CLAP
CLAP
CLAP
CLAP
CLAP
CLAP

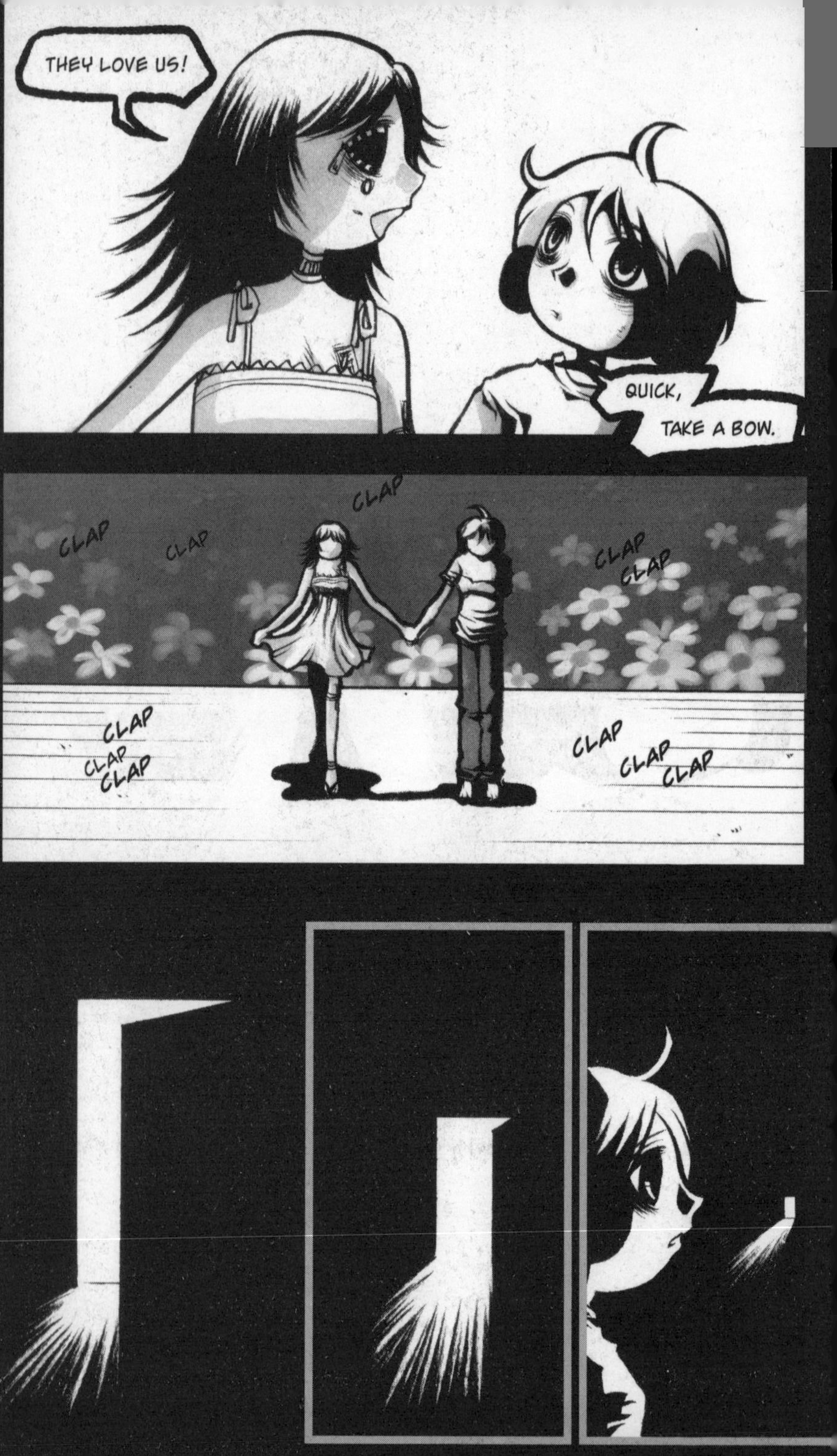
THEY LOVE US!
QUICK,
TAKE A BOW.
CLAP
CLAP
CLAP
CLAP
CLAP
CLAP
CLAP
CLAP
CLAP
CLAP
CLAP

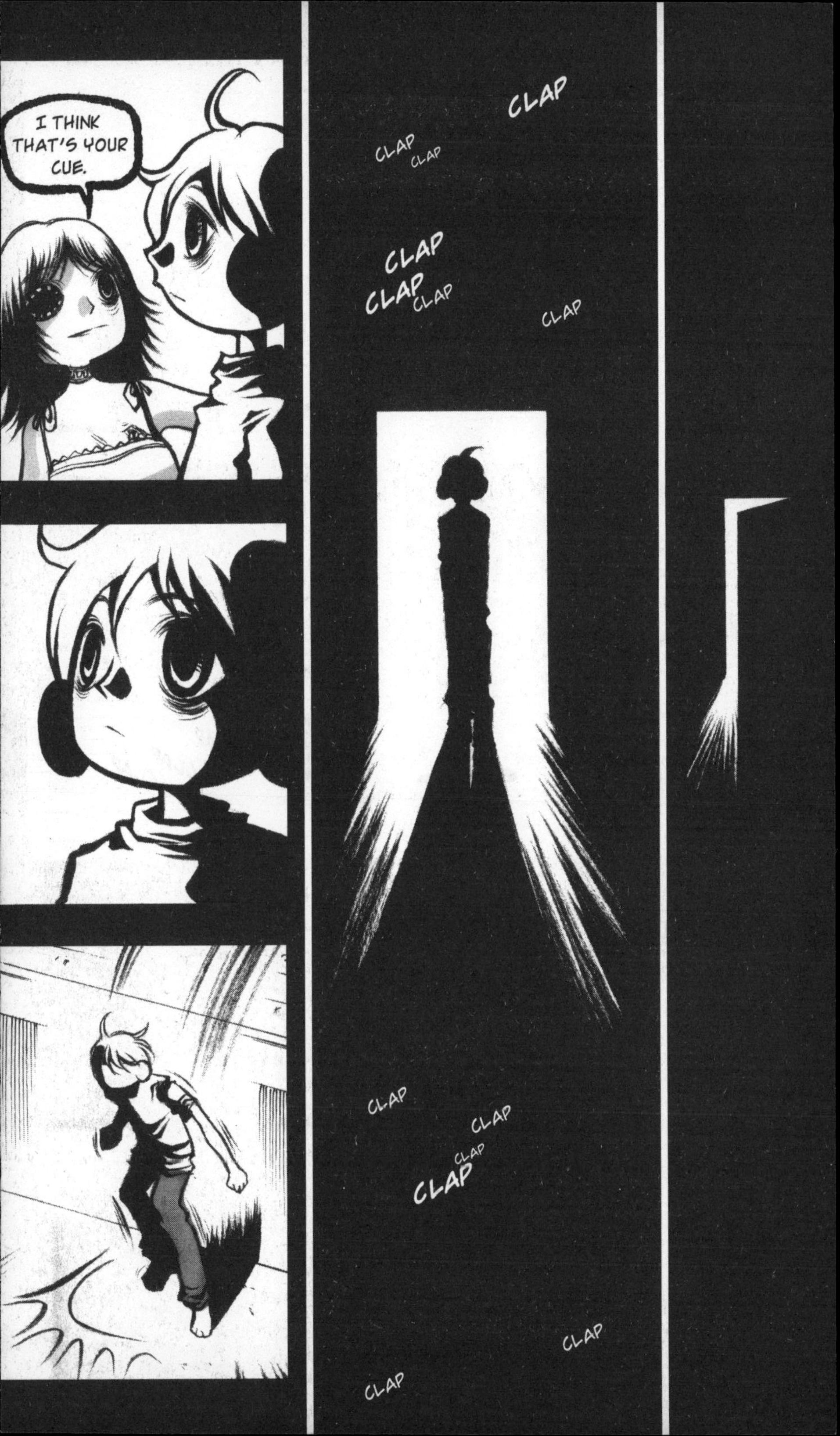
I THINK THAT'S YOUR CUE.
CLAP
CLAP
CLAP
CLAP
CLAP
CLAP
CLAP
CLAP
CLAP
CLAP
CLAP
CLAP
CLAP

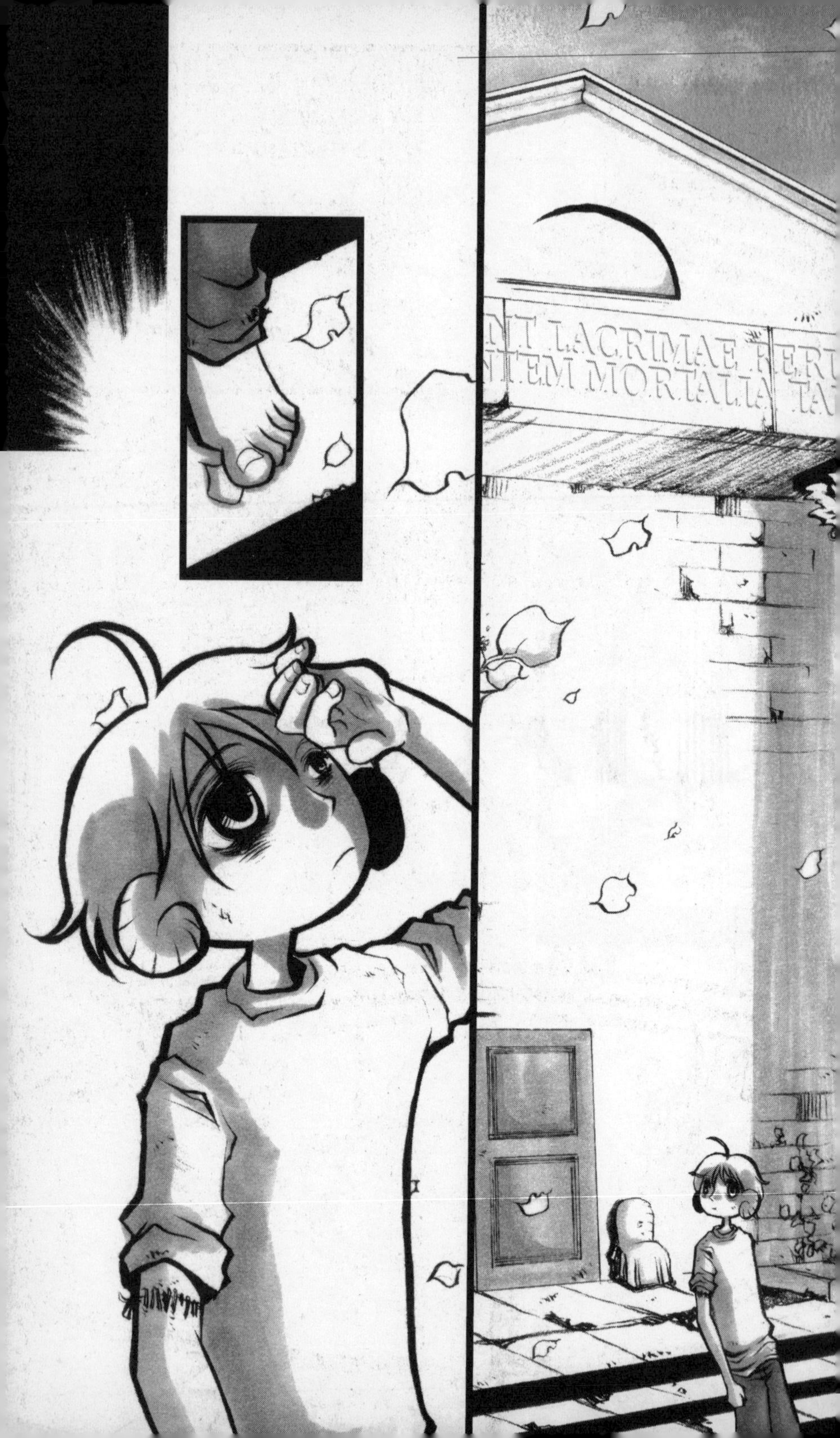
NT LACRIMAE RERU
NTEM MORTALIA TA

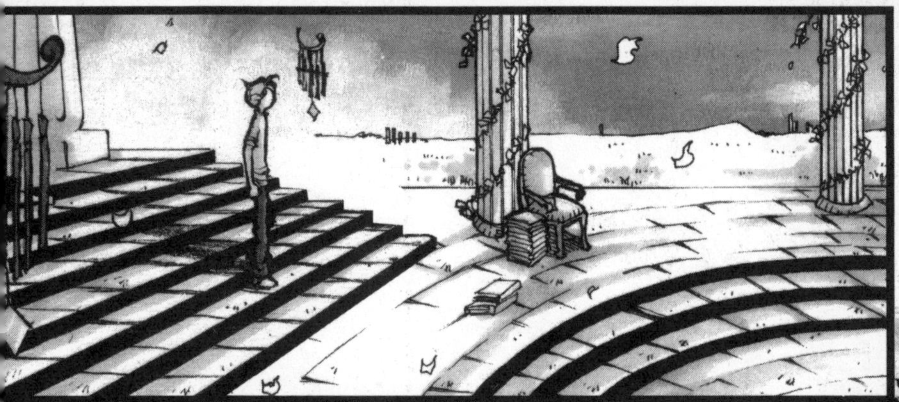

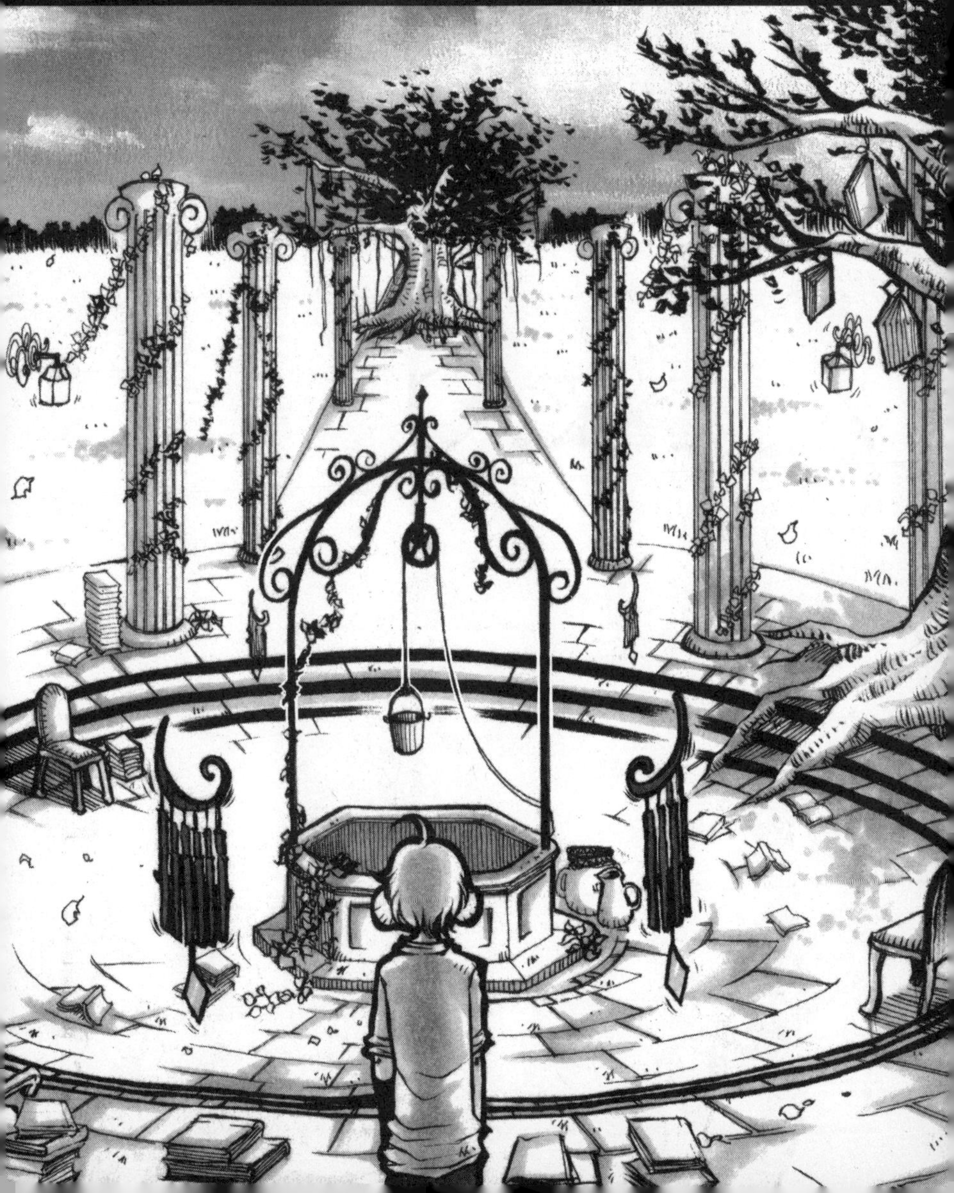

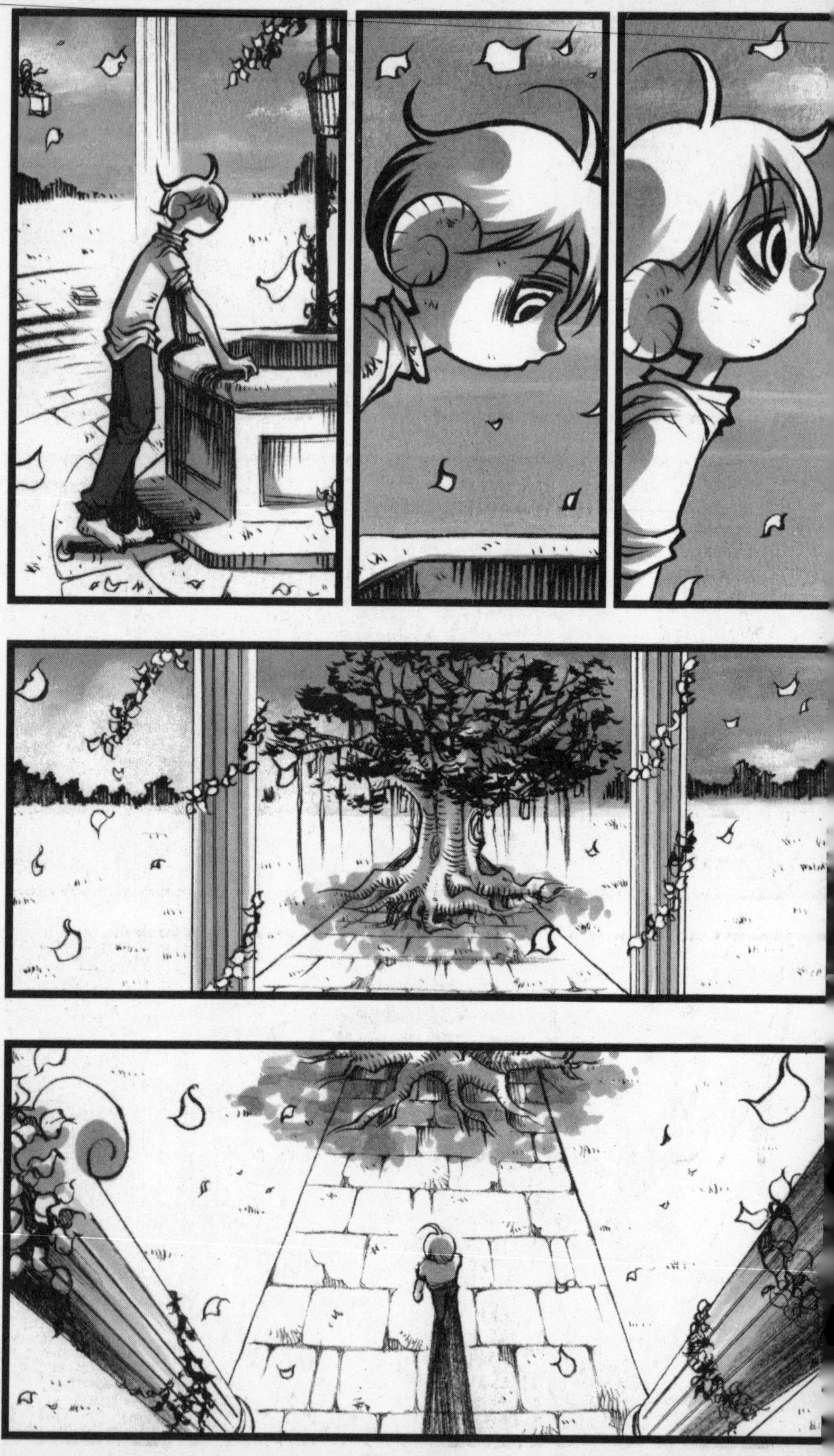

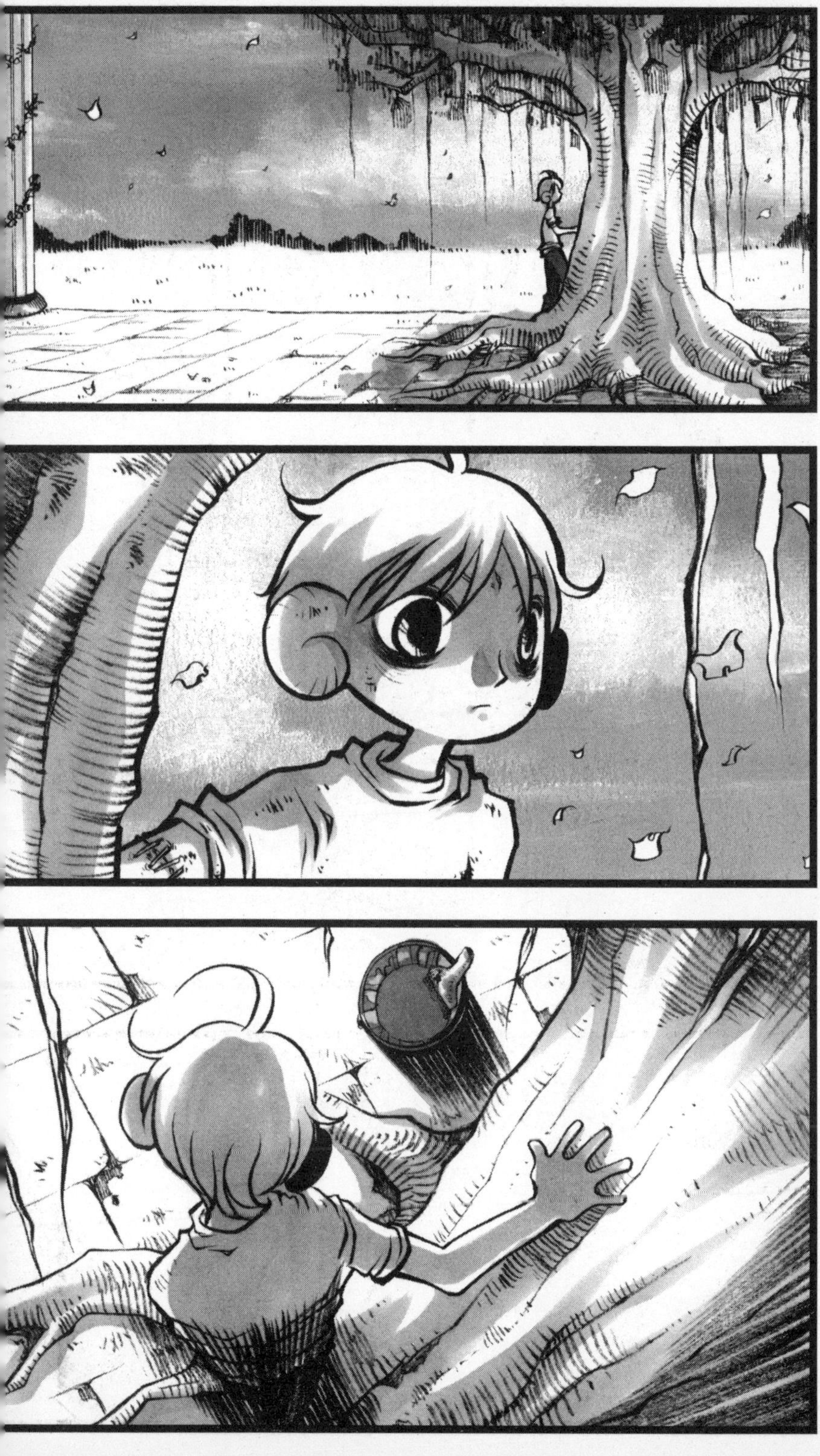

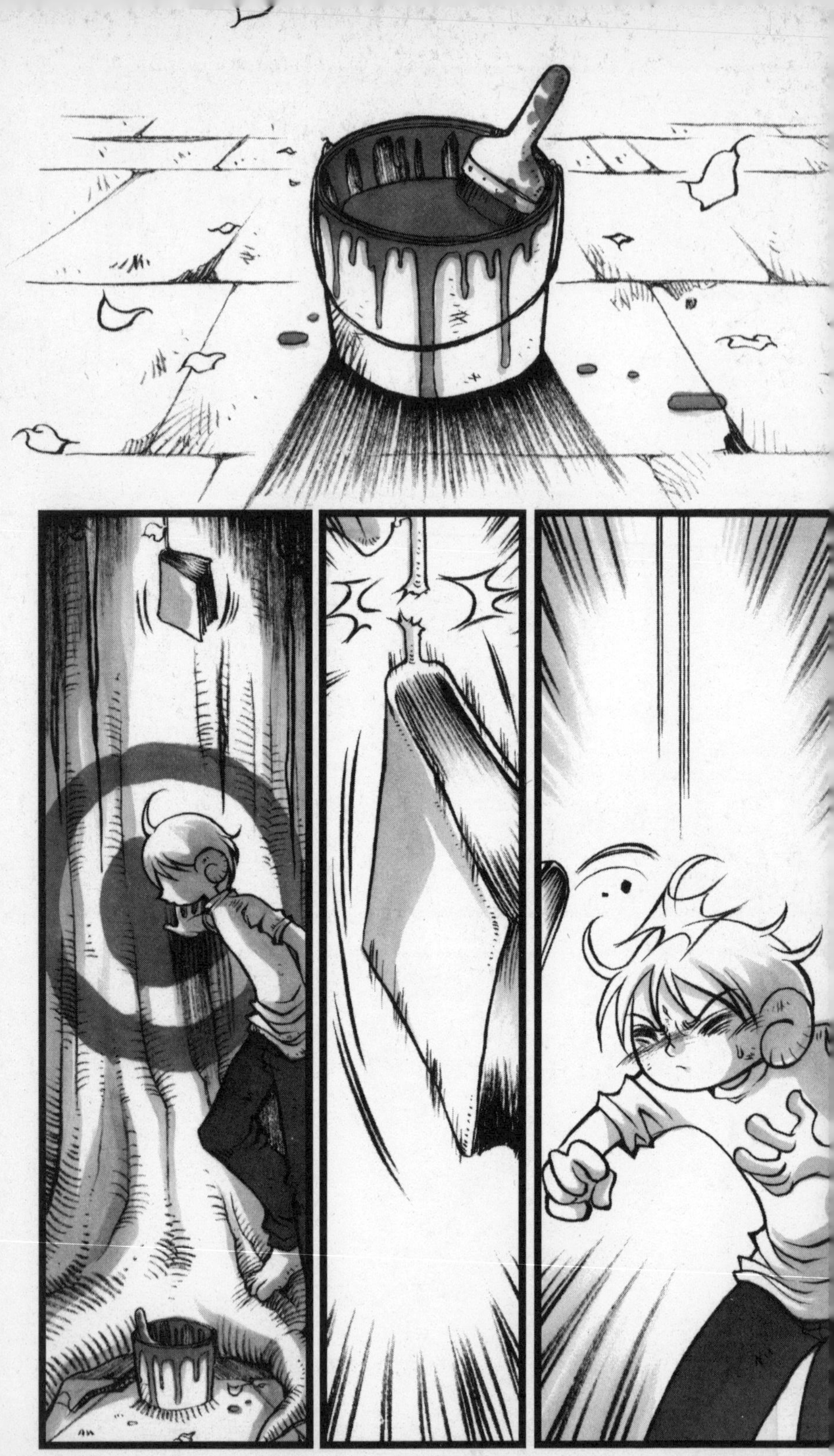

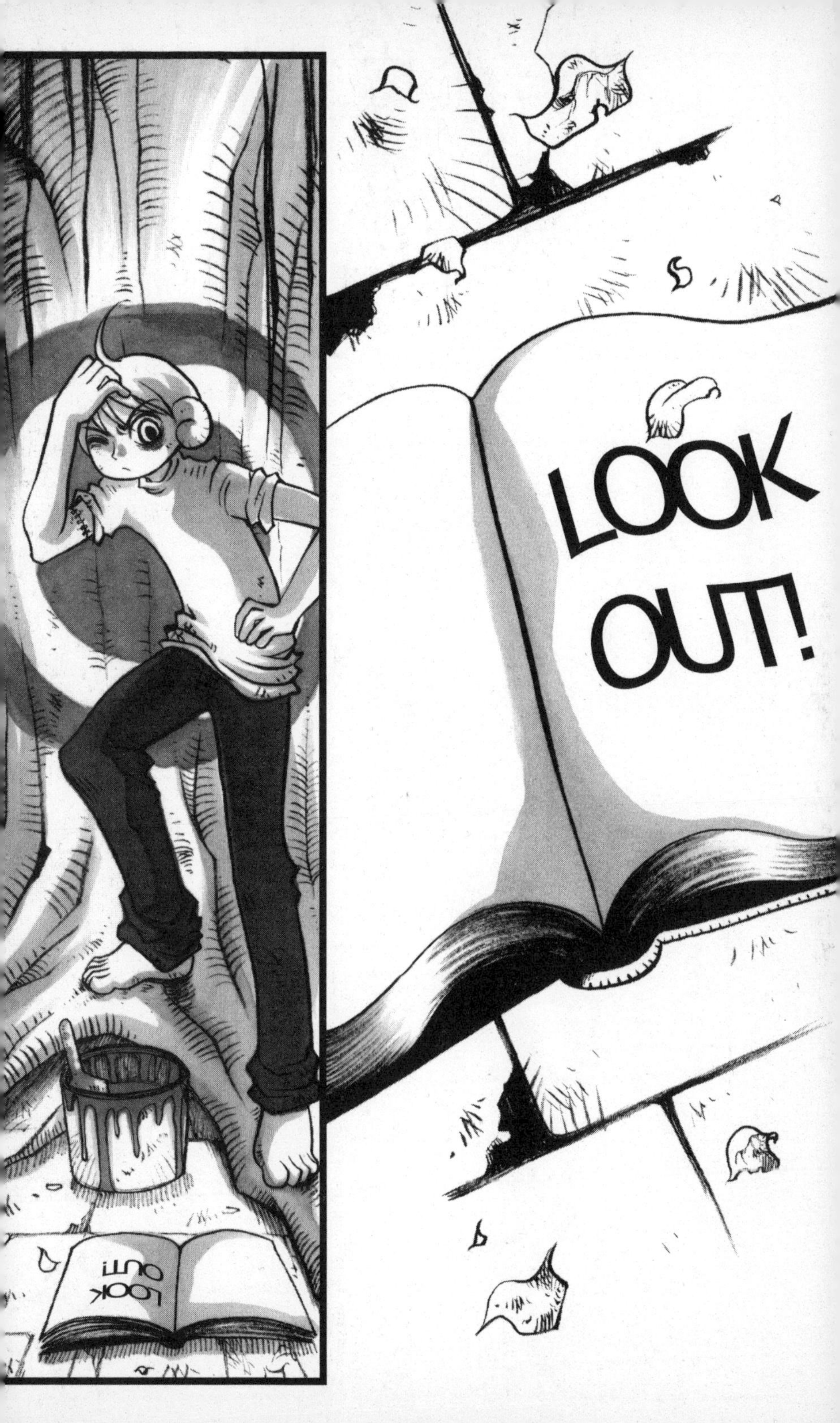
LOOK OUT!

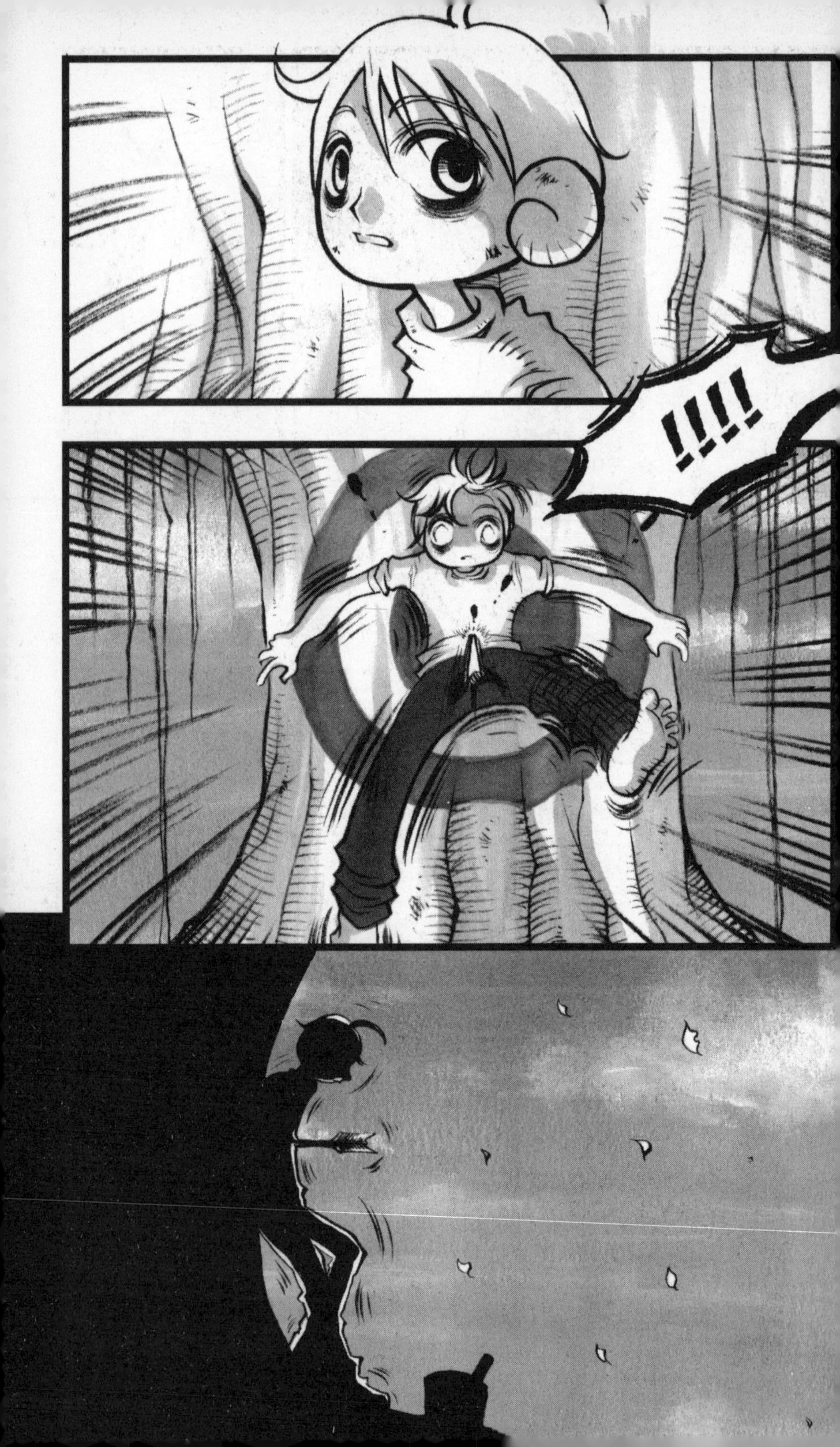
!!!!

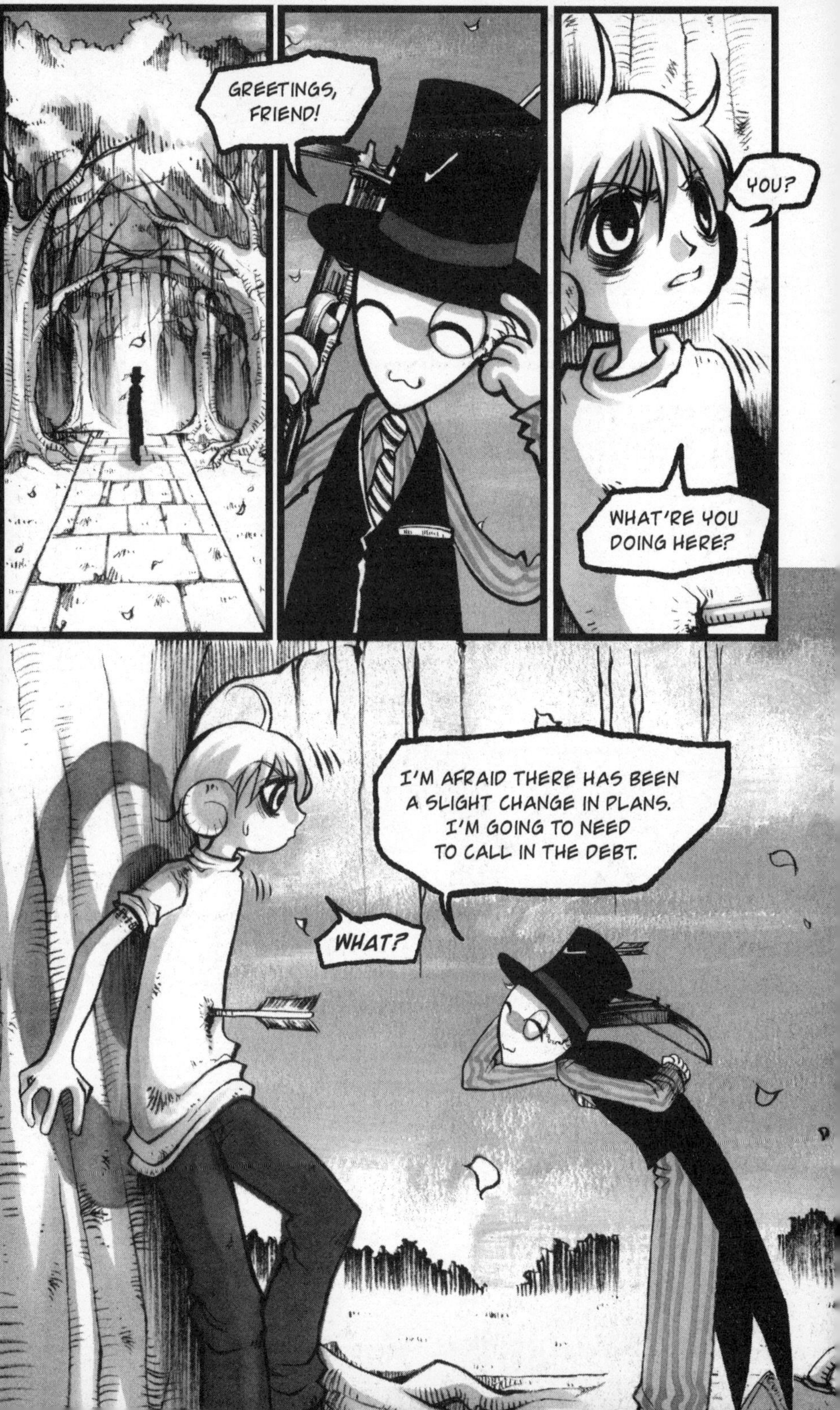
GREETINGS, FRIEND!
YOU?
WHAT'RE YOU DOING HERE?
I'M AFRAID THERE HAS BEEN A SLIGHT CHANGE IN PLANS. I'M GOING TO NEED TO CALL IN THE DEBT.
WHAT?

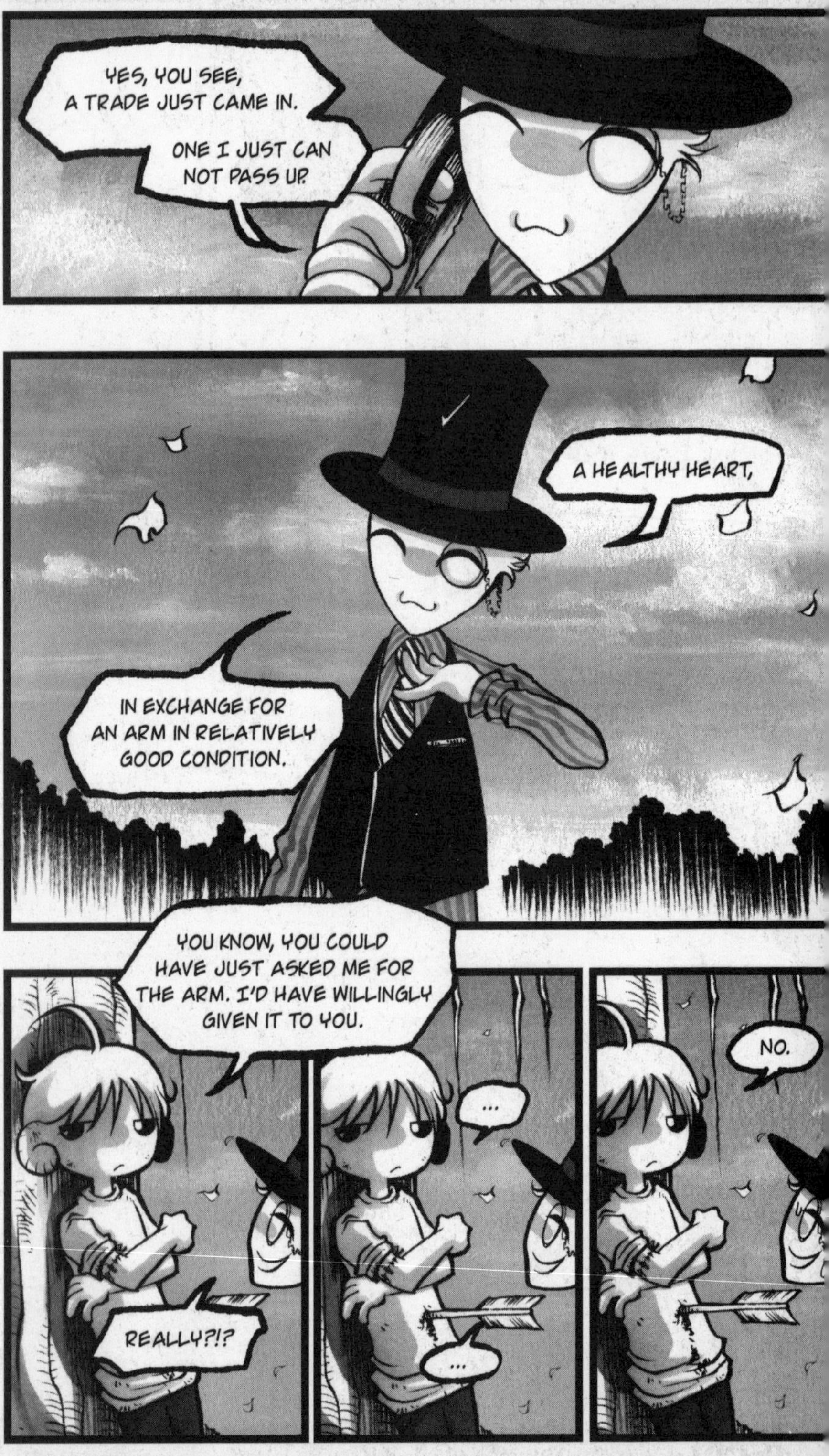
YES, YOU SEE, A TRADE JUST CAME IN.
ONE I JUST CAN NOT PASS UP.
A HEALTHY HEART,
IN EXCHANGE FOR AN ARM IN RELATIVELY GOOD CONDITION.
YOU KNOW, YOU COULD HAVE JUST ASKED ME FOR THE ARM. I'D HAVE WILLINGLY GIVEN IT TO YOU.
REALLY?!?
...
...
NO.

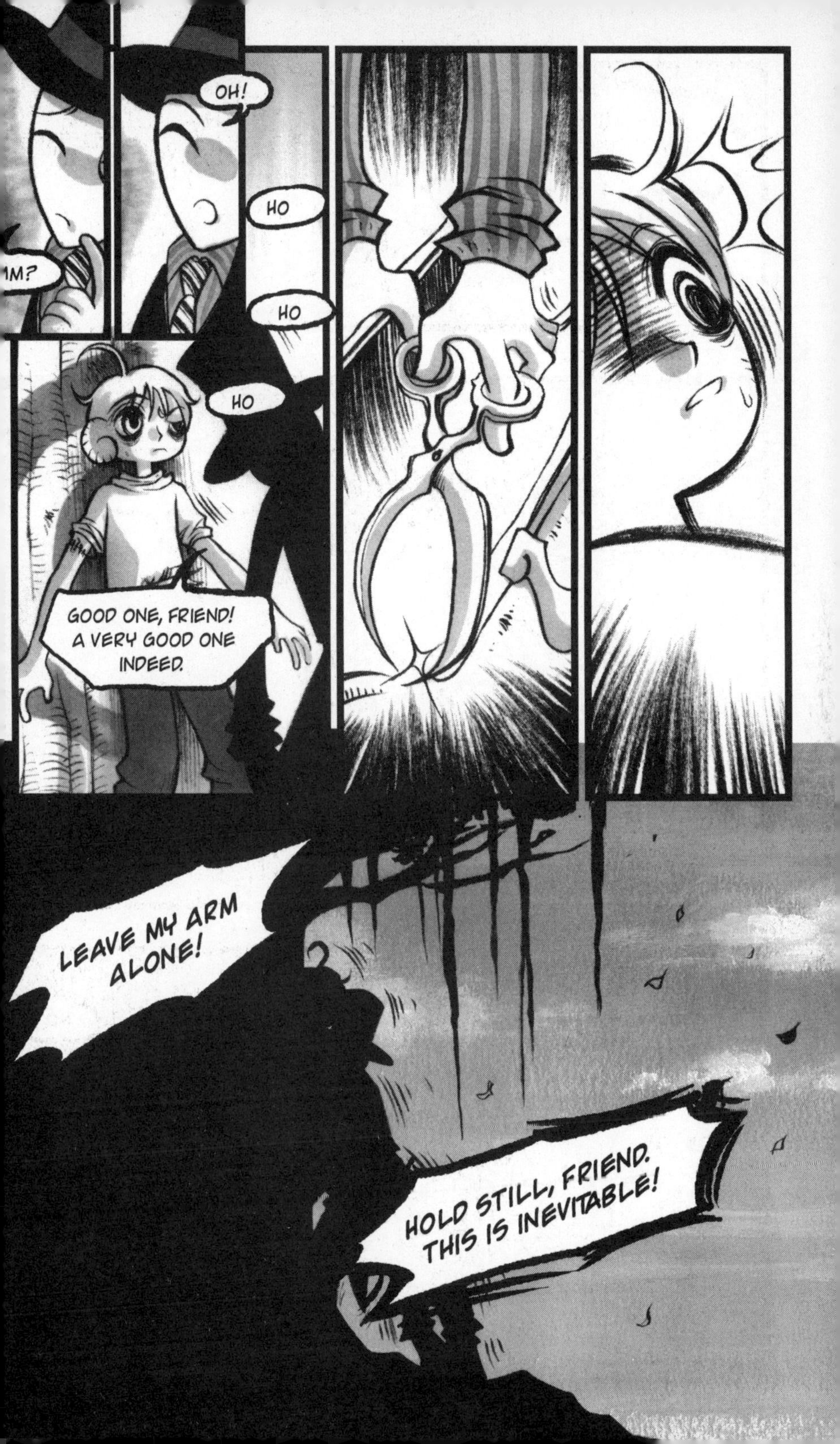
MM?
OH!
HO
HO
HO
GOOD ONE, FRIEND! A VERY GOOD ONE INDEED.
LEAVE MY ARM ALONE!
HOLD STILL, FRIEND. THIS IS INEVITABLE!

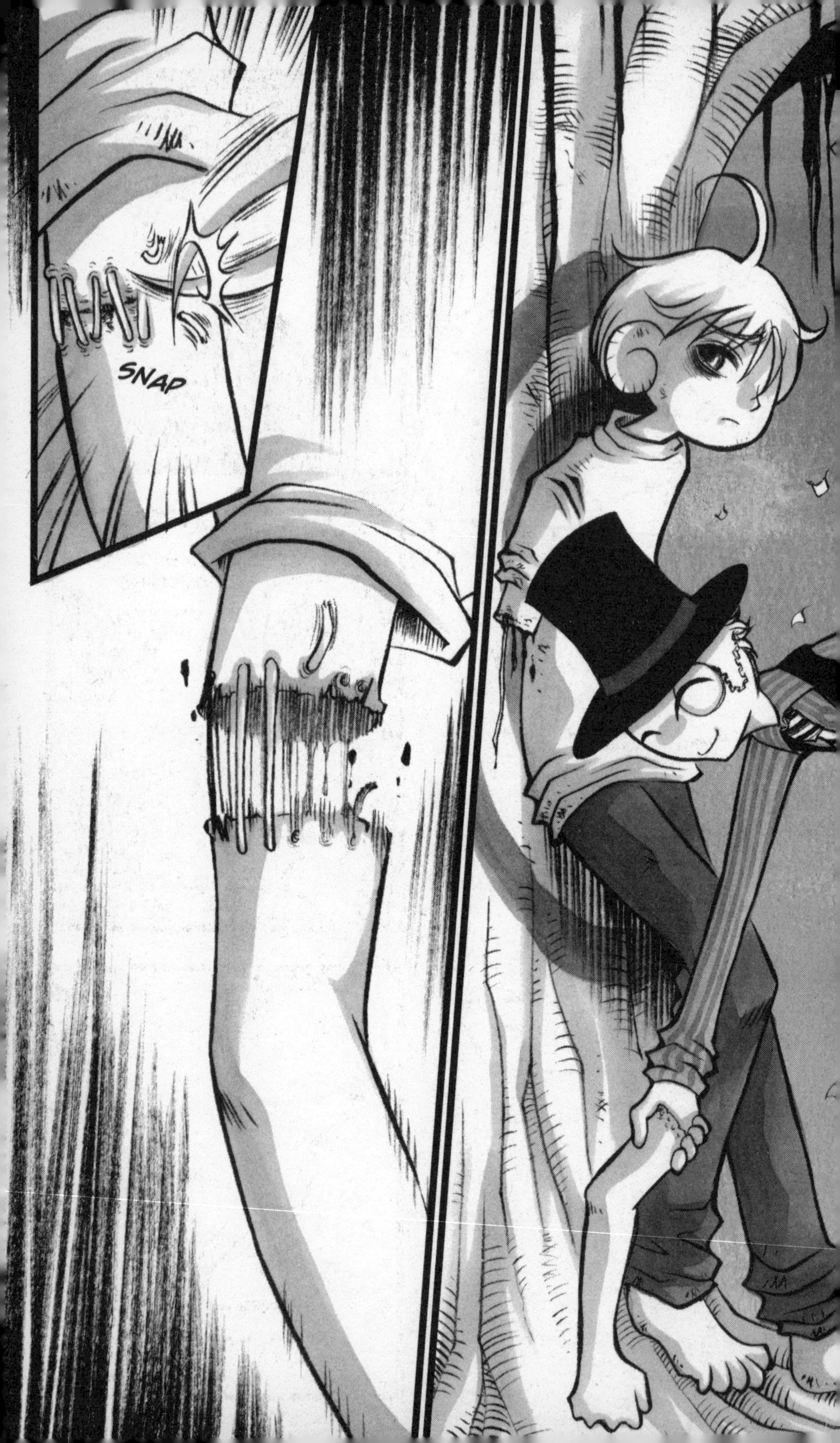
SNAP

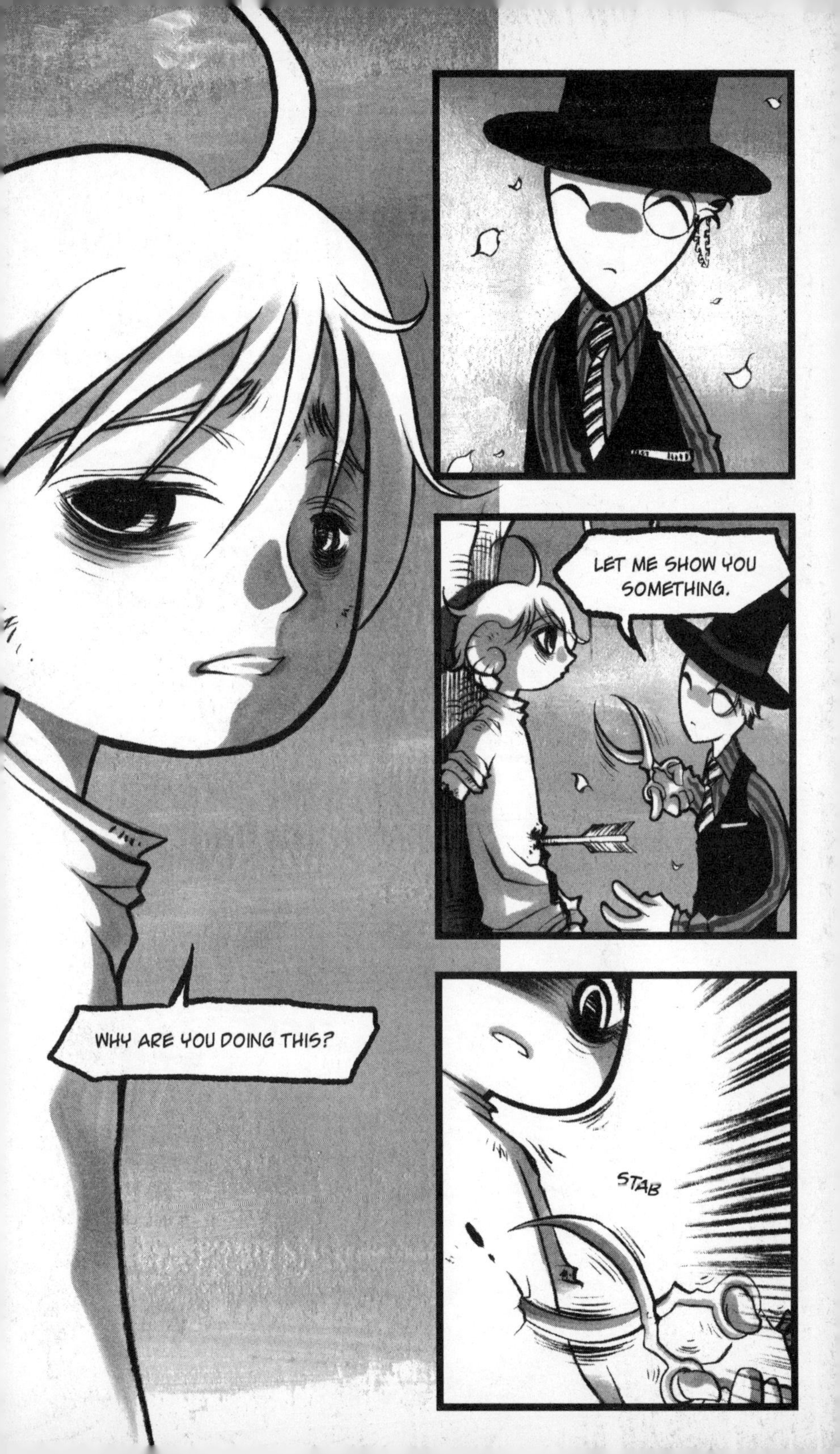
WHY ARE YOU DOING THIS?
LET ME SHOW YOU SOMETHING.
STAB

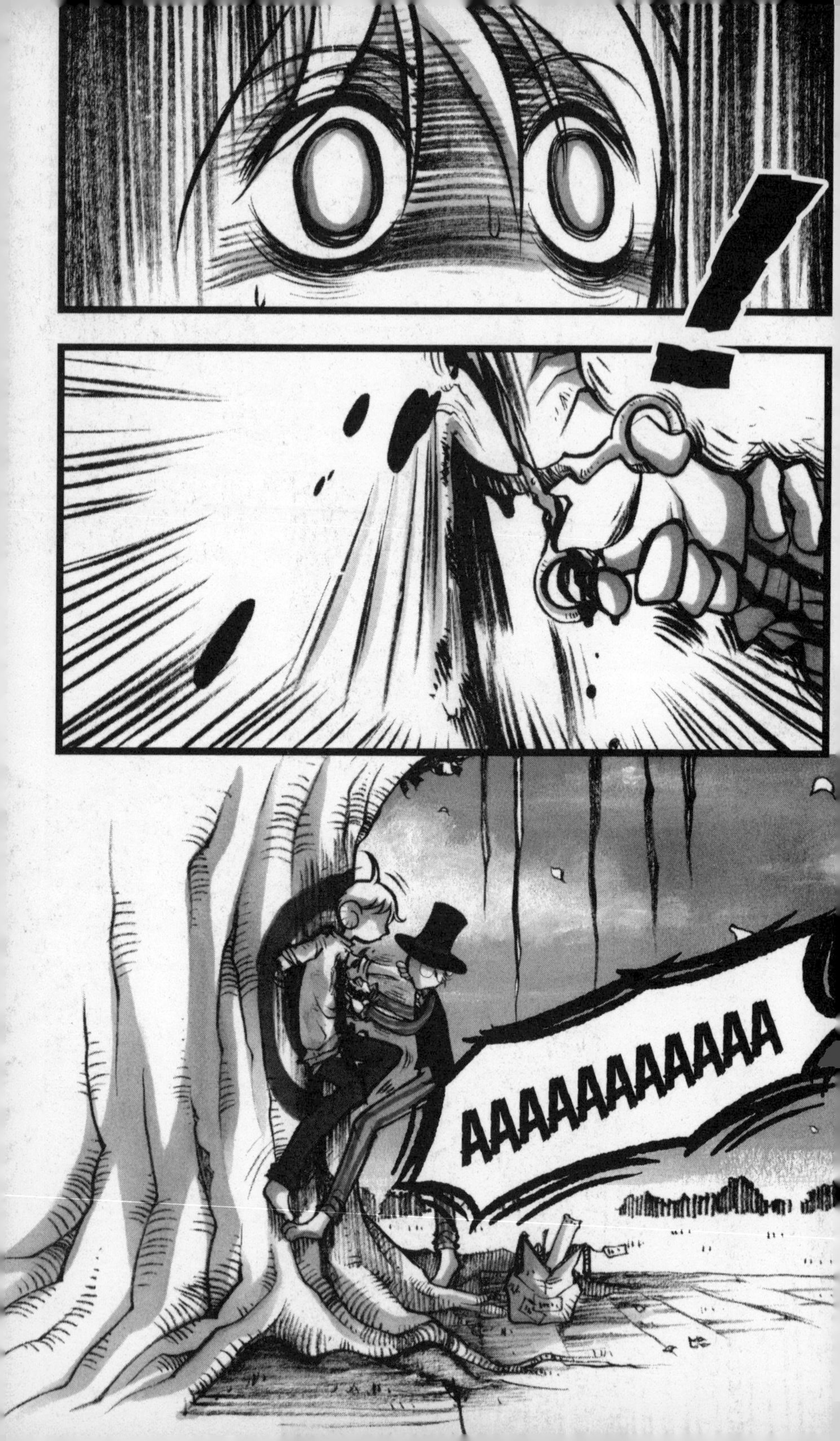
AAAAAAAAAAA

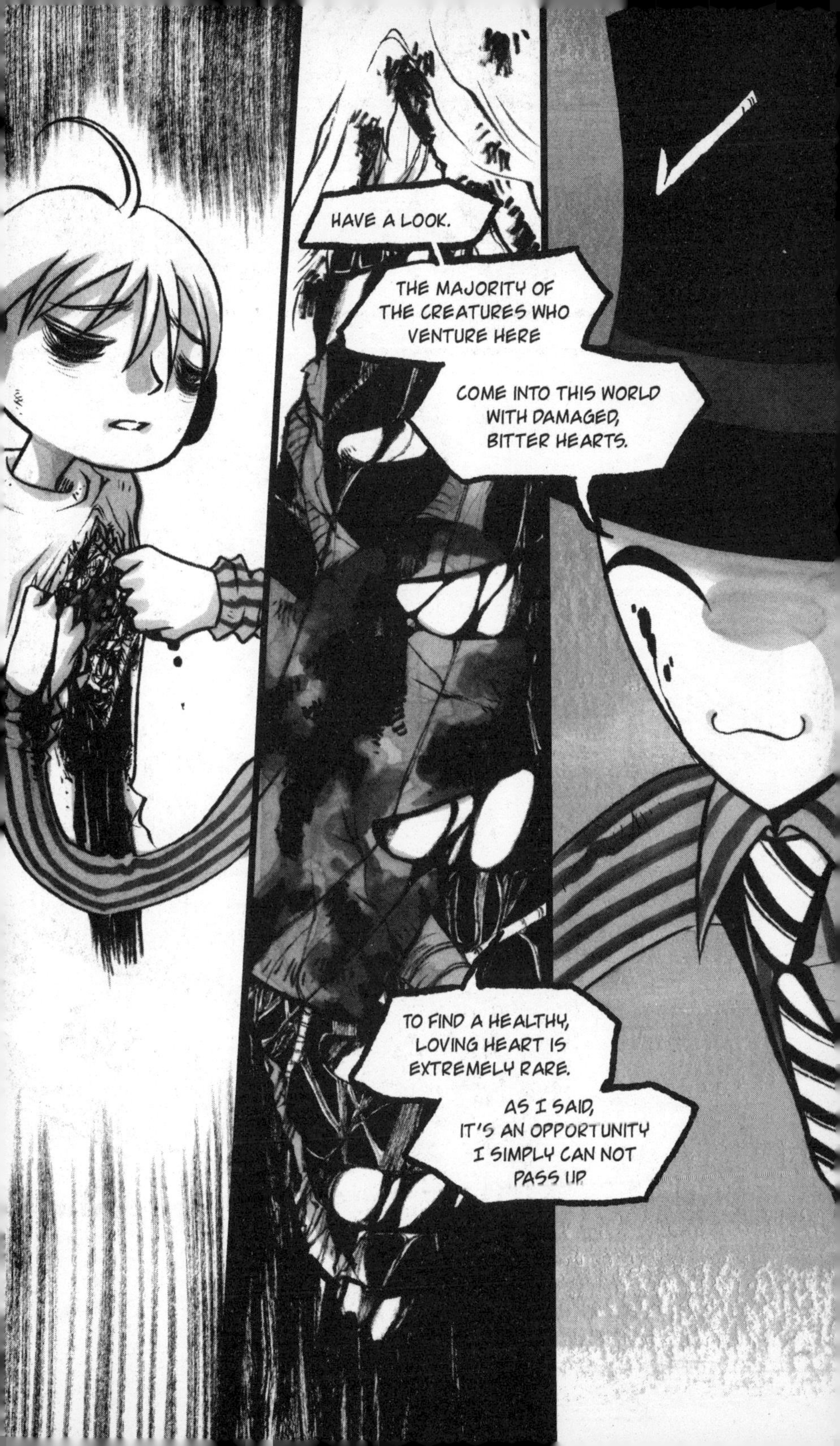

HAVE A LOOK.
THE MAJORITY OF THE CREATURES WHO VENTURE HERE
COME INTO THIS WORLD WITH DAMAGED, BITTER HEARTS.
TO FIND A HEALTHY, LOVING HEART IS EXTREMELY RARE.
AS I SAID, IT'S AN OPPORTUNITY I SIMPLY CAN NOT PASS UP

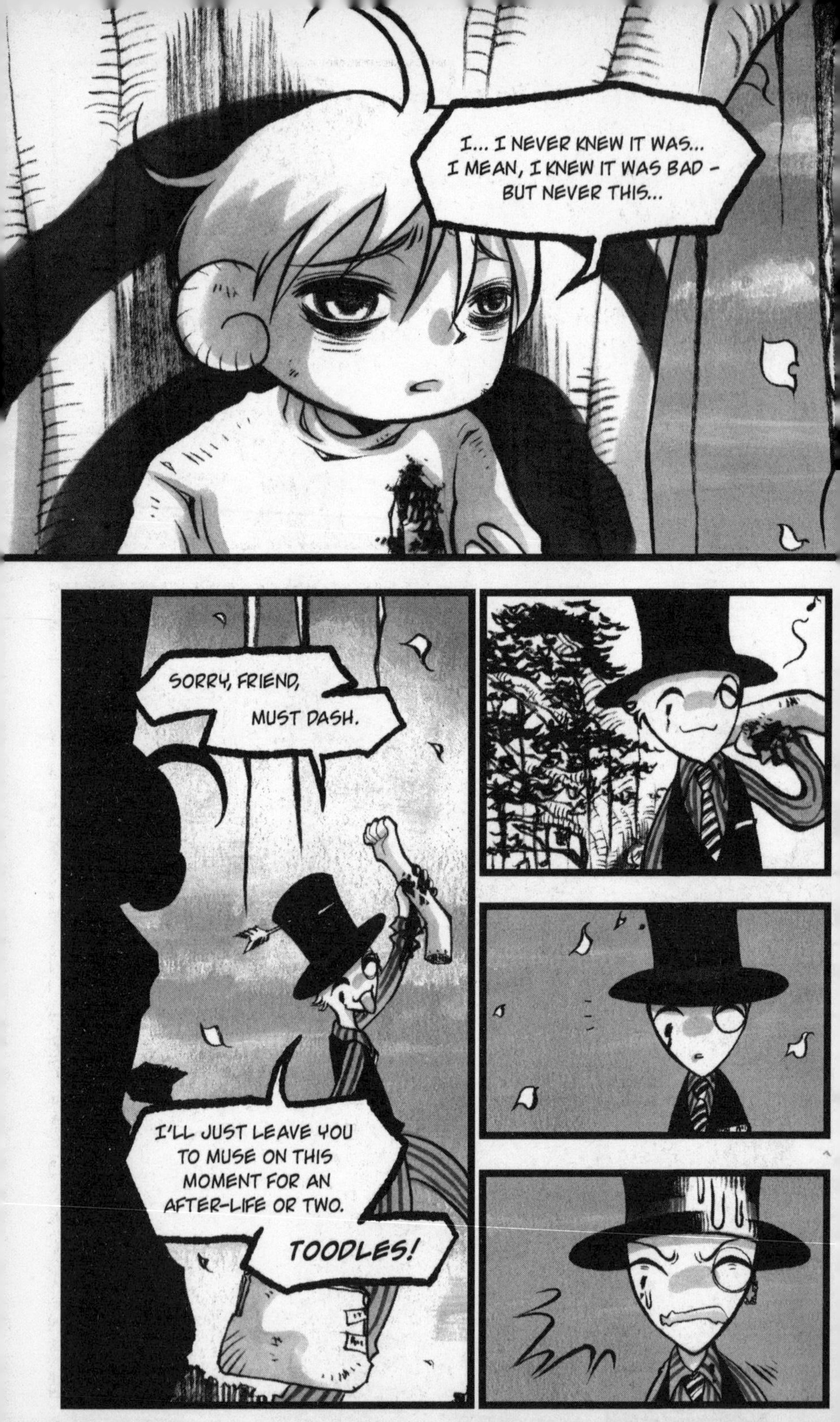
I... I NEVER KNEW IT WAS... I MEAN, I KNEW IT WAS BAD – BUT NEVER THIS...
SORRY, FRIEND, MUST DASH.
I'LL JUST LEAVE YOU TO MUSE ON THIS MOMENT FOR AN AFTER-LIFE OR TWO.
TOODLES!

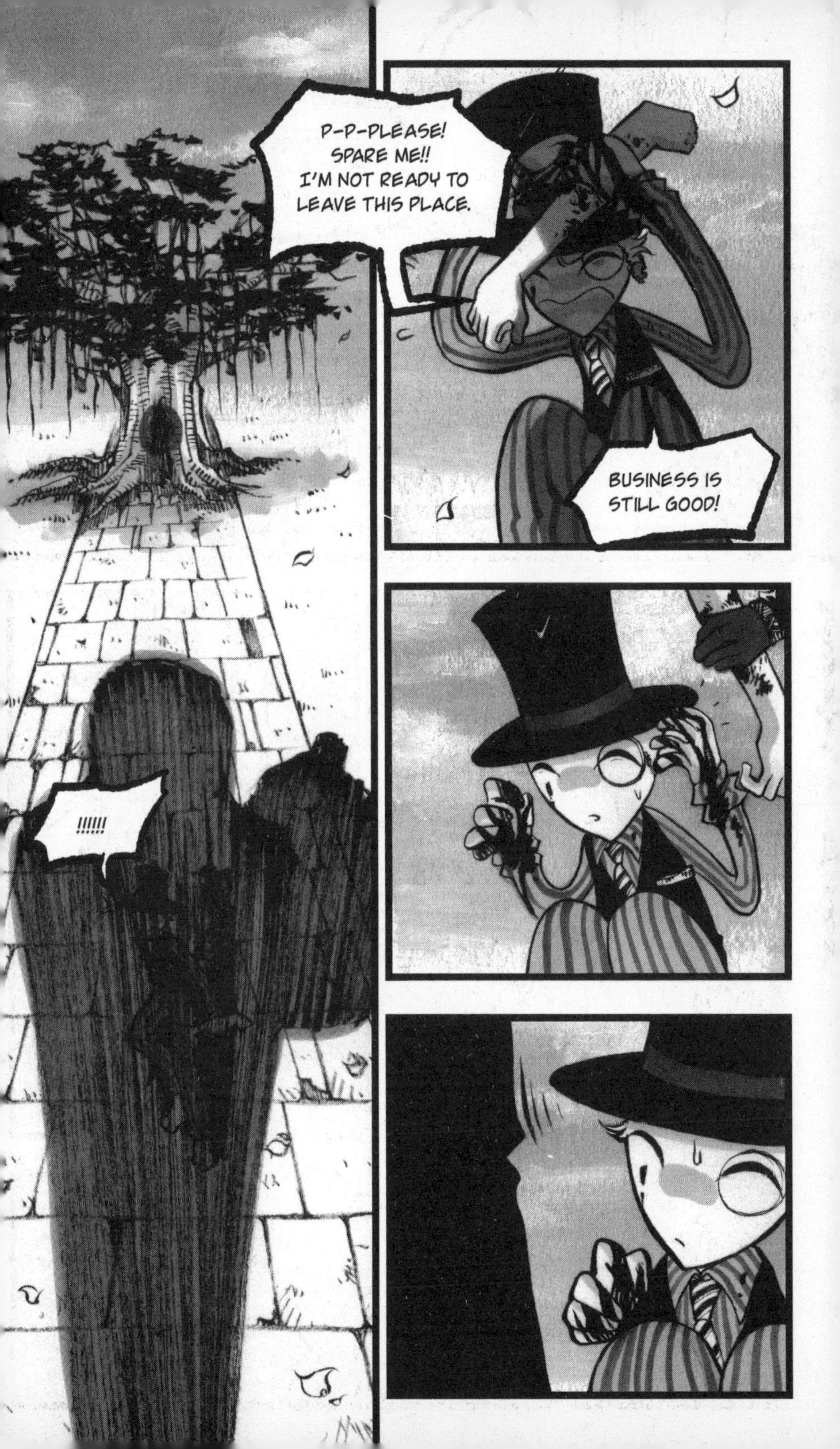
P-P-PLEASE! SPARE ME!! I'M NOT READY TO LEAVE THIS PLACE.
BUSINESS IS STILL GOOD!
!!!!!!

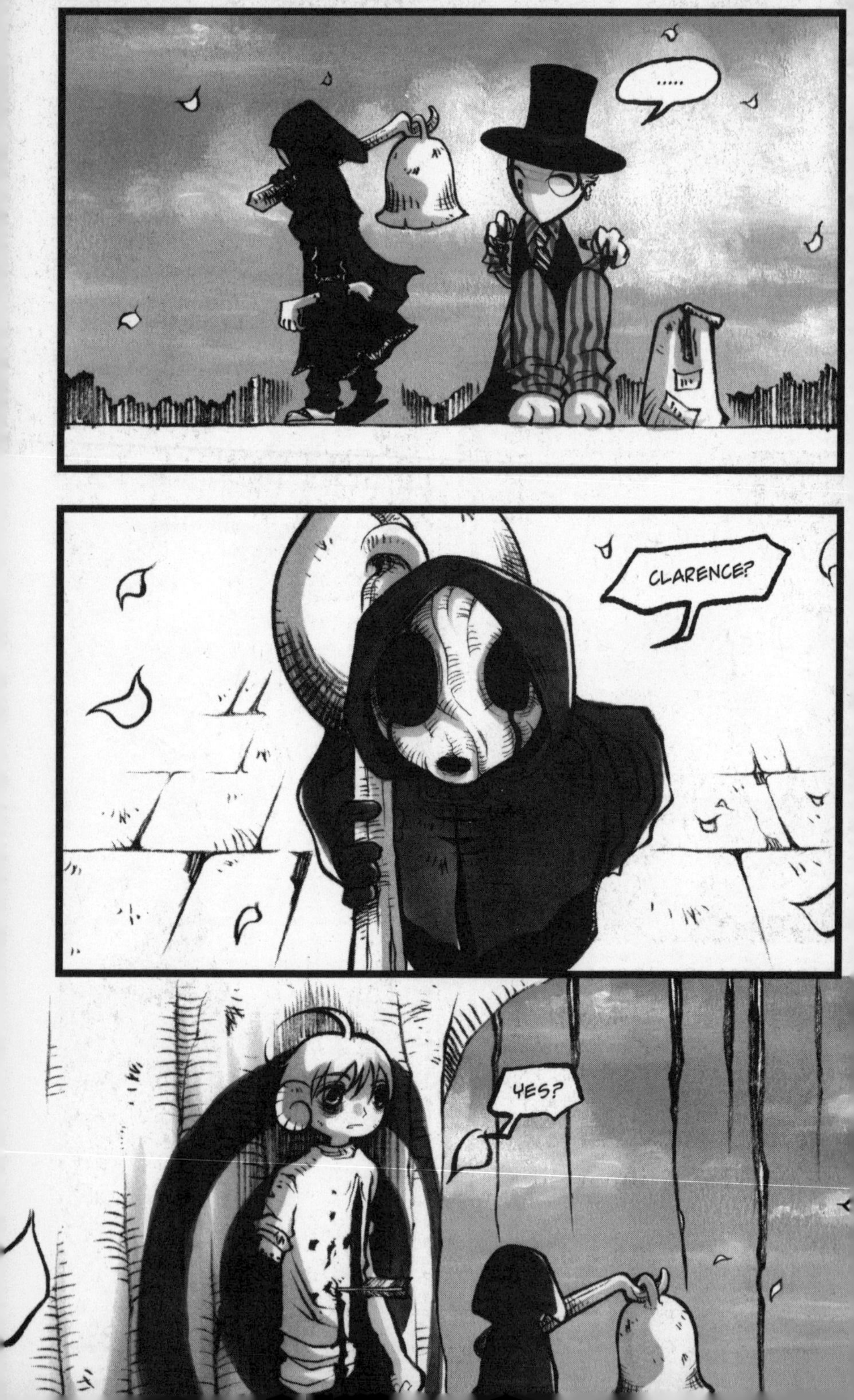
......
CLARENCE?
YES?

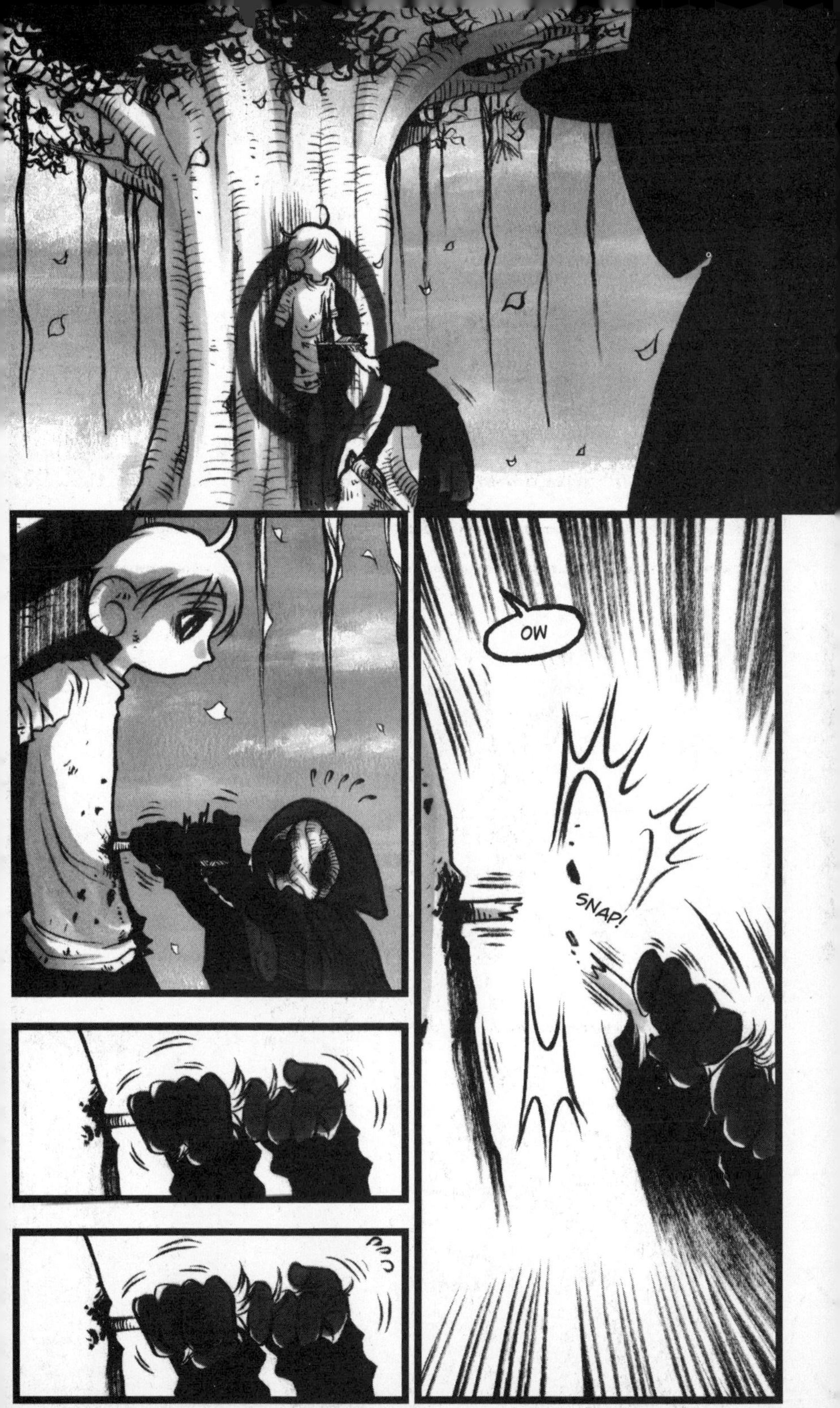
OW
SNAP!

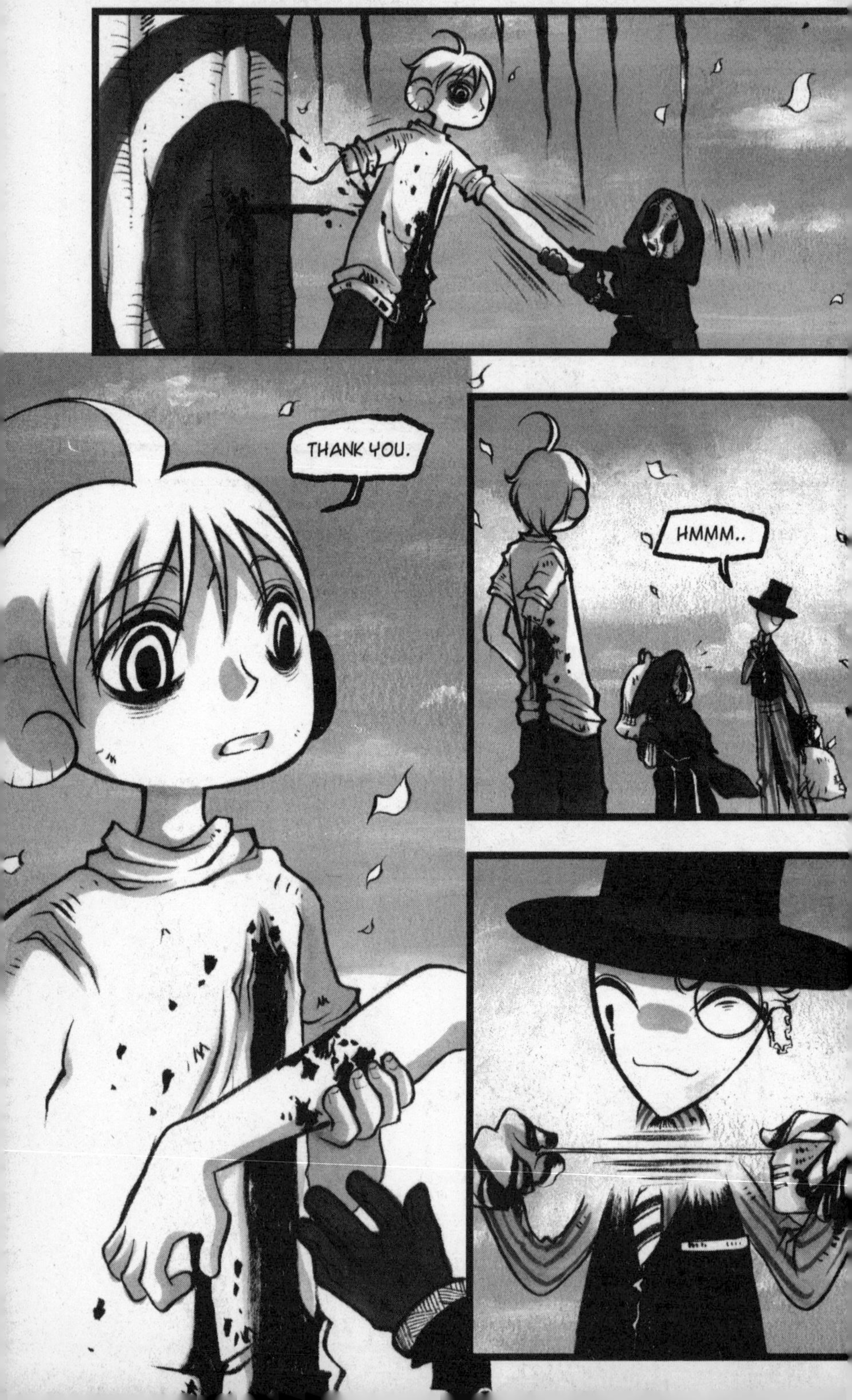
THANK YOU.
HMMM..

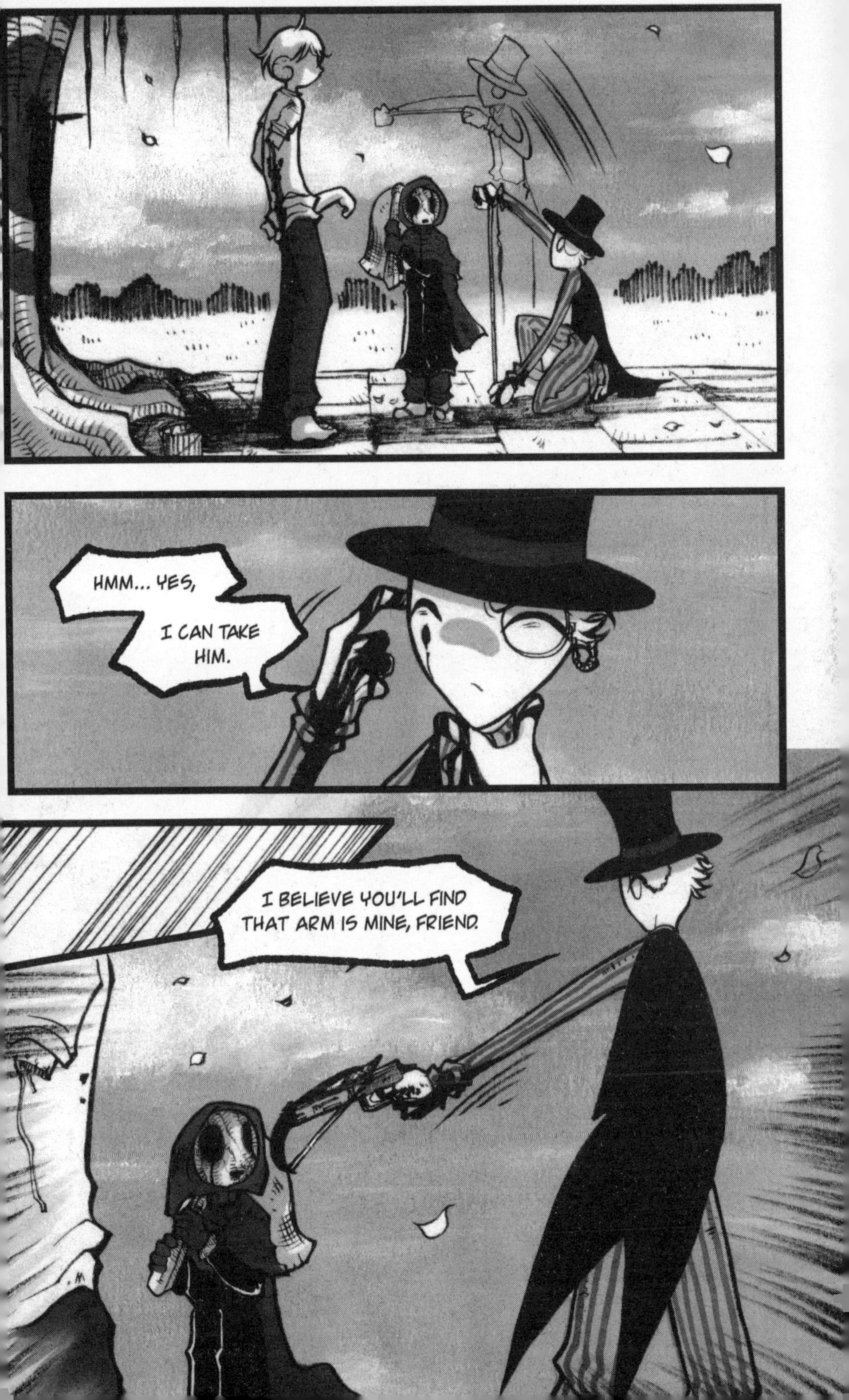
HMM... YES,
I CAN TAKE HIM.
I BELIEVE YOU'LL FIND THAT ARM IS MINE, FRIEND.

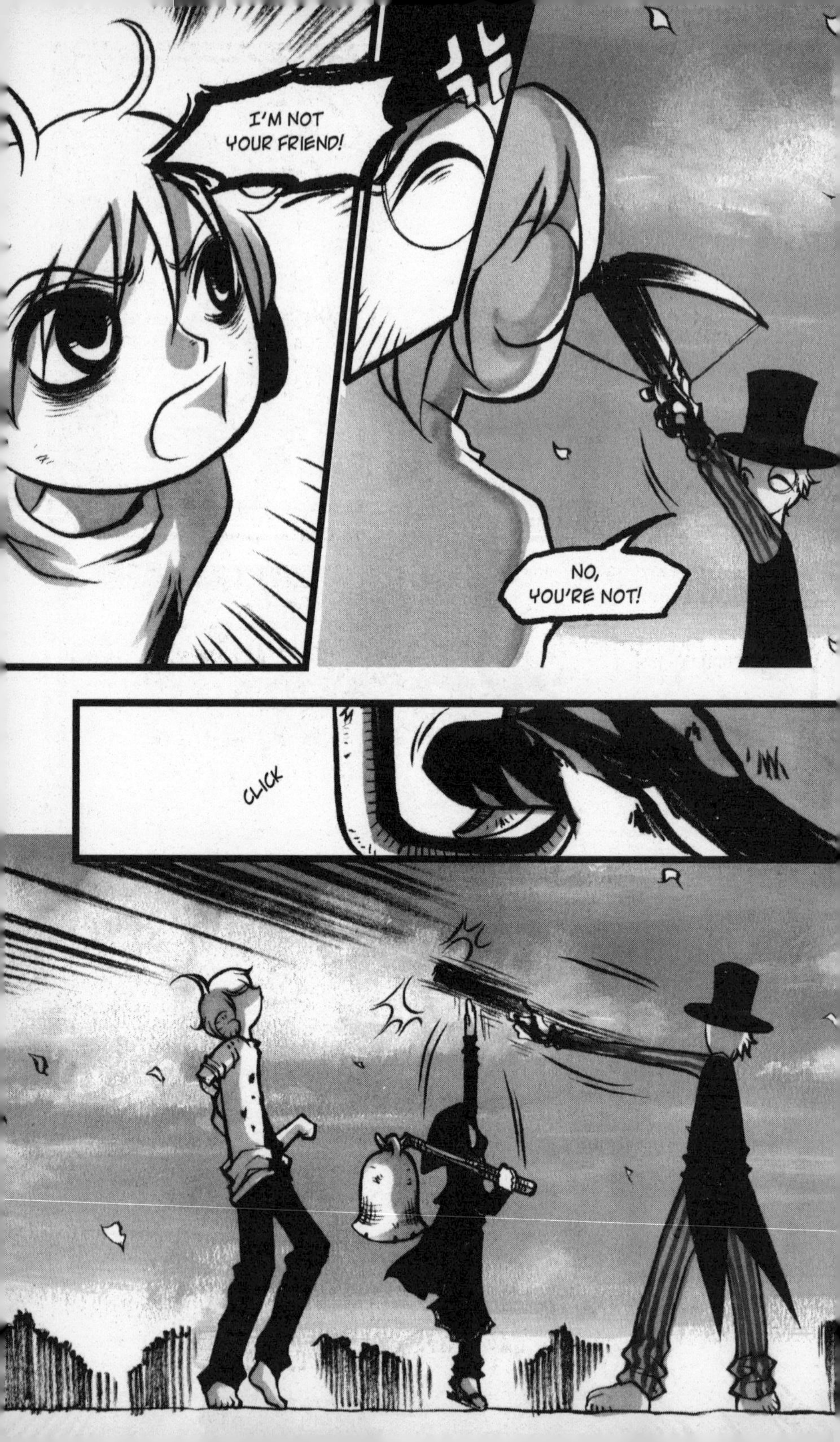
I'M NOT YOUR FRIEND!
NO, YOU'RE NOT!
CLICK

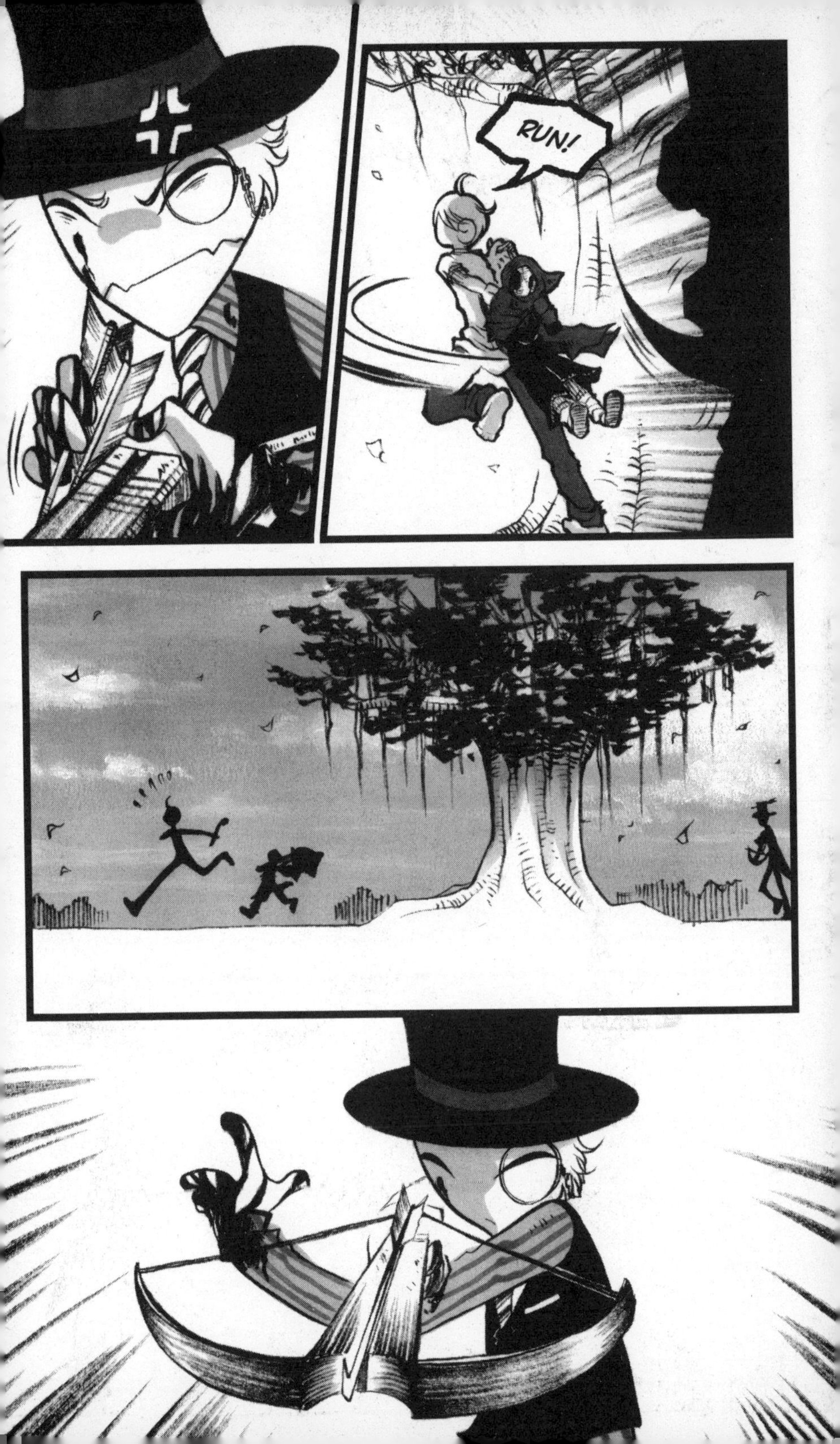
RUN!

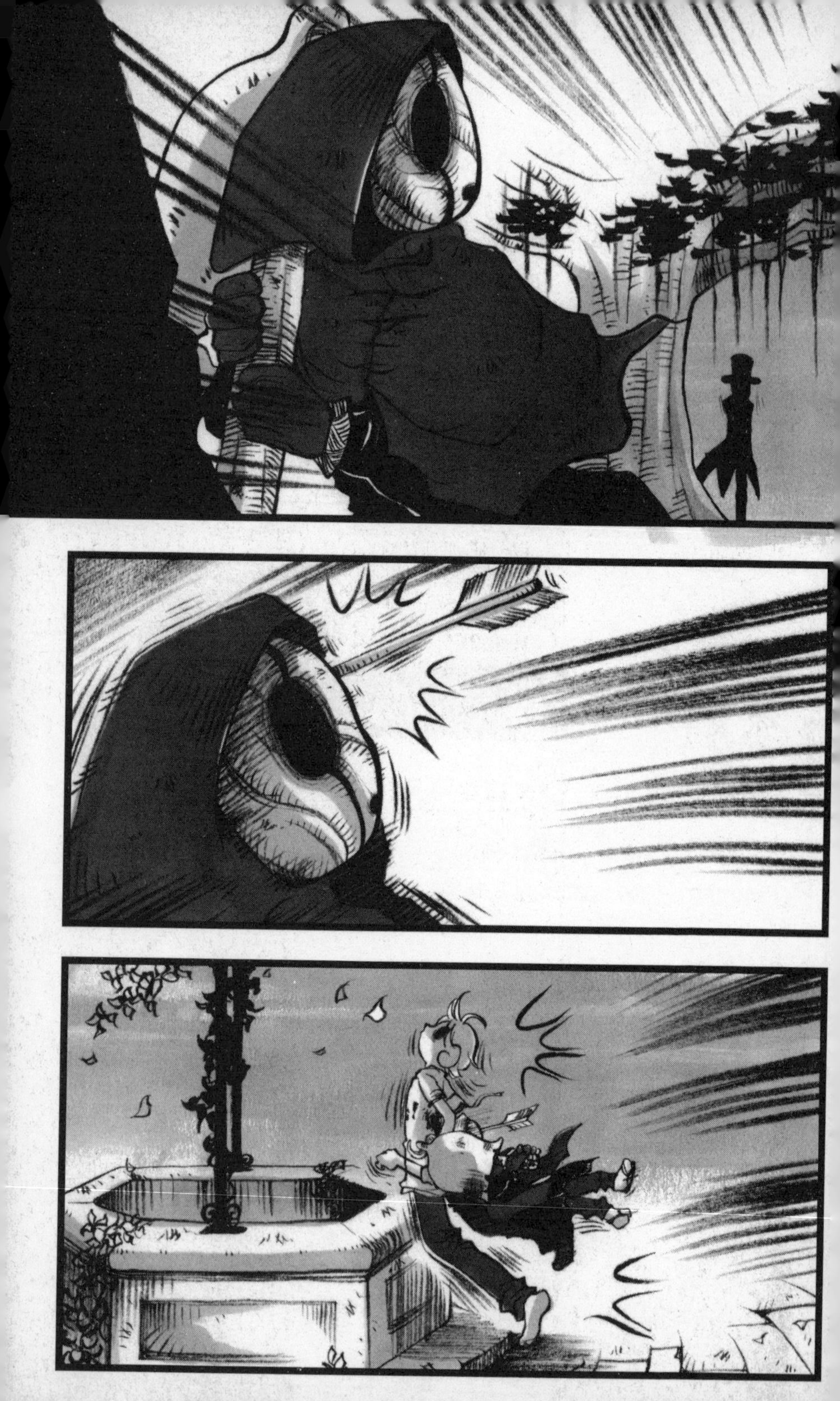

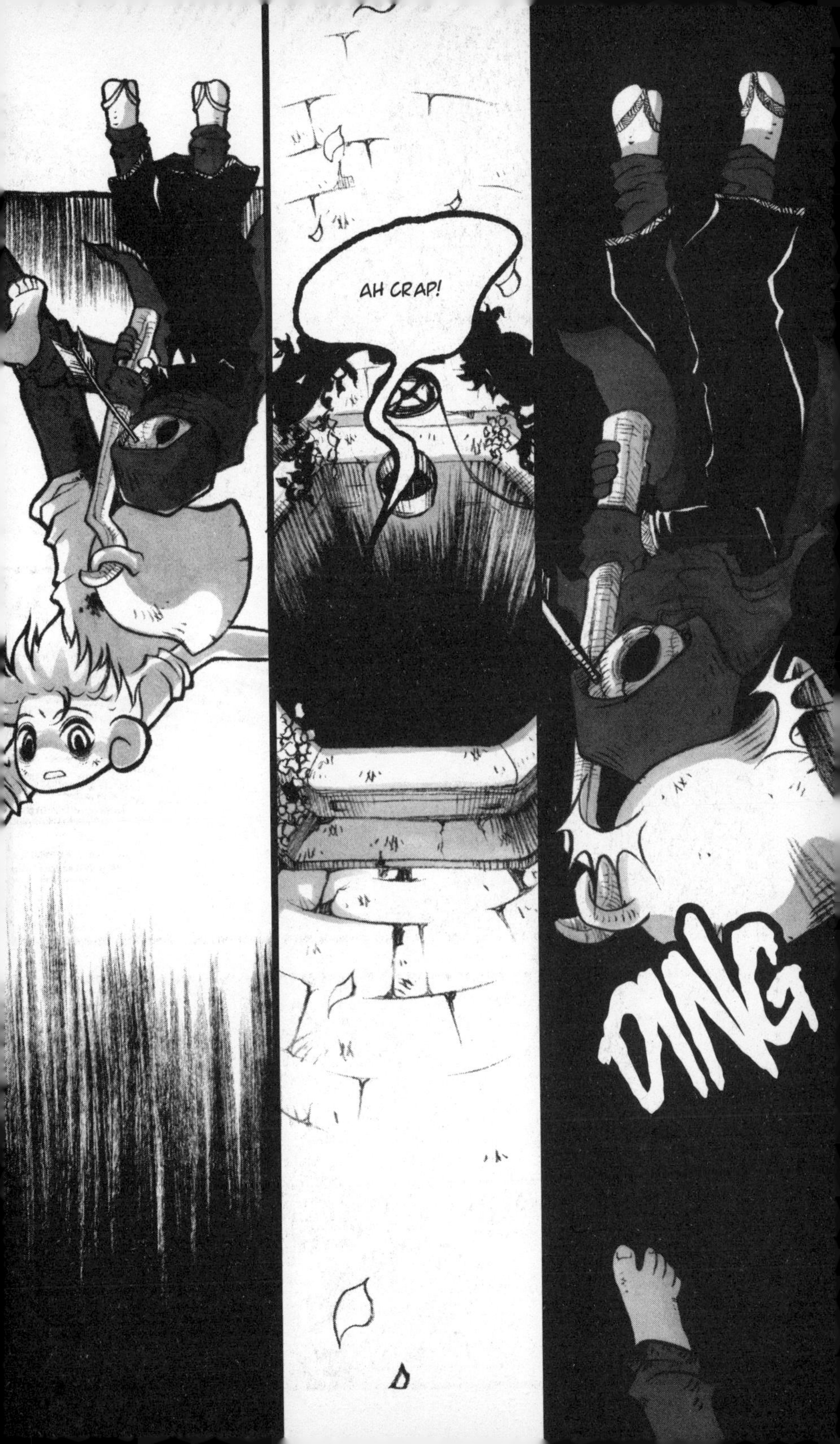
AH CRAP!
DING

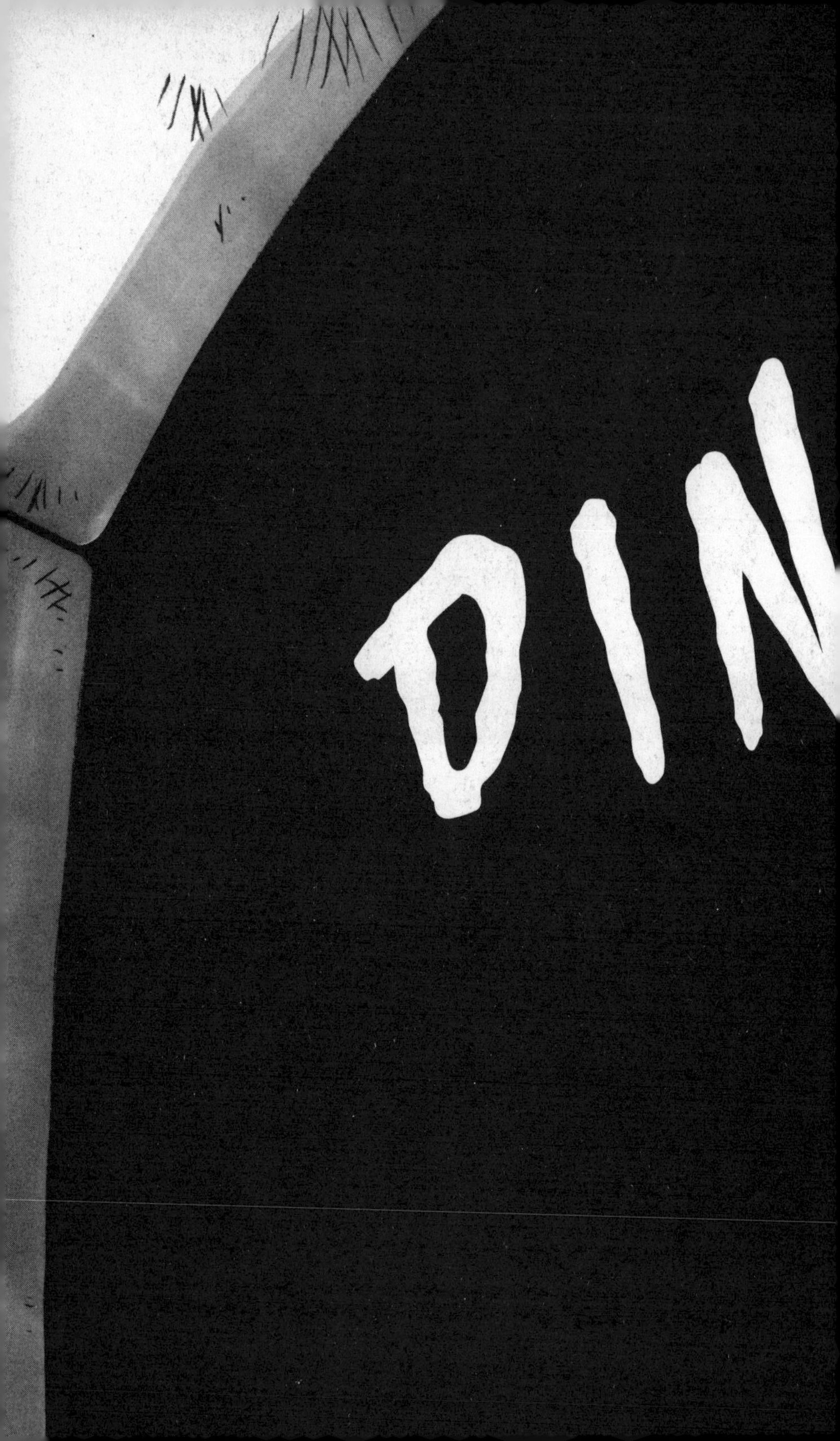
DIN

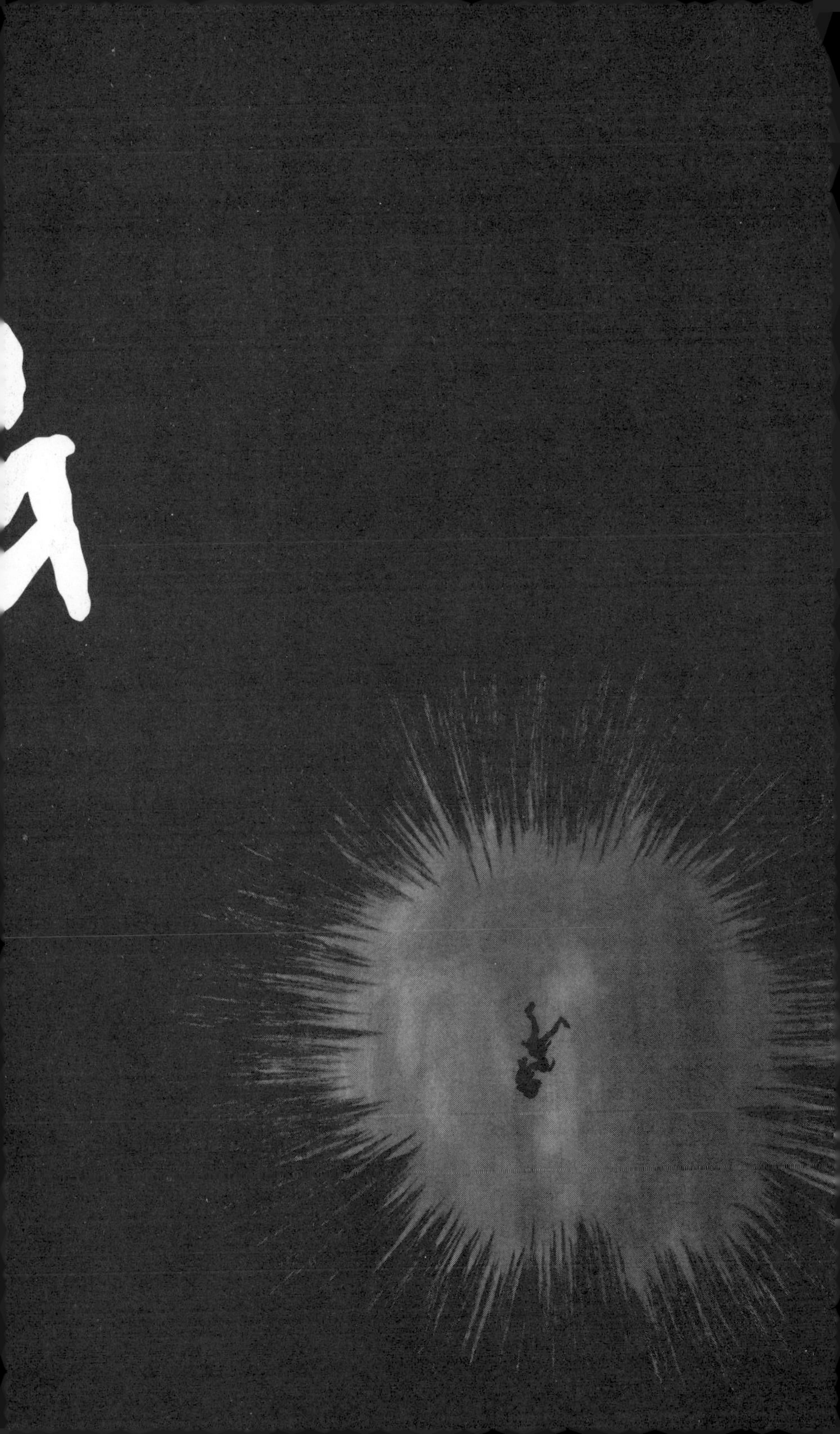

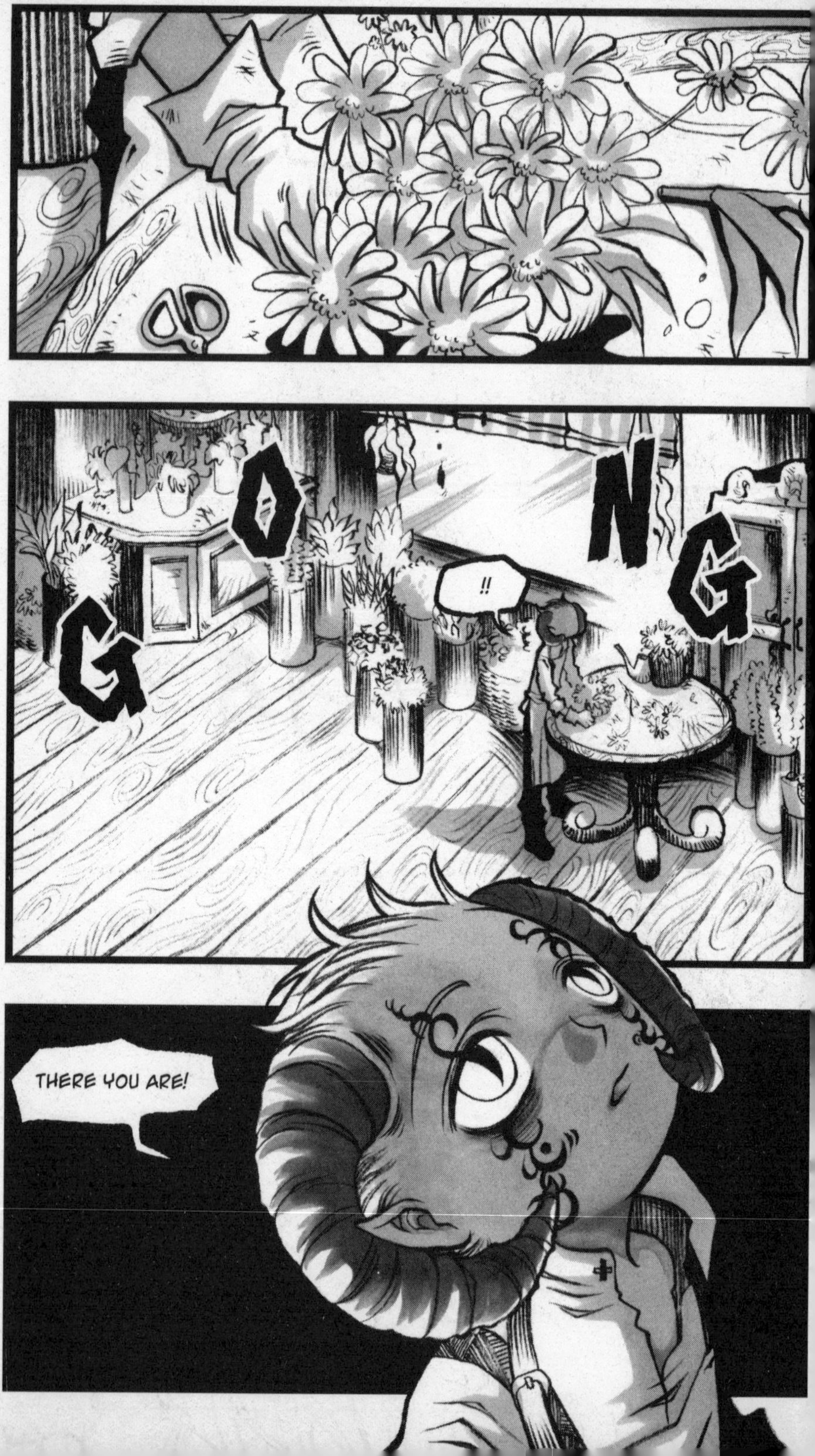
G
O
N
G
!!
THERE YOU ARE!

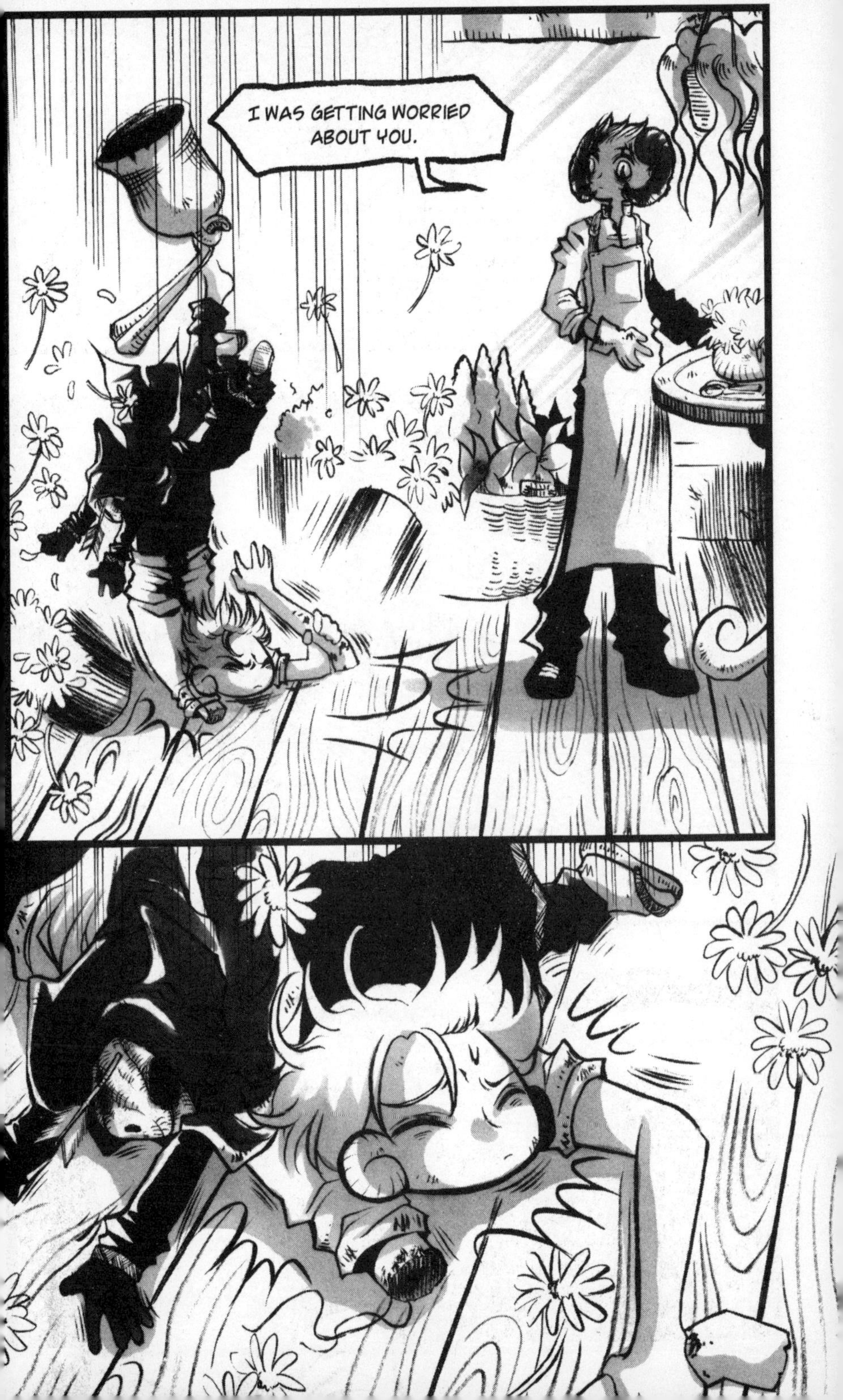
I WAS GETTING WORRIED ABOUT YOU.

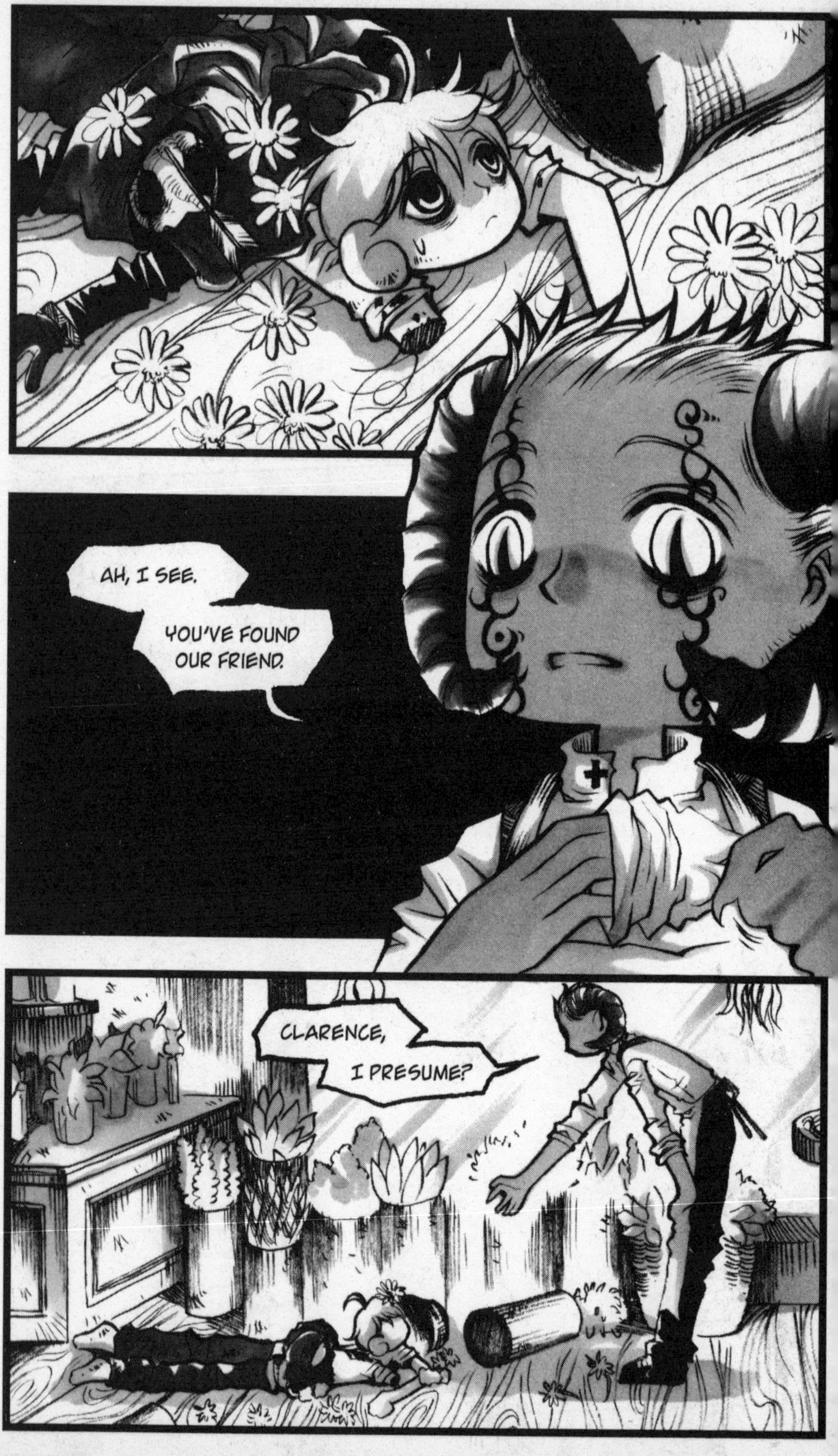
AH, I SEE.
YOU'VE FOUND OUR FRIEND.
CLARENCE,
I PRESUME?

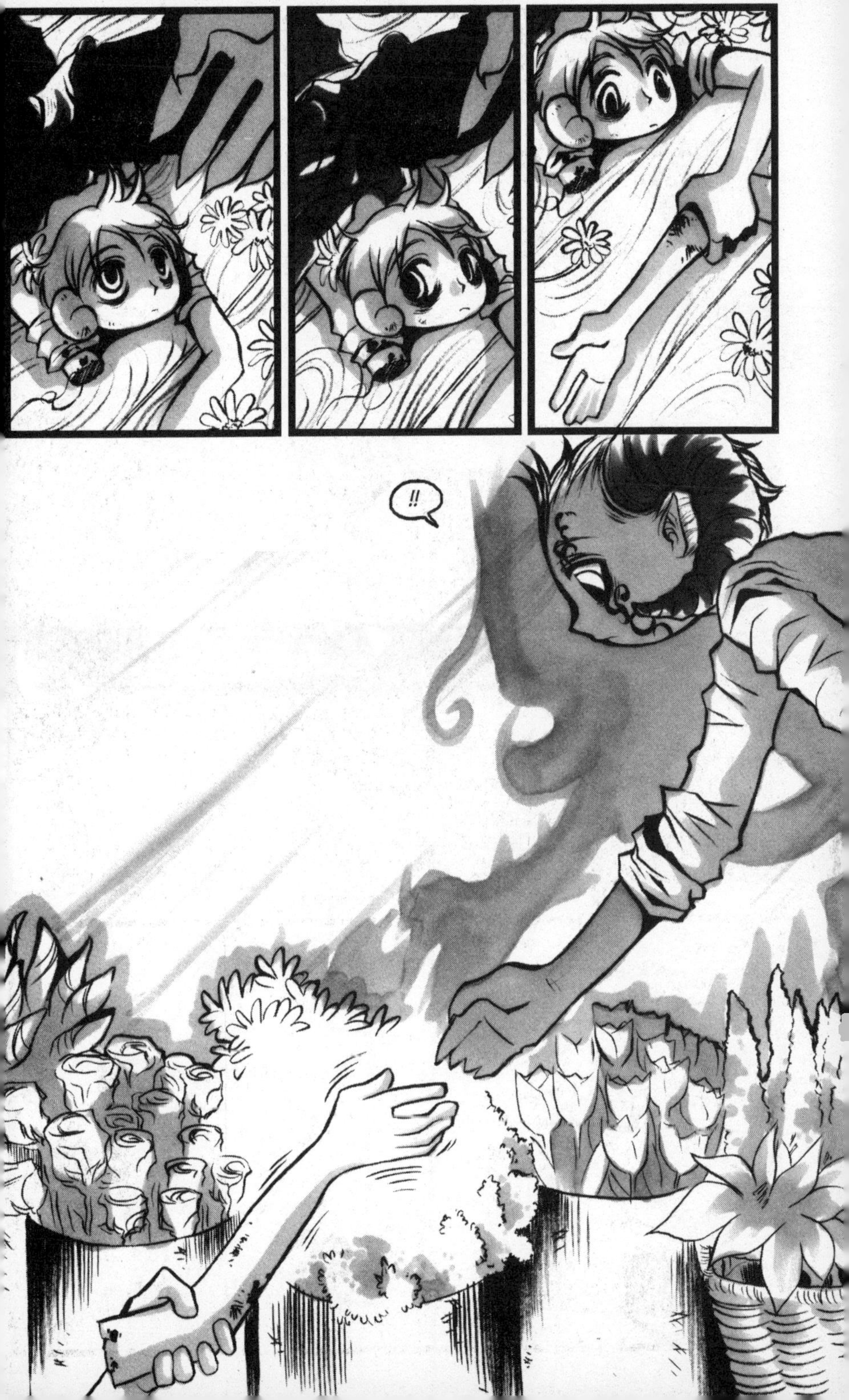
!!

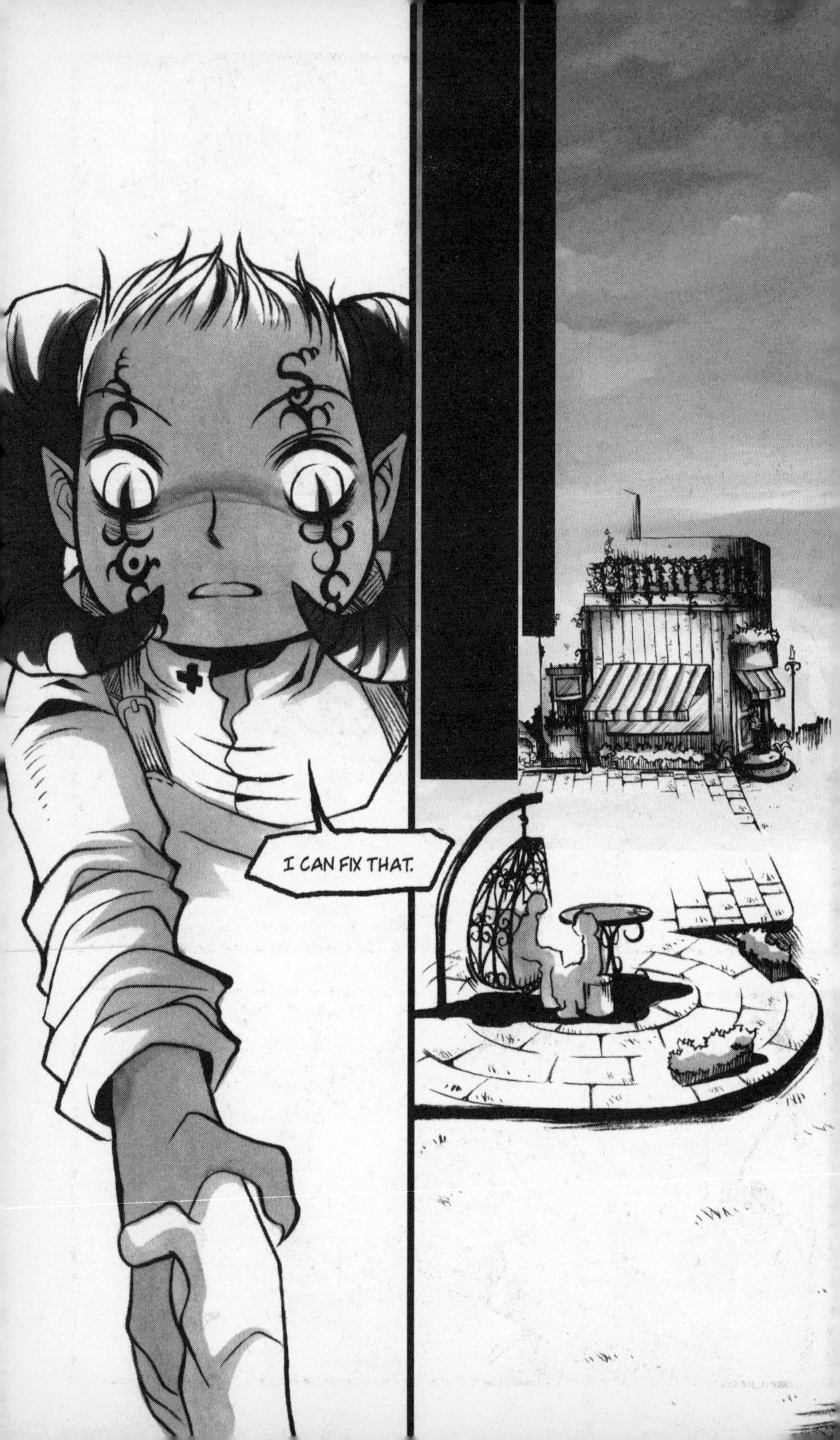
I CAN FIX THAT.

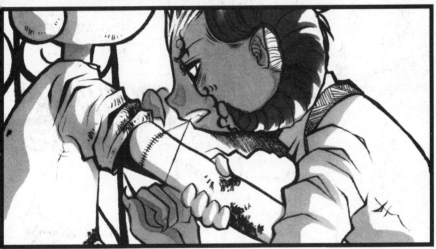

THERE.

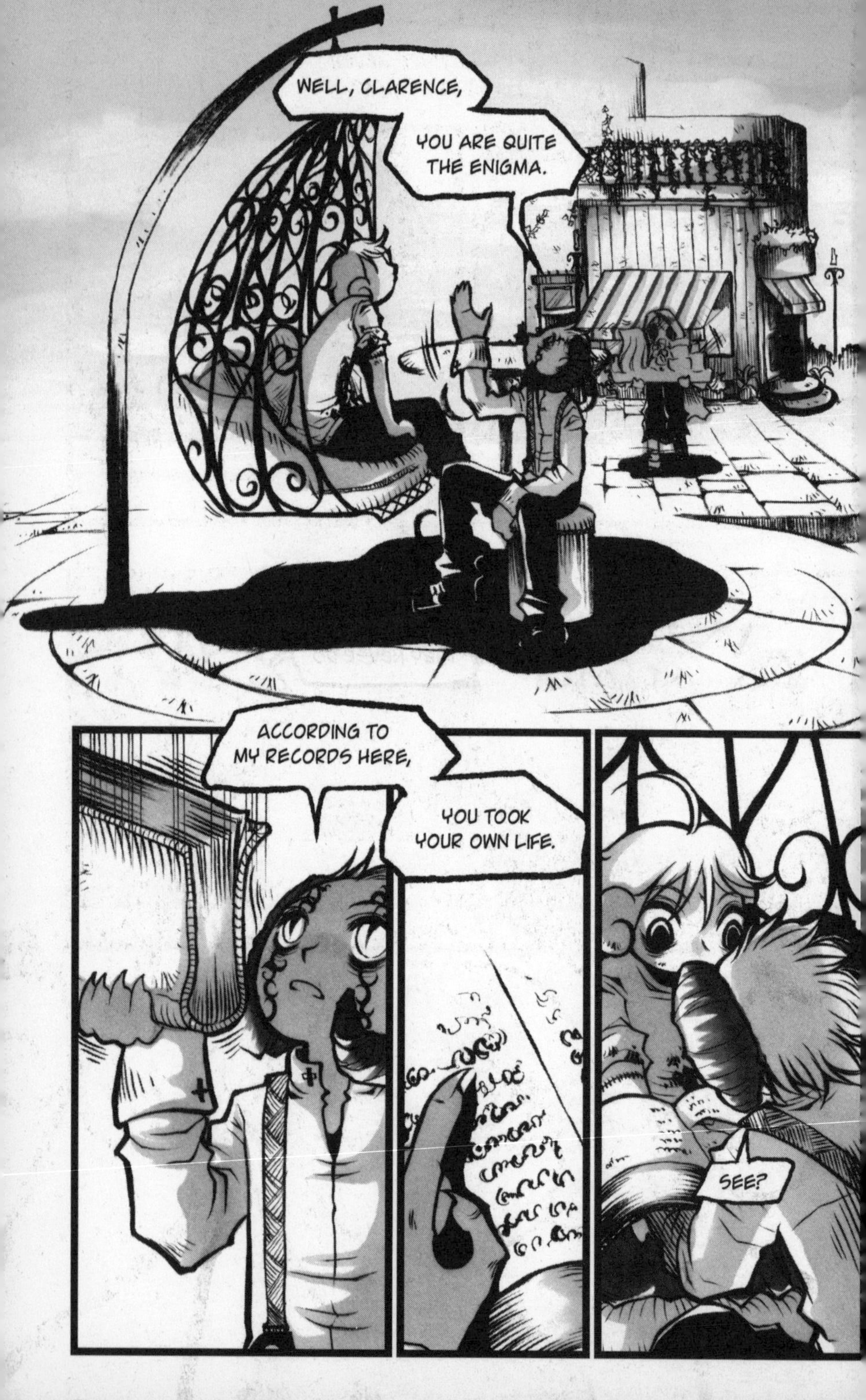
WELL, CLARENCE,
YOU ARE QUITE THE ENIGMA.
ACCORDING TO MY RECORDS HERE,
YOU TOOK YOUR OWN LIFE.
SEE?

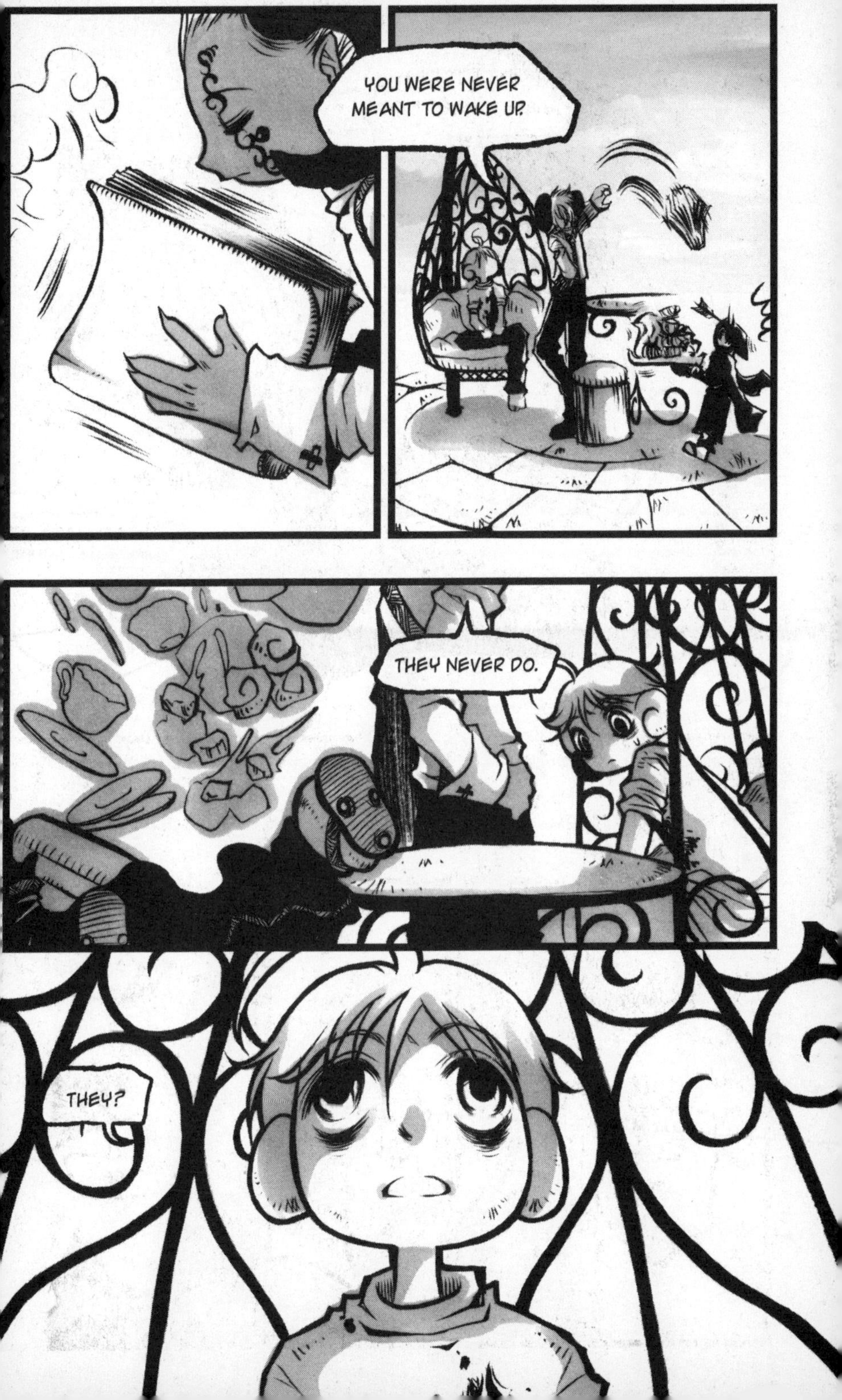
YOU WERE NEVER MEANT TO WAKE UP.
THEY NEVER DO.
THEY?

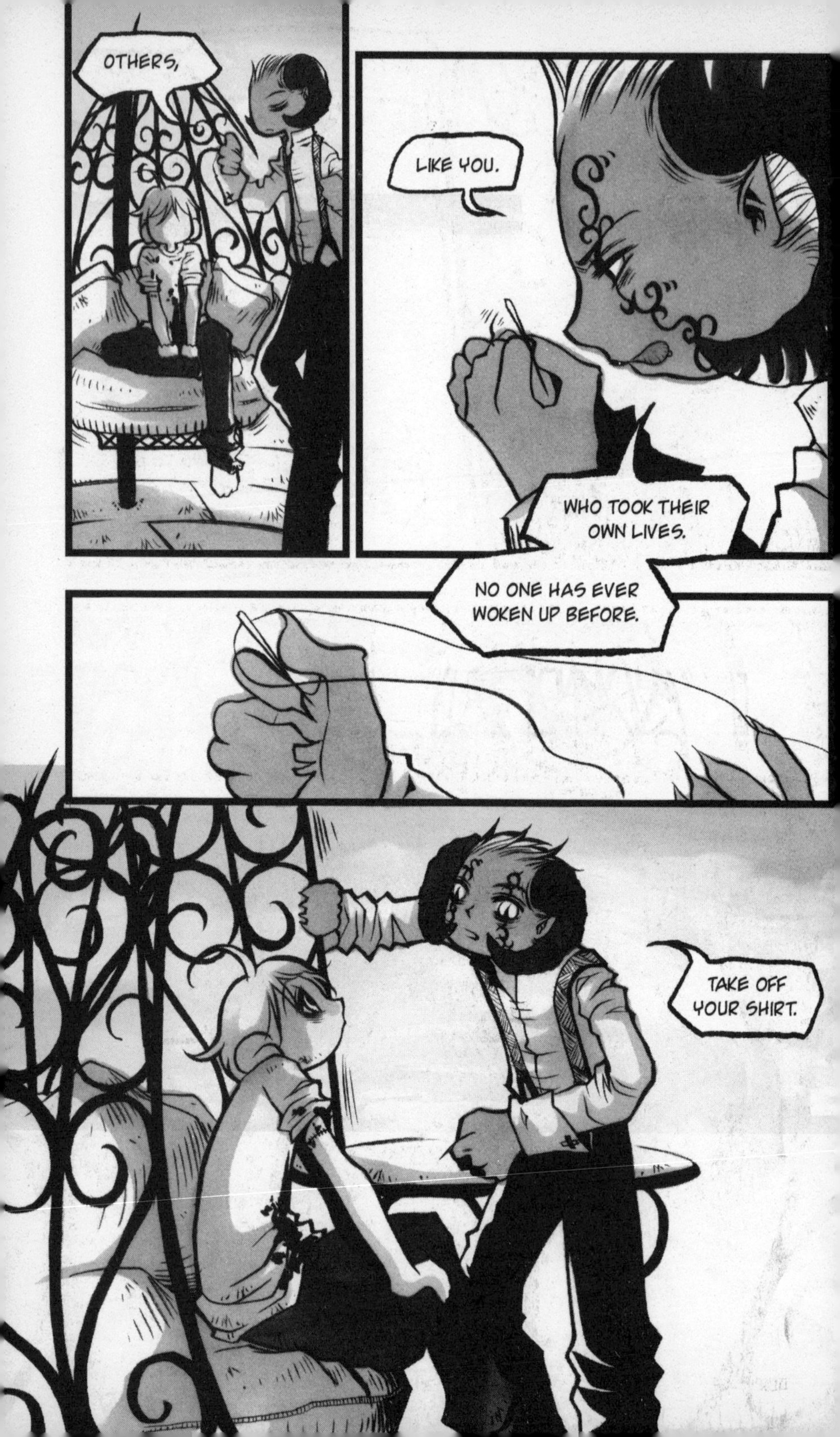
OTHERS,
LIKE YOU.
WHO TOOK THEIR OWN LIVES.
NO ONE HAS EVER WOKEN UP BEFORE.
TAKE OFF YOUR SHIRT.

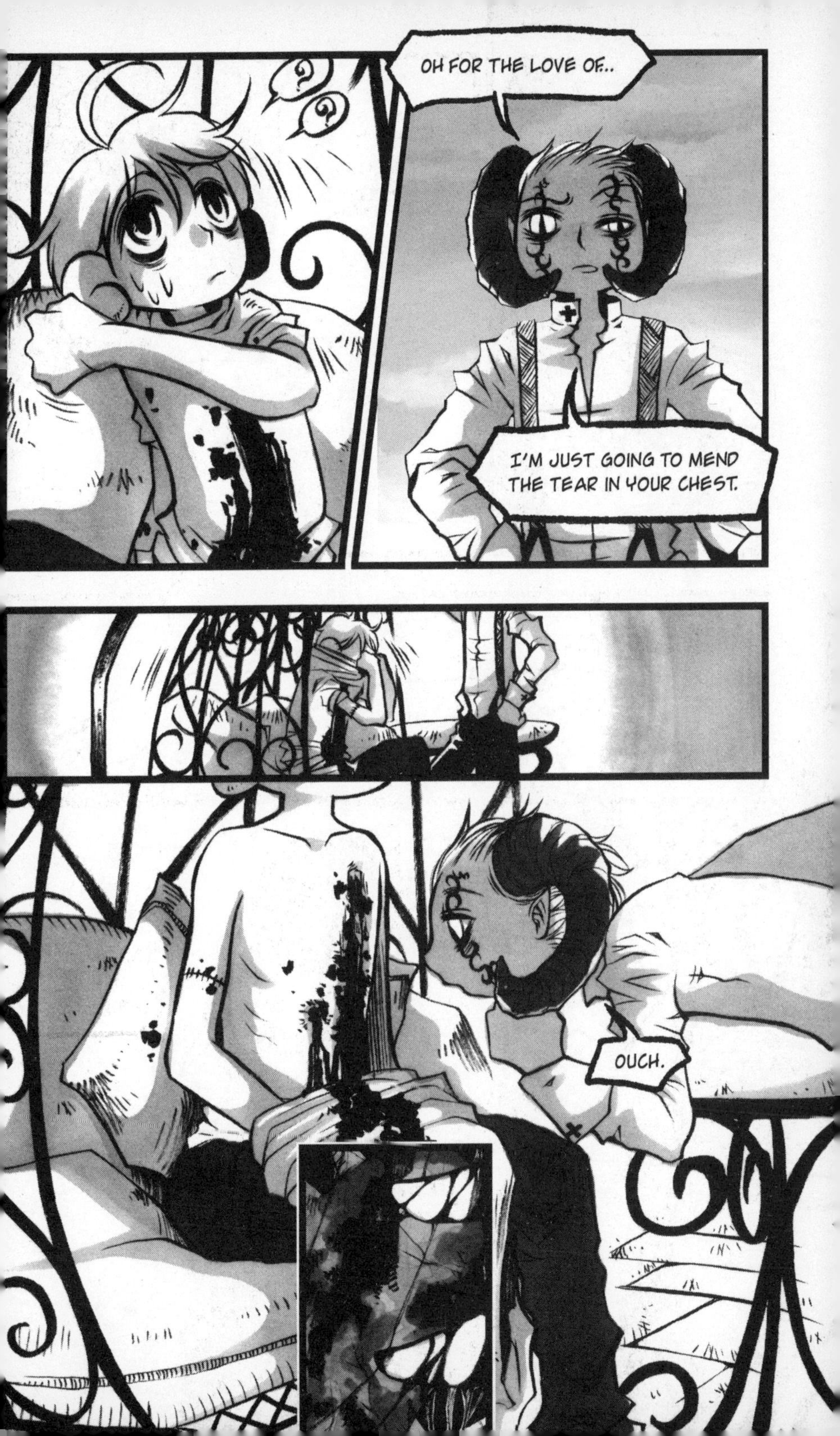
OH FOR THE LOVE OF...
I'M JUST GOING TO MEND THE TEAR IN YOUR CHEST.
OUCH.

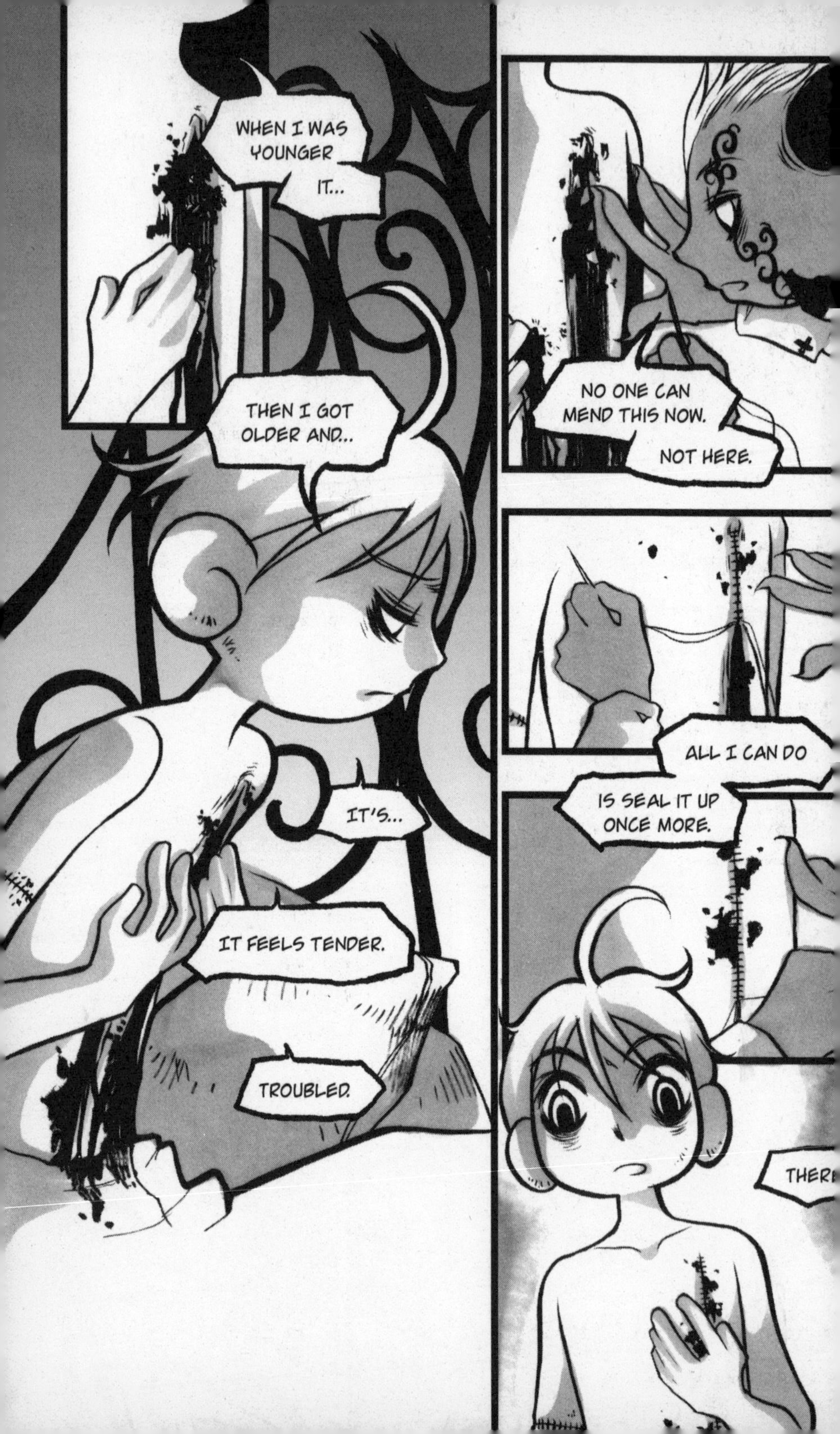
WHEN I WAS YOUNGER
IT...
THEN I GOT OLDER AND...
IT'S...
IT FEELS TENDER.
TROUBLED.
NO ONE CAN MEND THIS NOW.
NOT HERE.
ALL I CAN DO
IS SEAL IT UP ONCE MORE.

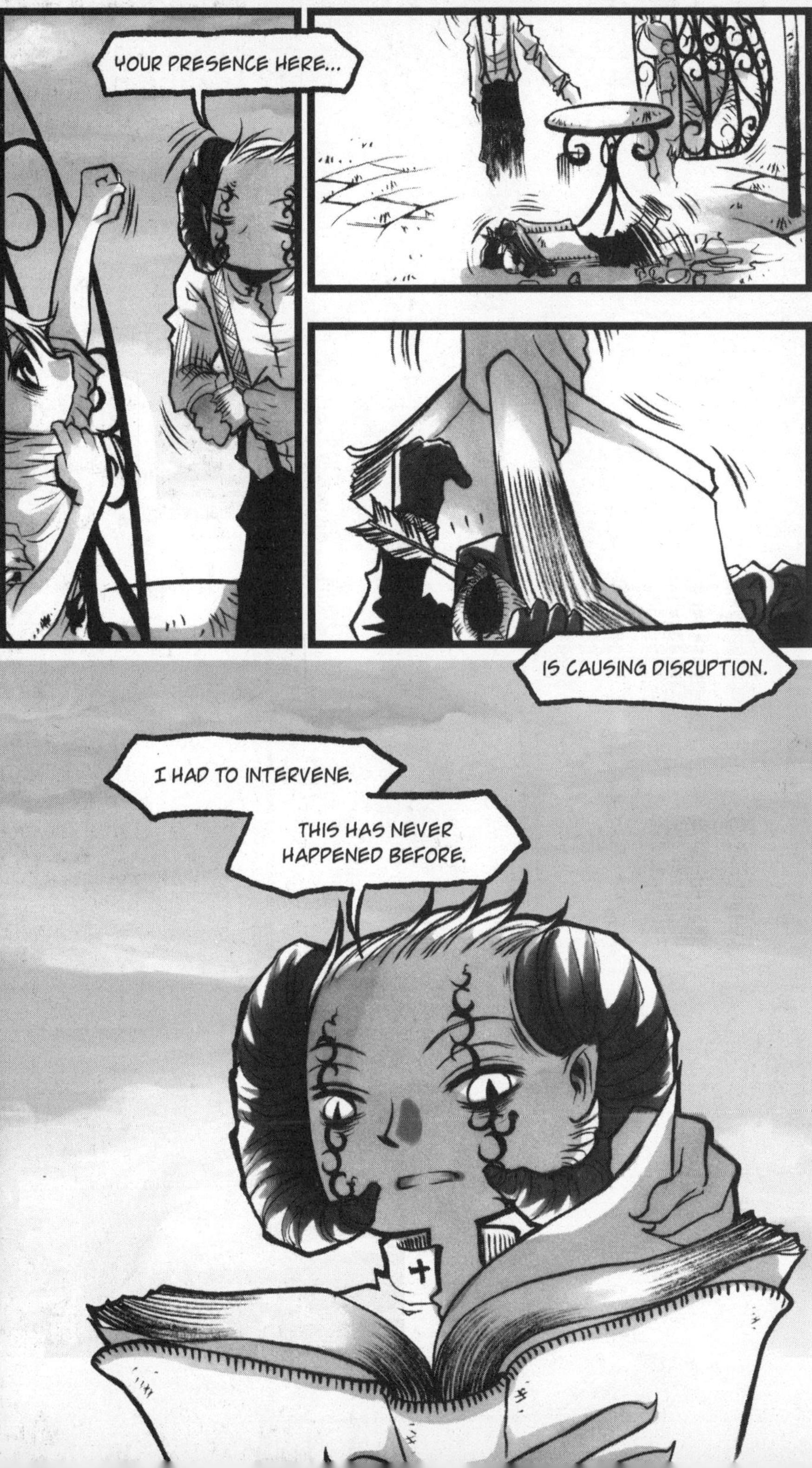
YOUR PRESENCE HERE...
IS CAUSING DISRUPTION.
I HAD TO INTERVENE.
THIS HAS NEVER HAPPENED BEFORE.

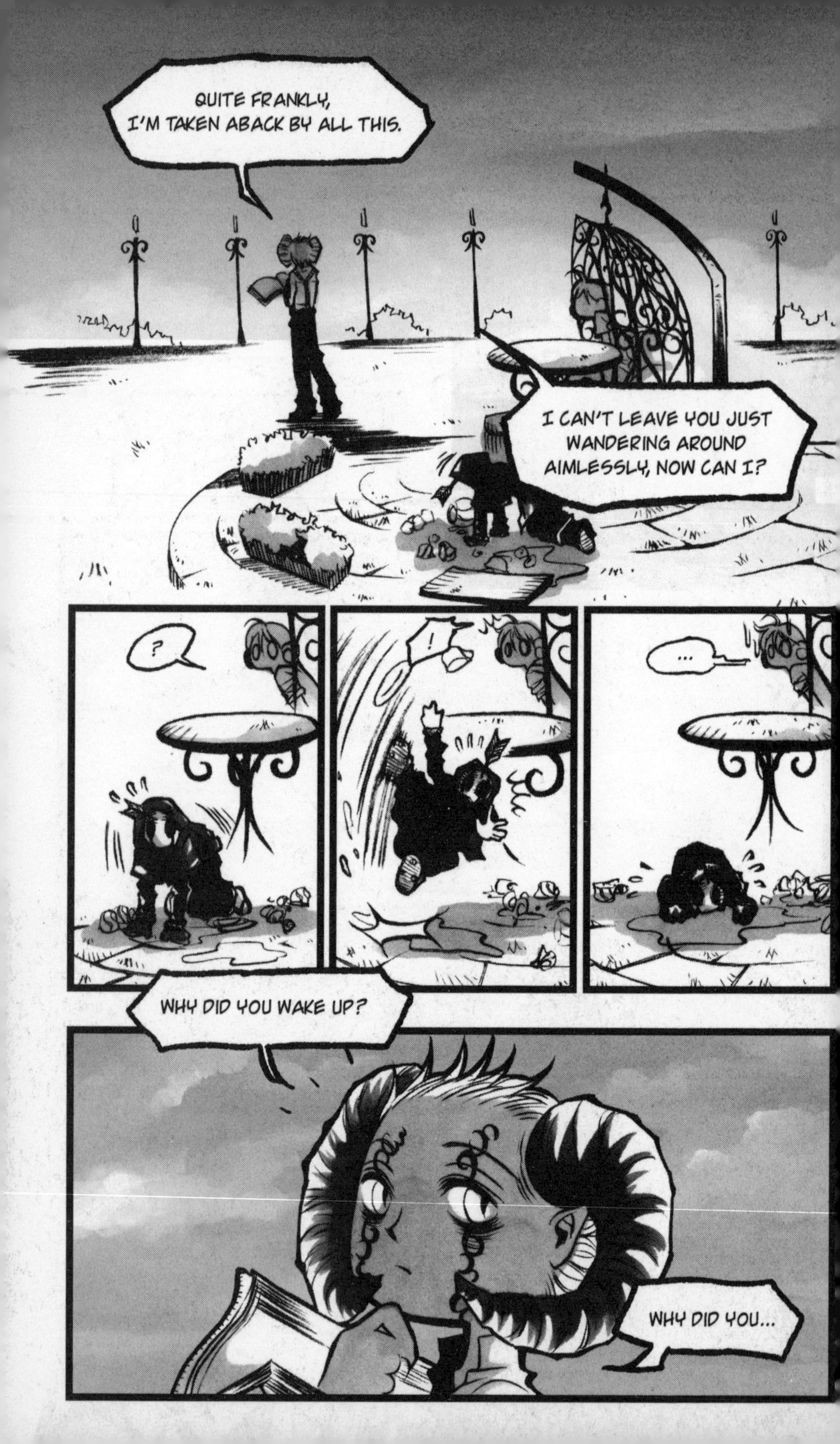
QUITE FRANKLY,
I'M TAKEN ABACK BY ALL THIS.
I CAN'T LEAVE YOU JUST WANDERING AROUND AIMLESSLY, NOW CAN I?
?
!
...
WHY DID YOU WAKE UP?
WHY DID YOU...

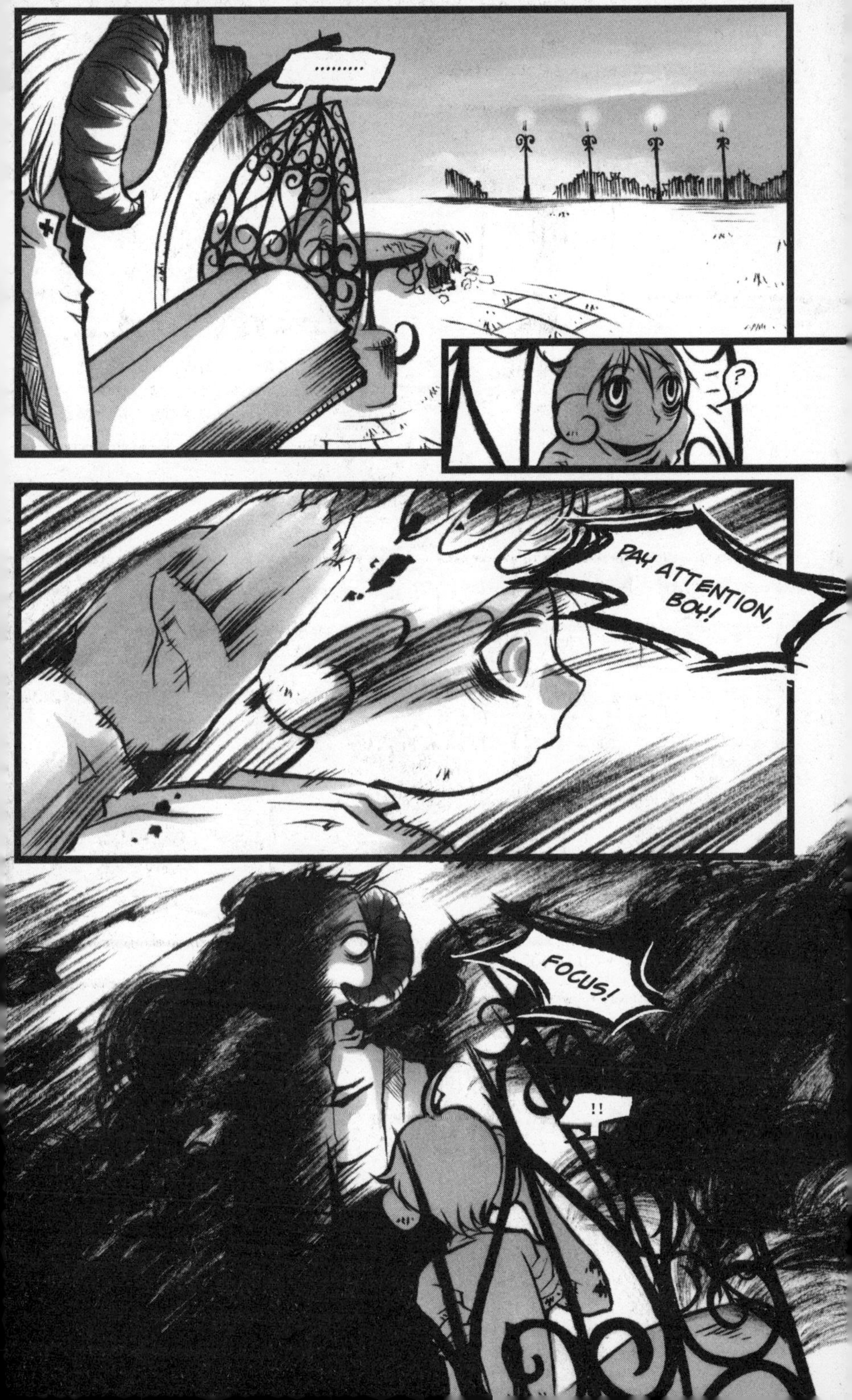
....
?
PAY ATTENTION, BOY!
FOCUS!
!!

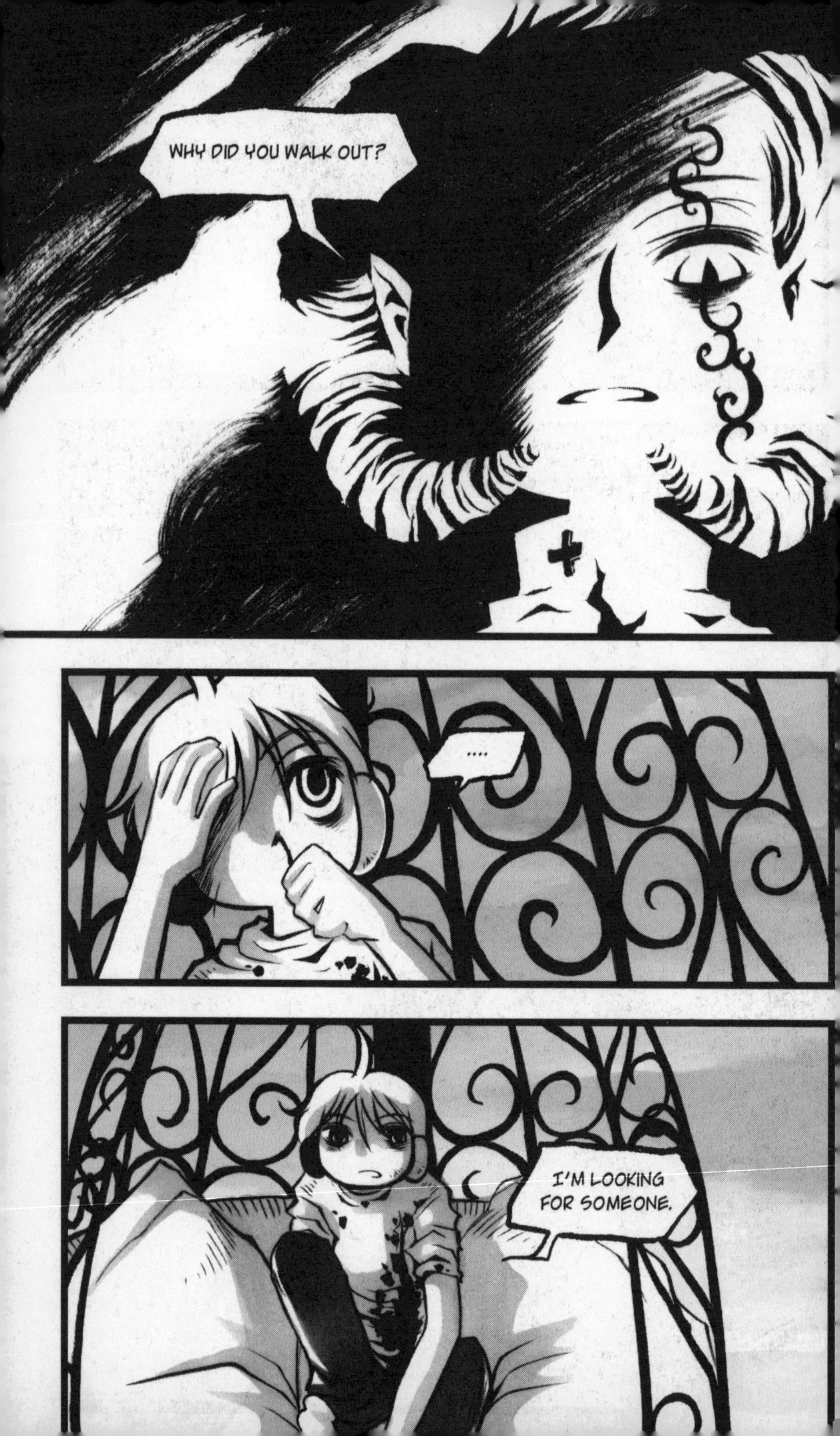
WHY DID YOU WALK OUT?
....
I'M LOOKING FOR SOMEONE.

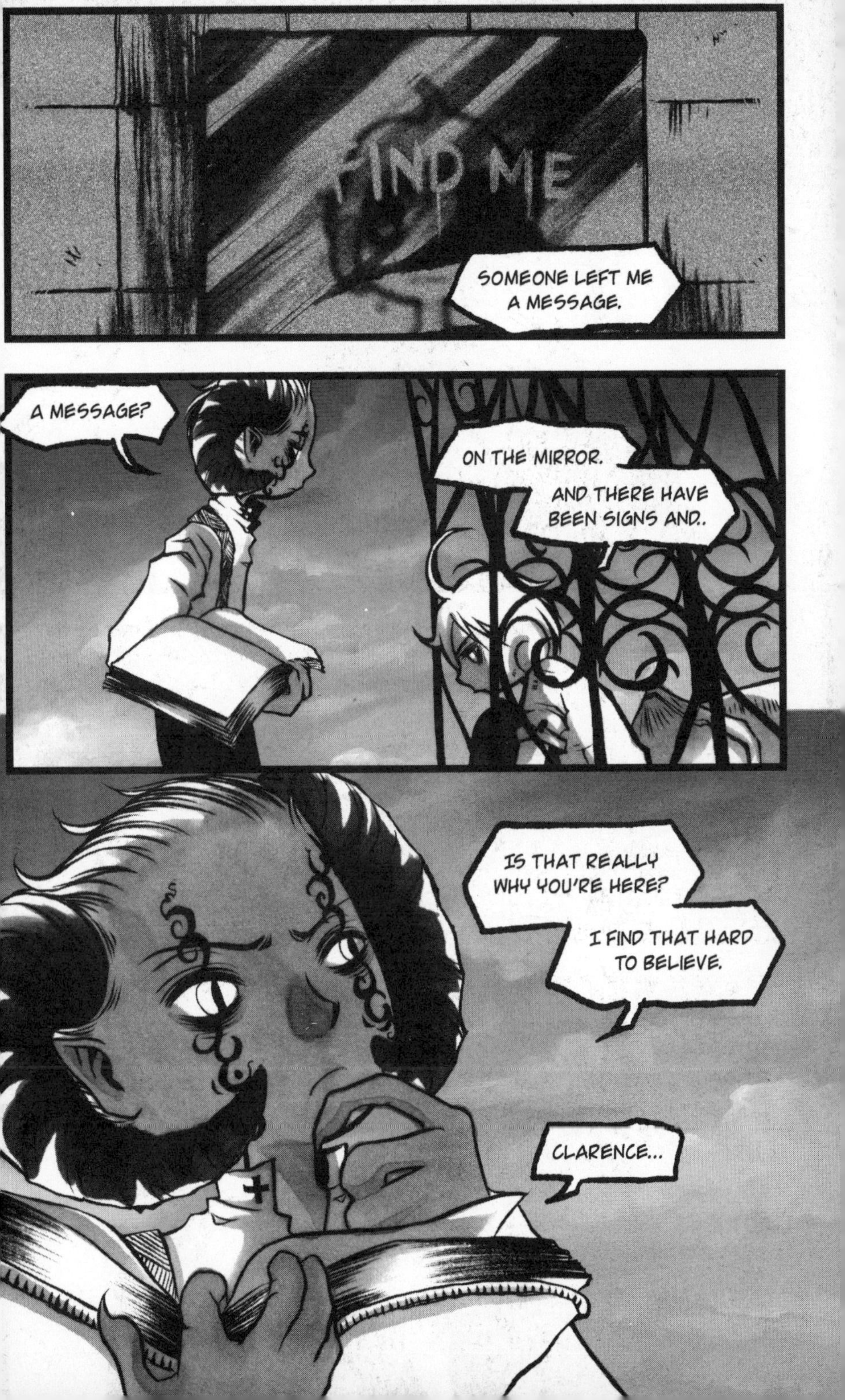
FIND ME
SOMEONE LEFT ME A MESSAGE.
A MESSAGE?
ON THE MIRROR.
AND THERE HAVE BEEN SIGNS AND..
IS THAT REALLY WHY YOU'RE HERE?
I FIND THAT HARD TO BELIEVE.
CLARENCE...

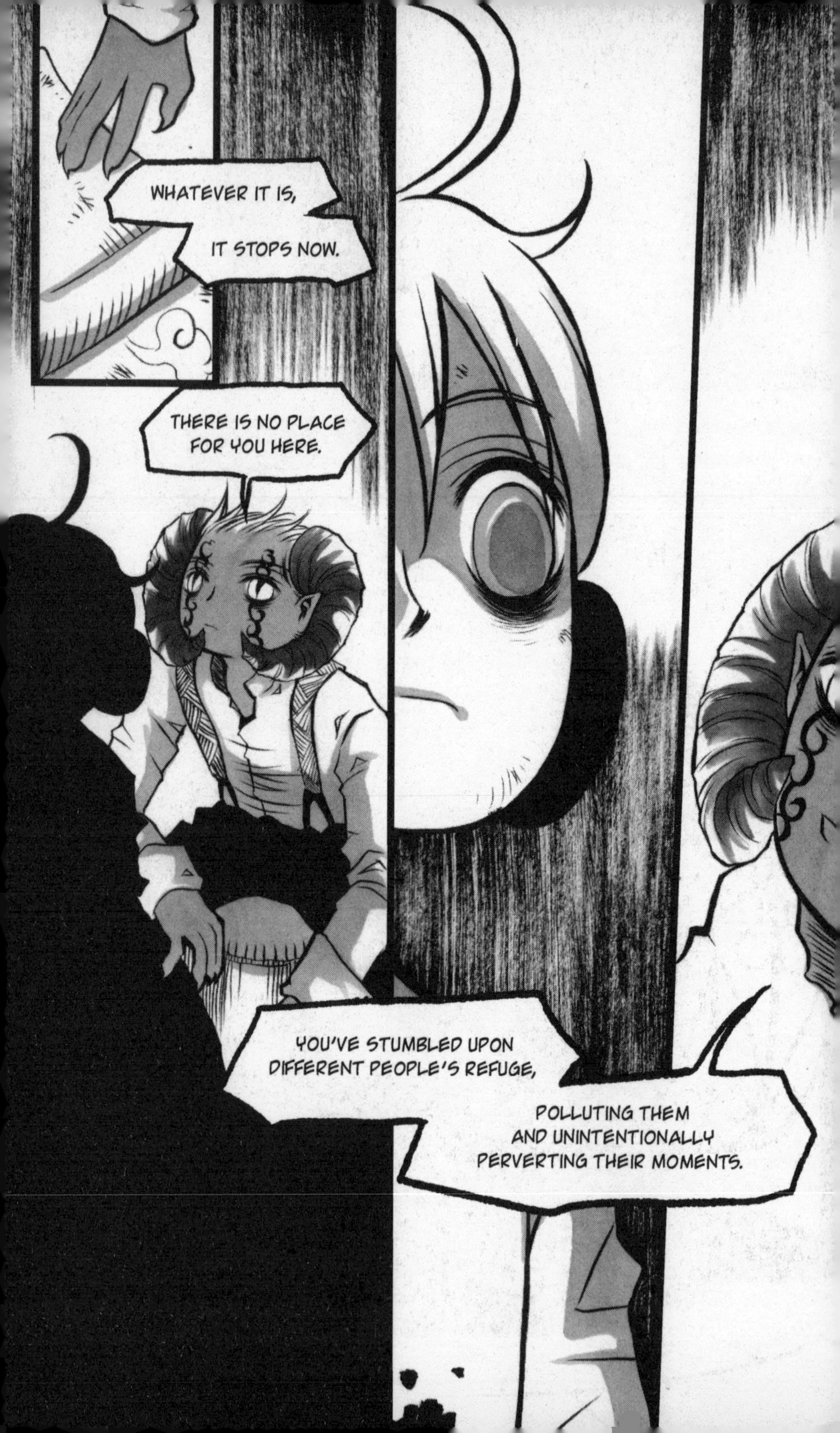
WHATEVER IT IS,
IT STOPS NOW.
THERE IS NO PLACE FOR YOU HERE.
YOU'VE STUMBLED UPON DIFFERENT PEOPLE'S REFUGE,
POLLUTING THEM AND UNINTENTIONALLY PERVERTING THEIR MOMENTS.

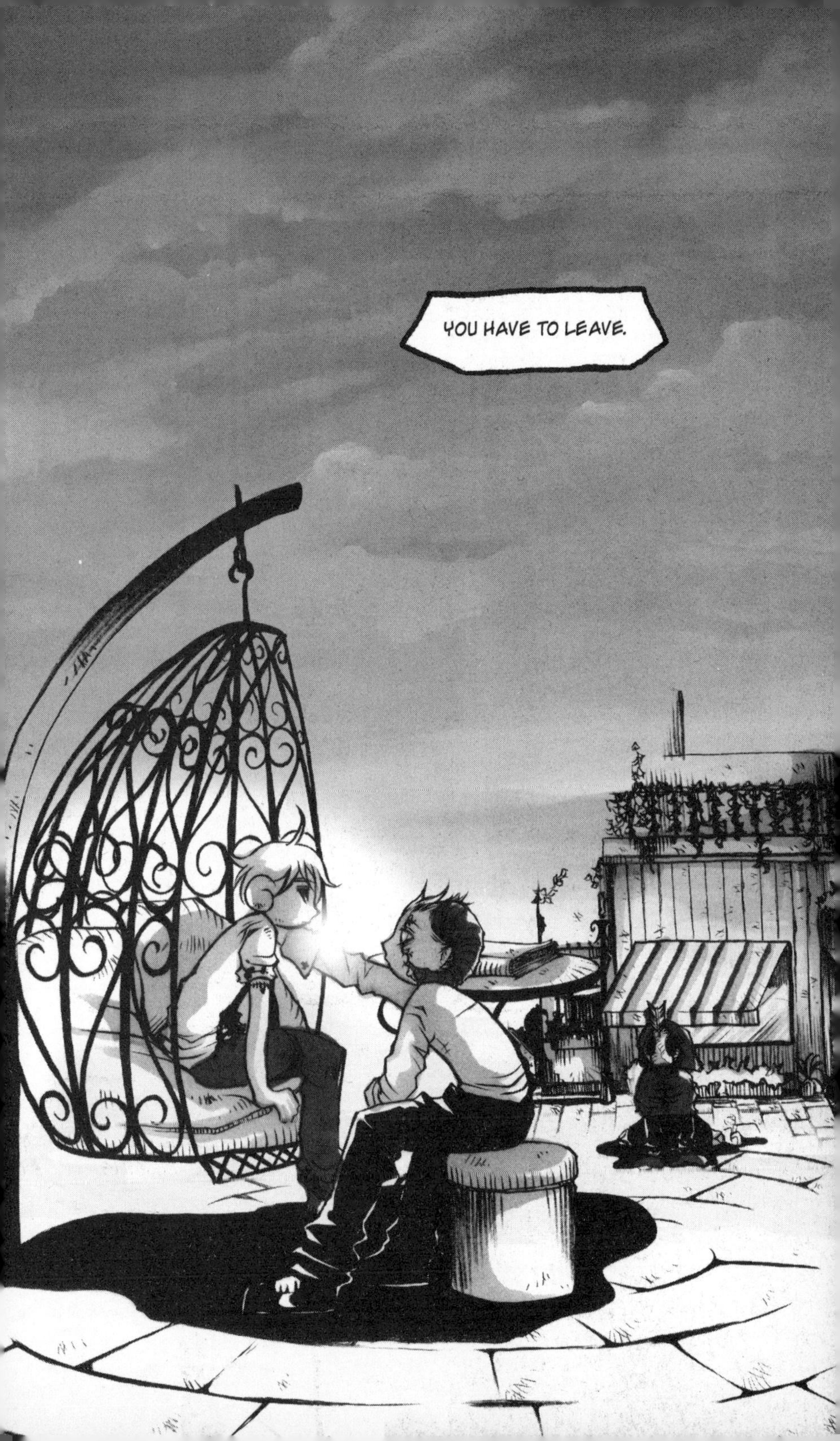
YOU HAVE TO LEAVE.

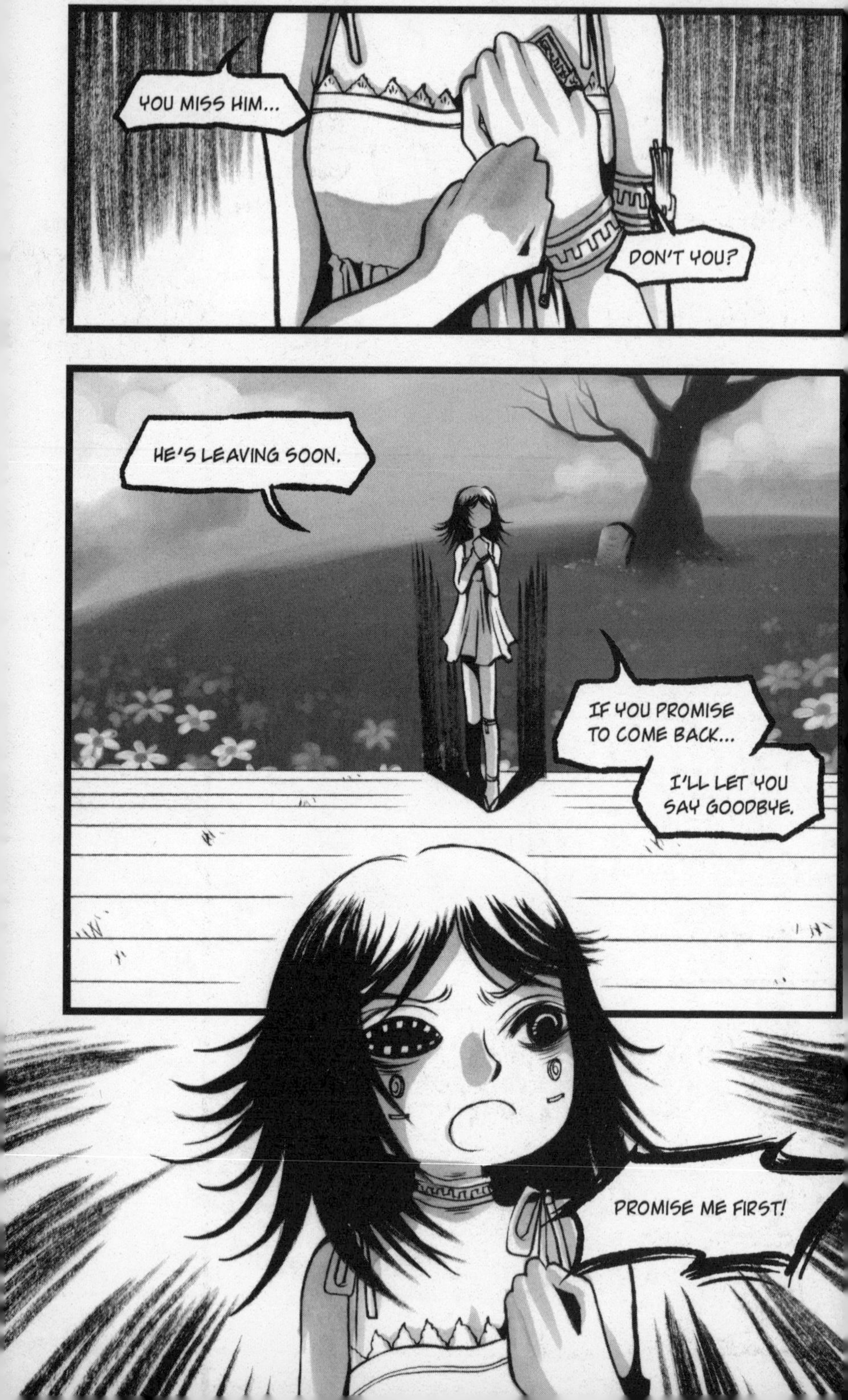
YOU MISS HIM...
DON'T YOU?
HE'S LEAVING SOON.
IF YOU PROMISE TO COME BACK...
I'LL LET YOU SAY GOODBYE.
PROMISE ME FIRST!

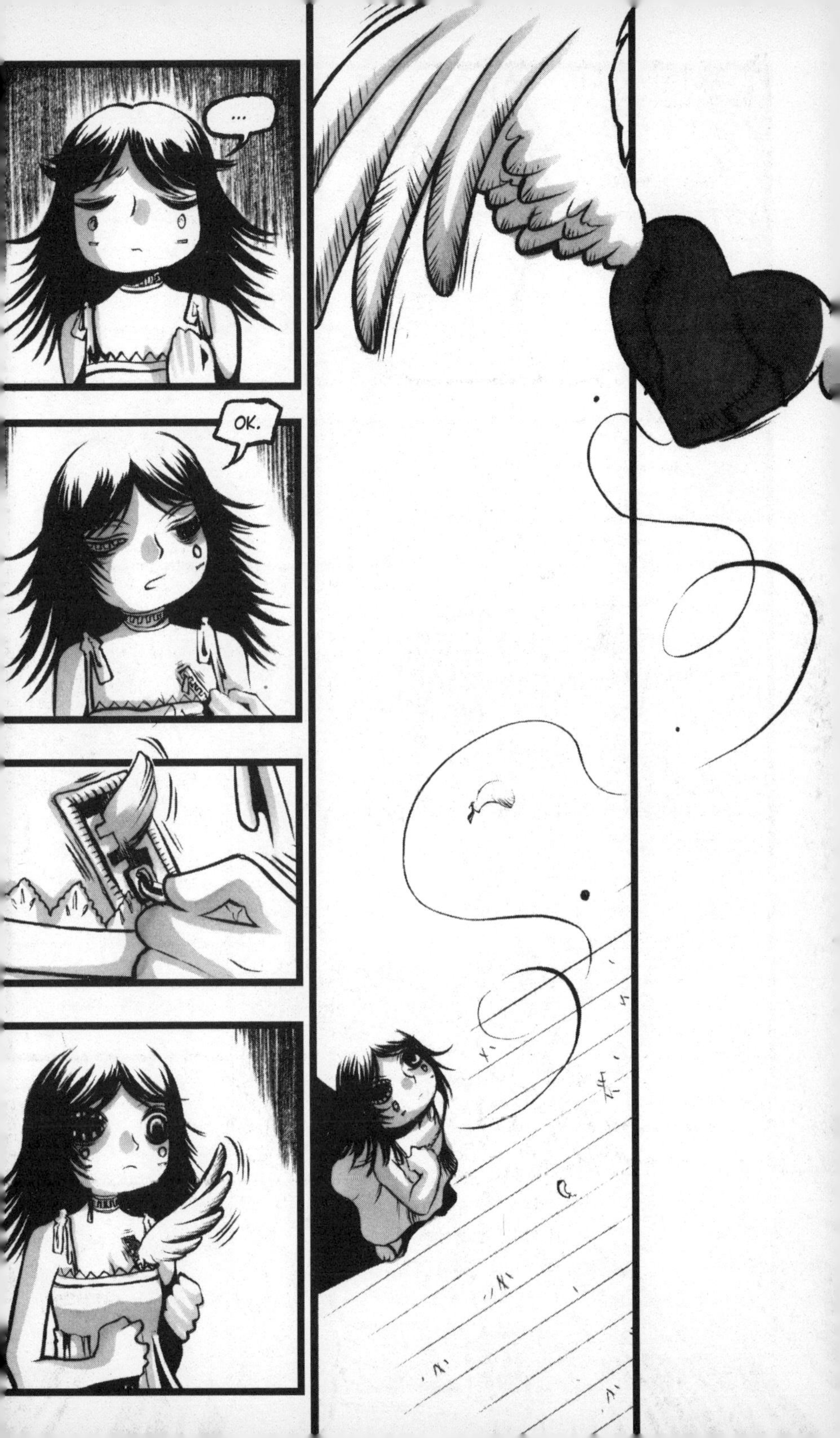
...
OK.

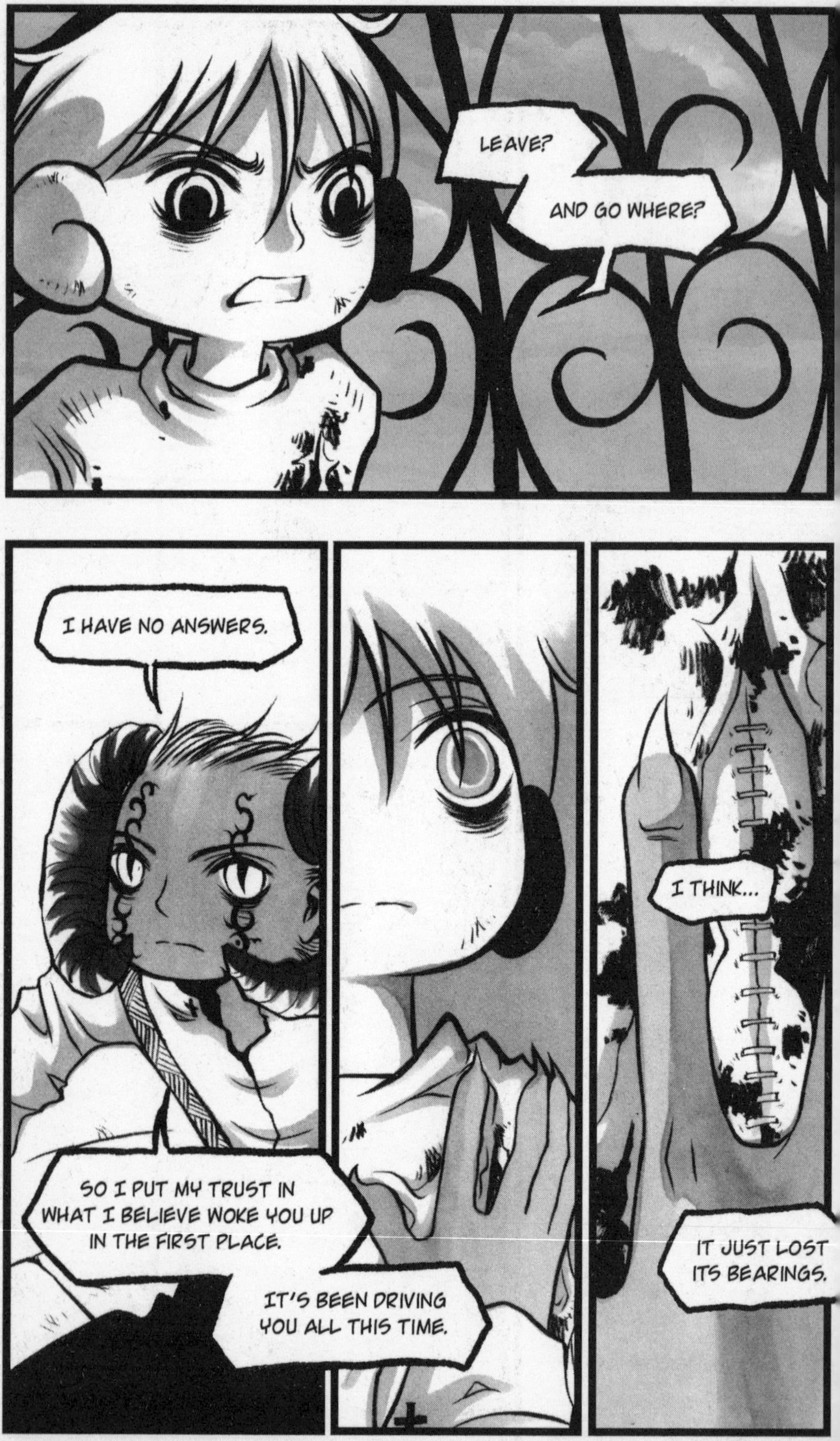
LEAVE?
AND GO WHERE?
I HAVE NO ANSWERS.
SO I PUT MY TRUST IN WHAT I BELIEVE WOKE YOU UP IN THE FIRST PLACE.
IT'S BEEN DRIVING YOU ALL THIS TIME.
I THINK...
IT JUST LOST ITS BEARINGS.

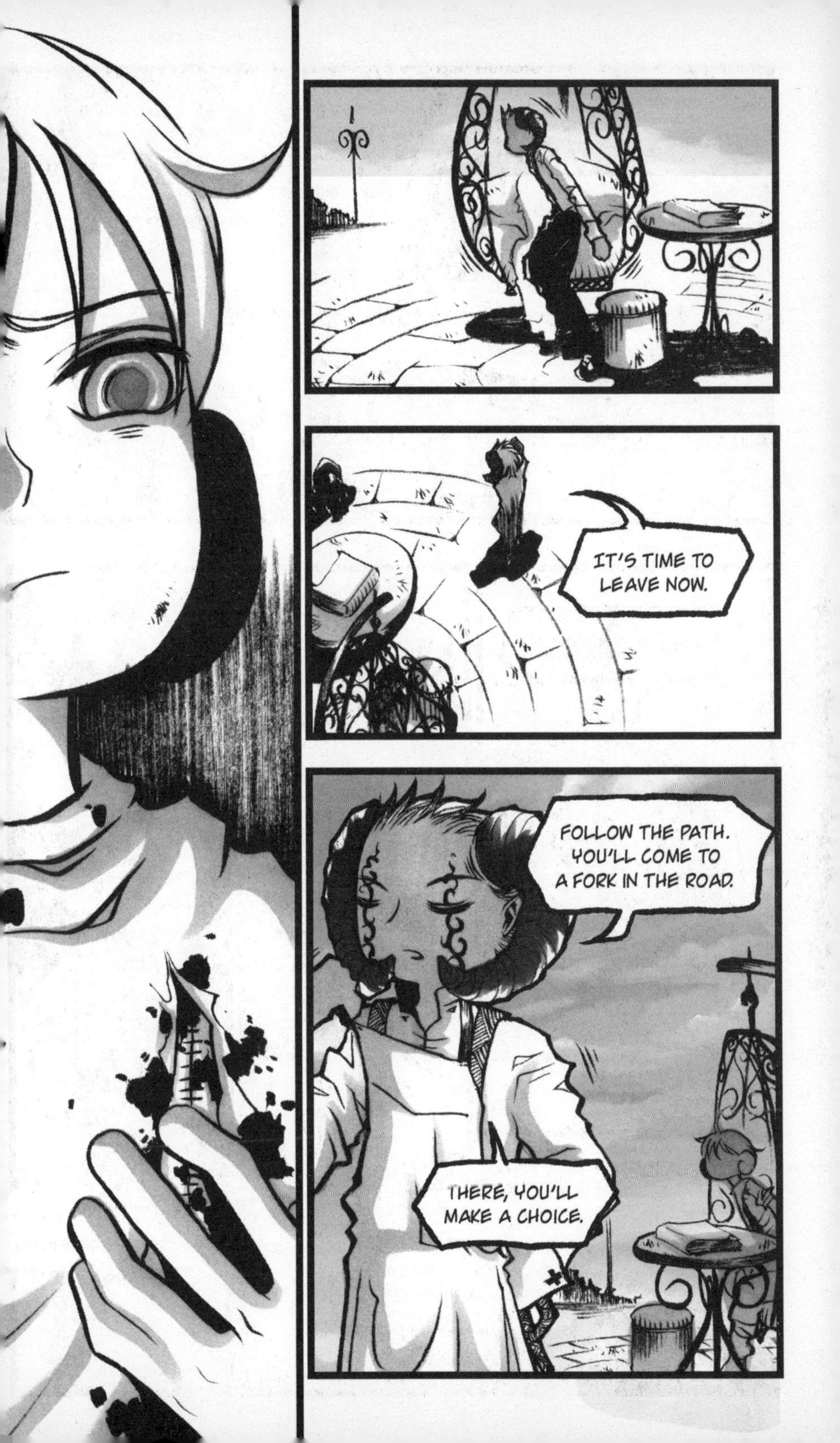
IT'S TIME TO LEAVE NOW.
FOLLOW THE PATH. YOU'LL COME TO A FORK IN THE ROAD.
THERE, YOU'LL MAKE A CHOICE.

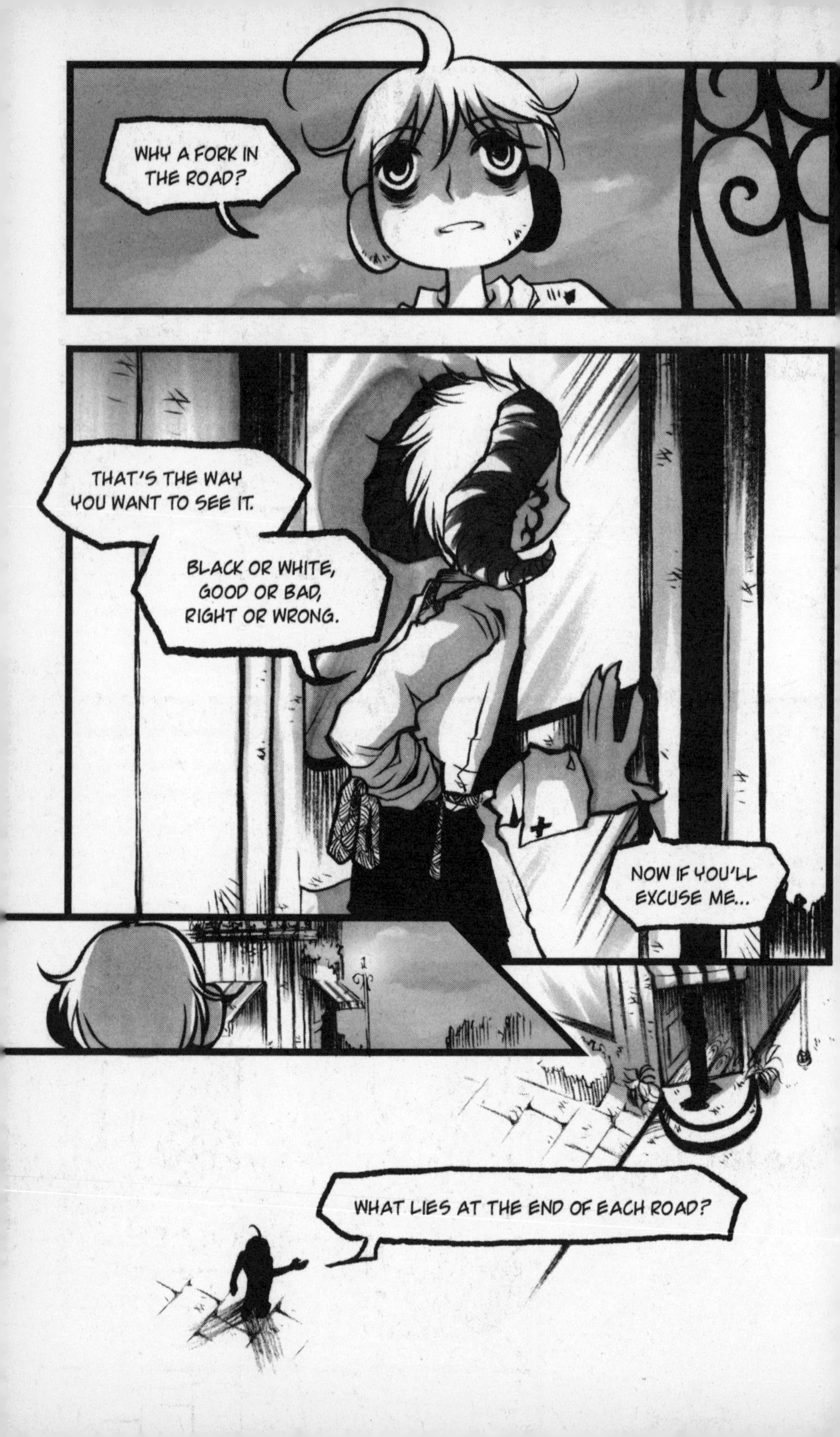
WHY A FORK IN THE ROAD?
THAT'S THE WAY YOU WANT TO SEE IT.
BLACK OR WHITE, GOOD OR BAD, RIGHT OR WRONG.
NOW IF YOU'LL EXCUSE ME...
WHAT LIES AT THE END OF EACH ROAD?

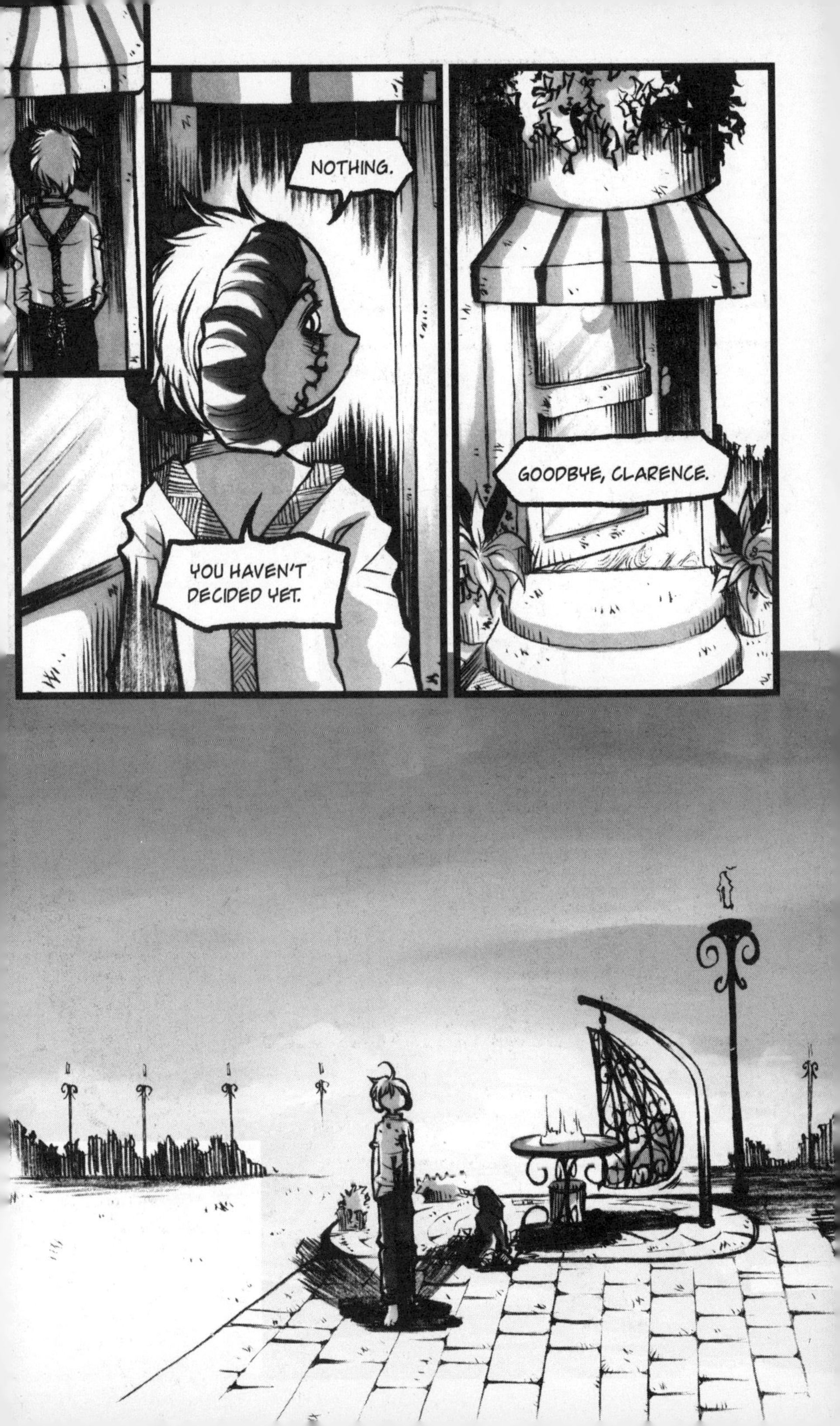
NOTHING.
YOU HAVEN'T DECIDED YET.
GOODBYE, CLARENCE.

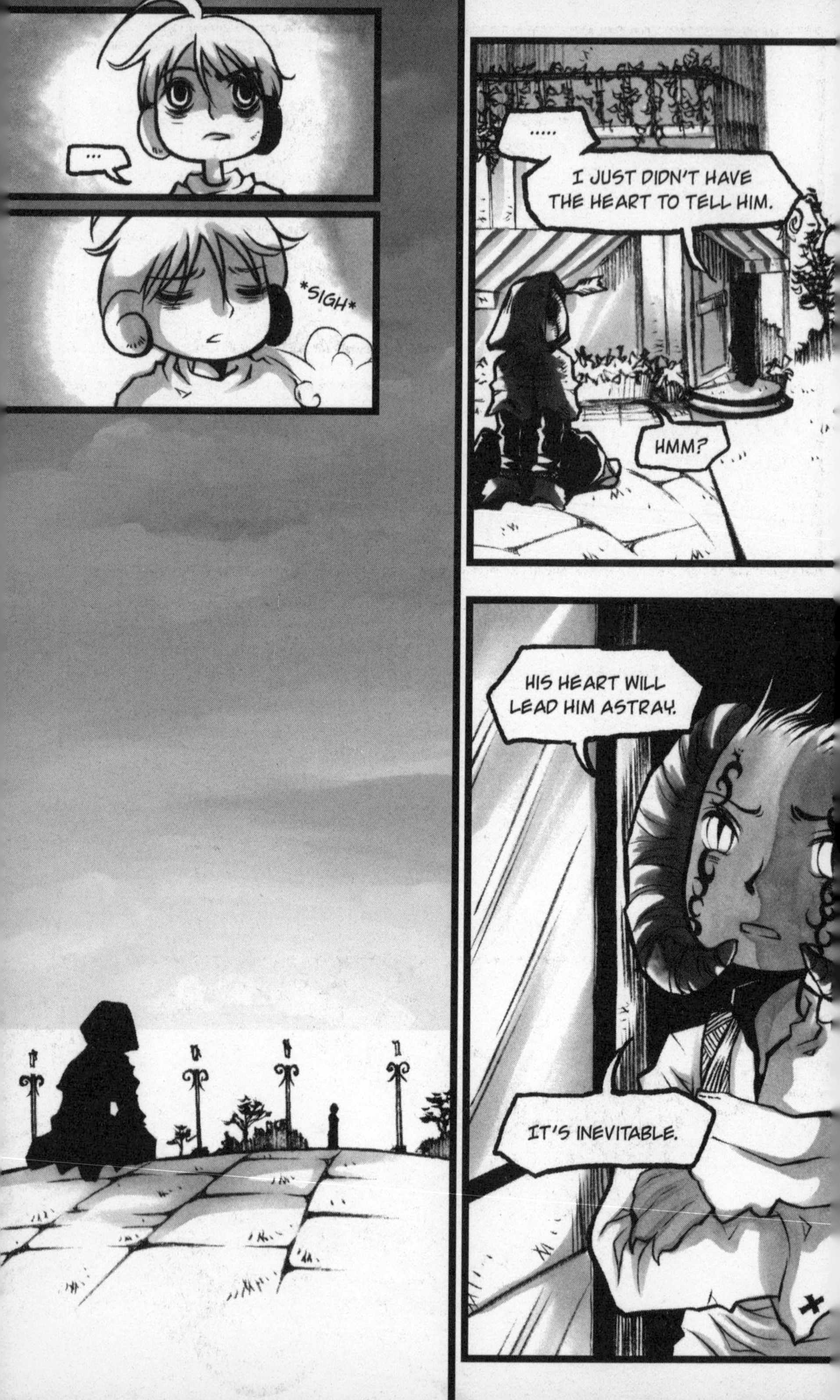
...
SIGH
.....
I JUST DIDN'T HAVE THE HEART TO TELL HIM.
HMM?
HIS HEART WILL LEAD HIM ASTRAY.
IT'S INEVITABLE.

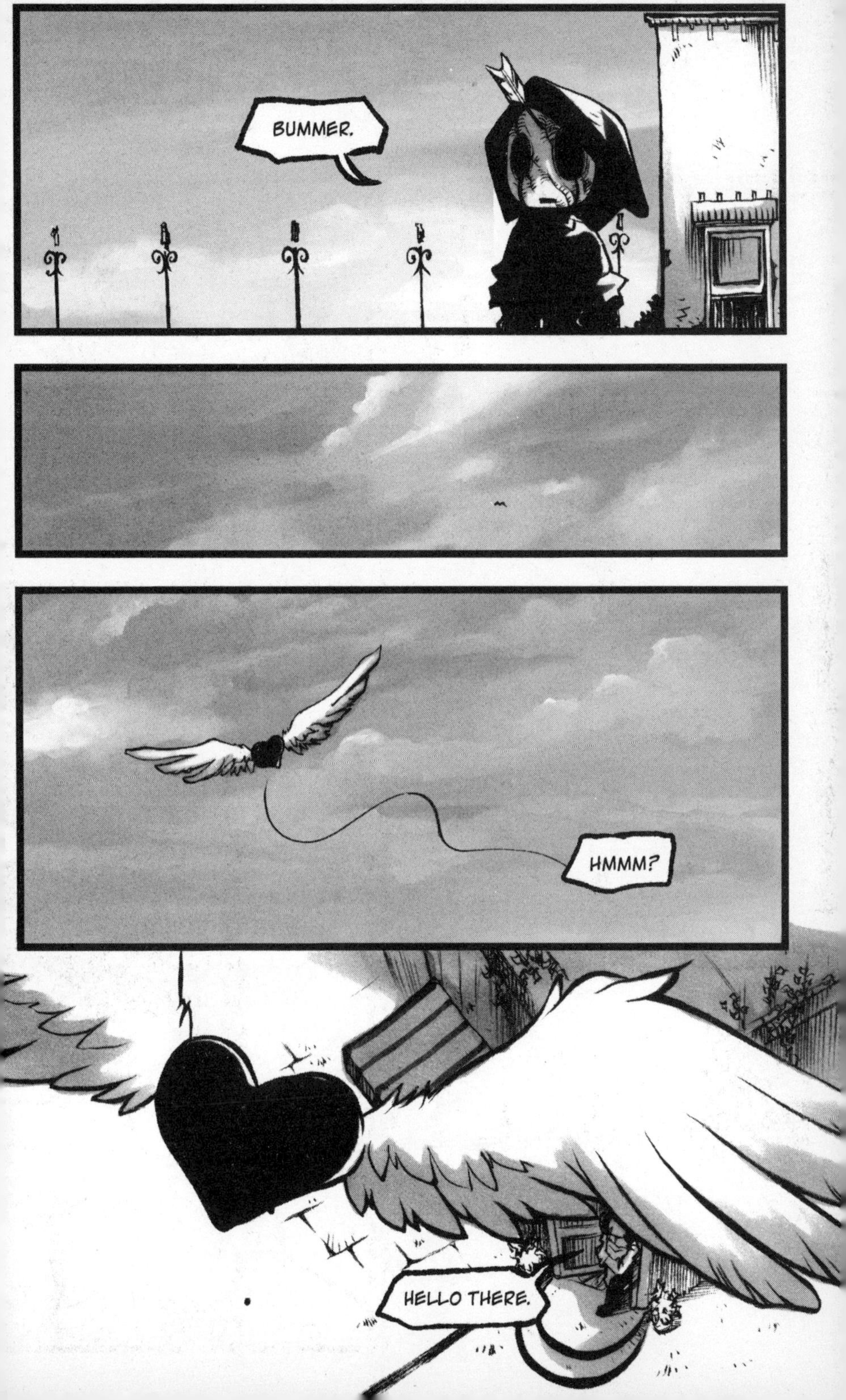
BUMMER.
HMMM?
HELLO THERE.

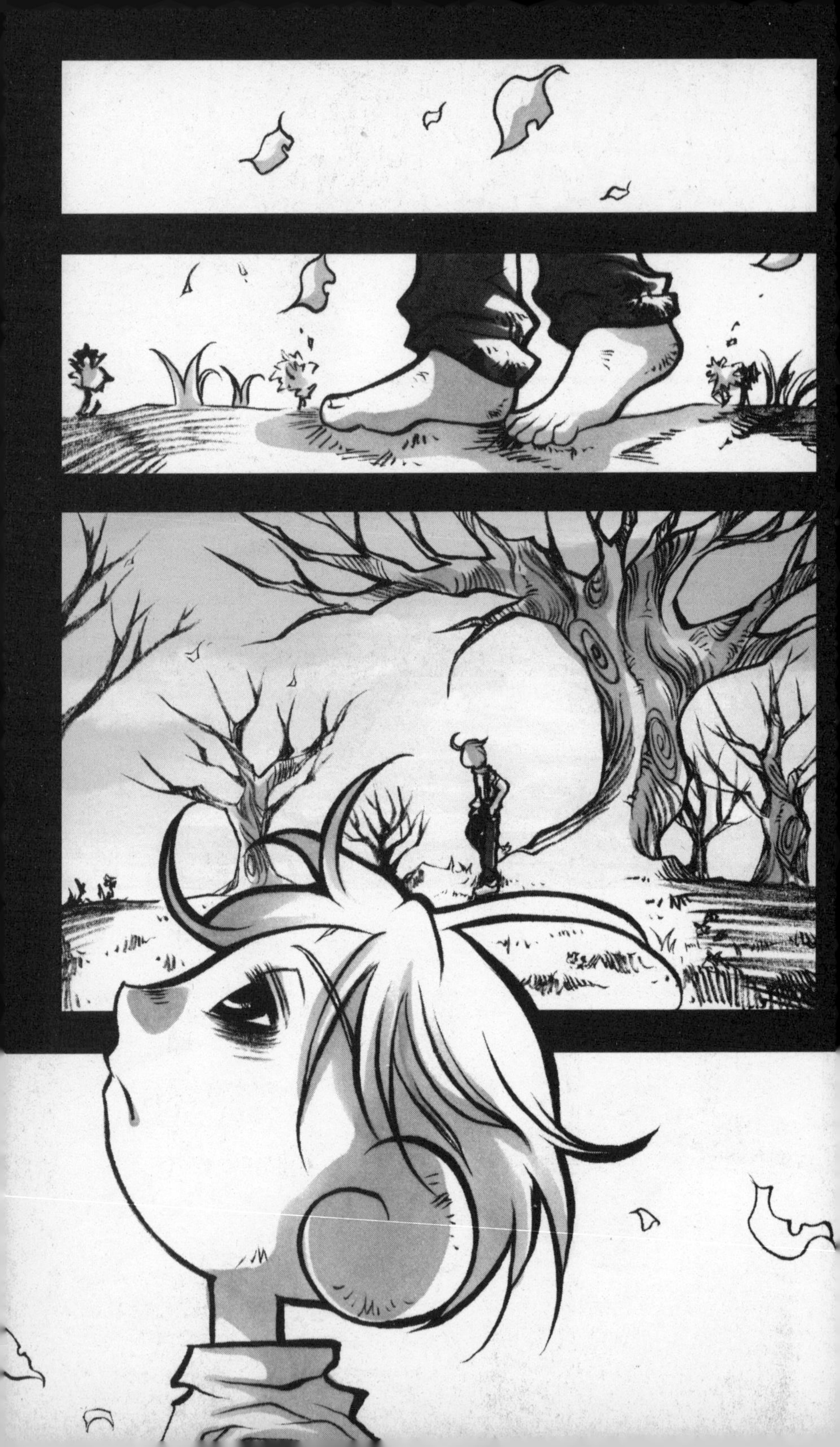

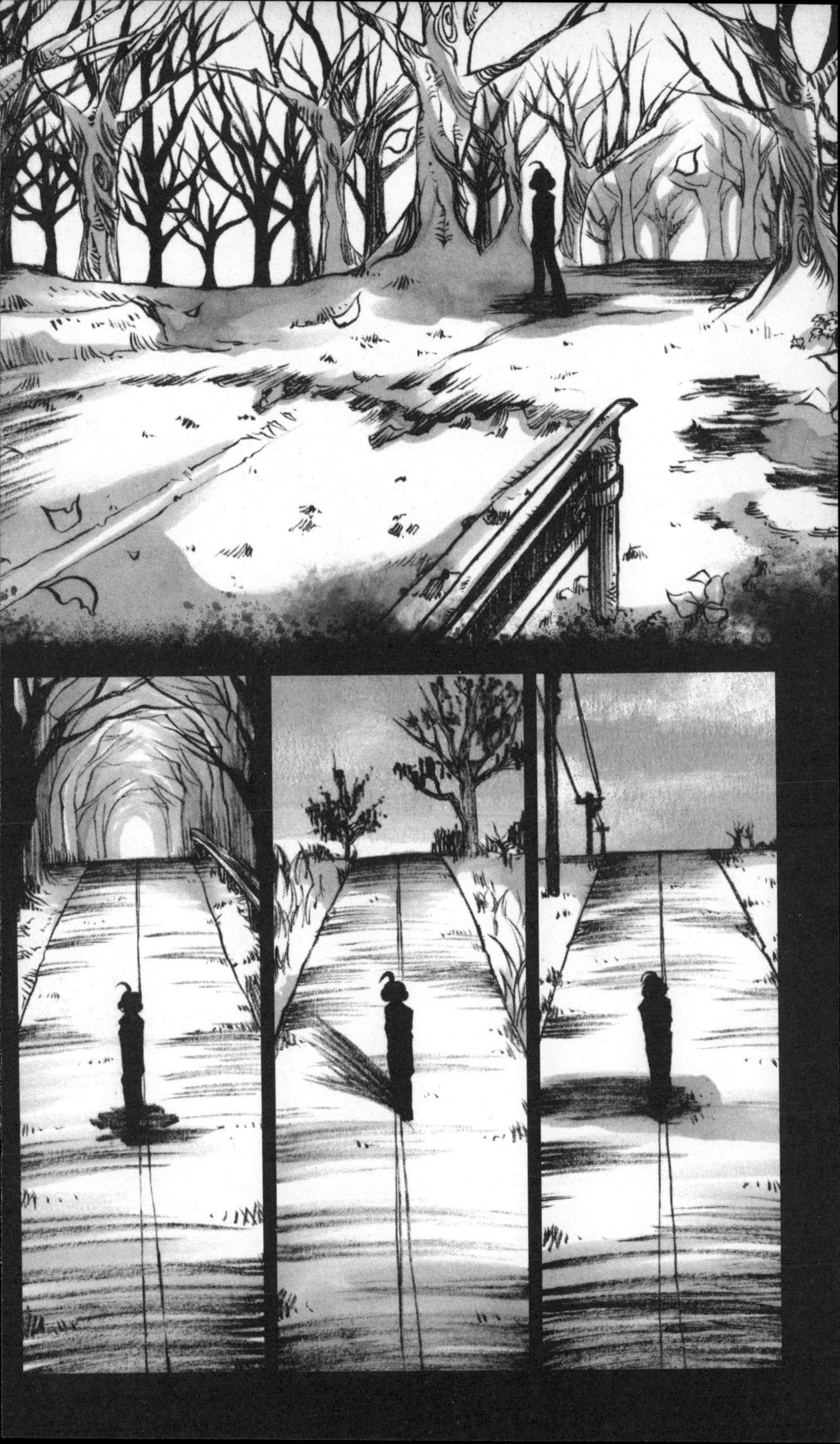

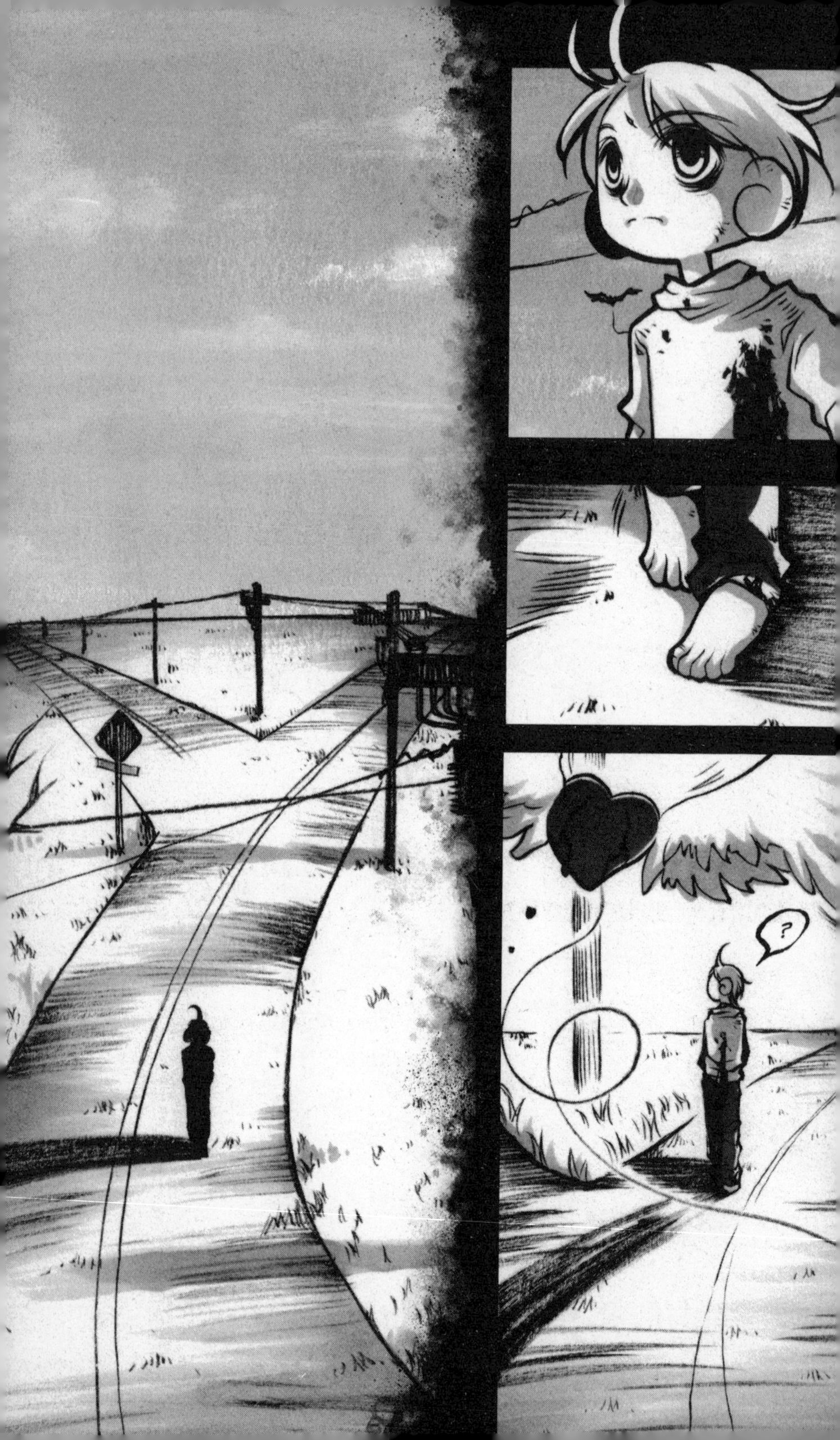
?

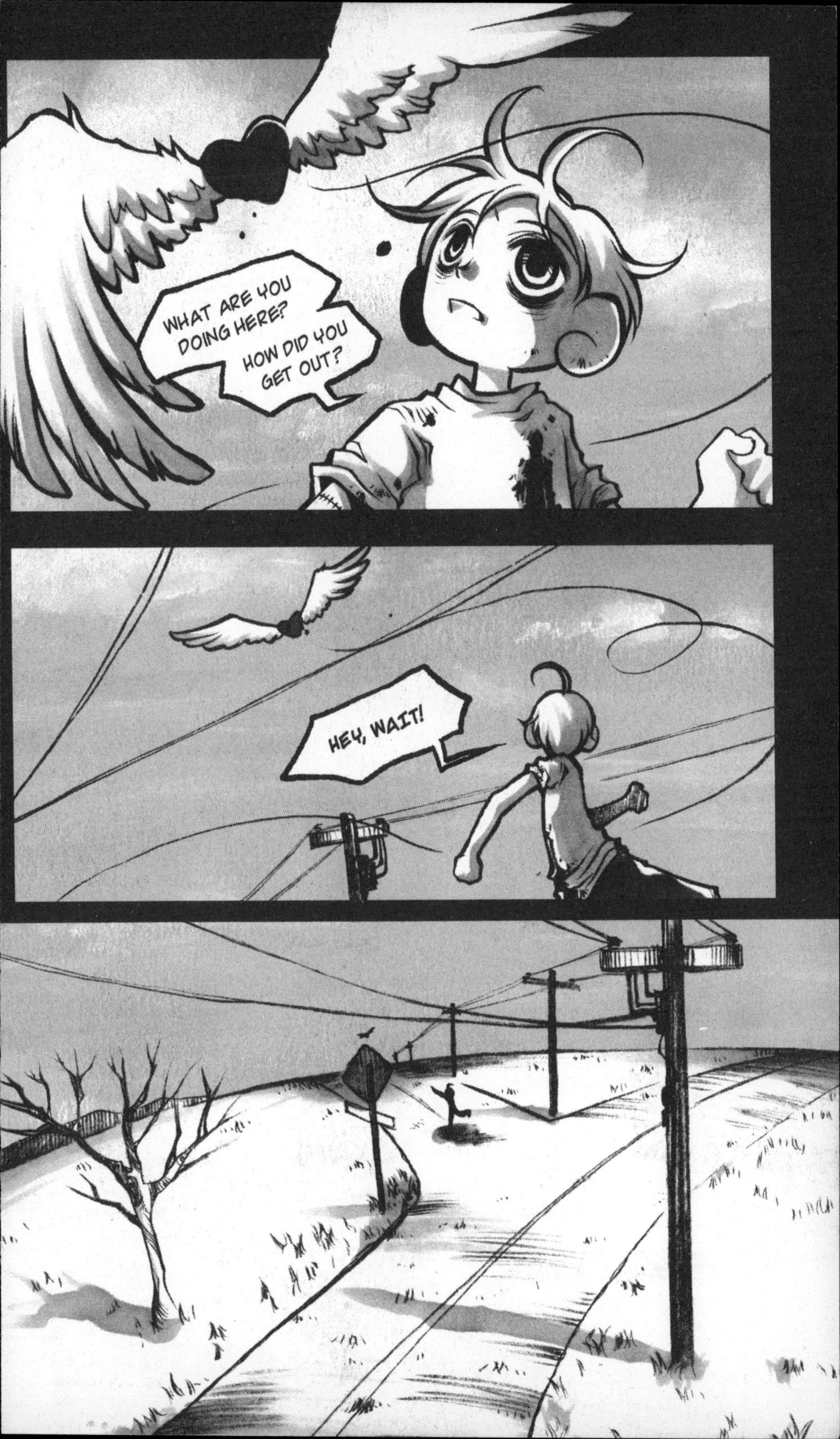
WHAT ARE YOU DOING HERE?
HOW DID YOU GET OUT?
HEY, WAIT!

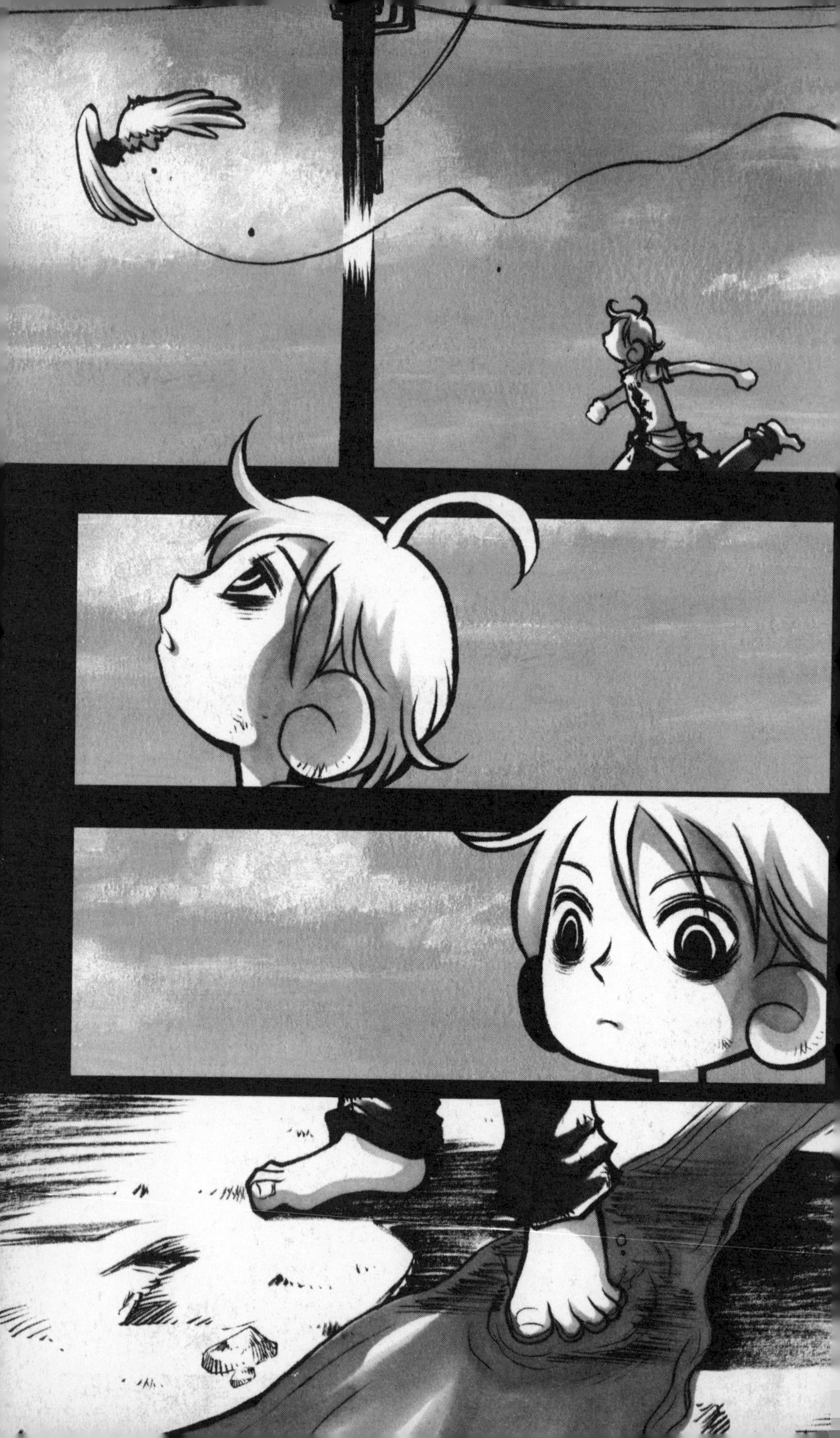

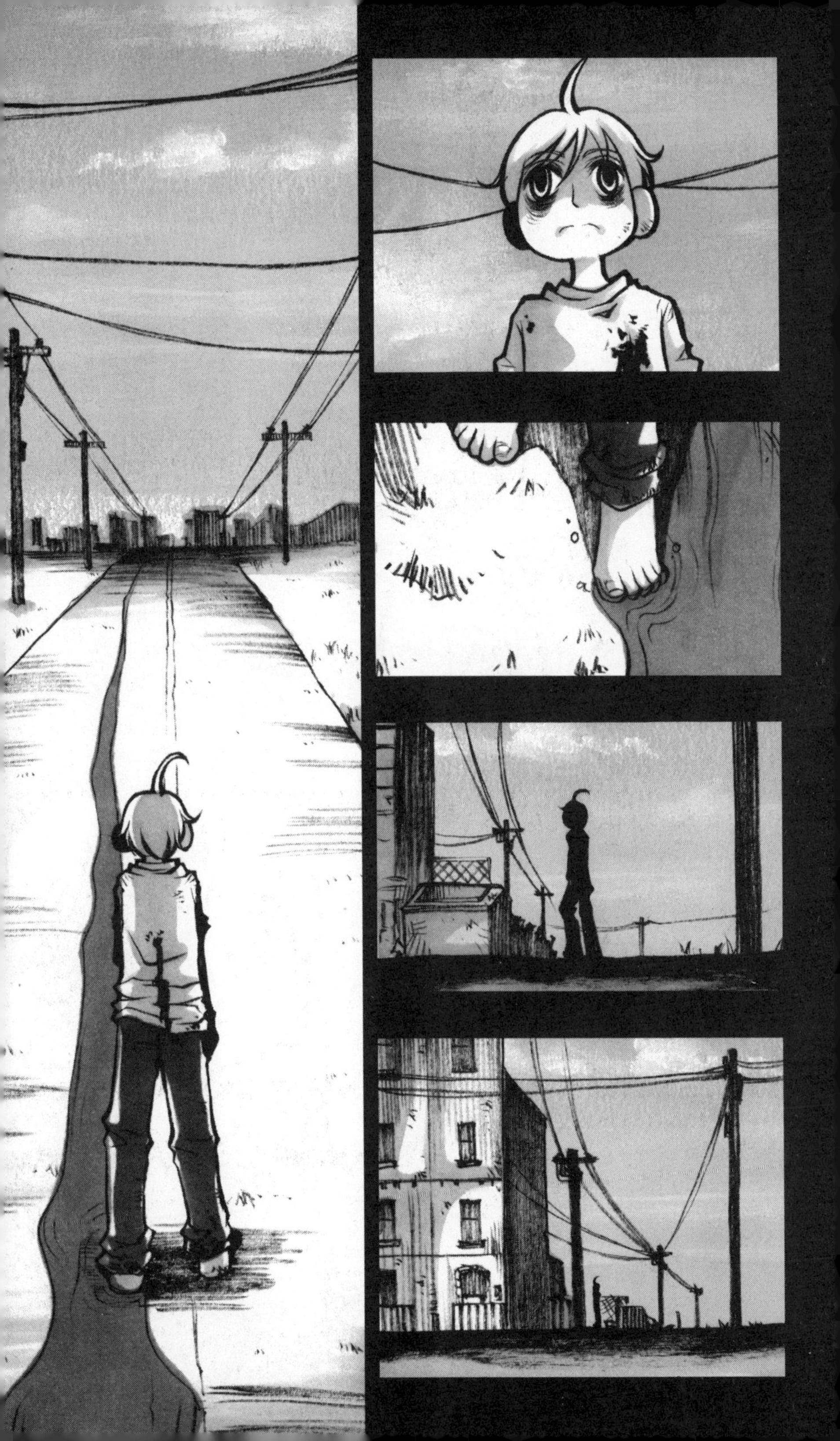

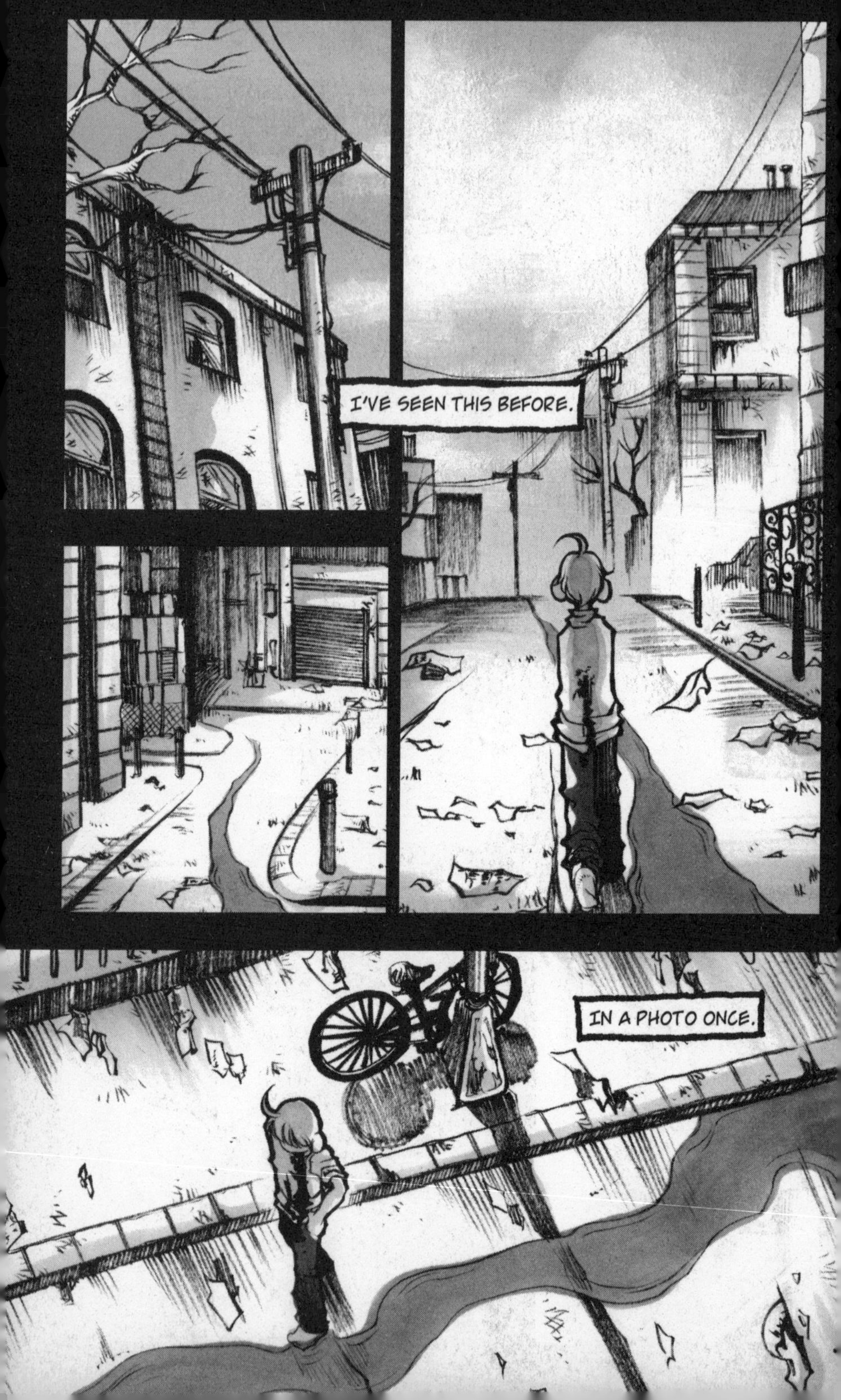
I'VE SEEN THIS BEFORE.
IN A PHOTO ONCE.

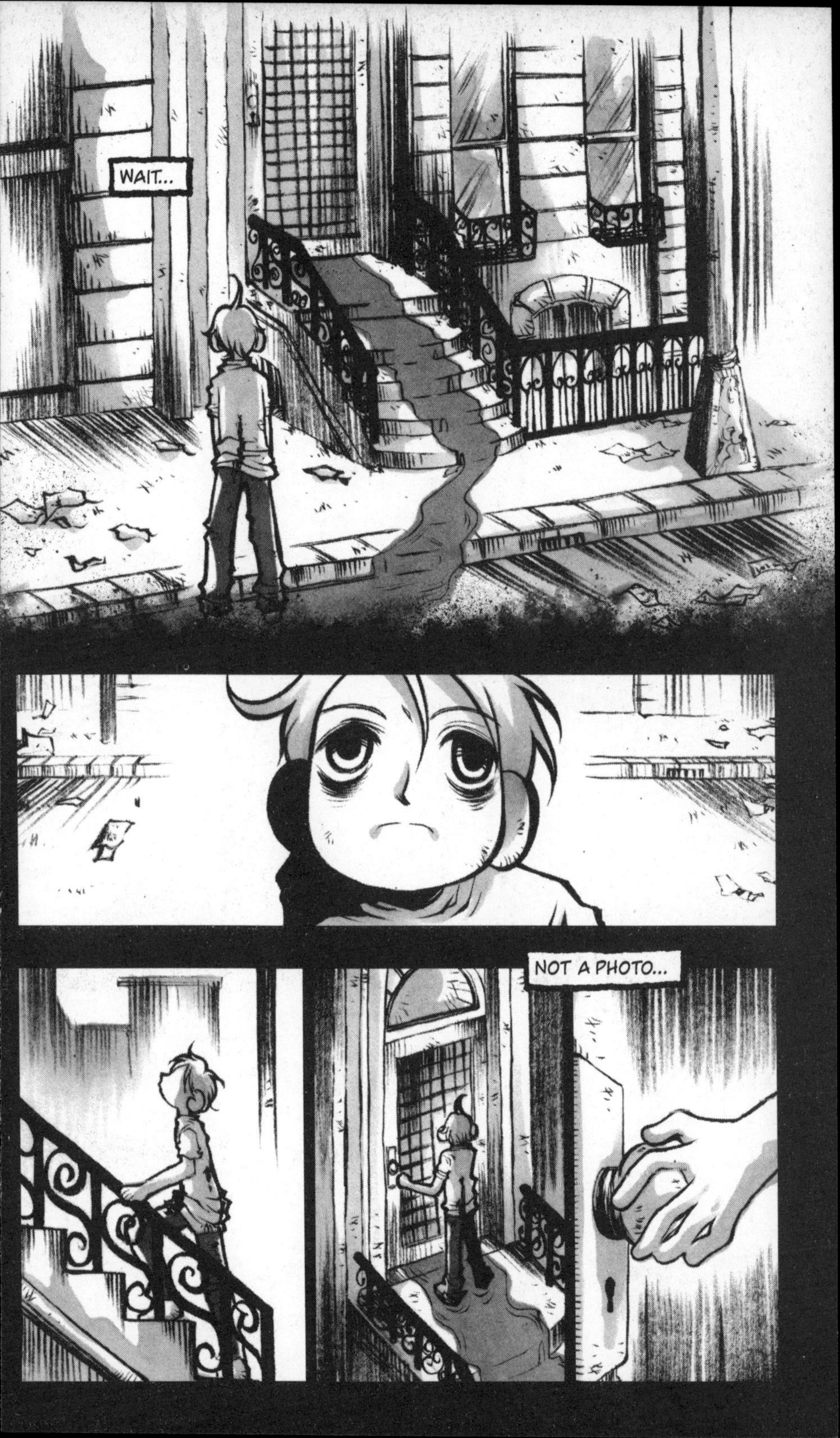
WAIT...
NOT A PHOTO...

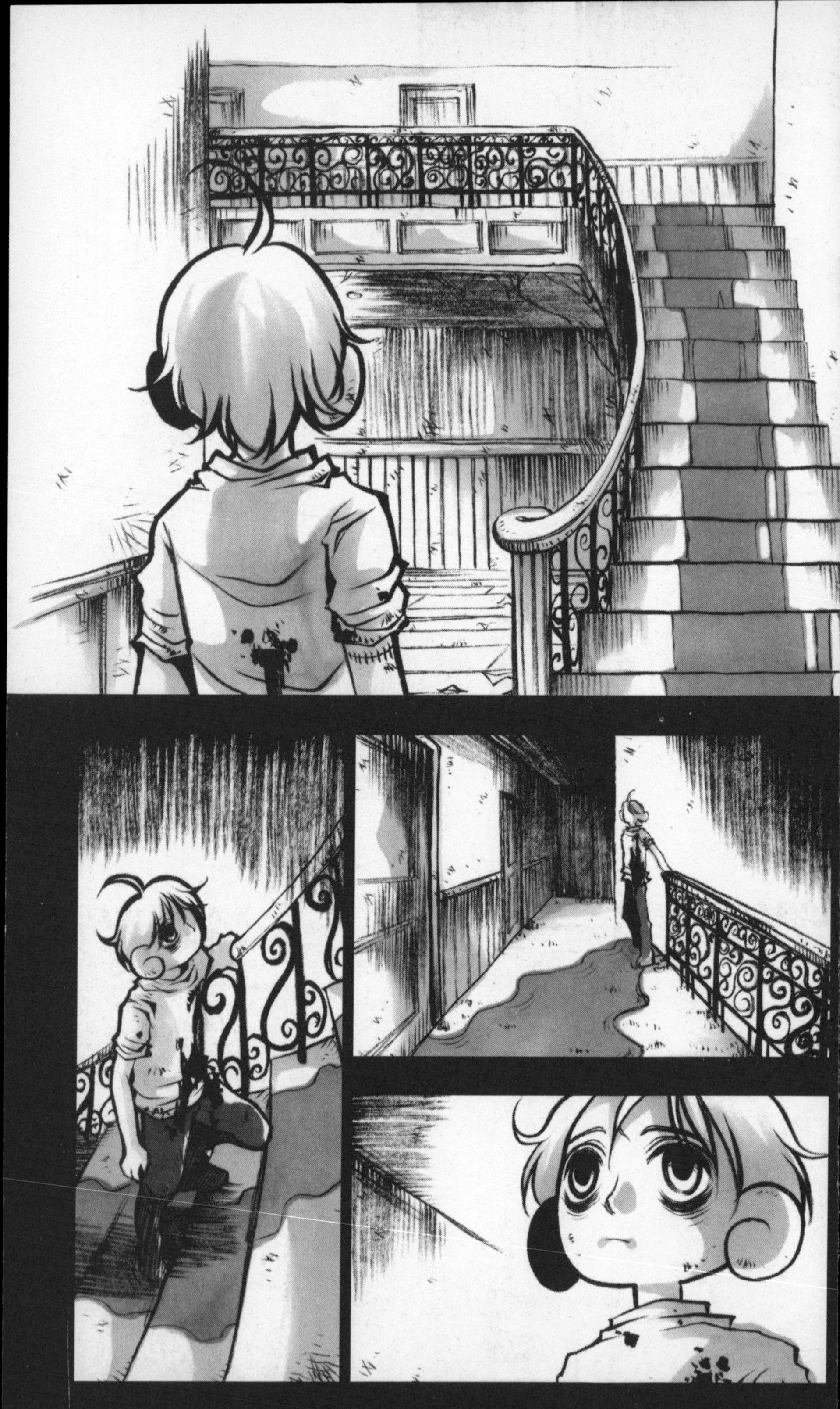

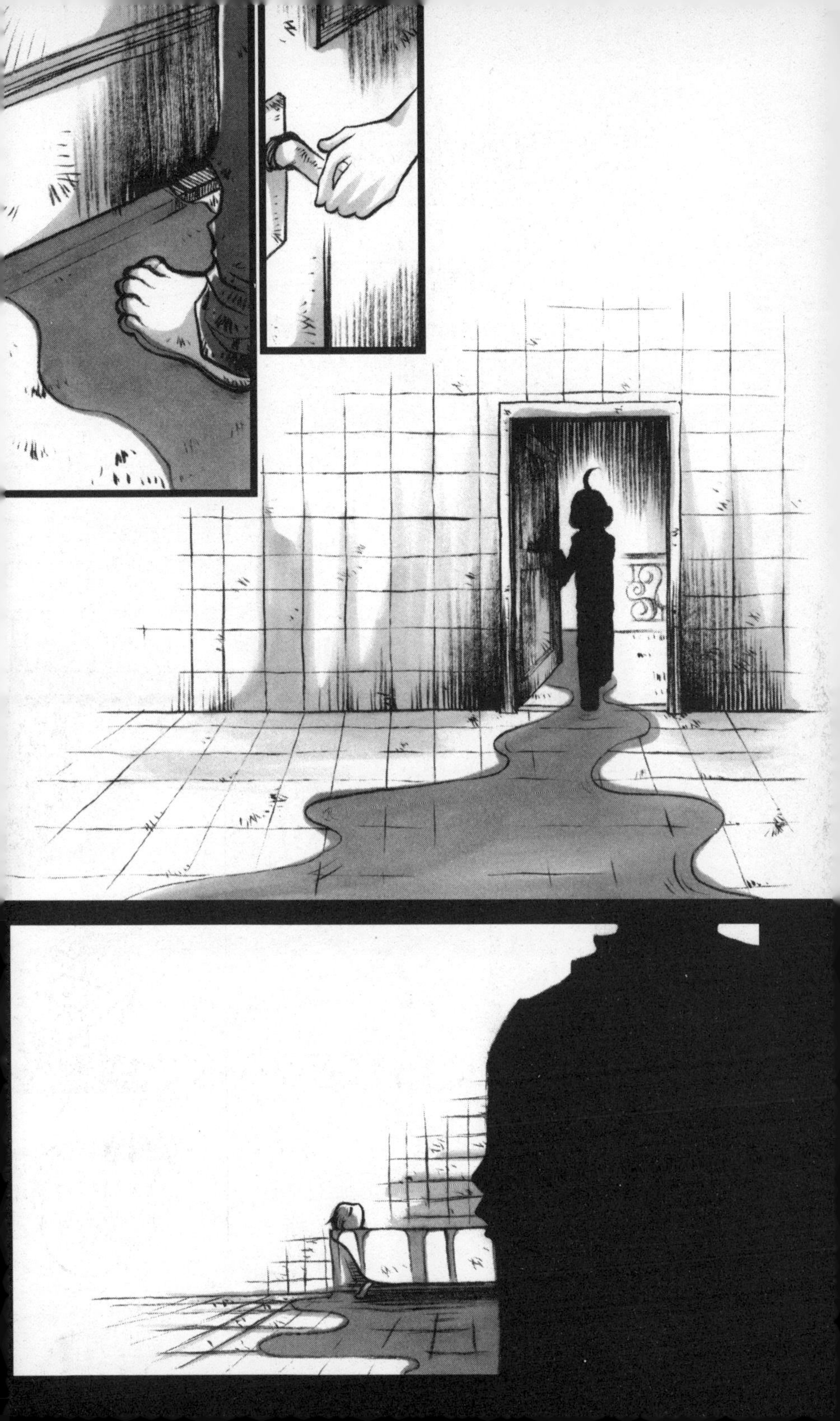

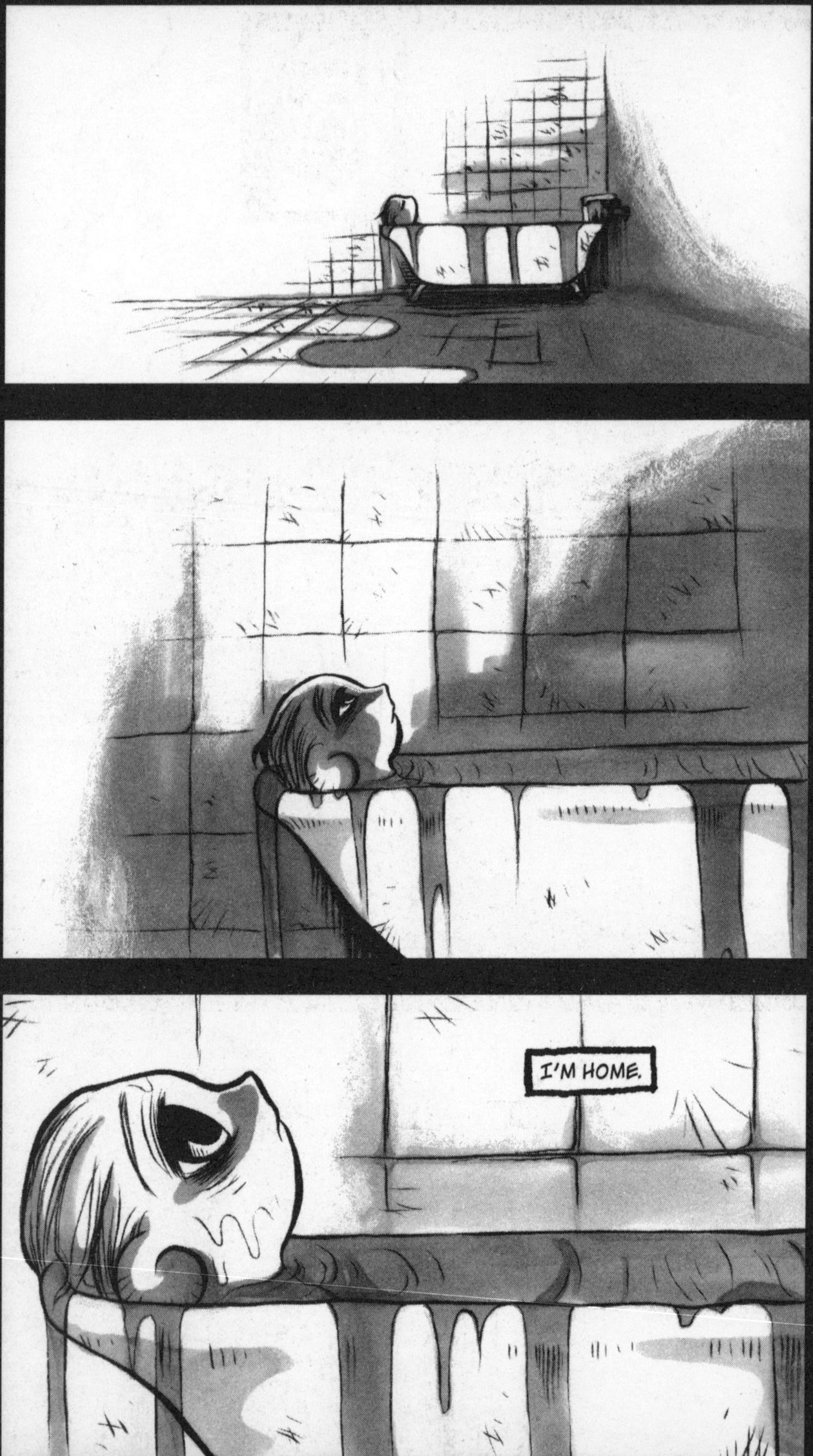
I'M HOME.

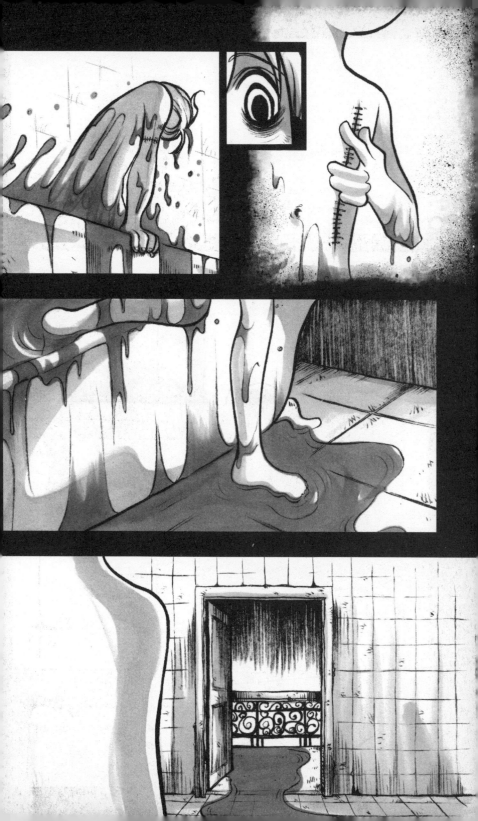

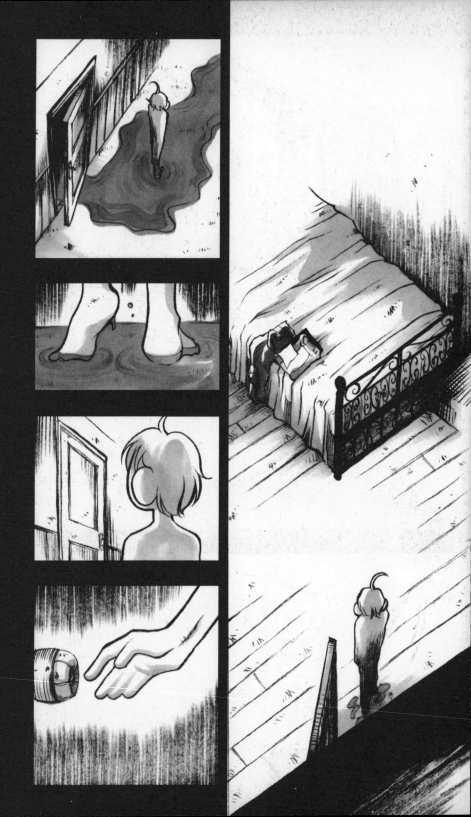

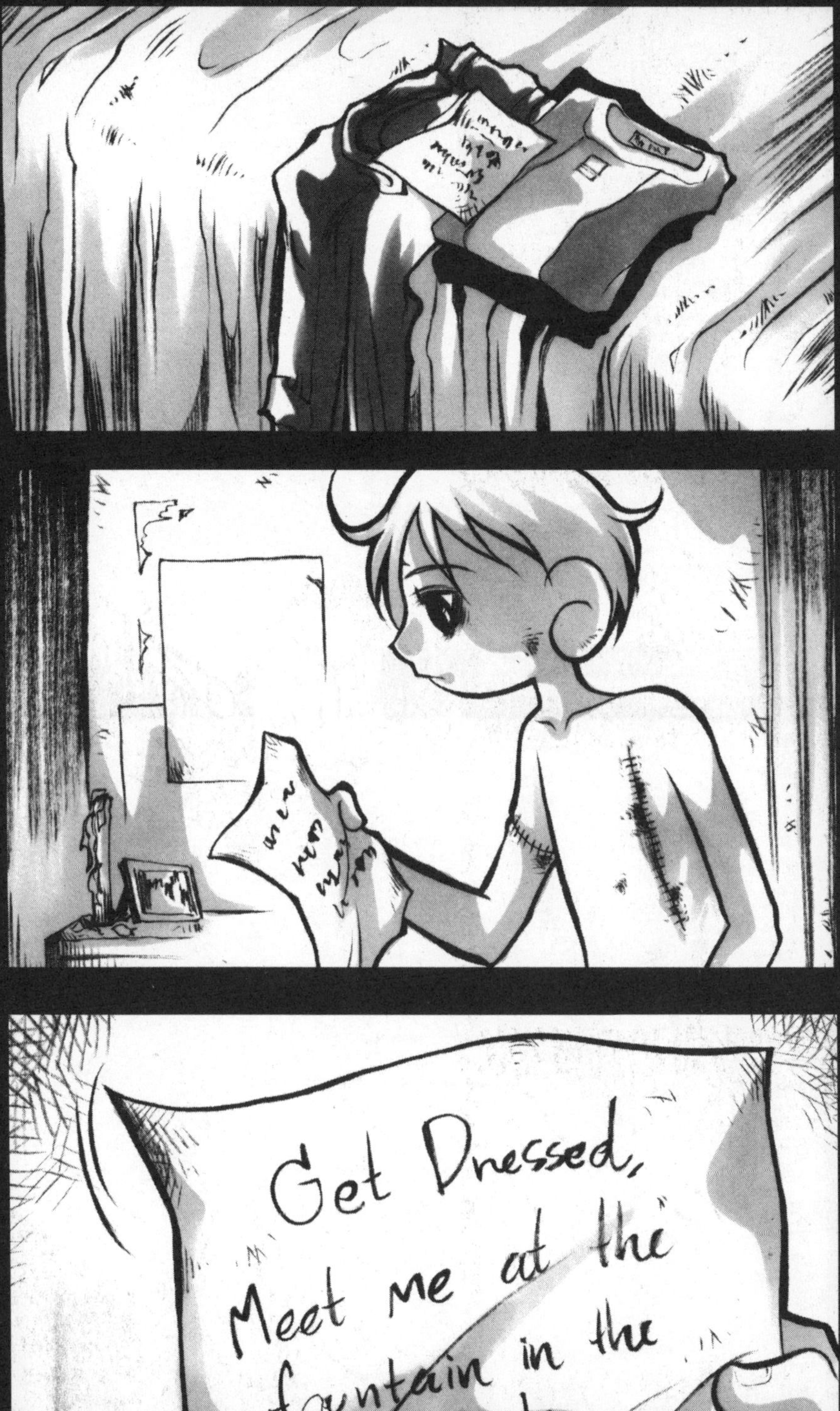
Get Dressed,
Meet me at the
fountain in the
Park.

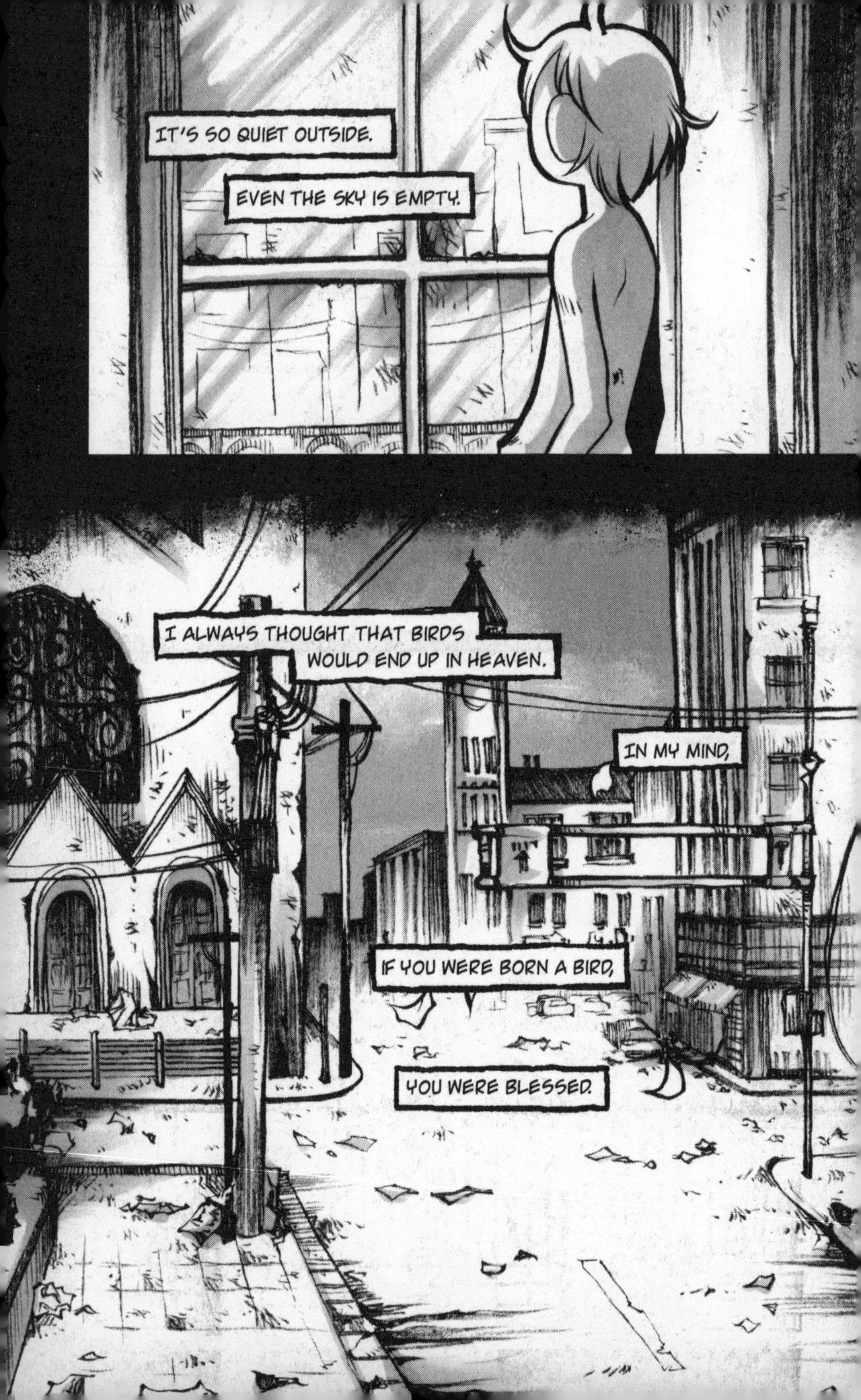
IT'S SO QUIET OUTSIDE.
EVEN THE SKY IS EMPTY.
I ALWAYS THOUGHT THAT BIRDS WOULD END UP IN HEAVEN.
IN MY MIND,
IF YOU WERE BORN A BIRD,
YOU WERE BLESSED.

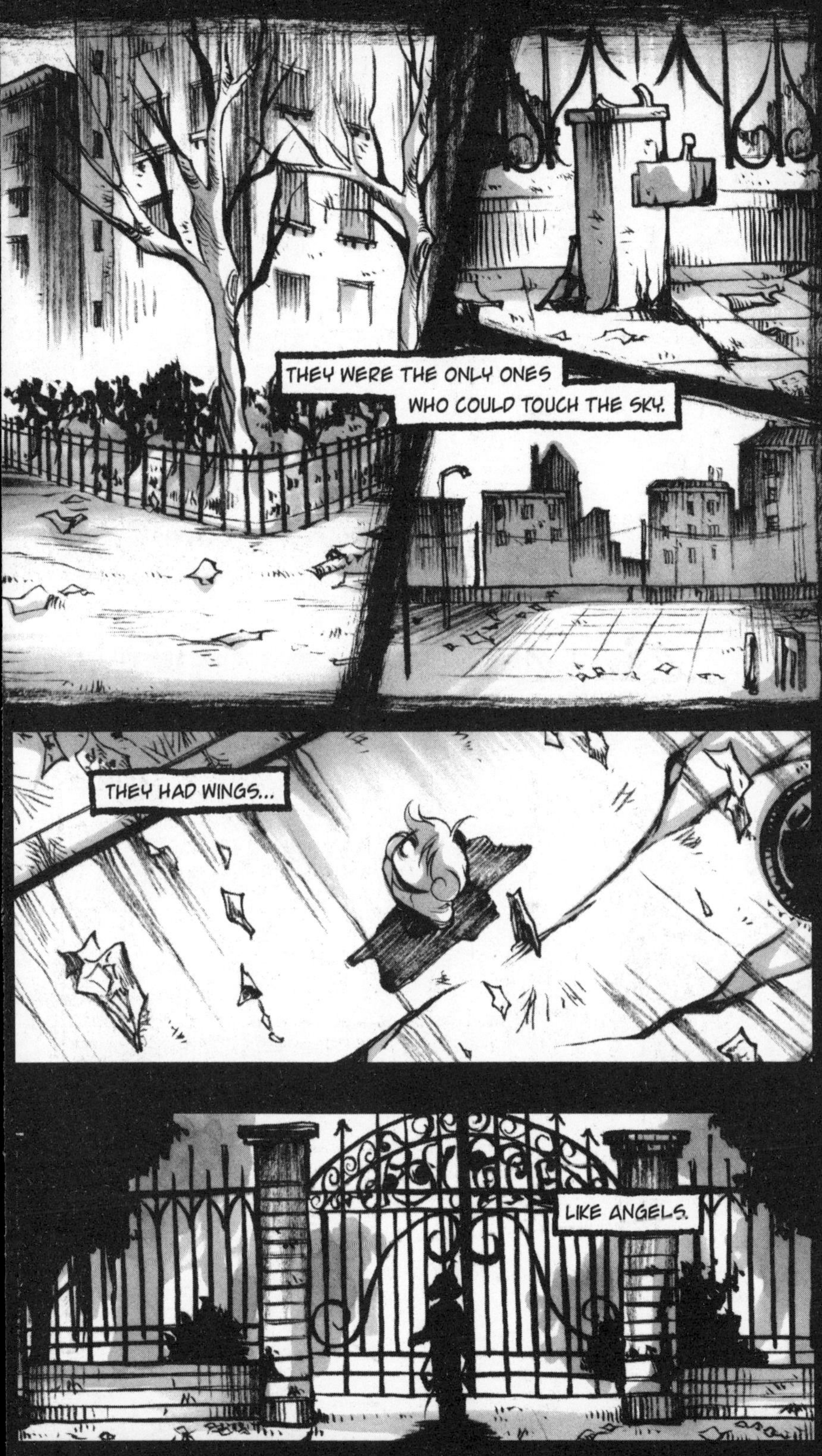
THEY WERE THE ONLY ONES
WHO COULD TOUCH THE SKY.
THEY HAD WINGS...
LIKE ANGELS.

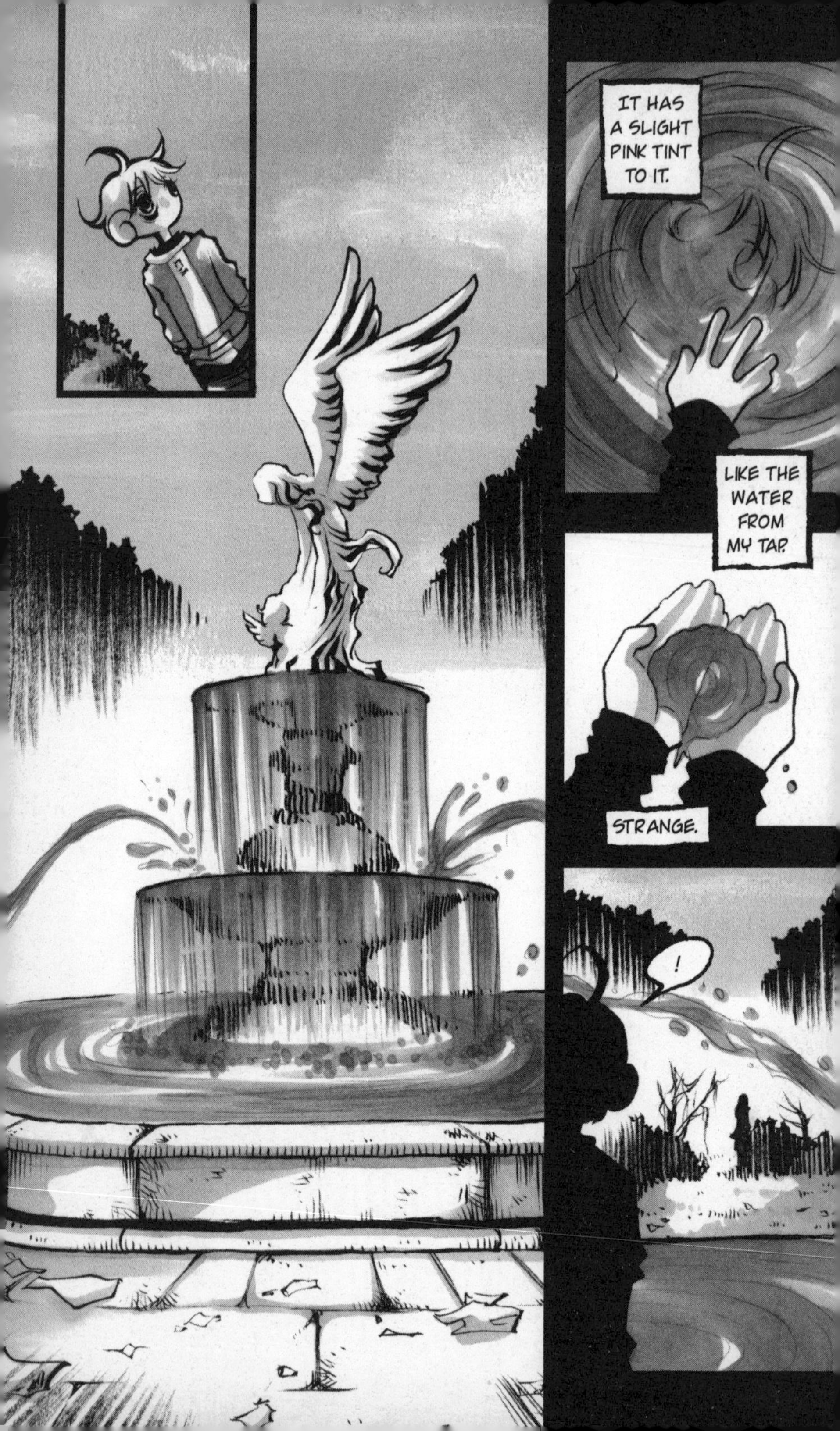
IT HAS A SLIGHT PINK TINT TO IT.
LIKE THE WATER FROM MY TAP.
STRANGE.
!

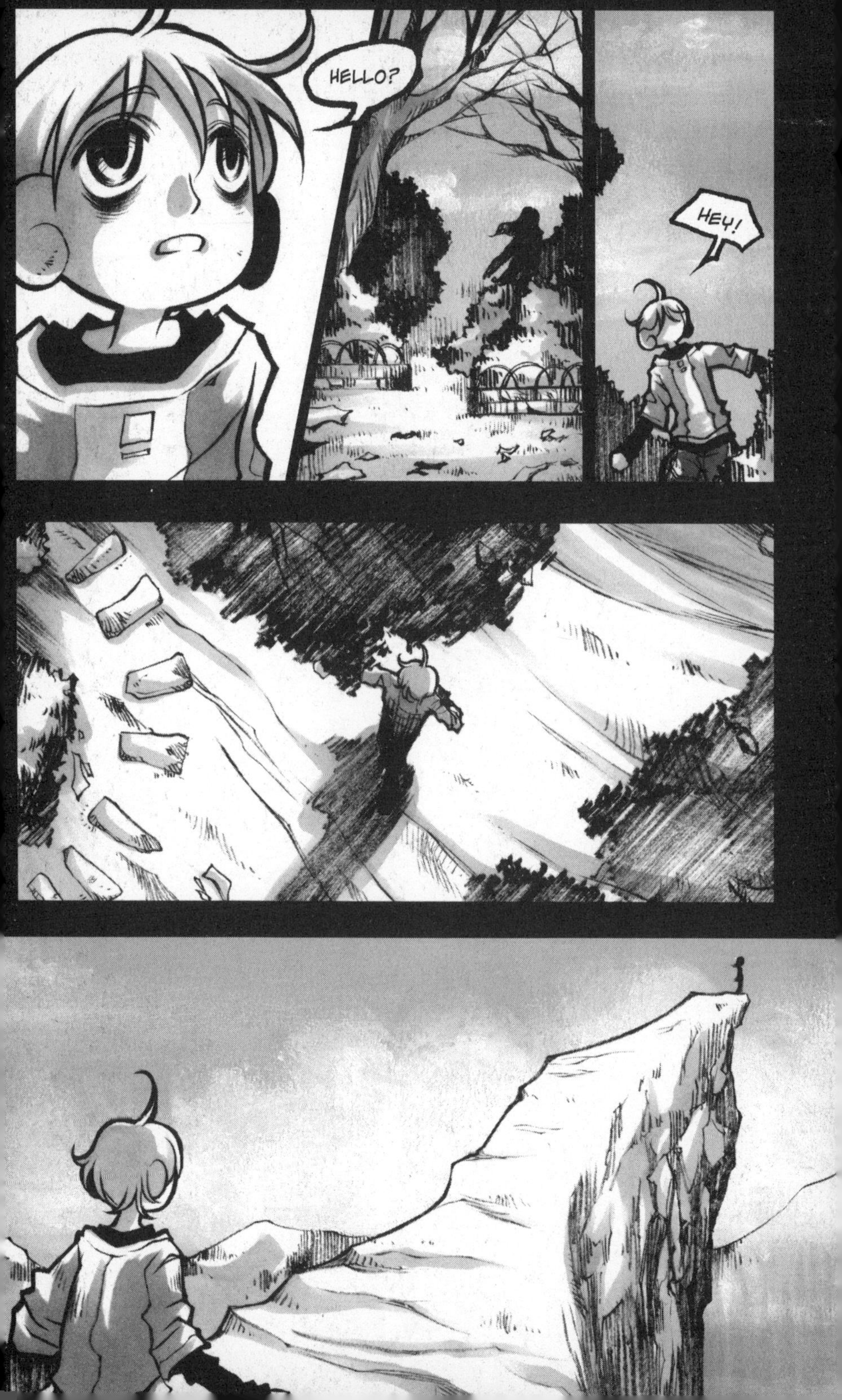
HELLO?
HEY!

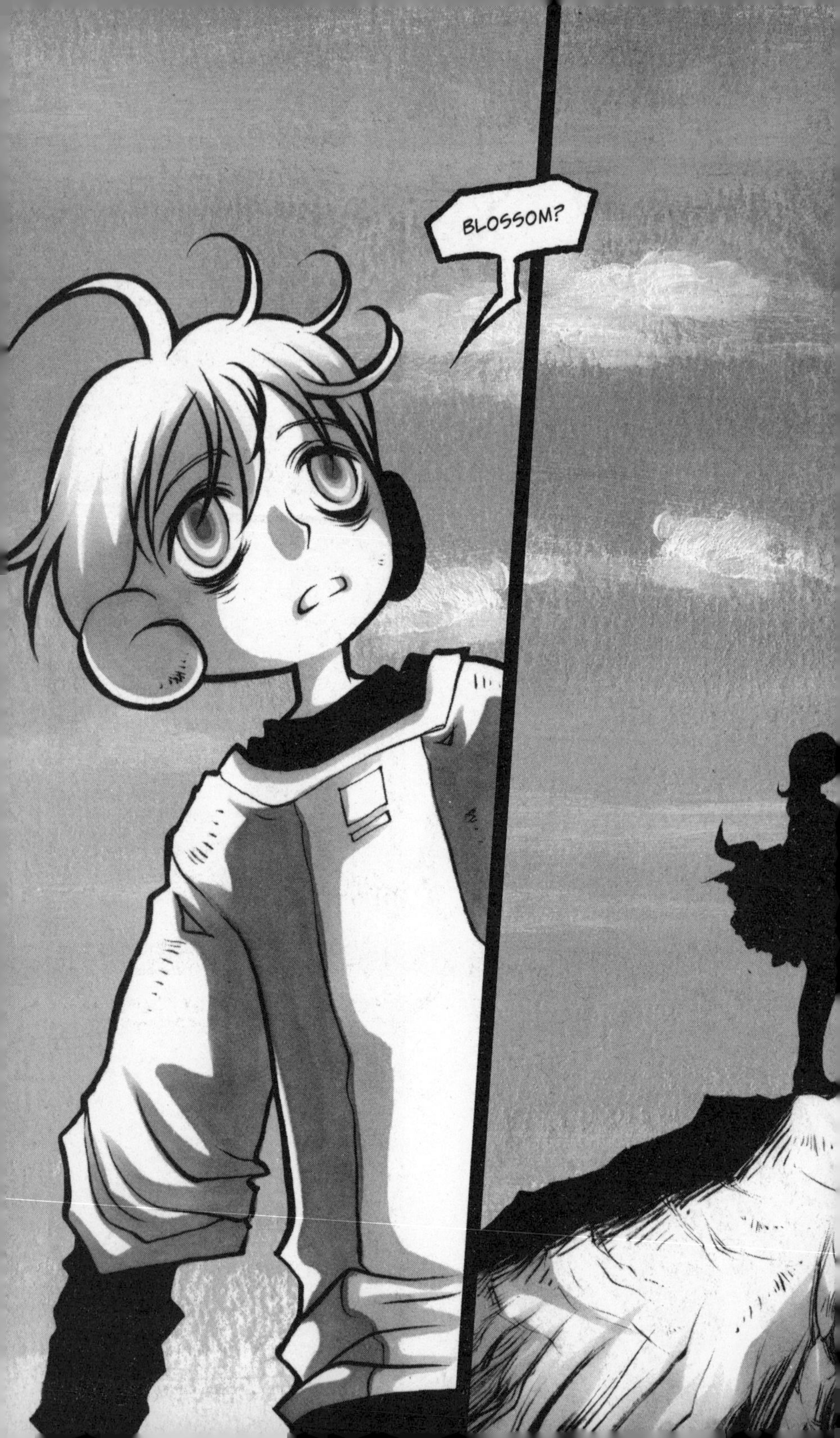
BLOSSOM?

WHO'S BLOSSOM?
ELISSA!
....
SHE'S A GIRL WHOSE HEART I MENDED.
YOU'VE BEEN CHEATING ON ME?
I COULDN'T WAIT FOREVER.

AFTER ALL MY FRIENDS HAD MOVED ON
YOU WERE THE ONLY ONE I HAD LEFT.
I WAS THERE FOR YOU THEN.
I SUPPORTED YOU!
YOU OWE ME FOR THAT.
YOU WAITED TO WATCH ME FAIL.
SO YOU COULD LEAVE ME,
WITHOUT A GUILTY CONSCIENCE.
HOW COULD YOU SAY THAT?
I CAN'T BELIEVE YOU SAID...

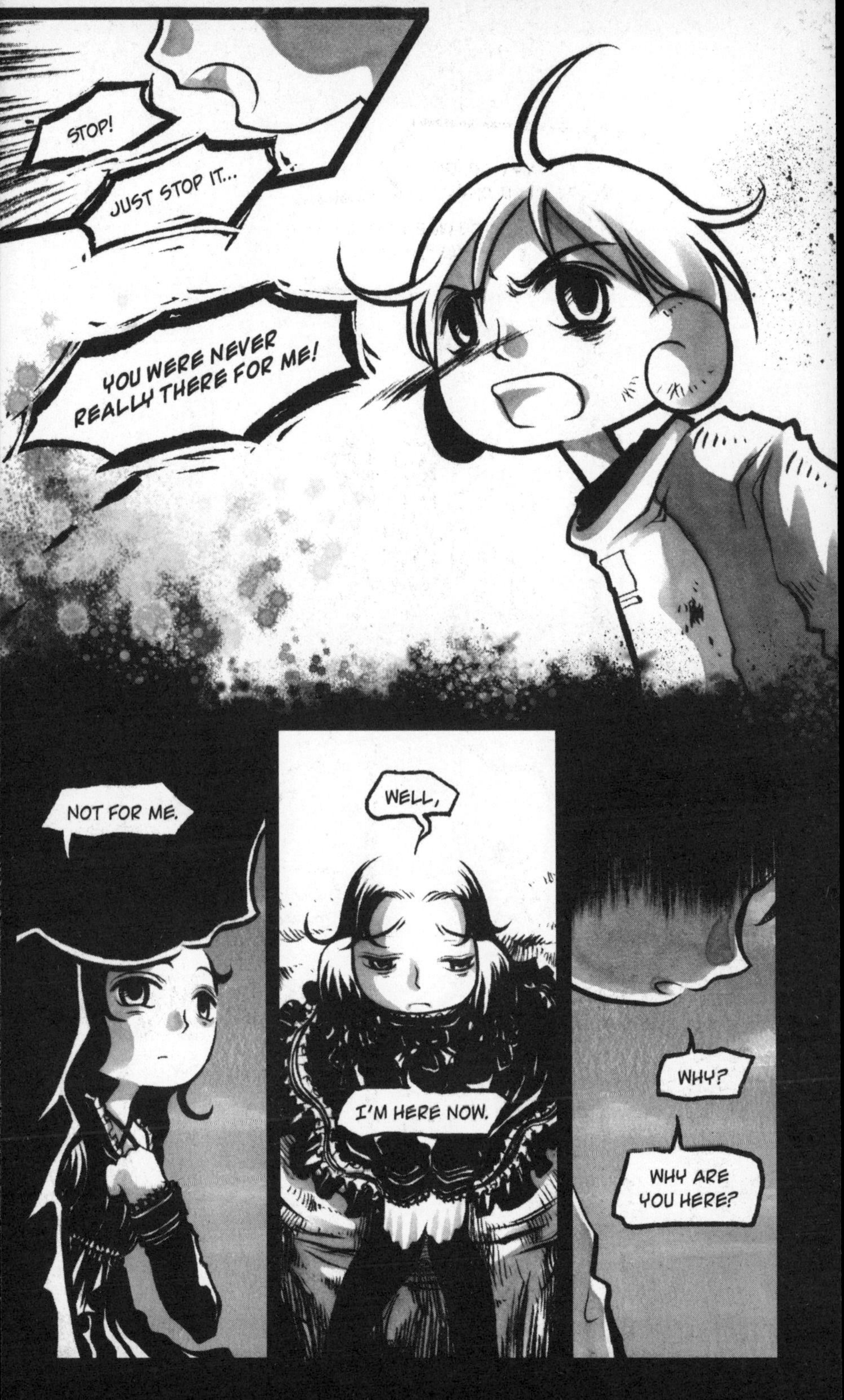
STOP!
JUST STOP IT...
YOU WERE NEVER REALLY THERE FOR ME!
NOT FOR ME.
WELL,
I'M HERE NOW.
WHY?
WHY ARE YOU HERE?

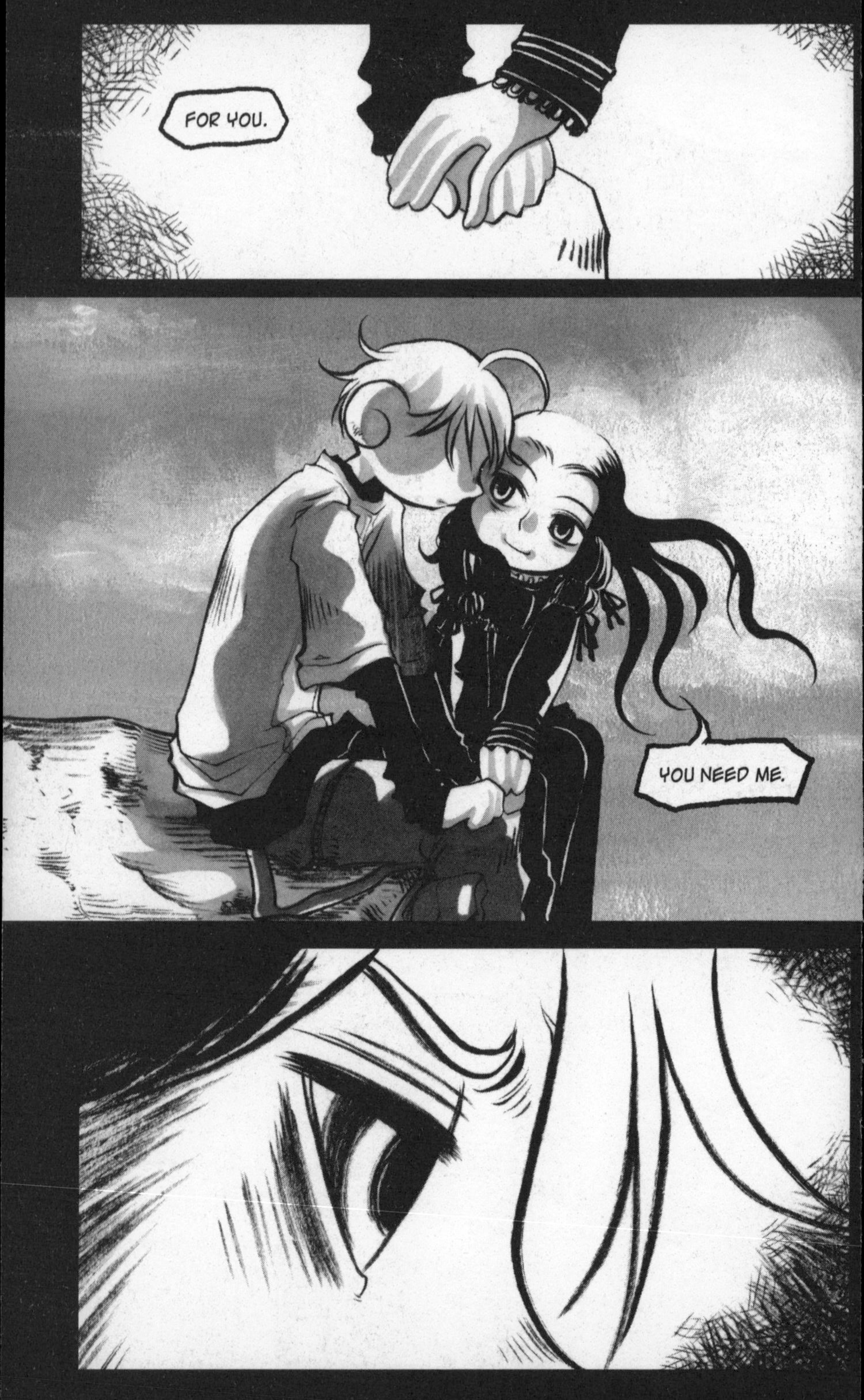
FOR YOU.
YOU NEED ME.

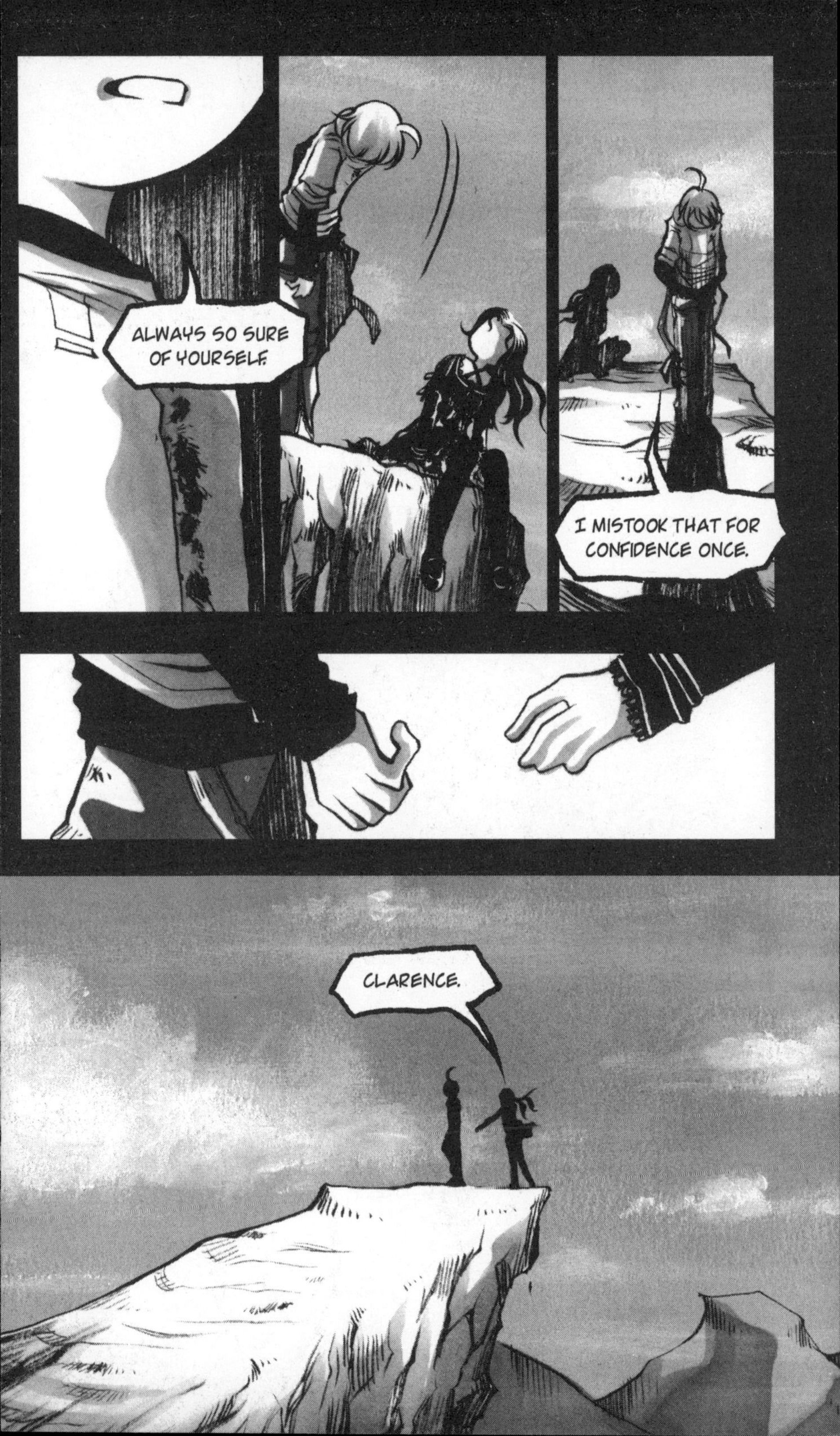
ALWAYS SO SURE OF YOURSELF.
I MISTOOK THAT FOR CONFIDENCE ONCE.
CLARENCE.

TAKE MY HAND.
WHAT'RE YOU DOING?
I'M GIVING YOU THE POWER TO CHANGE THINGS.
I WENT AWAY.

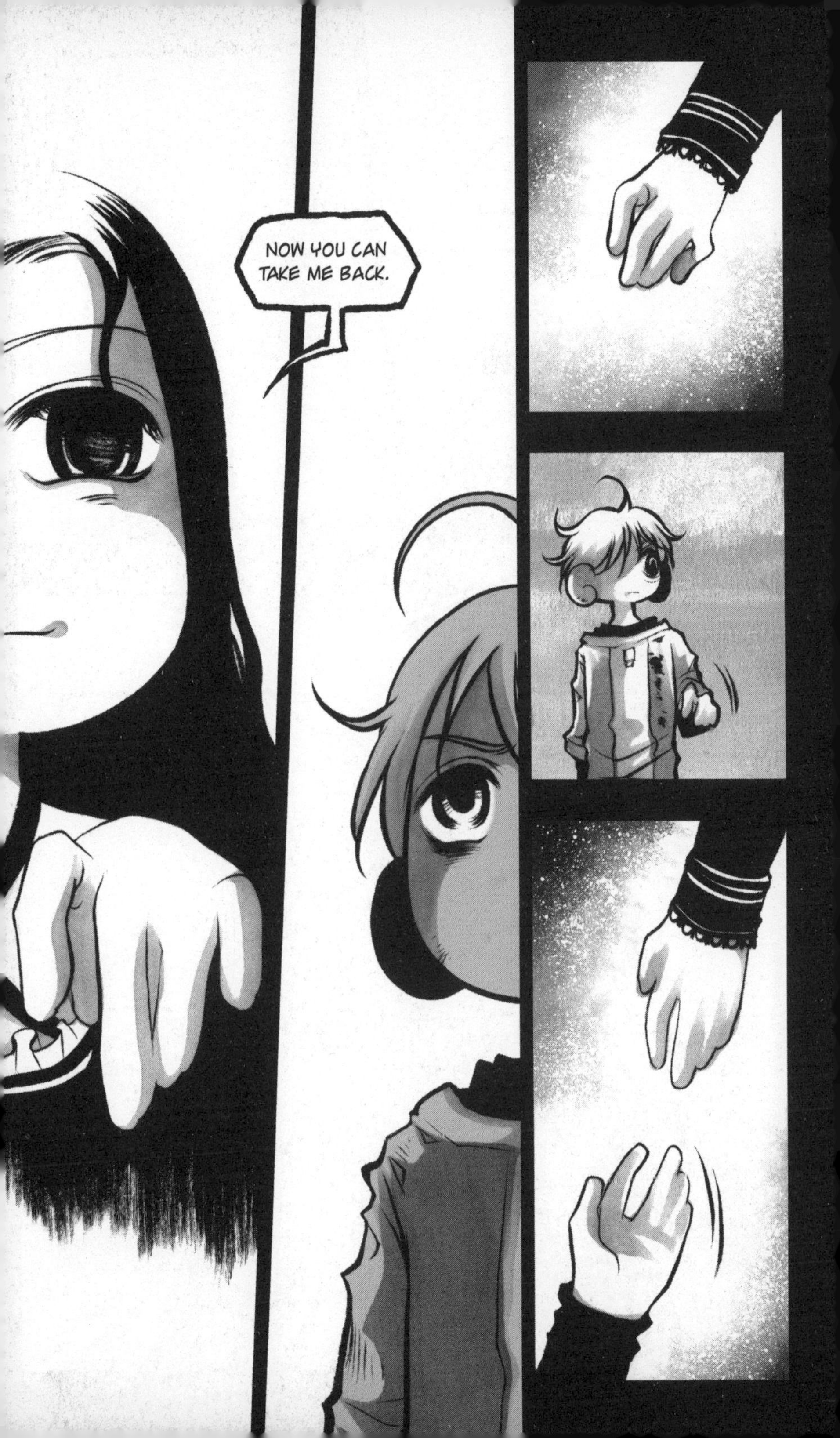
NOW YOU CAN TAKE ME BACK.

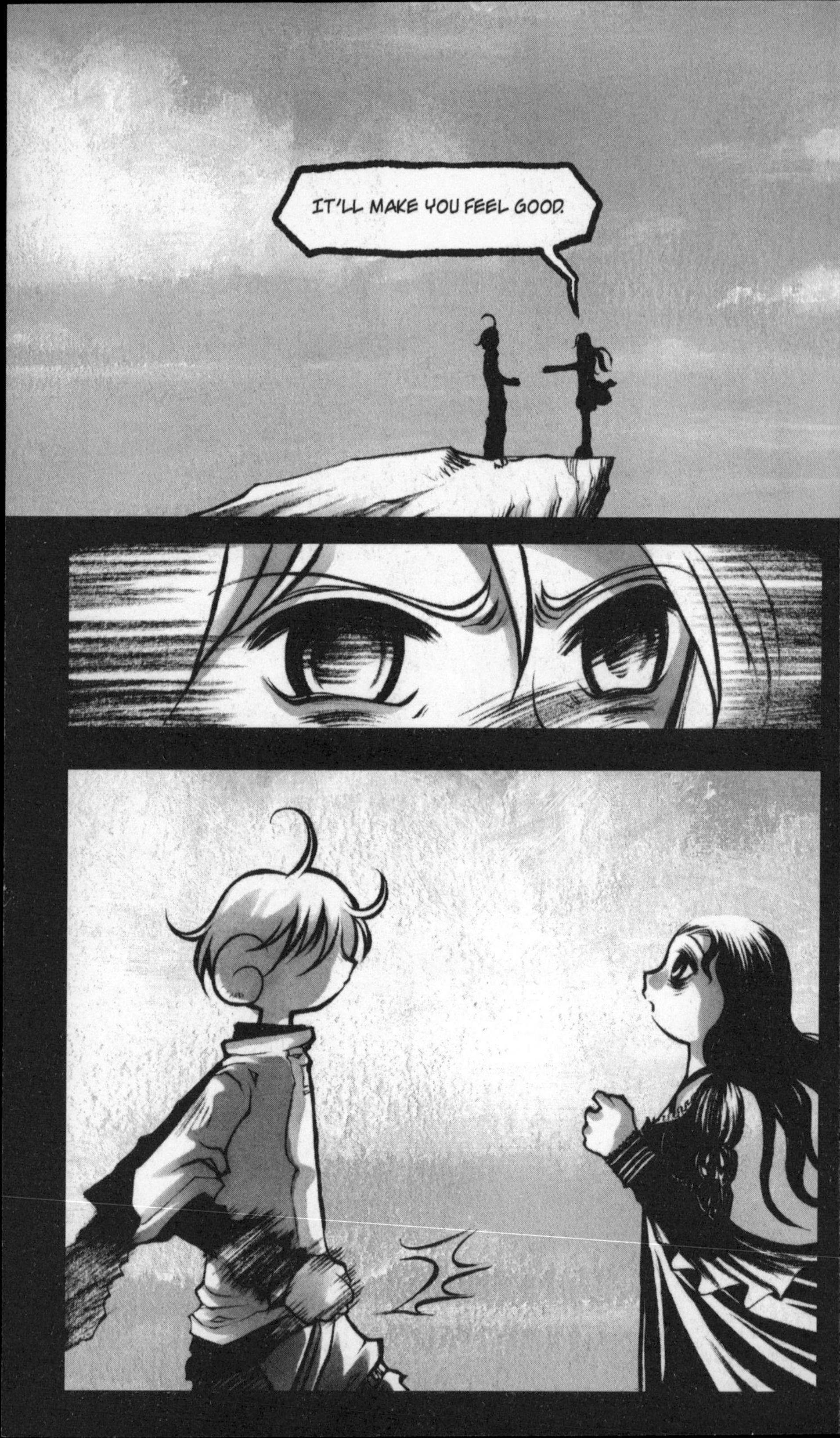
IT'LL MAKE YOU FEEL GOOD.

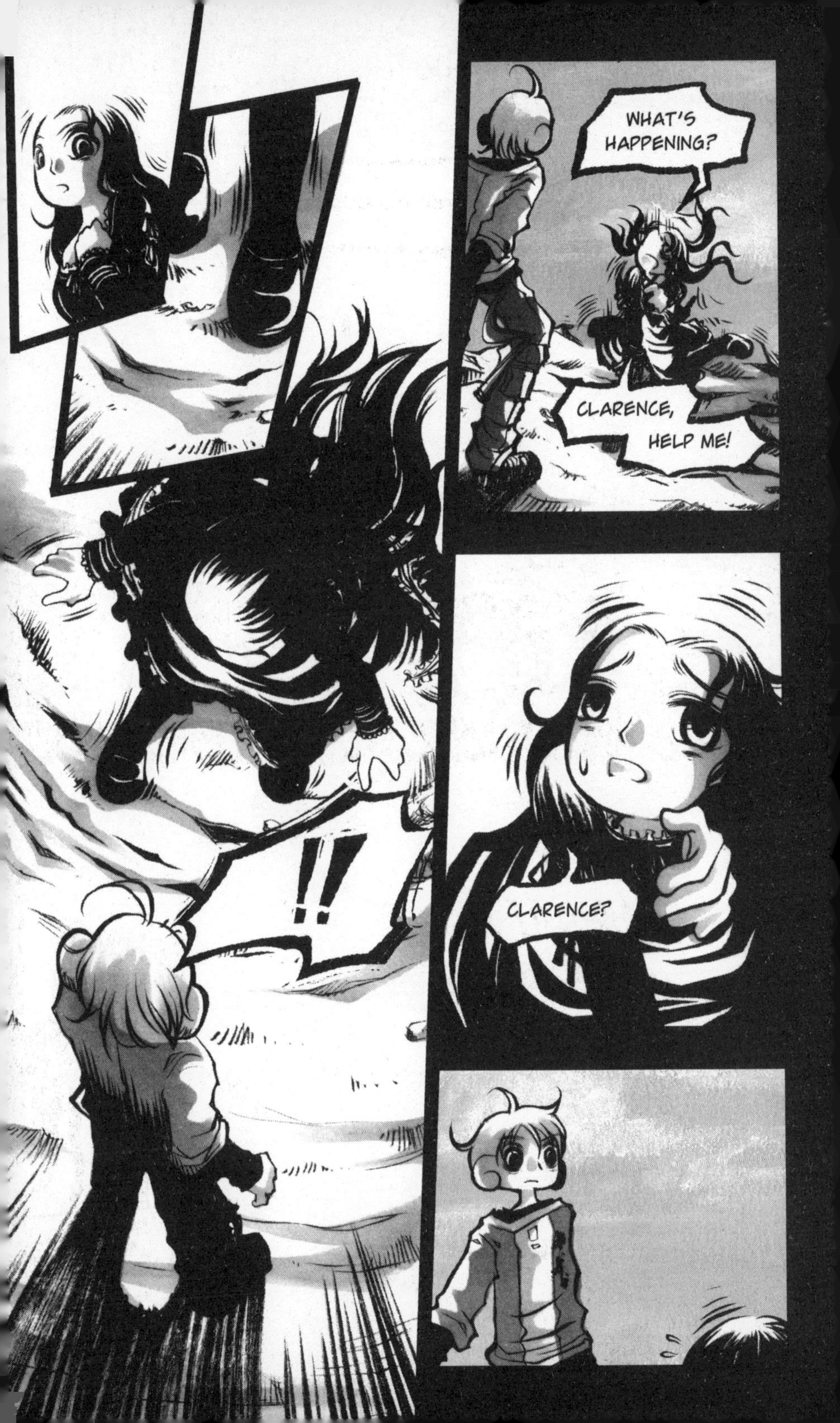
WHAT'S HAPPENING?
CLARENCE, HELP ME!
CLARENCE?
!!

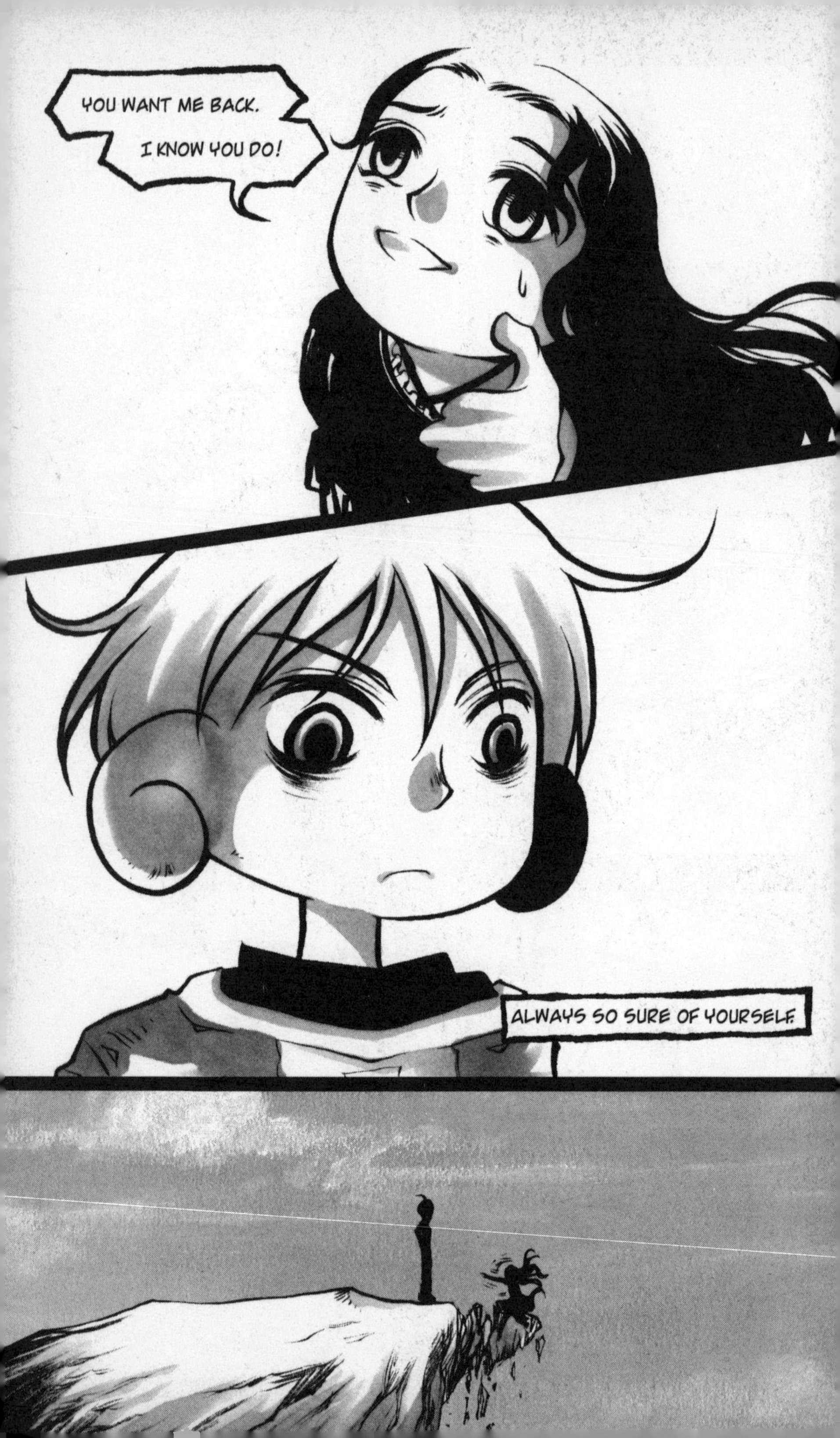
YOU WANT ME BACK.
I KNOW YOU DO!
ALWAYS SO SURE OF YOURSELF.

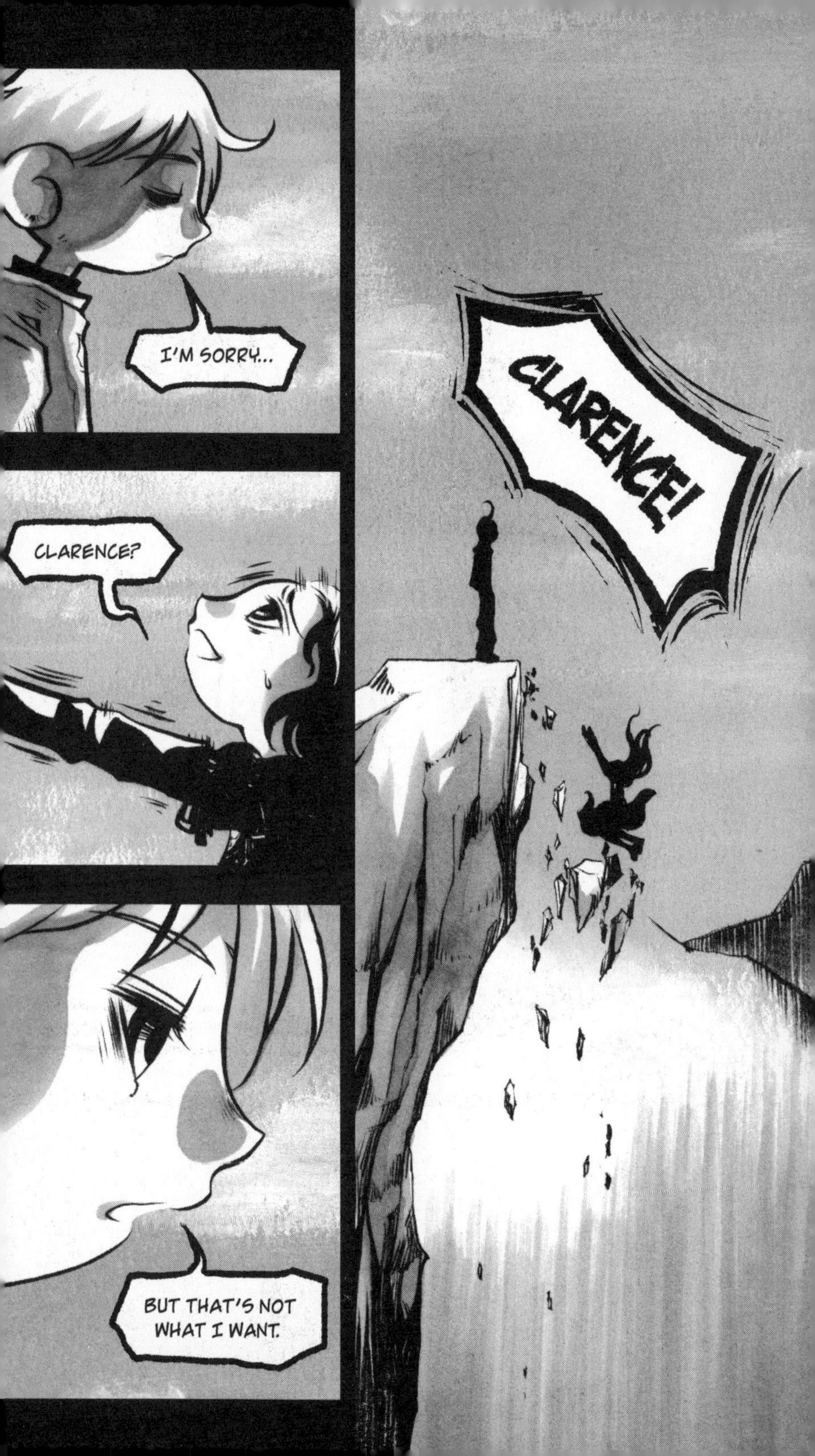
I'M SORRY...
CLARENCE!
CLARENCE?
BUT THAT'S NOT WHAT I WANT.

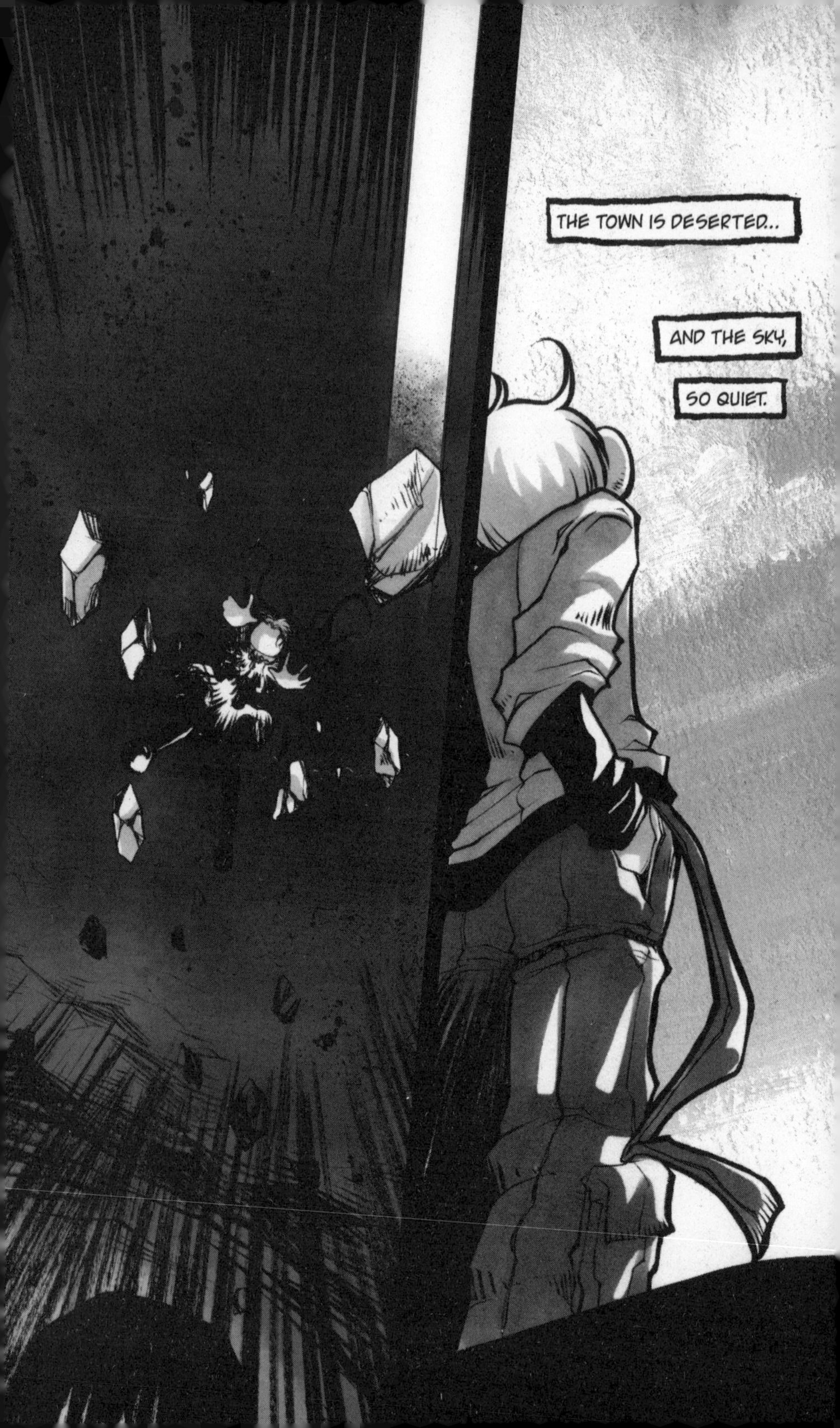
THE TOWN IS DESERTED...
AND THE SKY,
SO QUIET.

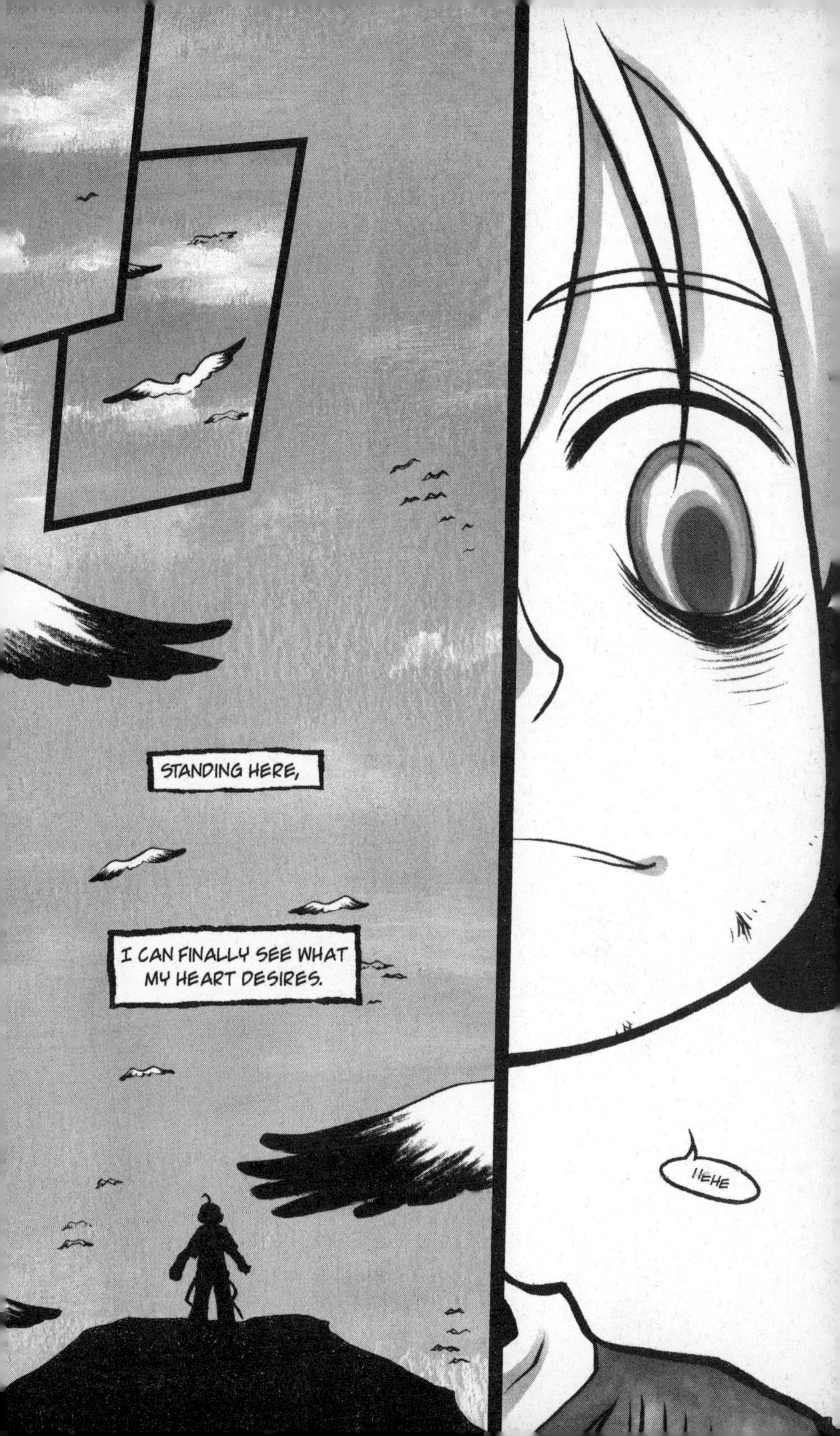
STANDING HERE,
I CAN FINALLY SEE WHAT MY HEART DESIRES.
HEHE

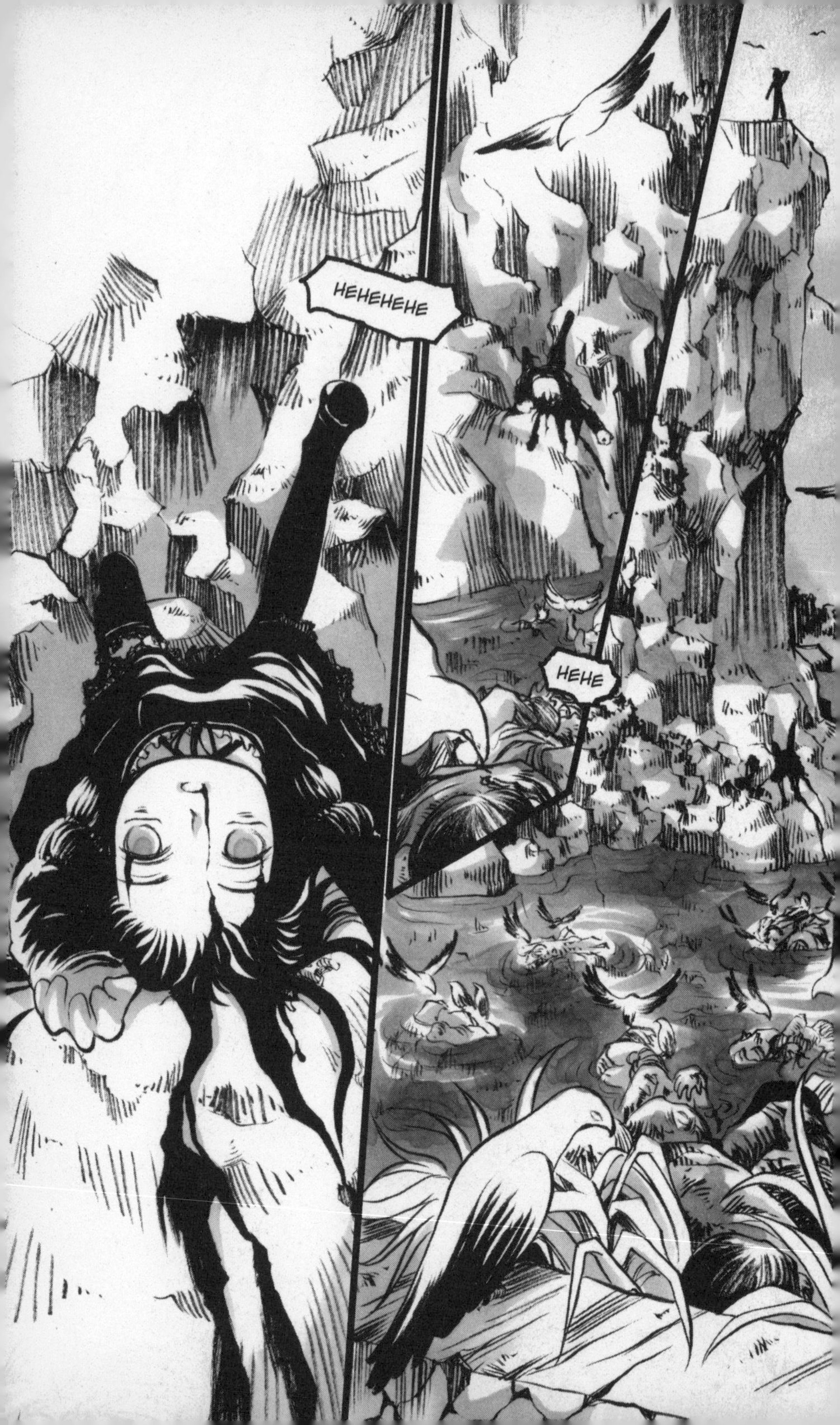
HEHEHEHE
HEHE

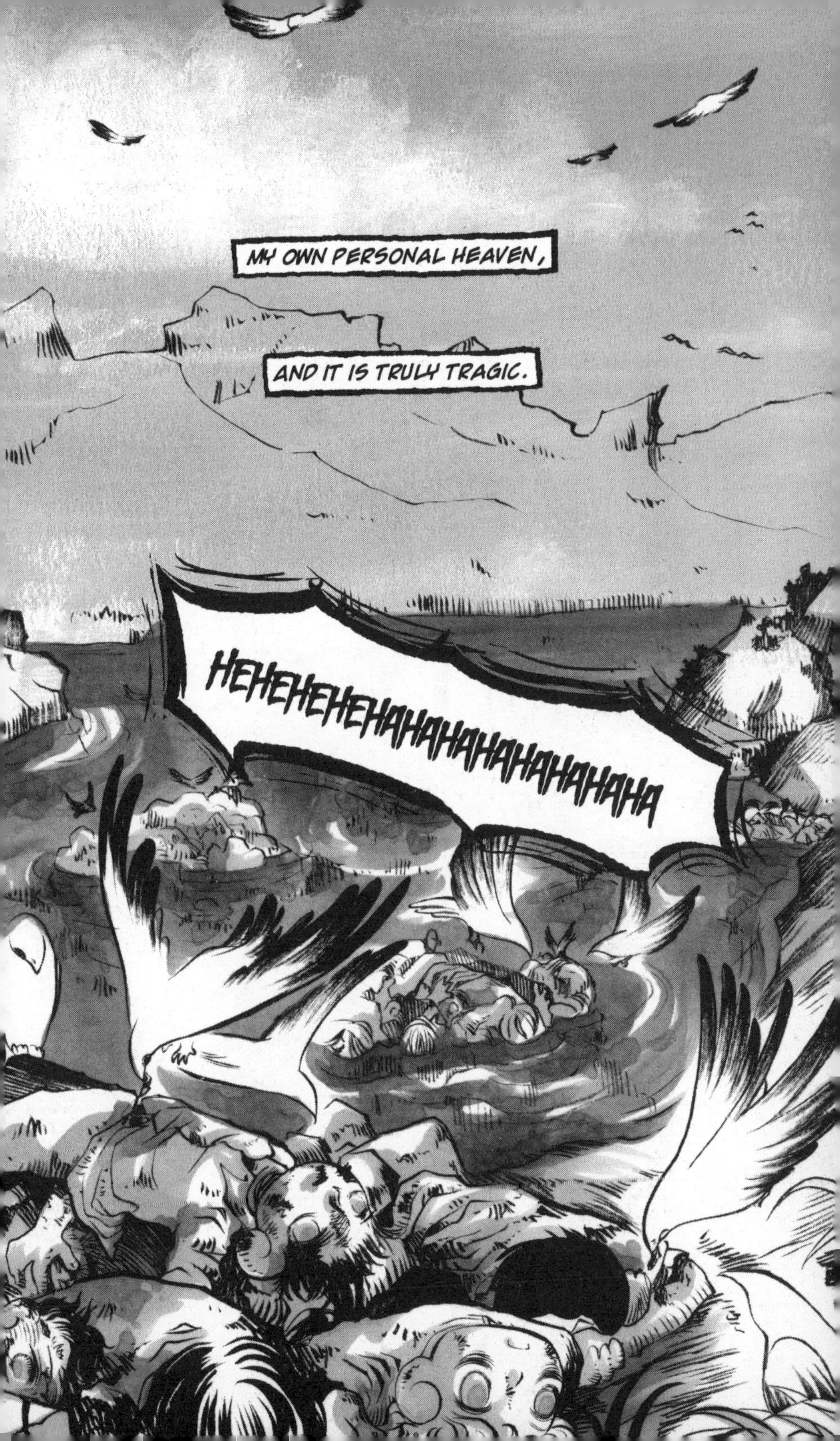
MY OWN PERSONAL HEAVEN,
AND IT IS TRULY TRAGIC.
HEHEHEHEHAHAHAHAHAHAHAHA

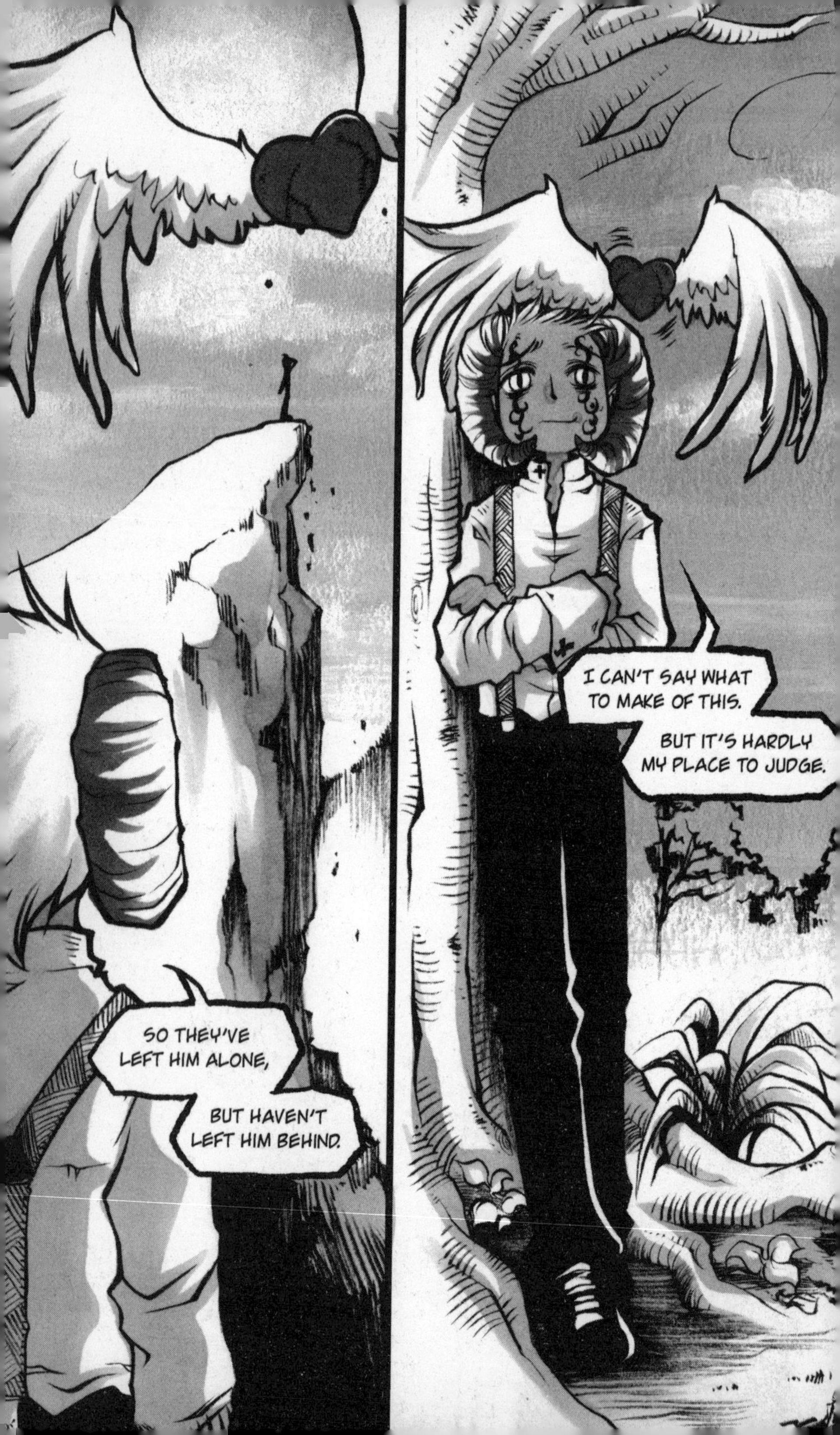
SO THEY'VE LEFT HIM ALONE,
BUT HAVEN'T LEFT HIM BEHIND.
I CAN'T SAY WHAT TO MAKE OF THIS.
BUT IT'S HARDLY MY PLACE TO JUDGE.

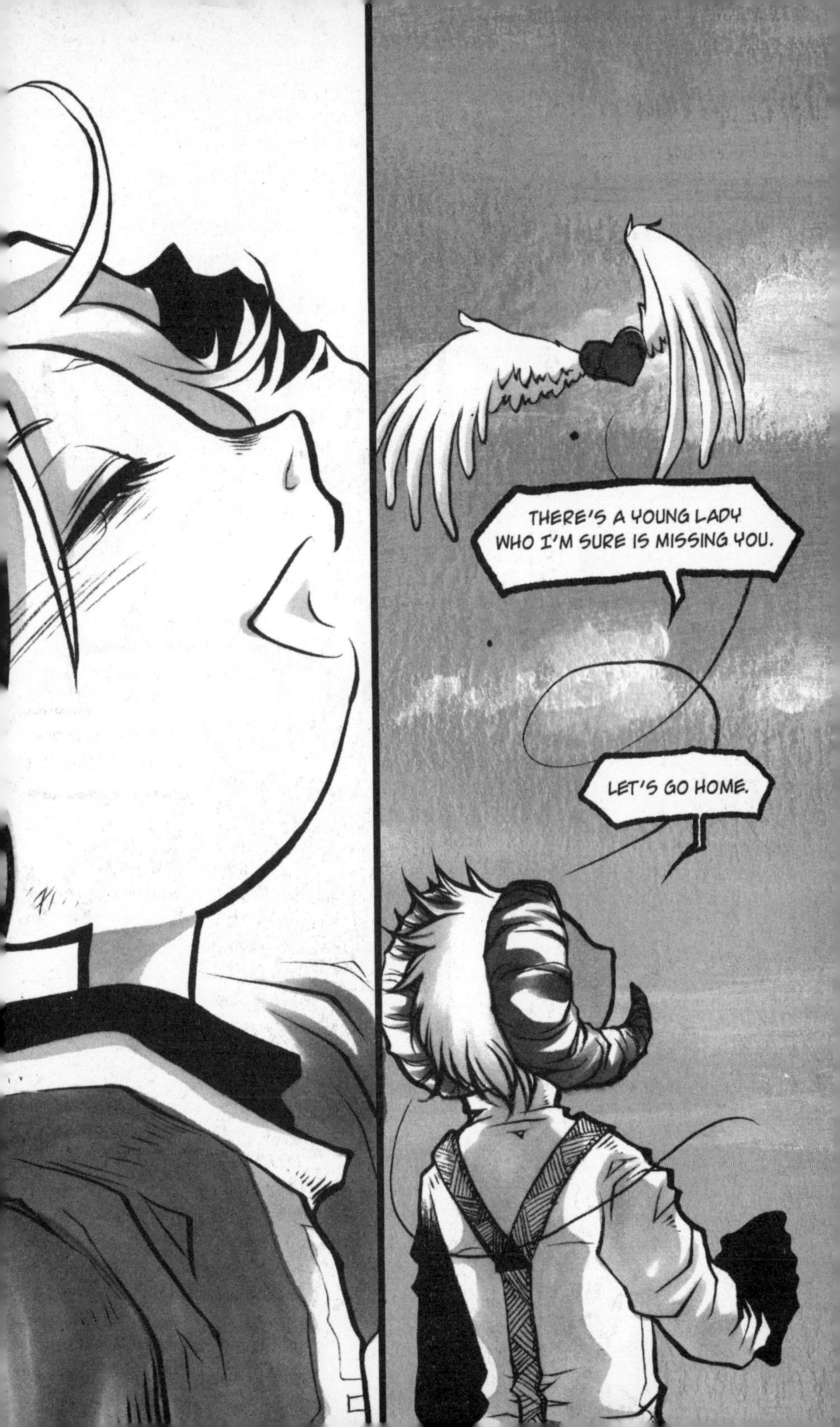
THERE'S A YOUNG LADY WHO I'M SURE IS MISSING YOU.
LET'S GO HOME.

... and they all lived happily ever after.

END

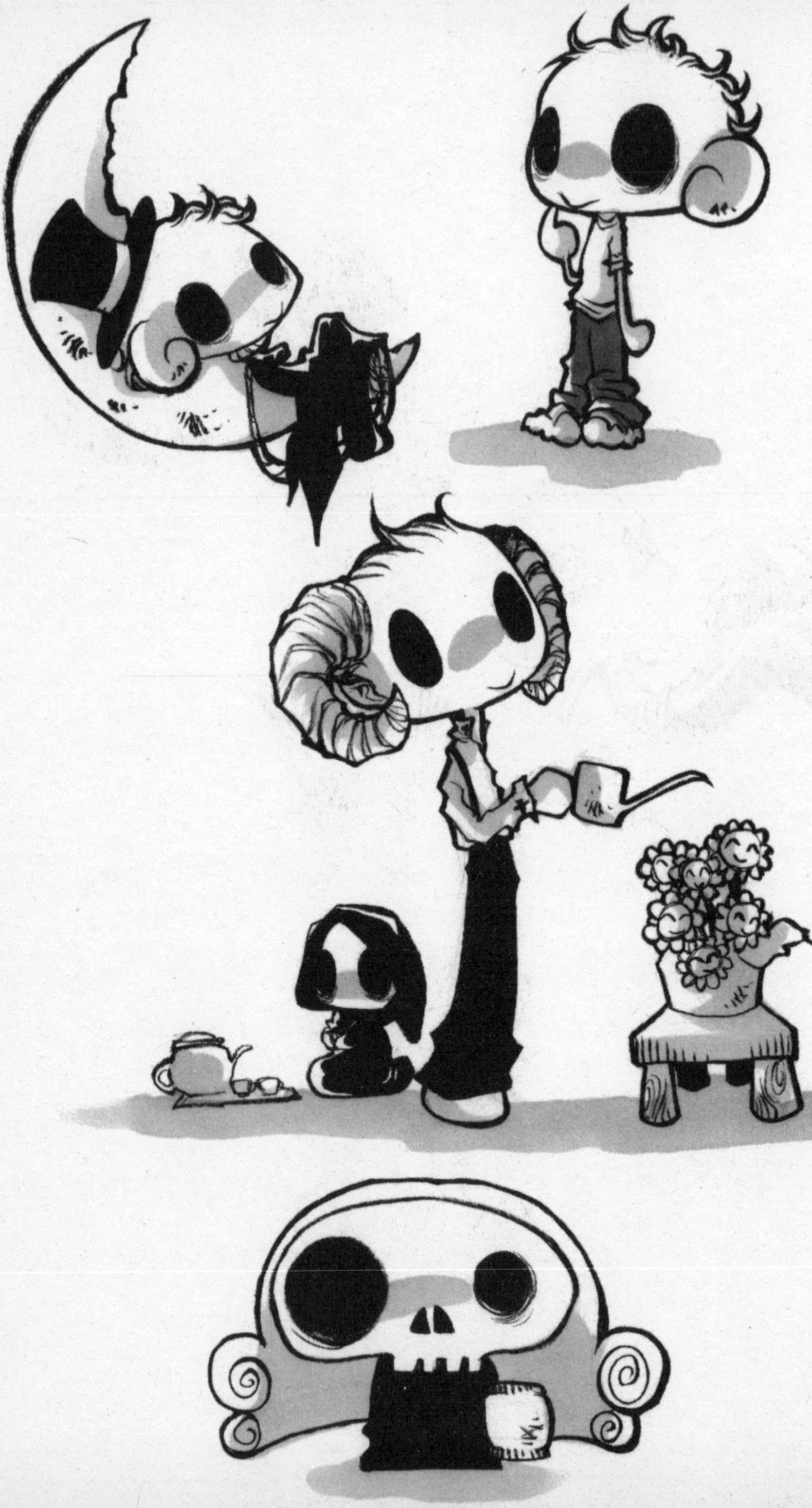

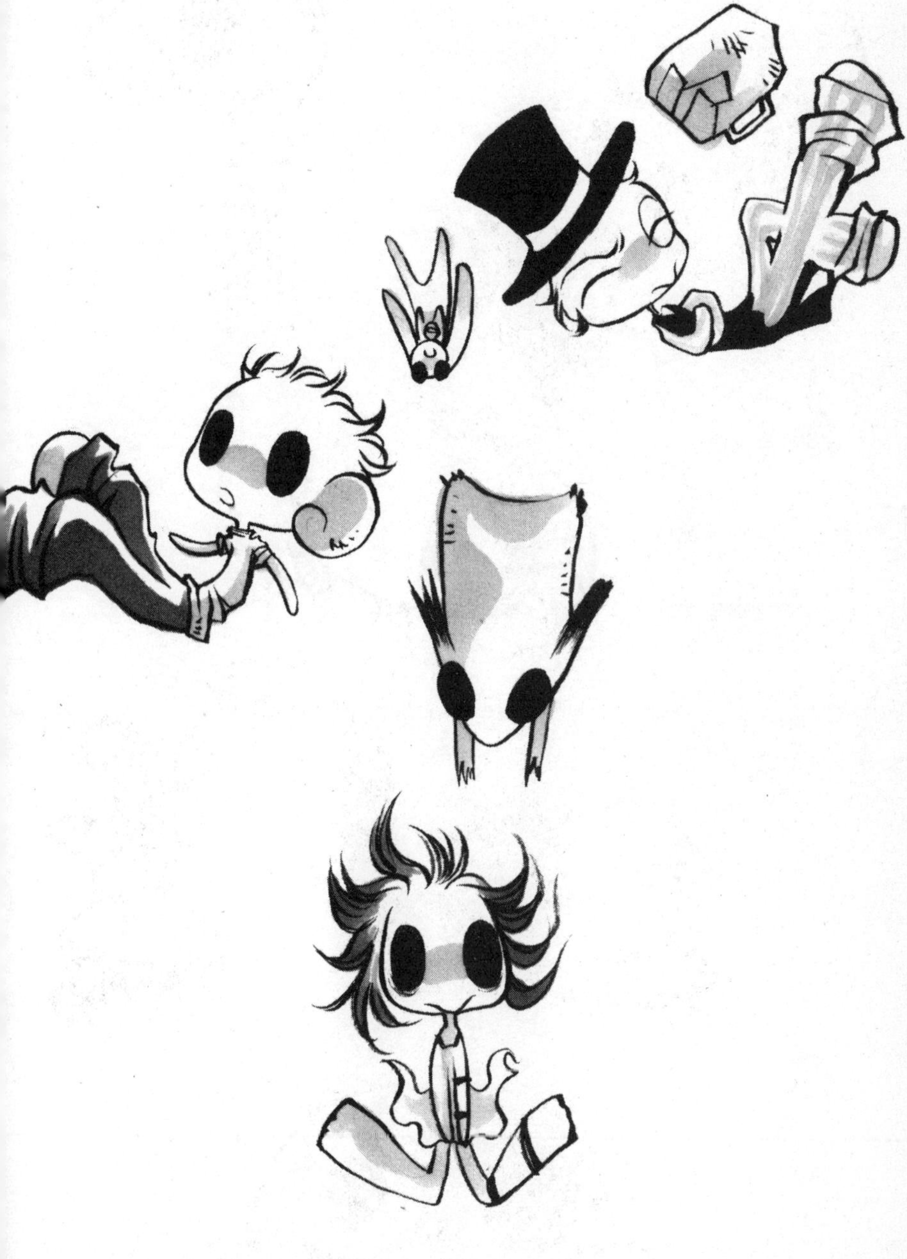

The courtyard and the book tree.

"... PILLARS ALL AROUND HIM, FALLEN LEAVES ON THE FLOORS. BOOKS ARE ON THE FLOOR TOO. ALL AROUDN HIM ARE GIANT BOOK SHELVES STACKED FULL OF BO HIGH ABOVE THE SHELVES WE SEE TOWERING TREES WITH BRANCHES THAT HAVE SPROUTED BOOKS, LIKE FRUITS." - SCRIPT EXTRACT

THE BOOKSHELVES WERE LATER SCRAPPED BECAUSE I FOUND IT TOO PROBLEMATIC FOR THE SCENE. THIS WAS PROBABLY THE HARDEST SCENE TO DESIGN.

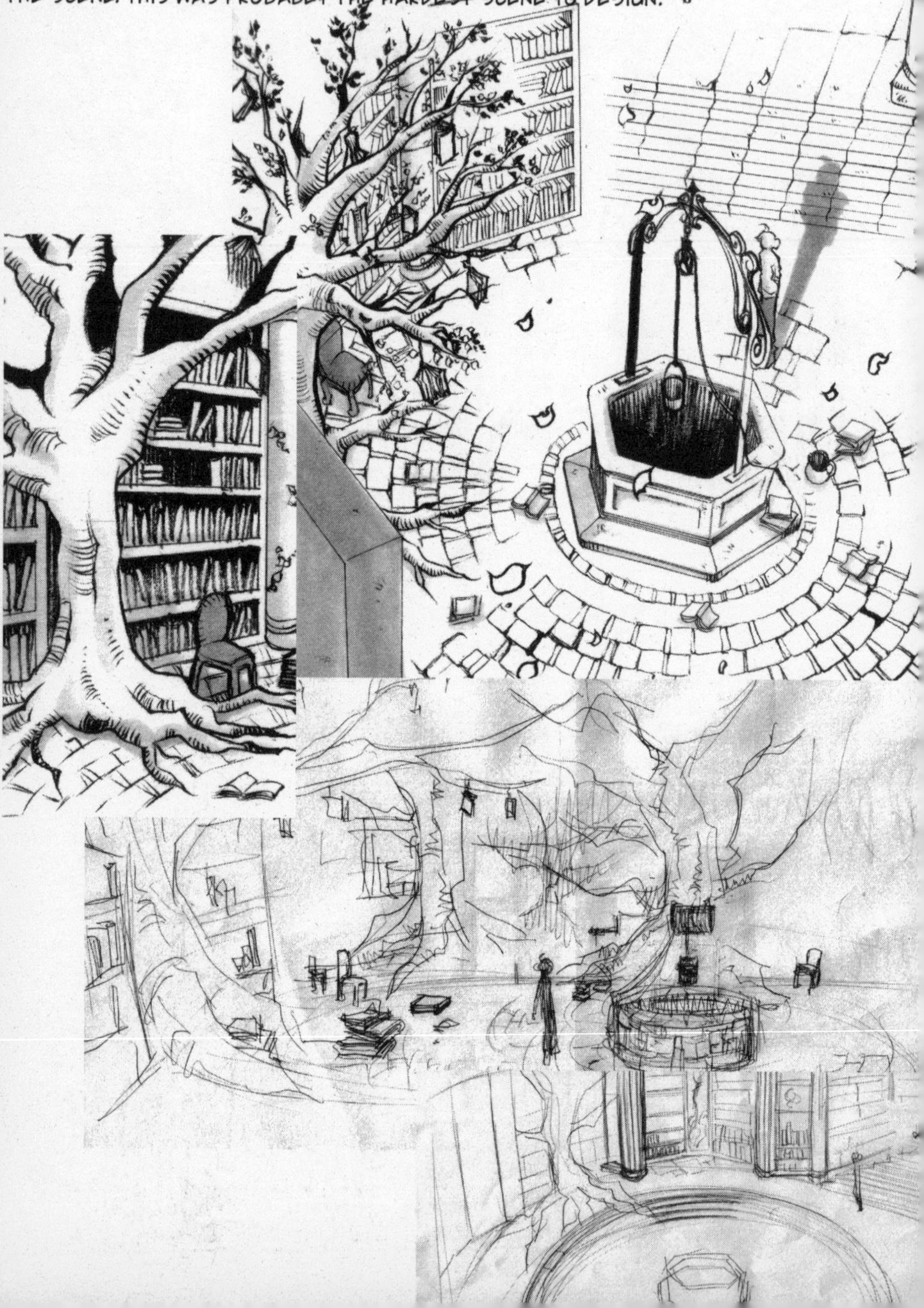

Death flower shop.

COMPARED TO THE COURTYARD, THIS IS THE
EASIEST SCENE TO DESIGN, THE VERY FIRST
SKETCH CAME OUT JUST THE WAY WE WANTED.

EARLY CONCEPT DESIGN FOR MAJOR SCENE

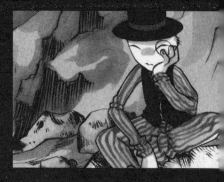

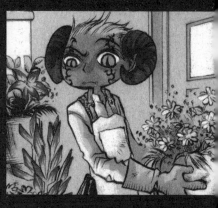

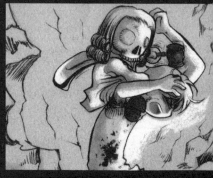

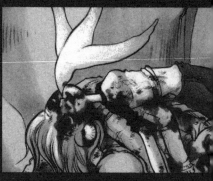

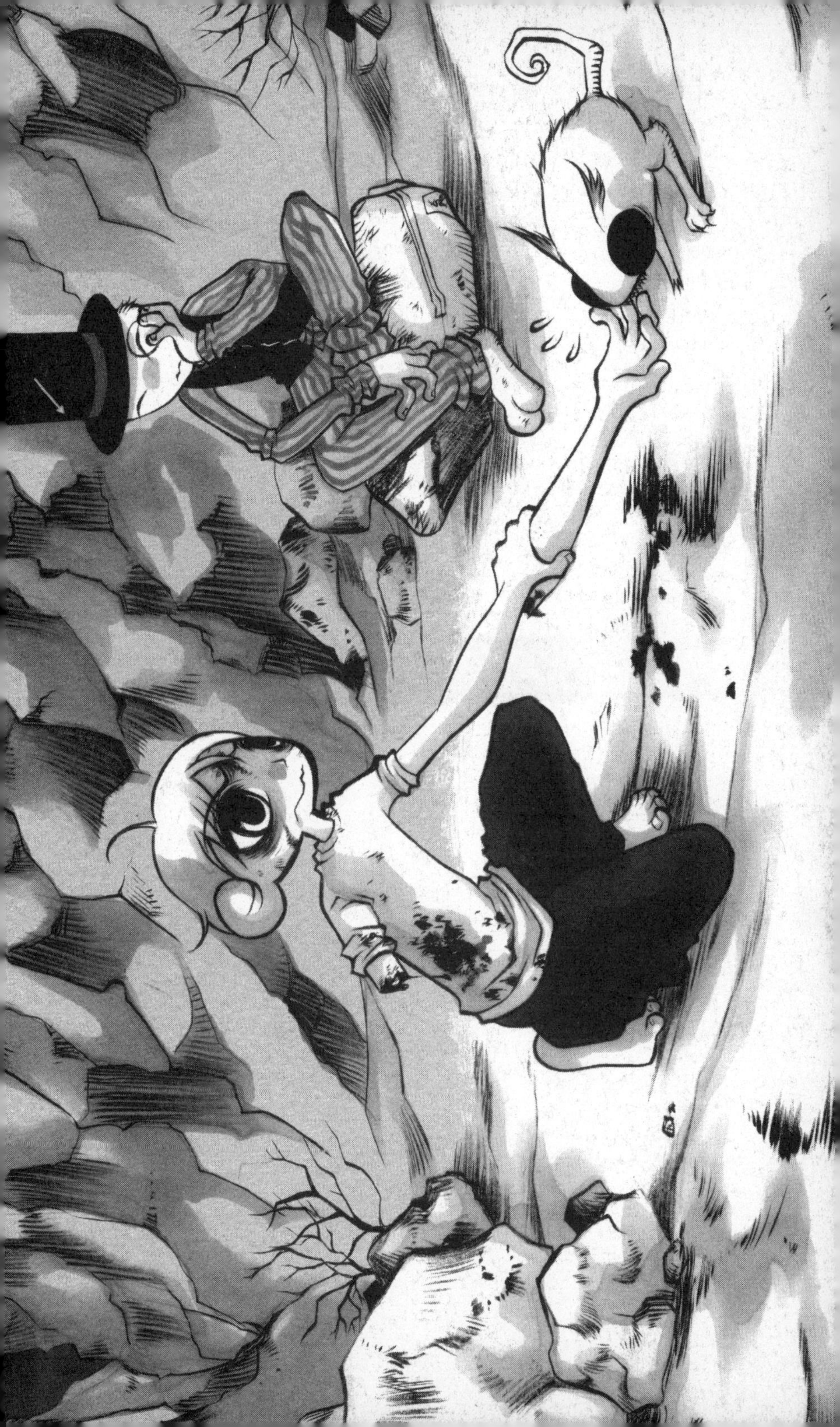

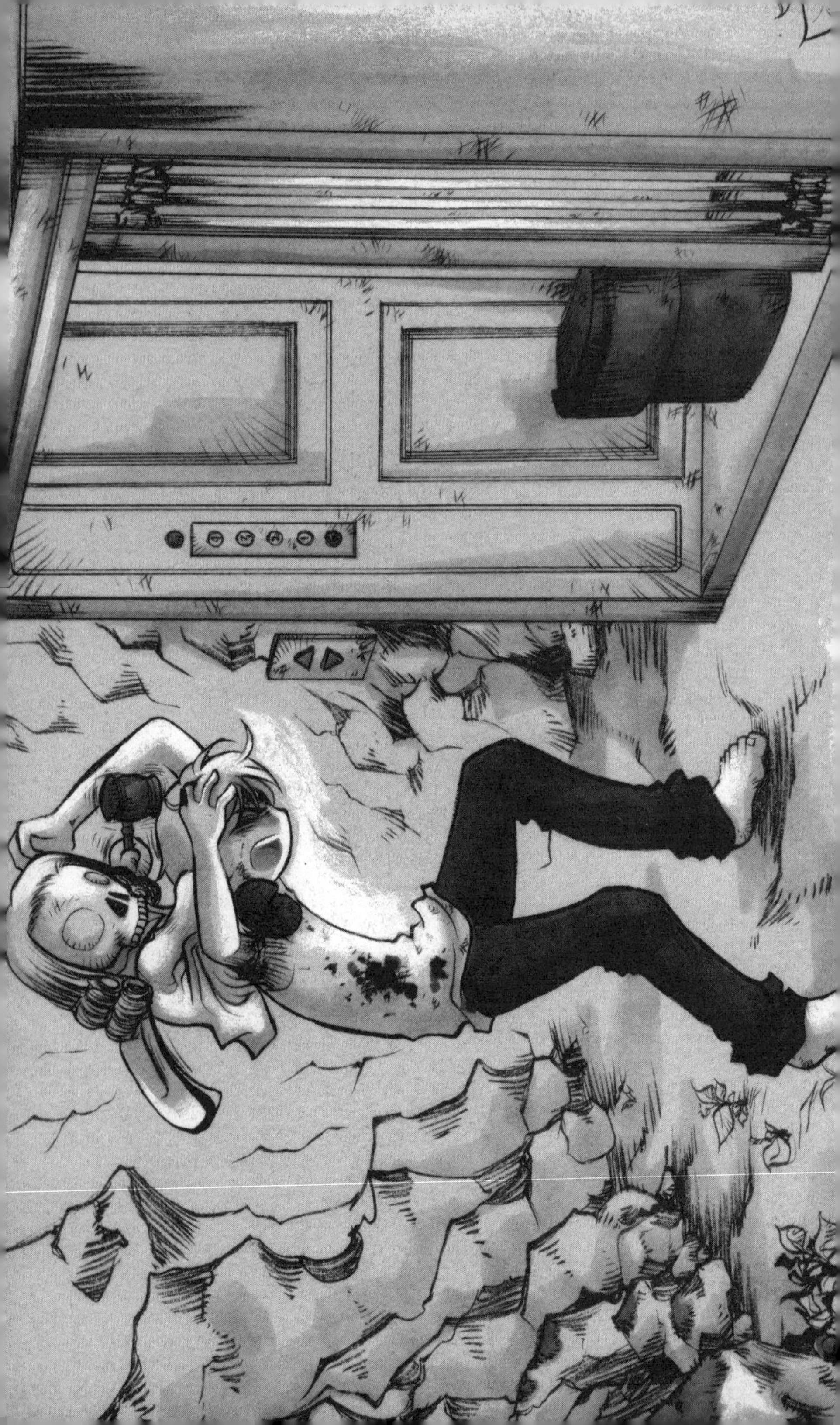

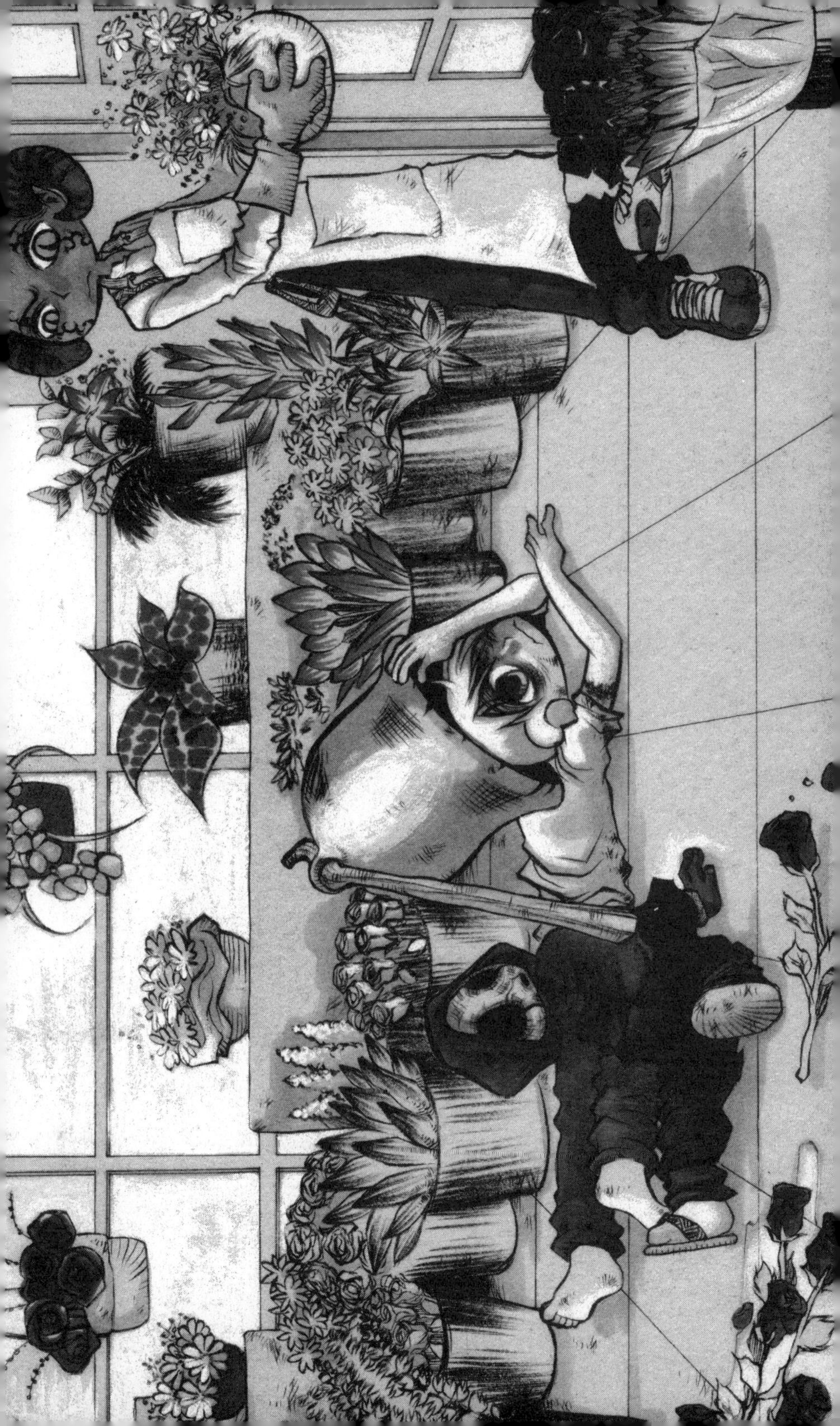

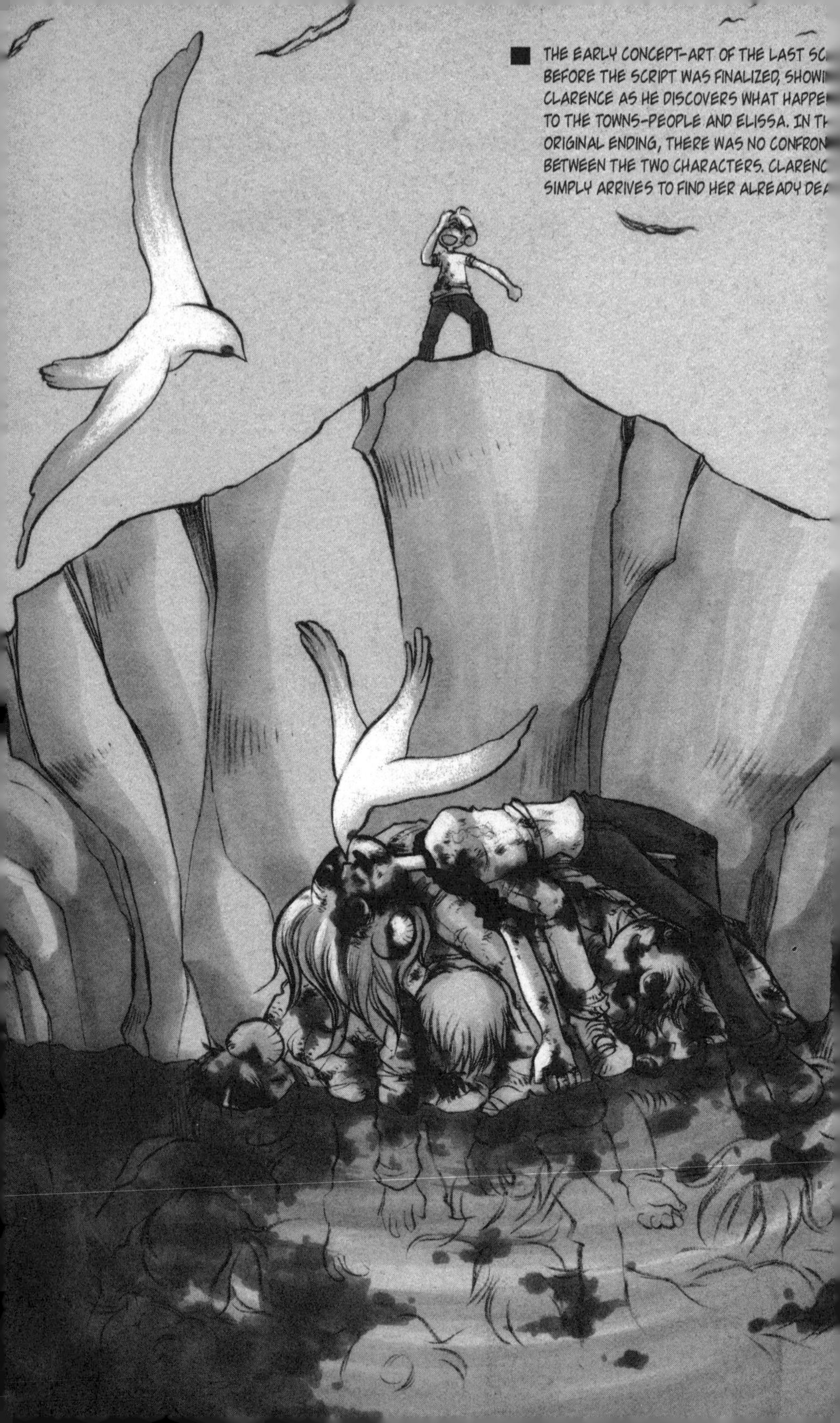

■ THE EARLY CONCEPT-ART OF THE LAST SC
BEFORE THE SCRIPT WAS FINALIZED, SHOWI
CLARENCE AS HE DISCOVERS WHAT HAPPE
TO THE TOWNS-PEOPLE AND ELISSA. IN T
ORIGINAL ENDING, THERE WAS NO CONFRON
BETWEEN THE TWO CHARACTERS. CLARENC
SIMPLY ARRIVES TO FIND HER ALREADY DE

The (almost) last page

Production of

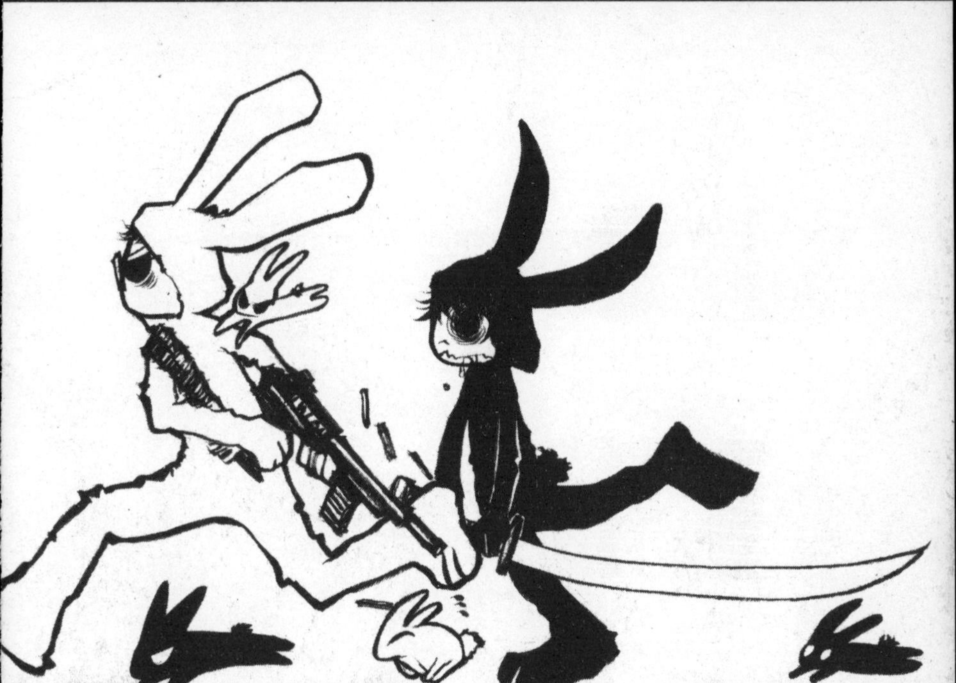

sixkillerbunnies.com

Did you dream?

No.

Tell me a dream?

I rarely dream.

You're broken.